THE SOURCE BOOK OF
WORLD WAR TWO
AIRCRAFT

THE SOURCE BOOK OF
WORLD WAR TWO
AIRCRAFT

John M.G. Emory

BLANDFORD PRESS
POOLE · DORSET

First published in the UK 1986 by Blandford
Press, Link House, West Street, Poole, Dorset,
BH15 1LL

Copyright © 1986 John M. G. Emory

Distributed in the United States by
Sterling Publishing Co., Inc.,
2 Park Avenue, New York, N.Y. 10016

Distributed in Australia by
Capricorn Link (Australia) Pty Ltd,
PO Box 665, Lane Cove, NSW 2066

British Library Cataloguing in Publication Data

Emory, John M.G.
  The source book of World War Two aircraft.
  1. Aeronautics—History
  I. Title
  629.133'09044   TL515

ISBN 0-7137-1722-X

Typeset by Poole Typesetting (Wessex) Ltd.
Printed in Great Britain by
Billings Ltd., Worcester

CONTENTS

INTRODUCTION

Military airpower played a decisive role in the outcome of World War Two. The effort for supremacy in the air created an unparalleled advance in aviation technology. Mobilization of every available aircraft, development of new types and application of aviation to entirely new roles all led to a wide variety of aircraft in service or proposed for service.

In recent years, an ever-increasing amount of information has been published on this variety of aircraft used or planned for use during World War Two. It has been difficult to maintain an organized record of these aircraft types, or conveniently to locate information in the literature. This Source Book of World War Two Aircraft has been compiled to remedy this situation.

For the first time a comprehensive listing of aircraft involved in World War Two has been assembled. This compilation provides brief descriptions of over three thousand aircraft types, more than three times as many as collected in a single work previously. Rather than include a general bibliography, this Source Book references each aircraft type to specific books and periodicals by page number and extent of material presented. References have been selected, where available, which include extensive aircraft descriptions, illustrations and accounts of technical development.

A broad definition has been applied to the category of World War Two aircraft, covering the years 1939 through 1945. This encompasses both combat and non-combat types, including fixed wing, rotary wing, gliders, lighter than air and certain classes of bombs and missiles; experimental and prototype aircraft are included, as are projects which proceeded beyond design study status; civil aircraft are included if operational in roles related to the war effort.

This Source Book consists of a comprehensive listing of aircraft, a bibliographical guide to the literature references and a complete index.

HOW TO USE
THIS SOURCE BOOK

Part One – *Listing of Aircraft*

1 Aircraft are listed alphabetically in the following sequence:
country of manufacture or design
name of manufacturer or designer
most commonly used designation

2 Alternative designations are listed in parentheses following the most commonly used designation.

3 The aircraft configuration and principal use are listed following the designation. Unless otherwise described, the aircraft configuration is single, forward-mounted piston engine, low or mid-wing landplane.

4 A letter is suffixed to each description to identify further the nature and extent of use:
A moderate to extensive operational use in role stated.
B limited operational use in role stated (typically in quantities fewer than 100 aircraft).
C small quantity produced; very limited use, if any.
D obsolete; limited second line use.
E experimental prototype(s); not selected or too late for production.
F experimental or research; not intended for production.

G completed or almost completed, but not flown.
H completed and/or flown post war.
I impressed civil/commercial/private aircraft; limited quantity.
J project continued beyond design study, but not completed.
K extent and nature of use not documented, probably limited if any.
L civil/commercial/private aircraft not known to have been impressed, but may have served in airline, training, civil air patrol or other civilian role.
M prototype(s) flown during war; operational post war.

5 Following the aircraft description, references are provided to the literature listings in Part Two: Bibliography. References are listed generally in order of completeness of aircraft description.

Part Two – *Bibliography*

1 The bibliography of literature references is divided into Sections A, B, C and D.

2 A number is suffixed to each reference to describe the illustrations accompanying the written material in the reference:

0 no illustrations.
1 includes photograph(s).
2 includes photograph(s) and 3-view drawing.
3 includes 3-view drawing.
4 includes photograph(s), cutaway and 3-view drawing.
5 includes photograph(s) and cutaway drawing.
6 includes drawing(s).
7 includes 3-view and other drawing(s).
8 includes cutaway and other drawing(s).

3 Section A includes English language books currently or recently in print, which include many of the listed aircraft and comprise a basic library. Unless otherwise stated, the reference consists of the 'A' listing number followed by the page number in parentheses, and then the suffix number; for example A13(284)-1.

4 Section B includes other English language books. Unless otherwise stated, the reference consists of the 'B' listing number followed by the page number in parentheses, and then the suffix number; for example B148(64)-4.

5 Section C includes non-English language books. Unless otherwise stated, the reference consists of the 'C' listing number followed by the page number in parentheses, and then the suffix number; for example C13(240)-2.

6 Section D includes magazines and other periodicals. Unless otherwise stated, the reference consists of the 'D' listing number followed by the month/year of issue and page number in parentheses, and then the suffix number; for example D20(10/69-73)-2.

7 A page number reference of 'P' indicates that a photograph appears in an unpaginated photograph section.

8 Page number references apply to the particular edition listed in the bibliography by place and date of publication. Other editions may have the reference material on different pages.

9 Many of the books listed also contain material on aircraft types for which they have not been referenced. Space considerations have limited the number of references listed for each aircraft.

Example of Aircraft Listing
A typical listing from Part One of this Source Book appears as follows:

ITALY
SAVOIA-MARCHETTI Societa Idrovolanti Alta Italia 'Savoia-Marchetti'
SM.89 Twin engine attack bomber-E D20(10/69-73)-2, C20(2-77)-2, A13(284)-1, C13(240)-2, C10(136 1, C88(227,P)-1

By following the explanation provided, complete information can be determined from this listing example:

The SM.89 was manufactured in Italy by Savoia-Marchetti (S.I.A.I.) and was a twin forward piston engine low or mid-wing experimental attack bomber. Information on this aircraft can be found on page 73 of the October 1969 issue of *Flying Review International* (reference D20) with a photograph and 3-view drawing, on page 77 of Vol. 2 of *Aerei Italiani Nella 2ª Guerra Mondiale* (reference C20) with a photograph and 3-view drawing, on page 284 of *Italian Civil and Military Aircraft 1930-1945*

9

(reference A13) with a photograph, on page 240 of *Guida Agli Aeroplani d'Italia* (reference C13) with a photograph and 3-view drawing, on page 136 of *Aireview's World War II Military Aircraft of France, Italy, Soviet and 21 Other Countries* (reference C10) with a photograph, and

on page 227 of *Vojenska Letadla 3 Letadla Druhe Svetove Valky* (reference C88) with a photograph in an unpaginated section.

A similar procedure will obtain complete information from all other listings.

EXAMPLE

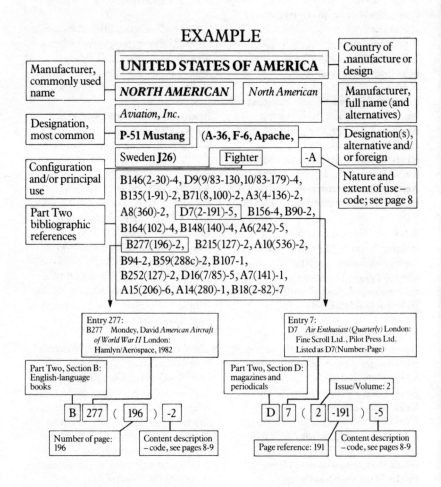

Part One:
LISTING OF AIRCRAFT

ARGENTINA

F.M.A. *Fabrica Militar de Aviones (Instituto Aerotecnia)*
Ae.C.1 Tourer -L
B152(3c)-1, D3(5-135)-1, B9(12)-0
Ae.C.2 Trainer -D
B152(3c)-1, B279(165)-1, D3(5-135)-1, B9(12)-0
Ae.C.3 Trainer, tourer -B
B152(4c)-1, D19(1/61-30)-1, D3(5-135)-1, B411(160)-0
Ae.M.B.1 Bomber -E
A10(42)-1, B279(165)-1, B9(12)-0
Ae.M.B.2 Bombi Bomber, observation -B
D25(6/63-49)-2, A10(42)-1, D26(117)-3, B411(160)-0, B9(12)-0
Ae.ME.1 Trainer, version Ae.C.2 -D
B9(12)-0
Ae.M.O.1 Trainer -B
B152(4c)-1, B279(165)-1, B397(358)-1, B411(160)-0, B9(13)-0
Ae.T.1 Light transport -B
B152(4c)-1, D3(5-147)-1, B411(160)-0
Curtiss Hawk 75-0 (H750) Fighter -B
A3(4-45)-2, B146(1-35)-2, B39(356)-1, A10(479)-1, B368(106)-1, B9(13)-0, B71(80-10)-0, A14(245)-0, A15(194)-0
Focke-Wulf Fw 44 Steiglitz Biplane trainer -A
C131(140)-1, B9(13)-0, B376(29)-0
Focke-Wulf Fw 58 Twin engine trainer -B
B9(13)-0, B376(40)-0
I.Ae.A.20 El Boyero High wing trainer -L
B139(18)-2, B58(3c)-1, B22(A-141)-1, D11(57/58-51)-1, D3(5-147)-1
I.Ae.21 (version North American NA-16) Trainer -E
B9(14)-0
I.Ae.D.L.22 'Dele-Dele' (version North American NA-16) Trainer -B
B139(59)-2, B60(3c)-1, D3(8-89)-2, D19(1/61-29)-1, C10(210)-1, C131(200)-1
I.Ae.23 (wood version Focke-Wulf Fw 44) Biplane trainer -E
B9(13)-0
I.Ae.24 Calquin Twin engine attack bomber -H
D9(10/77-203)-2, B60(3c)-1, A10(42)-1, B139(112)-2, D3(8-89)-2
I.Ae.25 Manque High wing transport glider -E
D6(4/72-207)-1, D20(10/63-62)-1, B286(177)-0

I.M.P.A. *Compania Industria Metalurgica & Plastica Argentinas S.A.*
Chorlito Trainer -L
D19(1/68-46)-1, B279(197)-0
LF-1 Tu-Sa Light tourer, trainer -L
D19(1/68-46)-1, D3(8-64)-1, B58(3c)-0,

11

B279(197)-0
RR-11 Light tourer -L
D19(1/68-45)-1, D10(3/67-90)-1,
D3(4-219)-1, B58(3c)-0, B279(197)-0
RR-12D Trainer -J
D19(1/68-45)-0
RR-13D Twin engine light transport -J
D19(1/68-46)-0

TUCAN Sociedad Anonima Sfreddo &
Paolini
T-1 High wing light plane -L
B59(3c)-1, D3(4-254)-1

AUSTRALIA

COMMONWEALTH Commonwealth
Aircraft Corporation Pty, Ltd
Boomerang (CA-12,13,14,19)
Fighter -A
B320-4, D6(2/72-91)-4, B71(178)-2,
A3(1-4)-2, A10(42)-2, A6(8)-2,
B164(88)-2, B59(82c)-2, B122(50)-1,
B18(2-258)-7, A15(81)-6, B88(5-23)-2
CA-15 Fighter -H
D6(10/72-178)-2, B88(7-50)-2,
D9(5/75-258)-2, B60(92c)-1, D3(7-99)-2,
B323(86)-1, D6(4/73-206)-1, B17(285)-7
Wackett (CA-2,6) Trainer -A
B323(42,47)-1, D9(12/79-305)-1,
B122(10)-1, B319(49,87)-2, B59(83c)-1,
B139(45)-1, B321(24)-1, B279(127)-1,
A7(247)-0
Wirraway (CA-1,3,16) Attack bomber,
trainer -A
B71(154)-2, A3(7-7)-2, B322-2,
B88(2-29)-2, D20(9/65-43)-2, B319(55)-2,
B58(63c)-1, A15(81)-6, B18(2-256)-7,
B279(128)-1
Woomera (CA-4,11) Twin engine
bomber -E
D7(1-52)-2, A3(7-14)-2, B60(92c)-1,
B319(110)-1, B122(32)-1, B321(61)-1,
B18(2-260)-7, B87(119)-6, B382(209)-1

D.A.P. Department of Aircraft
Production

Beaufighter Mk 21 (Bristol 156) Twin
engine fighter -A
B319(78)-2, B323(62)-1, A3(2-22)-1,
B144(1-29)-1, B27(303)-1, B316(82)-1,
B122(16)-1
Beaufort (Bristol 152) Twin engine
bomber, transport -A
A3(7-18)-2, B343(56)-1, B319(66)-2,
B27(284)-1, A10(333)-1, B122(18)-1,
D3(8-150)-1

D.C.A. Department of Civil Aviation
Fleep (Project Skywards) Rotary-wing
Jeep conversion -G
D9(7/75-19)-2, B209(68)-1, B326(87)-0

D.H.A. De Havilland Aircraft Pty, Ltd
D.H.82 Tiger Moth Biplane trainer -A
B201(305)-1, B323(43)-1, B319(49)-1,
B122(27)-1, B57(45a)-1
D.H.84 Dragon III Twin engine
biplane trainer -B
B201(332)-1, B323(84)-1, B321(100)-1,
B122(47)-1, A15(135)-0
D.H.98 Mosquito FB Mk 40 Twin
engine fighter, reconnaisance -B
B201(414)-1, B144(1-49)-1, B323(84)-1,
A3(2-32)-0, B369(109)-1, B122(59)-1
G1 High wing transport glider -E
D9(7/76-22)-2, B286(177)-2, B122(62)-1,
D6(4/72-207)-1, B323(57)-1

G2 High wing transport glider -C
D9(7/76-22)-2, B201(529)-1,
B319(120)-1, D3(7-112)-2, B60(94c)-1,
B122(62)-1, B286(177)-0
GLAS II High wing suction wing
glider -H
D9(7/76-26)-4, B286(178)-1,
D9(11/85-238)-1

TUGAN *Tugan Aircraft Coy (Wackett)*
Gannet Twin engine high wing survey -I
B323(34)-1, B122(23)-1, B319(48)-1,
D3(6-226)-1, A15(81)-0, B279(292)-0

AUSTRIA

BAUMGARTL *Paul Baumgartl*
Heliofly I Strap-on autogiro glider -E
C45(71)-1, C91(44)-1, C16(80)-6,
B381(586)-0, B228(16)-0, C142(52)-1
Heliofly III/57 (Heliofly II) Strap-on
helicopter -E
C45(71)-6, C91(44)-6, B381(586)-0,
B228(16)-0, C142(52)-1
Heliofly III/59 Light helicopter -E
C45(72)-1, C142(53)-1, C139(90)-1

DOBLHOFF *Friedrich Baron von
Doblhoff (WNF)*
WNF 342 Jet-driven helicopter -E
C45(61)-2, D3(8-5)-2, B381(587)-1,
B326(44)-1, C91(41)-1, B23(18)-1,
B53(146)-1, B228(17)-1, C16(82)-1,
C66(135,933)-1, B138(37)-1,
C139(170)-1, C142(57)-1

HIRTENBERG *Hirtenberger Patronen
Zundhutchen und Metallwarfenfabrik
A. G. (Theodor Hopfner)*
Focke-Wulf Fw 44 Steiglitz
Biplane trainer-B
C133(108)-2, C49(183)-1
HS.8 (HS 928) High wing trainer -D
C49(184)-1, C133(40)-2
HS.8 (HS 829) High wing trainer -D
B340(188)-1, B200(2-367)-1, C49(185)-1,
D3(4-194,7-83,7-131)-1, B279(192)-0,
B114(12-1317)-0, C133(48)-2

HS.10 (HS 1033) High wing liaison -D
C49(206)-1, C133(55)-2
HA.11
See WNF Wn 11
HM.13 (HM 1334) Biplane trainer -B
B340(188)-1, C49(199)-1, B397(362)-1,
D3(4-194)-1, C133(85)-2
HR.14 (HR 1434) Twin engine
transport -K
C49(87)-1, C133(93)-2
HV.15 (WNF Wn 15) Twin engine
trainer -B
B340(191)-6, C49(87)-1, D3(4-194)-1,
C133(98)-2, C66(485)-0

MEINDL *Erich Meindl*
A 7 Trainer -K
C49(87)-1
A 8 Liaison -K
C49(88)-1
M.XV
See WNF Wn 16

MUSGER *Ing. Erwin Musger*
Mg 12 Training glider -K
B82(14)-0

NAGLER-ROLZ *Nagler-Rolz
Flugzeugbau*
NR 54 Light helicopter -E
C45(71)-1, D25(9/57-28)-6, C16(80)-6,
B381(610)-0, B228(21)-0, C142(50,P)-1

13

NR 55 Light helicopter -E
C45(70)-0, D25(9/57-28)-0, B381(610)-0,
C91(44)-0, B228(21)-0, C142(50)-0

PHÖNIX *Phönix Flugzeugwerft GmbH*
L2c Biplane trainer -D
C49(188)-1

PINTSCH *Julius Pintsch AG*
Schwalbe II (Raab-Katzenstein) Biplane
trainer -B
B397(364)-1, C49(189)-1,
D20(12/69-51)-0, B279(253)-0

THALERHOF *Fliegerwerft Thalerhof
(Major Hammerle)*
U-12o (U-12S, version Udet U-12)
Biplane trainer -B

B71(257-114)-1, C49(191)-1,
D20(12/69-51)-6

WNF *Wiener Neustädter Flugzeugfabrik*
Lampich NL XXII Biplane trainer -D
C49(187)-1
Wn 11 (Hopfner HA 1133) Twin engine
high wing amphibian -C
C48(282)-2, C66(484,1048)-1,
C133(70)-2, C117(254)-1, B397(360)-1,
B340(191)-6
Wn 16 (Meindl M.XV) Twin boom
pusher lightplane -E
C66(485,1048)-1, C117(255)-1,
D11(57/58-54)-1
WNF 342
See Doblhoff

BELGIUM

FAIREY *Societe Anonyme Belge 'Avions
Fairey' S.G.B.A.*
Feroce (Fantome) Biplane fighter -C
B400(260)-2, D9(12/78-297)-2,
B234(238)-1, B153(4c)-1, A10(36)-1,
C112(4-61)-2, C78(209)-1, B20(A-110)-1,
B397(366)-1, B469(8)-1
Firefly IIM Biplane fighter -B
D20(9/66-86)-2, B400(170)-2,
D9(11/78-245)-2, B88(1-34)-2, A10(47)-1,
D23(74-28)-1, B411(17)-1, C44(119)-1
Fox Biplane bomber, reconnaissance -B
A3(7-26)-2, B400(196)-2, D25(6/63-23)-1,
B421(200)-2, A10(48)-1, D23(74-34)-2,
B153(3c)-1, B88(1-35)-2, C44(118)-1,
B289(24)-6, B411(18)-1
Fox VI C Biplane fighter -B
D9(12/78-296)-2, D25(6/63-22)-2,
B278(86)-1, D18(7/71-3)-1
Kangourou (Mono-Fox, Fox VII)
Biplane fighter -E
D9(12/78-296)-2, B400(203)-1,

A10(49)-1, A3(7-31)-6, B153(4c)-1,
B20(A-109)-1, B88(1-87)-2, B278(86)-3,
B234(239)-1
Tipsey See Tipsey

LACAB *Les Ateliers de Constructions
Aeronautiques Belges*
GR.8 Twin engine sesquiplane multi-
role -E
D9(1/77-46,5/77-230)-2, B397(370)-1,
C110(181)-1, C114(98)-1, B97(P)-1,
D3(4-291)-1, B279(84)-0,
B114(11-1159)-0

RENARD *Constructions Aeronautiques
G. Renard*
R-31 High wing reconnaissance, ground
support -B
A3(7-34)-2, D18(10/72-22)-2,
D23(74-36)-2, B153(5c)-1, C50(36)-2,
C44(131)-1, C10(211)-1, C114(98)-1,
A15(81)-6, B18(1-286)-7

R-32 High wing reconnaissance, ground support -E
A3(7-35)-1, C50(46)-2, D23(74-36)-1, B20(A-111)-1, A15(81)-0
R-34 Biplane trainer -E
C50(50)-2
R-35B Three engine bomber -J
D9(9/78-148)-6, C50(53)-0
R-36 Fighter -E
D9(4/77-185)-2, A3(1-6)-1, C50(57)-2, D20(3/67-452)-1, B152(8c)-1, C44(123)-1, D23(74-44)-1, B20(A-110)-1, D14(3-34)-3, B397(372)-1
R-37 Fighter -E
D9(4/77-187)-1, A3(1-6)-1, C50(64)-2, B153(5c)-1, D23(74-45)-1, D20(3/67-452)-1
R-38 Fighter -E
D9(4/77-187)-1, A3(1-6)-2, C50(64)-2, D20(3/67-452)-2, B153(6c)-1, C44(123)-1, D23(74-45)-1, C10(212)-1
R-40 Fighter -G
C50(70)-3, D9(4/77-188)-0, A3(1-6)-0, D23(74-45)-0

SABCA *Societe Anonyme Belge de Constructions Aeronautiques*
S.40E Trainer -C
B153(6c)-1, C44(126)-1, B20(A-112)-1, D3(6-51)-1
S.47 (Caproni Bergamaschi Ca.335)
Attack bomber -E

A3(7-38)-2, B153(7c)-1, A13(117)-1, B20(A-112)-1, D23(74-46)-1, D3(6-51)-1

STAMPE *Societe Stampe et Vertongen (Renard)*
RSV.26-180 Biplane trainer -D
C50(13)-2
RSV.32-120 Biplane trainer, liaison -I
D25(5/62-43)-1, D4(11/75-56)-1, A15(81)-0, C50(9)-0
S.V.4 Biplane trainer, liaison -B
C64-2, D4(11/75-54)-1, B153(7c)-1, D3(3-142)-2, C50(72)-2, C44(123)-1, C74(38)-2, B293(59)-6, B97(P)-1, A15(82)-0
S.V.5 Biplane trainer, reconnaissance -B
B153(8c)-1, D23(74-64)-1, C10(212)-1, B97(P)-1, B397(374)-1, A15(82)-0, D7(18-74)-0, B279(283)-0
S.V.6 Biplane trainer -K
B153(8c)-0, B20(A-113)-0

TIPSEY *Avions Tipsey (Avions Fairey)*
BC (Belfair) Communications -I
B400(41)-1, B200(2-297)-1, B139(50)-1, D3(8-41)-2, B152(11c)-1, B284(3-150)-0
M (Fairey Primer) Trainer -E
B400(378)-2, B153(9c)-1, D3(9-41)-2, B20(A-114)-1
S.2 Light tourer -L
B200(2-293)-2, B400(40)-1, B420(62)-2, B153(9c)-1, D3(9-23)-1

BRAZIL

C.N.N.A. *Companhia Nacional de Navegacao Aerea (Fabrica Brasiliera de Aviones)*
HL-1 High wing club trainer -B
C106(89)-2, B58(4c)-1, B60(8c)-1, D11(57/58-56)-1, C131(159)-1
HL-6 Caure Trainer -B

B139(30)-2, C106(95)-2, B60(7c)-1, C131(195)-1
HL-8 Three engine transport -E
B139(130)-1, C106(132)-1, D3(5-168)-1, D9(5/77-248)-1
Muniz M-7 Biplane trainer -B
B56(4c)-2, C106(35)-1, B153(18c)-1,

D3(5-171)-1, C10(213)-1, C131(135)-1
Muniz M-9 Biplane trainer -B
C106(37)-2, B153(18c)-1, D3(5-183)-1,
B22(A-143)-1, B57(6a)-1,
C131(139,153)-1
Muniz M-11 (TP-1) Trainer -E
C106(41)-1, C131(282)-1

GALEAO Fabrica de Galeao
1 FG Pintassilgo (Focke-Wulf Fw 44)
Biplane trainer -B
C106(45)-1, B279(173)-0, C131(52)-1
2 FG (Focke-Wulf Fw 58) Twin engine
trainer -B
C106(47)-2, C131(53,156)-1, B376(40)-0,
A15(108)-0, B279(173)-0
3 FG (Fairchild PT-19) Trainer -A
C106(99)-1, B279(173)-0, C131(163)-1

*I.P.T. Instituto de Pesquisas
Technologicas de Sao Paulo*
IPT-0 Bichinho Lightplane -F
D9(6/76-300)-2, C106(61)-2,
D11(57/58-51,53)-1
IPT-1 Gafanhoto High wing training
glider -E
C106(64)-3
IPT-2 Aratinga High wing training
glider -E
C106(65)-3

IPT-3 Saracura High wing training
glider -B
C106(65)-1
IPT-4
See Paulisata CAP-1
IPT-5 Jaragua Training sailplane -E
C106(119)-2
IPT-6 Stratus High wing training
glider -E
C106(120)-2

*PAULISTA Companhia Aeronautica
Paulista*
CAP-1 Planalto (IPT-4) Trainer -E
B57(5c)-1, C106(71)-2, B60(7c)-1,
D3(5-243)-1, B59(5c)-1
CAP-3 Planalto Trainer -C
C106(71)-1, C131(197)-1
CAP-4 Paulistinha High wing
observation, ambulance -A
B60(6c)-1, B139(12)-2, C106(77)-1,
D3(5-243)-1, B59(5c)-1, C131(182)-0
CAP-5 Carioquinha High wing
tourer -B
C106(79)-2, B60(6c)-0
CAP-8 Tourer -E
C106(82)-2

TORRES Mario Torres
Torres-5 Mutuca Biplane trainer -E
C106(101)-2

BULGARIA

CBSA Caproni Bulgara SA
**Ka.B.3 Tchoutchouliga (Caproni
Ca.113)** Biplane trainer, liaison -B
A15(154)-0
Ka.B.11 (L.W.S.3 Mewa) High wing
reconnaissance -B
A1(338)-1, A15(182)-0, D9(6/84-306)-0

*D.A.R. Darjavna Aeroplanna
Rabotilnitza*

D.A.R.3 Garvan (LAZ-3) Biplane
reconnaissance -B
D6(10/71-277)-1, A15(82)-0
D.A.R.6 Sinigier Biplane trainer -B
B153(19c)-1, C10(213)-1, B397(376)-1,
A15(82)-0
D.A.R.10 Reconnaissance bomber -E
D9(6/84-306)-2, A3(7-50)-2, A10(49)-1,
B279(138)-1, D25(12/61-45)-3,
A15(82)-6, B114(7-694)-0, A7(247)-0

LAZAROV *Prof. Ing. Cvietan Lazarov*
LAZ-3
See D.A.R.3

LAZ-7 Trainer -H
D20(4/66-489)-1, B279(210)-0

CANADA

BOEING *Boeing Aircraft of Canada Ltd*
Canso A (Consolidated PBY-5A)
Twin engine high wing patrol
amphibian -B
B37(240)-1, B155(8,81)-1, B276(203)-0,
A14(312)-0
Catalina IVB, VI (PB2B) Twin engine
high wing patrol flying boat -A
B37(240)-2, B276(203)-1, B298(82)-1,
A9(78)-1, A3(5-154)-1, B360(35,38)-1,
B122(35)-1, A14(312)-0, A15(191)-0,
D22(17-69)-1
Shark III (Blackburn) Biplane torpedo
floatplane -B
B427-2, B276(108)-1, B37(239)-1,
B199(374)-2, B298(70)-1, B155(6,46)-1,
B227(25)-1, D19(2/60-162)-1

C.A.A. *Canadian Associated Aircraft Ltd*
Handley Page Hampden (H.P.52)
Twin engine bomber -A
B276(375)-1, B155(13,139)-1, B79(67)-1,
B56(51c)-1, B233(276)-1, B71(58-5)-0

CANADIAN VICKERS *Canadian
Vickers Ltd*
Bellanca CH-300 Pacemaker High
wing photographic -B
B276(104)-1, B155(6,44)-1, B227(28)-1,
B385(56)-1, D19(2/60-162)-1, B279(96)-1
Canso A (PBV, PBY-5A, 0A-10A)
Twin engine high wing patrol
amphibian -A
B276(206)-1, B155(8,81)-1, A3(5-143)-1,
A14(312)-1, D22(17-65)-1, B111(53)-1

Delta (Northrop) Patrol,
reconnaissance, also floatplane -B
A3(7-57)-2, B276(415)-1, D20(9/65-61)-1,
B155(16,169)-1, B55(124)-2,
B153(77c)-1, B121(163)-1, B227(493)-1,
A15(206)-0, D19(2/60-162)-1
Vancouver II Twin engine biplane
patrol flying boat -B
B276(198)-1, B155(8,69)-1, A10(52)-1,
B11(493)-1, B279(114)-1, B152(19b)-1,
B114(23-2553)-0
Vedette Biplane pusher patrol
amphibian -B
B276(174)-1, B155(8,75)-1, B11(489)-1,
D21(1/2-92)-1, B402(483)-1

C.C.F. *Canadian Car & Foundry Co, Ltd*
CBY-3 Loadmaster Twin engine twin
boom transport -E
D20(4/65-44)-2, D3(7-68)-2,
D11(4/65-46)-2, B276(170)-1,
B60(96c)-1, B317(53)-1
FDB-1 Gregor Fighter Biplane
fighter -E
D2(2/1-30)-2, D3(7-256)-2,
D9(9/75-137,10/75-201)-2, B276(168)-1,
B22(A-201)-1
G-23 Goblin (Grumman FF-1)
Biplane patrol, reconnaissance -B
D7(9-26)-4, A3(7-52)-2, D9(2/81-101)-2,
B276(524)-1, A10(499)-1,
D21(1/4-150,1/5-181,1/6-239)-2,
B411(63)-1, C78(254)-2, B254(9)-1
Hawker Hurricane XII Fighter -A
B276(378)-1, B250(253)-1, B144(2-28)-1,
B155(14,143)-1, B227(60)-1, A3(2-66)-1

Maple Leaf II (Ares Num.2) Biplane
trainer -E
B276(165)-1, B22(A-201)-1, D3(2-230)-1
SBW Helldiver (Curtiss SB2C)
Carrier dive bomber -A
B39(430)-1, B65(96)-1, B59(85c)-1,
B389(24)-1, A15(195)-0

CURTISS-REID Curtiss Reid Aircraft
Co, Ltd
Rambler Biplane trainer -I
B276(236)-1, B155(9,91)-1, B39(315)-1,
B279(135)-0, D19(2/60-161)-1

DeHAVILLAND The de Havilland
Aircraft of Canada Ltd.
**D.H.82C Tiger Moth (Menasco
Moth)** Biplane trainer -A
B276(246)-1, B201(306)-1, B155(9,96)-1,
B88(2-27)-2, B57(56c)-1,
D3(3-122,8-76)-1, B191(60)-1,
B172(31)-1, B208(30)-0
D.H.98 Mosquito (USAAF **F-8**) Twin
engine fighter, bomber, trainer,
reconnaissance -A
B191(68)-5, B276(253)-1, B201(408)-1,
B143(1-75)-1, B144(1-50)-1, A8(548)-1,
B155(10,99)-1, A3(2-32)-1, B369(96)-1
D.H.C.1 Chipmunk Trainer -H
B191(94)-2, B60(98c)-2, D3(8-33)-2,
B276(262)-1, A11(176)-2, B139(33)-2,
B155(10,105)-1, B201(532)-1,
B17(149)-7, B172(57)-1
Sparrow (W.W.S.1 Salamandra)
High wing training glider -L
B191(64)-2, A1(725)-1, D3(7-224)-1

FAIRCHILD Fairchild Aircraft Ltd
Bolingbroke (Bristol Blenheim)
Twin engine bomber -A
A3(7-62,6-2)-2, B276(120)-1, B27(278)-1,
B155(6,50)-1, B44(111)-1, D7(28-72)-1,
D25(8/63-39)-2, B143(1-59)-1,
B134(2-15)-1, B233(268)-1
Model 51
See United States: Fairchild

Model 71 High wing utility, also
floatplane -B
B276(310)-1, B155(11,116)-1,
D19(2/74-97)-2, B139(26)-1, B227(26)-1,
D22(17-36)-1, B468(34)-1
Super 71 High wing utility, also
floatplane -C
D7(4-208)-2, B276(316)-1, D3(3-242)-1,
B155(11,118)-1, D19(2/74-99)-1
Model 82 High wing utility, also
floatplane -B
B55(126)-2, B276(320)-1,
D19(2/74-98)-1, B153(79c)-1, B139(26)-1
SBF Helldiver (Curtiss SB2C) Carrier
dive bomber -A
B276(234)-1, B39(430)-1, B71(126-4)-0,
B389(42)-1, A15(195)-0
X-1, X-2 High wing pusher tailless
lightplane -J
B276(514)-1

FEDERAL Federal Aircraft Ltd.
Anson (Avro 652A, USAAF **AT-20)**
Twin engine trainer -A
B276(56)-1, B59(87c)-2, B198(324)-1,
A8(550)-1, B155(5,30)-1, B191(61)-1,
D3(5-233)-1, B177(129)-1, B111(41)-1,
B170(44)-1

FLEET Fleet Aircraft Ltd
Cornell II (Fairchild PT-26)
Trainer -A
B276(326)-1, B59(88c)-1,
B155(12,121)-1, A6(222)-7, D3(5-63)-2,
D21(1/5-177)-1
Model 7 Fawn Biplane trainer -B
B276(336)-1, B155(12, 129)-1,
D3(3-302)-1, D21(1/1-26)-1,
B218(4-229)-1, B227(35)-1
Model 10 Biplane trainer -B
B276(341)-1, B430(150)-1
Model 16 Finch Biplane trainer -A
B57(58c)-2, B88(2-26)-2, B276(341)-1,
B155(13,130)-1, A7(197)-1, B139(154)-1,
D19(1/68-56)-1, B463(P)-1

Model 21 (Consolidated Y1BT-7)
Biplane trainer -B
B276(347)-1, B358(2-24)-3, B88(4-35)-2,
B55(130)-2
Model 50K Twin engine biplane
transport, also floatplane -B
B55(132)-2, B276(345)-1,
D20(4/65-44)-1, B56(55c)-1,
B155(13,131)-1, A15(82)-0
Model 60 Fort Wireless trainer -B
D21(1/1-50)-2, D6(3/72-151)-1,
B56(54c)-2, B276(352)-1, B48(1-54)-1,
D3(3-63)-2, B88(2-25)-2, B155(13,132)-1,
A7(197)-0

*NATIONAL STEEL CAR National
Steel Car Corp. Ltd*
Westland Lysander High wing army
cooperation -A
B276(449)-1, B345(26)-1,
B155(18,191)-1, B154(61c)-1,
B71(159-13)-1, B279(235)-0

NRC National Research Council
Flying wing research glider -H
B439(79)-1

NOORDUYN Noorduyn Aviation Ltd
**Harvard II (North American NA-59,
USAAF AT-16)** Trainer -A
B276(404)-1, B58(218c)-2, B394(21)-1,
B155(16,164)-1, A8(349)-0, B463(P)-1
Norseman (UC-64, JA-1) High wing
transport, also floatplane -A
D7(29-11)-4, B276(396)-1, B59(89c)-2,
B88(6-44)-2, A3(6-6)-2, A8(557)-1,
B155(15,159)-1, A7(225)-1, B16(259)-7,
B408(260)-2, A15(82)-6, D3(5-135)-2

NOURY Noury Aircraft Ltd
N-75 (Fleet Model 80 Canuck) High
wing tourer -M
B276(419,354)-1, B279(163)-1,
B60(101c)-1, B218(8-305)-1, B139(16)-2,
B420(73)-1
T-65 Noranda High wing tourer -H
B276(420)-1, B139(29)-1, D3(7-84)-1

VICTORY Victory Aircraft Ltd
Lancaster X (Avro 683) Four engine
bomber -A
B276(65)-1, B143(1-40)-1, B155(5,33)-1,
B134(1-131)-1, B344(38)-1, B198(341)-0

CHINA

CHU C. J. Chu
Humming Bird Model A Coaxial rotor
helicopter -H
B228(30)-1, C16(110)-0
XP-O Fighter -K
D9(7/85-33)-1

SHANGHAI Naval Air Establishment
Ning Hai (Nin Hia) Biplane
reconnaissance floatplane -K
B15(290)-7, B397(378)-1, D3(5-194)-1

CZECHOSLOVAKIA *(Bohemia-Moravia)*

AERO Aero Tovarna Letadel Dr Kabes
A11 Biplane reconnaissance bomber -D
A10(53)-1, B411(6)-1, B370(13)-1,
C69(110)-1, C85(73,P)-2

A32 Biplane close support -B
A10(35)-1, B411(7)-1, C69(112)-2,
C70(78)-1, C85(76,P)-1, B416(15)-1,
B370(13)-1, C121(1-34)-1, A15(82)-0

A38 Biplane transport, ambulance -D
B391(35)-1, B340(197)-1, C85(90,P)-1,
C113(1-174)-1

A100 (A430) Biplane reconnaissance -B
A3(7-41)-2, A10(55)-1, B18(1-271)-7,
C85(82,P)-2, B416(15)-1, B397(380)-1,
A15(83)-6, B380(13)-1, B152(88c)-1,
D18(7/70-22)-1

A101 (Ab 101) Biplane light bomber -B
A3(7-41)-1, A10(55)-1, B411(7)-1,
C85(83,P)-1, D18(7/70-22)-1,
C112(1-68)-2, C78(244)-1, A15(83)-0

A104 High wing attack bomber -E
C85(83,P)-1

A204 Twin engine transport -L
B16(272)-7, C85(95,P)-1, B153(10c)-1,
A15(83)-0

A211 Biplane trainer -K
C85(77,P)-1

A300 Twin engine bomber -E
D20(11/63-47)-1, C85(97,P)-2,
B416(19)-1, C10(216)-1, B153(10c)-1,
C87(30)-6, A15(83)-0

A304 Twin engine reconnaissance
bomber -B
A3(7-44)-2, A10(56)-1, C85(96,P)-1,
B416(19)-1, C10(217)-1, B153(11c)-1,
B87(82)-6, A15(83)-0

MB200 (Bloch MB200 BN) Twin
engine high wing bomber -B
A10(55)-1, B411(131)-1, C85(85,P)-1,
B387(42)-1, D18(7/70-20)-1

*AVIA Avia Akciova Spolecnost Pro
Prumysl Letecky*
BH-25J Biplane transport -I
C85(121,P)-2, B391(37)-1,
B287(23,105)-6, A15(83)-0
BH-33L (Ba33) Biplane fighter -D
D6(7/72-36)-2, C85(119,P)-2, A10(58)-1,
B411(17)-1, B416(17)-1
B35 (Av35) Fighter -E
D6(8/72-104)-2, D20(4/68-229)-1,
A10(60)-1, C85(133,P)-1, B416(21)-1,
B153(11c)-1, B387(38)-1, A15(83)-0

B71 (Tupolev SB-2) Twin engine
bomber -A
A10(58)-1, C85(157,P)-2, B411(132)-1,
B340(208)-1, B416(29)-6, A5(311)-1,
C66(1048)-1, D16(5/83-52)-1,
A15(218)-0, D18(7/70-20)-1

B122 (Bal22) Biplane trainer -B
B152(89c)-1, C85(137,P)-2, B340(198)-1

B135 (Av135) Fighter -C
D6(8/72-105)-2, A3(1-10)-2,
C85(135,P)-2, D20(4/68-228)-2,
A10(60)-1, B340(207)-1, B416(21)-1,
C74(61)-2, A15(83)-6

B158 (Av158) Twin engine bomber -E
D9(1/81-48)-2, D20(7/65-59)-1,
C85(146,P)-1, B416(19)-1

B534 Biplane fighter -A
D9(7/74-25)-4, B71(152)-2, B148(72)-4,
A3(1-8)-2, A10(59)-2, A6(8)-7,
B280(20)-2, B18(1-272)-7,
D16(11/83-38)-2, A15(83)-6

B634 Biplane fighter -E
D6(8/72-104)-2, B71(152-4)-1,
C85(133,P)-1

F39 (Fokker F.IX) Three engine high
wing bomber -B
A10(58)-1, C85(153,P)-1, B328(96)-1,
B416(18)-1, B391(38)-1, B340(208)-1,
D18(7/70-20)-1, B411(161)-0, A15(179)-0

*BENES-MRAZ Ing. Pavel Benes & Ing.
Jaroslav Mraz Tovarna Na Letadla*
Be 50 Beta Minor Trainer -I
B153(11c)-1, C85(196,P)-1, A15(83)-0
Be 51 Beta Minor Liaison, trainer -I
B153(12c)-1, C85(198,P)-1, B340(202)-1,
C113(3-171)-1, A15(83)-0
Be 252 Beta Scolar Trainer -I
B153(13c)-1, C85(200,P)-1, D3(2-134)-1
Be 550 Bibi Tourer -L
B153(12c)-1, C85(203,P)-2,
B200(1-425)-1, B139(44)-1, B420(68)-1
Be 551 Superbibi (Be 555) Tourer -I
B153(13c)-1, C85(204,P)-2, B340(202)-1

FGP *Flugtechnische*
Fertigungsgemeinschaft Prag
FGP-227 Scale model Blohm und Voss
BV 238 flying boat -F
A4(97)-2, C48(169)-2, C85(242,P)-1,
C96(40)-2, A3(5-64)-3, C139(116)-1

LETOV *Vojenska Tovarna Na Letadla*
'Letov'
S16 Biplane observation -D
C85(40,P)-2, D18(7/70-21)-1
S50 Twin engine bomber -E
D25(1/63-47)-2, B153(14c)-1,
C85(57,P)-2, D3(4-303)-1, B416(19)-1,
B397(388)-1
S218 Smolik Biplane trainer,
communications -B
C69(126)-2, C70(77)-1, C85(37,P)-1,
B241(P)-1, A15(83)-0
S228 Biplane bomber, trainer -B
D7(18-69)-1, C85(53,P)-1
S231 Biplane fighter -D
D9(2/75-103)-2, D9(7/84-41)-2,
C85(46,P)-2, C78(220)-2, A15(83)-6,
C74(67)-2, B416(26)-6, B351(186)-1,
C112(1-73)-3, D3(4-303)-1
S239 High wing sport -L
C85(51,P)-1, D18(7/70-23)-1
S328 Biplane reconnaissance bomber,
also floatplane -A
A3(7-46)-2, A10(63)-2, C85(53,P)-2,
D20(11/66-214)-1, A6(8)-7, B18(1-270)-7,
B280(152)-1, B411(86)-1, C74(68)-2,
A15(84)-6
S528 Biplane reconnaissance bomber -B
B152(92c)-1, C85(57,P)-1, A3(7-46)-6,
B397(390)-1, B279(300)-1, A15(84)-0,
A10(63)-0

MIEIK *Milos Mieik*
Mimi-2-SS Tourer -H
D3(8-8)-1

MRAZ *Tovaren Na Letadla Ing. J. Mraz*
(Automobilove Zavody)
M-1 Sokol Tourer -H
D3(8-241)-2, B60(106c)-2, B139(62)-2,
B403(331)-1
Zobor (Be 555 Superbibi) Tourer -I
C85(237,P)-1, D18(7/70-23)-1

PRAGA *Ceskomoravska-Kolben-Danek*
E39 (BH-39) Biplane trainer -B
C85(162,P)-1, B340(201)-1,
C113(3-171)-1
E40 Biplane trainer -L
B153(16c)-1, C85(175,P)-1, D3(5-291)-1,
B279(125)-0
E51 Twin engine twin boom
reconnaissance -E
D20(7/65-59)-1, C85(176,P)-2,
B416(21)-1
E210 Twin engine high wing pusher
light transport -L
B153(15c)-1, B60(107c)-1, C85(173,P)-1,
D3(5-291)-1
E241 Biplane trainer -B
B152(95c)-1, C85(163,P)-1, B340(198)-1,
D20(6/64-57)-1, C113(3-170)-1,
D3(5-291)-1, B380(11)-1, D18(7/70-22)-1

SKODA-KAUBA *Skoda-Kauba*
Flugzeugbau
SK L6 Twin boom pusher -F
C85(242)-3, D3(8-295)-6, C66(483)-0
SK P14 Ramjet fighter -J
B381(632)-3, D20(11/65-172)-6,
D3(8-295)-6, B253(136)-6, B364(136)-6,
C85(242)-0
SK V1 Piloted flying bomb -E
D20(11/65-169)-1, C85(240,P)-1,
D3(8-294)-6, C66(482)-0, B381(582)-0
SK V2 Piloted flying bomb -E
D20(11/65-169)-1, C85(240,P)-1,
D3(8-294)-6, C66(482)-0, B381(582)-0
SK V3 Sports -F
D20(11/65-171)-1, C85(240,P)-1,
D3(8-294)-6, C66(482)-0, B381(582)-0

SK V4 Trainer -E
D20(11/65-169)-1. D25(4/63-43)-2,
C85(240,P)-2, D3(8-294)-1, C66(482)-0,
B381(582)-0, B279(275)-0

SK V5 Fighter -J
D20(11/65-171)-6, D3(8-295)-6,
C66(483)-0, C85(241)-6, B381(583)-0

SK V6 Twin boom pusher -F
D20(11/65-171)-1, C85(241,P)-1,
D20(9/64-46)-1, D3(8-295)-1,
C66(483)-0, B381(583)-0

SK V7 Canard pusher -J
D20(11/65-171)-0, D3(8-295)-6,
C85(242)-6, C66(483)-0, B381(583)-0

SK V8 Trainer -E
B381(583)-1, D3(8-295)-1, C85(242,P)-1,
D20(11/65-171)-1, C66(483)-0

SK 257 Fighter trainer -C
D20(11/65-171)-1, B381(582)-1,
D25(4/63-43)-2, D3(8-294)-2,
C85(240,P)-1, C66(483,1047)-1

TATRA *Moravskoslezska Vagonka*
'Tatra'
T-101 Tourer -L
C85(182,P)-2
T-126 (Avro 626) Biplane trainer -B
C85(181,P)-1, B279(232)-0
T-131 (Bücker Bü 131) Biplane
trainer -B
B71(222-256)-1, C85(183,P)-1
T-301 Tourer -L
C85(183,P)-1

ZLIN *Zlinska Letecka A.S.*
Z-XII Trainer -L
C85(187,P)-2, D3(7-40)-1, B152(98c)-1,
B420(62)-1, C100(6-162)-1,
D11(5/72-51)-1
Z-XV Tourer -L
B153(17c)-1, C85(191,P)-1, D3(7-40)-1,
B20(A-120)-1
Z-212 Trainer -L
B153(17c)-1, C85(189,P)-1, D3(7-40)-1,
B20(A-120)-1

DENMARK

FLYVERTROPPERNES
VAERKSTEDER *Army Air Service*
Workshops
I O (Fokker C.I) Biplane trainer,
communications -B
B328(118)-1, D25(12/61-28)-1,
C73(33)-1, A15(84)-0
II O Biplane trainer, communications -B
C73(34)-1, A15(84)-6

ORLOGSVAERFTET *Royal Danish*
Shipyard
Dankok (L.B.II, Hawker Danecock)
Biplane fighter -B
B250(98)-2, D9(3/82-152)-1, A10(64)-1,
C73(13)-1, C74(74)-2, D25(12/61-27)-1,
B173(16)-1, B279(244)-0

S.A.I. *Skandinavisk Aero-Industrie A/S*
(Kramme & Zeuthen)

KZ II Sport, Coupe (L.M.II)
Trainer -B
B60(110c)-2, D11(2/64-30)-1,
B153(84c)-1, B139(40)-2, C73(45)-1,
B20(A-205)-1, D25(2/61-28)-1,
C10(219)-1, D3(7-210)-1, B279(275)-0

KZ III Laerke High wing ambulance -B
B60(111c)-2, D11(2/64-31)-1,
B139(21)-2, C73(44)-1, B420(73)-1,
D3(6-72)-1, B279(275)-0

KZ IV Twin engine ambulance -C
B60(111c)-2, D3(5-123)-2,
D11(2/64-31)-1, B391(43)-1, B139(128)-1

ESTONIA

OGL Ohu-ja Gaasikaitse Liit
OGL-1 (PON-1, Latvia **KOD-1)**
Biplane trainer -B
D7(18-70)-1

PN-3 Fighter trainer -E
D7(18-70)-1
PTO-4 Trainer, liaison -B
D7(18-70)-1, C12(2-74)-1, A15(84)-0

FINLAND

V.L. Industria Valtion Lentokonetekdas
Blackburn Ripon IIF Biplane
reconnaissance bomber, also floatplane -B
A3(7-68)-2, B199(223)-1, C70(51)-2,
B241(P)-1, B370(45)-1, D1(8-16)-1

Bristol Blenheim Twin engine
bomber -B
C70(57)-2, D7(28-71)-1, B143(1-58)-1,
B27(268)-1, B44(43)-1, B370(18)-1,
B71(93-11, 218-179)-1, B134(2-10)-1

Fokker C.X Biplane reconnaissance -B
A3(7-72)-2, C70(39)-2, B328(117)-1,
A6(126)-2, A10(275)-1, D1(8-16)-1,
C121(1-49)-2

Fokker D.XXI Fighter -A
A3(1-12)-2, D9(3/80-151)-1, C70(9)-2,
B241(205,P)-2, B370(24)-1

Humu (Brewster B-239 Buffalo wood
wing version) Fighter -E
C70(89)-1, C68(95)-1, D9(7/82-35)-1,
B147(10)-0, A15(191)-0

Kotka Biplane reconnaissance, also
floatplane -D
C69(128)-1, A10(65)-1, B370(11)-1,
C70(52)-1, C121(1-36)-1, A15(84)-0

Kukko (Gloster Gamecock II)
Biplane fighter trainer -D
C69(100)-2, B205(120)-1, B370(14)-1,
A10(366)-1, B71(33)-1, D9(7/80-36)-1,
B293(36)-6, B408(270)-3, B101(68)-1,
D7(21-61)-1

**Morko-Moraani (Morane-Saulnier
M.S.406)** Fighter -B
D25(3/61-19)-2, D6(10/73-188)-1,
A3(1-56)-1, C70(20)-1, B370(53)-1,
A15(96)-6, B61(48)-1, B241(217)-6,
C121(1-62)-1

Myrsky Fighter -B
D7(23-10)-4, A3(1-15)-2, A10(66)-1,
C70(29)-2, B18(1-287)-7, A7(258)-1,
D3(9-169)-1, A15(85)-6, B292(38)-6,
B370(39)-1

Pyorremyrsky Fighter -H
D6(10/71-273)-4, A3(1-18)-2,
D6(3/73-150)-1, D3(9-168)-1, C70(89)-1,
D9(7/82-34)-1, A15(85)-0

Pyry Trainer, liaison -B
D20(12/65-253)-2, C70(86)-2, A7(258)-1,
B370(2,48)-1, B139(50)-1, B153(87c)-1,
B22(A-207)-1, A15(85)-6, B241(P)-1

Saaski Biplane trainer,
communications -B
C69(116)-2, C70(78)-1, B370(10)-1,
C121(3-35)-1, A15(84)-0, B279(296)-0

Tuisku Biplane trainer,
reconnaissance -B
C69(130)-1, C70(82)-1, B139(156)-1,
B397(396)-1, B153(86c)-1, B370(19)-1,
C121(1-35)-1, B22(A-206)-1, A15(85)-0,
B279(296)-0

Viima Biplane trainer, liaison -B
C69(136)-2, C70(83)-1, B139(156)-1,
B370(2)-1, B153(86c)-1, B22(A-206)-1,
C121(1-36)-1, A15(85)-0, B279(296)-0

FRANCE

AMIOT *Avions Amiot (Societe d'Emboutessage le Constructions Mecaniques)*
143 Twin engine high wing bomber -A
A3(7-76)-2, D20(6/65-49)-2, A10(67)-2,
C23(127)-1, A6(10)-2, A7(245)-1,
B411(9)-1, B422(1-104)-1, B18(1-244)-7,
A15(85)-6
144 Twin engine high wing bomber -E
B397(402)-1, C25(133)-1, C18(118)-1,
A3(7-80)-0, A15(85)-0
150 BE Twin engine high wing bomber
floatplane -E
B152(119c)-2, B397(404)-1,
B20(A-186)-1, A3(7-81)-0, A15(85)-0
340 Twin engine bomber -E
B152(120c)-2, D18(10/72-2)-4,
C25(152)-1, A3(7-83)-6, C18(146)-1,
A15(86)-0
350 (351, 353, 354, 356) Twin engine
bomber -B
A3(7-83)-2, A10(68)-1, B279(79)-1,
B18(1-265)-7, B73(34)-1, B422(1-131)-1,
B153(105c)-1, C10(56)-2, C25(186)-1,
A15(85)-6
370 Twin engine record, postal -F
D25(8/56-15)-2, A3(7-89)-1, C10(6)-1,
B402(505)-1, B153(105c)-3, B436(206)-2

ARSENAL *Arsenal de l'Aeronautique*
Delanne 10-C2 Tandem wing fighter -E
A3(1-24)-2, D6(5/72-254)-2, C24(158)-2,
D25(9/56-31)-1, B61(12)-1, B42(32)-1,
C10(35)-3, C87(94,P)-1, B279(142)-0
VB 10 Tandem engine fighter -H
D6(7/71-94)-4, D6(4/72-218)-2,
D3(7-295)-2, B279(84)-1, D14(4-56)-3,
B60(117c)-0
VB 15 Tandem engine fighter -J
D26(196)-3

VG 30 Fighter -E
D6(4/72-217)-1, A3(1-20)-0, A15(86)-0
VG 32 Fighter -E
A3(1-21)-6, C24(182)-3, D14(2-25)-3,
A15(86)-0
VG 33 Fighter -C
A3(1-20)-2, D6(4/72-217)-2,
B18(1-266)-7, D25(7/56-17)-1, B73(31)-1,
C24(118,182)-1, B61(11)-1, C114(101)-1,
A15(86)-0
VG 34 Fighter -E
A3(1-22)-6, D6(4/72-218)-0, A15(86)-0
VG 36 Fighter -E
A3(1-22)-1, D6(4/72-218)-1,
D25(7/56-17)-1, C23(168)-1, A15(86)-0
VG 39 Fighter -E
D6(4/72-218)-2, A3(1-22)-1,
D20(3/65-43)-1, D25(7/56-17)-1,
D3(8-296)-1, C24(158)-1, A15(86)-0

BESSON *Societe de Constructions
Aeronautiques et Navales Marcel Besson*
MB-411 Sub-borne observation
floatplane -C
A3(6-8)-2, D20(8/67-812)-2,
C87(128,P)-1, D23(60-44)-1, A15(97)-0,
D29(2/84-44)-0, D9(2/86-98)-1

BLERIOT *Societe Aeronautique Bleriot
(SNCASO)*
SPAD 510 Biplane fighter -B
D6(10/73-192)-2, A10(130)-1,
D7(4-216)-2 B422(1-92)-1, C23(111)-1,
B411(163)-1, B14(117,128)-7,
C112(3-5)-2, C24(133)-1, A15(86)-0

BLOCH *Societe des Avions Marcel Bloch
(SNCASO)*
81 Ambulance -B
C23(167)-1, C87(135,P)-1, A15(86)-0

120 Three engine high wing transport -B
B162(115)-2, B391(58)-1, B15(52)-7,
C23(189)-1, C25(116)-1, D3(2-146)-1,
D23(102-23)-1

130 Guynemer Twin engine bomber -E
D29(2/82-49)-1, C25(109)-1, A3(7-93)-0

131 Twin engine bomber -A
A3(7-93)-2, A10(69)-1, B153(92c)-2,
C74(150)-2, B279(99)-1, B411(134)-1,
B422(1-110)-1, B18(1-253)-7, A15(86)-6,
B73(23)-1

133 Twin engine bomber -E
A3(7-94)-1, B397(408)-1, D3(2-158)-1,
C18(139)-1

134 Twin engine bomber -E
A3 (7-98)-3, B18(1-267)-6

135 Four engine bomber -E
A3(7-100)-2, C25(183)-1, D25(2/57-9)-1,
C10(57)-1, D3(2-158)-1

150 Fighter -E
D9(4/78-179)-2, D6(11/73-246)-2,
A3(1-26)-1, D7(2-220)-2, B71(201-228)-1,
C24(102)-1, B61(14)-1, C30(8,77)-1

151 Fighter -B
D9(4/78-182)-1, D6(11/73-246)-1,
A3(1-27)-1, D25(6/57-43)-2, A10(70)-3,
A6(10)-2, B88(1-73)-2, D3(2-30)-2,
A15(87)-0

152 Fighter -A
D9(4/78-179)-4, B148(106)-4, A3(1-26)-2,
B71(201)-2, B252(16)-2, A10(70)-1,
D6(11/73-247)-2, B164(20)-2, B61(16)-2,
A15(87)-6, B18(1-256)-7

153 Fighter -E
D6(11/73-247)-1, D9(4/78-187)-0,
B61(16)-1, A15(87)-0, C30(21)-0

155 Fighter -B
A3(1-31)-2, D9(4/78-188)-2,
D6(11/73-247)-2, B71(201-232)-1,
A10(70)-1, A7(246)-1, C24(167)-1,
A15(87)-6, B61(20)-1

157 Fighter -E
A3(1-33)-2, D6(12/73-296)-2,
D25(6/57-43)-1, C24(157)-1, C10(38)-1,
B61(25)-1, C30(22,123)-1

160 Four engine transport -E
B422(2-17)-1, B391(192)-1, C23(153)-1,
B153(93c)-1, C18(166)-1, A15(87)-0

161 (Sud-Est 161) Four engine
transport -I
B388(P)-1, D3(2-146)-1, B391(192)-0,
B162(132)-0, A15(87)-0

162 Four engine bomber -E
A3(7-104)-2, D25(2/57-9)-1, D3(2-154)-1,
C87(46,P)-1, A15(87)-0, B436(211)-3

170 Twin engine bomber -E
A3(7-107)-2, D25(2/57-11)-1,
B422(1-108)-1, C25(142)-1,
D18(9/70-13)-1, A15(87)-0

174 Twin engine reconnaissance
bomber -A
A3(7-107)-2, A6(10)-2, A10(71)-1,
C23(177)-1, B18(1-261)-7, C25(206)-1,
A15(87)-6, C87(25,P)-1, B73(34)-1,
D18(11/69-28)-2

175 Twin engine attack bomber -B
A3(7-116)-2, A10(71)-1, B139(125)-2,
D25(2/57-13)-1, C10(66)-3, B5(30)-1,
D18(10/70-15,11/70-14)-2, A15(87)-0

176 Twin engine attack bomber -C
A3(7-117)-1, D18(10/70-17)-1, A15(88)-0

177 Twin engine attack bomber -E
A3(1-118)-6, D18(11/70-14)-1, A15(88)-0

200 Twin engine high wing bomber -B
D6(1/72-35)-2, A10(71)-1, B422(1-96)-1,
B411(22)-1, B73(8)-1, B279(99)-1,
B14(145,155)-7, B416(19)-1,
C112(3-8)-2, A15(86)-0

210 Verdun Twin engine bomber -B
A3(7-123)-2, A10(72)-2, B411(23)-1,
B422(1-103)-1, B18(1-246)-7,
C112(3-11)-2, B73(8)-1, B297(66)-1,
C23(115)-1, A15(86)-0

218HY Twin engine bomber
floatplane -E
C25(144)-1

220 Twin engine transport -B
B162(116)-2, D3(3-75)-2, B153(94c)-2,
B391(60)-1, C23(162)-1, B16(188)-7,

C74(149)-2, B445(253)-1, B431(116)-8,
A15(86)-0, C15(108)-1

300 Pacifique Three engine transport -L
C18(138)-1, B153(95c)-3, C78(309)-1,
D3(2-158)-1

480 Twin engine reconnaissance bomber
floatplane -E
A3(6-10)-2, C25(186)-1, C10(70)-1,
B153(95c)-0

700 Fighter -E
A3(1-35)-2, D6(12/73-296)-2,
D25(7/61-46)-1, C24(120)-1, C18(193)-3,
C10(39)-1

800
See Sud-Ouest S.0.90

BREGUET *Societe Anonyme des Ateliers
d'Aviation Louis Breguet (SNCAO)*
Bre 19 Biplane bomber -B
D7(7-161)-4, A10(74)-2, C83(182)-2,
B411(28)-1, C74(152)-2, B422(1-80)-1,
C18(240)-2, B15(36)-7, C114(192)-1,
A15(88)-6

Bre 270 Sesquiplane reconnaissance,
trainer -B
B422(1-106)-1, B73(13)-1, C23(93)-1,
D29(2/82-48)-1, C18(243)-2, C25(92)-1,
A15(88)-6

Bre 413 Twin engine sesquiplane
bomber, reconnaissance -D
C25(102)-1, C18(144)-1, D3(8-248)-1,
D29(2/82-48)-1, C87(23,P)-1

Bre 462 Vultur Twin engine bomber -D
B422(1-106)-1, C25(133)-1,
B152(121c)-1, D16(2/76-40)-1,
C74(153)-2, B397(410)-1, C18(182)-1,
B436(218)-1, C78(251)-1, C100(6-144)-1

Bre 470 Fulgur Twin engine
transport -L
D9(6/84-306)-2, C78(310)-1, C18(133)-1,
C112(3-14)-6, D3(2-194)-1

Bre 482 Four engine bomber -E
A3(7-129)-2, D25(9/58-20)-2, C10(58)-1,
C87(23,P)-1, B18(1-267)-0

Bre 500 Colmar Twin engine
transport -E
D25(3/62-45)-1, C10(78)-1, C23(231)-1,
B60(119c)-0

Bre 521 Bizerte Three engine
sesquiplane patrol flying boat -B
A3(5-6)-2, A10(75)-1, D3(3-126)-2,
D23(61-68)-1, B411(136)-1,
D25(5/62-47)-2, C18(204)-1,
B18(1-247)-7, C74(152)-2, A15(88)-6,
B294(54)-6, B440(185)-1, C114(113)-1

Bre 522 Three engine sesquiplane
reconnaissance flying boat -E
B73(14)-1, A3(5-7)-0, A15(88)-0

Bre 690 Twin engine fighter -E
D9(10/74-200)-2, A3(7-132)-1,
A10(76)-1, B88(1-79)-2, B153(106c)-1,
B422(1-126)-1, C18(188)-1, A15(88)-0

Bre 691 Twin engine bomber -B
A3(7-134)-1, D25(5/63-34)-2,
D3(2-150)-2, A10(76)-1, A6(12)-7,
B18(1-257)-7, B411(136)-1, B436(217)-3,
B289(82)-6, A15(88)-0

Bre 693 Twin engine bomber -A
A3(7-135)-2, A10(76)-1, D25(5/63-35)-1,
C23(178)-1, A6(12)-1, B422(1-127)-1,
C25(242)-1, B73(32)-1, B279(105)-1,
A15(88)-0

Bre 695 Twin engine bomber -B
A3(7-135)-1, C23(179)-1,
D25(9/59-19)-1, A15(88)-6

Bre 700 Twin engine fighter -J
C24(126)-3

Bre 730 Four engine high wing
reconnaissance flying boat -C
A3(5-10)-2, B60(119c)-1, B197(212)-1,
B440(188)-1, C10(75)-1

Br 731 Four engine high wing
reconnaissance flying boat -H
A3(5-11)-1, B139(150)-1, B440(187)-1

Bre 790 Nautilus High wing pusher
reconnaissance flying boat -C
A3(5-13)-2, C10(8)-1

Bre 820 Twin engine fighter -J
D14(6-96)-3, C24(160)-3

Bre 910 Glide bomb -E
B163(100)-0
G.11E Coaxial rotor helicopter -H
D3(7-295)-2, B60(119c)-1, B228(41)-1,
B23(60)-3
Gyroplane-Laboratoire (Rene
Dorand) Coaxial rotor helicopter -F
B296(108)-6, B443(69)-1, B355(91)-1,
B127(72)-1, B408(213)-1, B53(14)-1,
B23(14)-6, B228(40)-0, B447(36)-1

BUGATTI Automobiles E. Bugatti
100P Tandem engine fighter, racer -G
D18(1/70)-2, C36(147)-1, B84(389)-0

*C.A.M.S. Chantiers Aero Maritimes de la
Seine*
37 Biplane pusher observation, trainer
flying boat -B
A3(5-15)-2, C25(146)-1, B197(209)-1,
B114(5-524)-1, A15(88)-0
55 Tandem engine biplane
reconnaissance flying boat -B
A3(5-17)-2, A10(79)-1, C25(206)-1,
B411(137)-1, B73(15)-1, B114(5-525)-6,
A15(88)-6, B279(113)-1, B387(44)-1,
D1(3-31)-1

*C.A.O. Societe Nationale de Constructions
Aeronautiques de l'Ouest (SNCAO)*
30 (LN-30) High wing pusher trainer
flying boat -E
A3(5-20)-2
200 Fighter -E
A3(1-37)-2, D20(6/67-679)-2,
D9(6/75-306)-2, C27(27)-1, B153(90c)-1,
C24(117)-1, C10(53)-2, A15(99)-0,
B114(5-531)-0
600 Twin engine high wing torpedo
bomber, reconnaissance -E
A3(7-145)-2, C87(79,P)-1
700 Four engine bomber -G
A3(7-148)-2, D25(1/58-41)-1, B87(71)-6,
C87(46)-6, B18(1-267)-0
720 Four engine transport -J
A3(7-151)-0

C.A.P.R.A. (Bernard)
RR Racer -G
D14(1-16)-3

CASTEL-MAUBOUSSIN
Etablissements Fouga et Cie.
C.M.10 High wing transport glider -H
B286(182)-2, D6(4/72-209)-1, D3(9-14)-1

*CAUDRON Societe Anonyme des Avions
Caudron*
C.272 Luciole Biplane liaison -I
B153(107c)-1, C23(146)-1, B139(153)-1,
D10(2/67-51)-1, D3(3-26)-1,
C112(3-16)-1, A15(88)-0, C78(332)-0
C.400 (C.282 Phalene) High wing
liaison -B
C23(155)-1, C112(3-17)-2, C18(79)-1,
D3(3-26)-1, A15(88)-0
C.445 Goeland (C.440) Twin engine
transport, liaison -A
D3(2-243)-2, D25(12/61-45)-1,
B391(90)-1, A7(246)-1, B139(114)-2,
C23(144)-1, B153(109c)-1, B16(190)-7,
C10(8,79)-2, B293(95)-6
C.480 Fregate (de Havilland D.H.85)
High wing liaison -K
D3(3-26)-1, C18(172)-1
C.510 Pelican High wing liaison,
ambulance -I
B139(25)-1, B152(123c)-0, A15(90)-0
C.570 Twin engine transport -E
C18(150)-1
C.600 Aiglon Liaison -I
B153(107c)-1, B139(44)-1, C112(3-22)-2,
C23(156)-1, C18(176)-1, C78(332)-1,
D3(7-211)-1, A15(90)-0
C.635 Simoun (C.620, C.630) Light
transport -A
D3(2-219)-2, B391(88)-1, B153(108c)-1,
B422(2-39)-1, B139(44)-1, C23(166)-1,
C18(144)-2, B16(187)-7, B279(118)-1,
A15(90)-0
C.670 Twin engine fighter trainer -E
B397(414)-1, B114(5-494)-0

C.690 (Japan **KXC**) Trainer -B
B73(16)-1, B397(416)-1, D10(2/67-59)-2,
C23(154)-1, C18(173)-1, D3(3-26)-1,
C100(6-166)-1, B114(5-494)-0
C.710 Cyclone Fighter -E
D9(9/75-136)-2, B152(124c)-1,
D25(11/56-11)-1, C24(104)-1,
C18(163)-1, A3(1-39)-0, A15(90)-0
C.713 Cyclone Fighter -E
D9(9/75-136)-3, C24(137)-1, A3(1-39)-0,
A15(90)-0, C110(196)-1
C.714 Cyclone Fighter -B
D9(9/75-136)-2, A3(1-39)-2, B164(18)-2,
A10(79)-1, C23(182)-1, B422(1-135)-1,
B411(161)-1, C24(183)-1, B18(1-258)-7,
A15(90)-6

***CAUDRON-RENAULT** Societe
Anonyme des Avions Caudron-Renault*
C.R.760 Fighter -E
D9(9/75-137)-2, A3(1-41)-2
C.R.770 Fighter -E
A3(1-43)-2, D9(9/75-137)-1,
D25(11/56-11)-1

***CENTRE** Societe Nationale de
Constructions Aeronautiques du Centre
(SNCAC)*
NC-130 Twin engine high altitude -F
D25(10/57-47)-1, C87(66,P)-1, C10(82)-0
NC-150 Twin engine high altitude
bomber -E
A3(7-151)-2, C25(184)-1, C87(66,P)-1,
C18(192)-1, D14(3-38)-3
NC-410 (Farman F.410) Twin engine
torpedo, patrol floatplane -E
A3(6-15)-2, C25(74)-1, C87(74,P)-1,
C10(73)-1, C130(197)-1
NC-470 (Farman F.470) Twin engine
high wing trainer floatplane -B
A3(6-13)-2, A15(91)-0, C130(204)-1
NC-701 Martinet (Siebel Si 204D)
Twin engine trainer -B
B422(2-80)-1, C23(258)-1, B401(32)-3,
C76(343)-1, B387(16)-1

NC-702 Martinet (Siebel Si 204A)
Twin engine transport -B
B60(113c)-1, B391(191)-1, D3(7-292)-2,
C23(259)-1, B139(126)-1, B401(32)-1
NC-900 (Focke-Wulf Fw 190)
Fighter -B
A10(123)-1, D20(4/64-59)-1, C23(246)-1,
B305(123)-1, B114(18-1974)-0
NC-2001 Abeille (Rene Dorand) Twin
rotor helicopter -H
D3(7-292)-2, B228(54)-1, B60(115c)-0,
B23(124)-0, B53(149)-0
**NC-3021 Belphegor (Sud-Ouest
S.O.3020)** High altitude research -H
D20(7/67-748)-2, D3(8-53)-2, B405(6)-1,
B60(116c)-3

***DEWOITINE** Societe Anonyme
Dewoitine (SNCAM)*
D.21 High wing fighter -D
A10(86)-1, B411(141)-1, D9(1/78-32)-1,
B279(144)-1, C26(39)-1, C24(34)-1
D.333 Three engine transport -L
C26(395)-2, B391(96)-1, C112(3-24)-2,
C110(214)-1
D.338 Three engine transport -I
B162(101)-2, B391(97)-1, C26(401)-2,
D3(3-87)-2, B153(103c)-1, B15(54)-7,
D23(102-96)-1, C23(145)-1, B431(117)-8,
A15(90)-0, C15(129)-1
D.342 Three engine transport -L
C26(419)-2, B391(98)-1, B153(104c)-1
D.371 (D.372) High wing fighter -D
D9(2/78-72)-2, A10(87)-1, D7(4-216)-2,
C26(138)-2, C78(204)-2, B422(1-94)-1,
C24(131)-1, D29(10/82-16)-1, A15(90)-0
D.373 High wing carrier fighter -B
A10(87)-1, B411(142)-1, B441(76)-1,
C26(144)-1, A15(90)-0, D9(2/78-72)-0
D.376 High wing carrier fighter -B
C26(144)-2, D23(60-86,61-77)-1,
A15(90)-0, D9(2/78-72)-0
D.482 Trainer -I
C26(284)-2

D.500 Fighter -D
D7(1-17)-1, D9(1/78-33)-1,
B14(117,128)-2, C26(85)-2, A10(88)-1,
C27(15)-1, B148(64)-1, B73(7)-1,
B422(1-93)-1, C23(117)-1, B167(34)-1
D.501 Fighter -D
D7(1-86)-1, C26(92)-1, C27(15)-1,
C23(118)-1, B411(42)-1, B73(7)-1,
B422(1-93)-1, C24(165)-1, A15(90)-0,
B114(7-680)-6, D7(29-66)-1

D.503 Fighter, trainer -E
D9(2/78-73)-1, C26(104)-1, C27(18)-1,
A15(90)-0
D.510 (Japan **AXD**) Fighter -B
D7(1-89)-4, B148(64)-4, D9(2/78-73)-2,
A10(88)-2, C26(100)-2, C27(15)-2,
B159(54)-8, B422(1-94)-1, B73(7)-1,
A15(90)-6
D.514 LP Fighter, parachute test
launcher -E
C26(169)-2, D25(12/59-42)-2, C27(24)-1,
D9(3/78-124)-0
D.520 Fighter -A
B148(120)-4, A3(1-45)-2, B71(135)-2,
C27-4, B164(19)-2, A10(89)-2, A6(13)-2,
D9(3/78-124)-2, B61(28)-2, C26(175)-1,
A15(91)-6, A7(248)-1, B18(1-262)-7
D.520Z Fighter -E
A3(1-49)-1, C27(200)-2, C26(321)-1,
B61(37)-1, A15(91)-0
D.521 (Merlin-engine version D.520)
Fighter -E
D9(7/82-125)-0, A3(1-47)-6, C27(177)-6,
C26(178)-1, A15(91)-0
D.550 Speed record -F
D9(7/82-47)-2, D20(4/67-515)-2,
C27(180)-2, C26(334)-1, A3(1-50)-0
D.551 (**D.560**) Fighter -G
A3(1-50)-2, C27(184)-2, D9(6/78-305)-1,
B61(37)-1, C24(157)-2
D.580 Trainer -J
C26(288)-3
D.600 (Hispano-Suiza HS 50)
Fighter -J
C27(206)-2, D20(6/67-679)-1,

C26(189)-1, C10(253)-1
D.600 Twin engine high altitude
bomber -J
C26(242)-3
D.720 Twin engine high wing
reconnaissance bomber -E
A3(8-20)-2, C26(253)-2, B18(1-260)-7,
C87(119,P)-1
HD.730 Observation floatplane -E
A3(6-18)-2, C26(256)-2,
D25(10/57-47)-1, C10(70)-1
HD.731 Observation floatplane -E
A3(6-19)-2, C26(256)-1
D.750 Twin engine carrier bomber -E
A3(8-23)-2, C26(262)-2, C87(79)-6
D.770 Twin engine attack bomber -E
A3(8-26)-2, C26(231)-2, C87(115,P)-1
HD.780 Floatplane fighter version
D.520 -G
D9(10/75-203)-2, C27(190)-2, B61(37)-1,
D14(1-4)-3, A15(91)-0
D.790 Carrier fighter version D.520 -J
C27(192)-3
D.800 Four engine bomber -J
C26(239)-2
High wing glide bomb -C
C26(297)-2

FARMAN *Avions Henri et Maurice*
Farman (SNCAC)
F.190 High wing transport,
ambulance -B
B391(116)-1, B15(34)-6, C78(294)-1,
C112(3-36)-1, C130(115)-1
F.220 Twin tandem engine high wing
transport -I
B391(122)-1, D23(102-26)-1,
D18(5/69-19)-1, C130(148)-1
F.221 Twin tandem engine high wing
bomber -C
A10(92)-1, B411(52)-1, C25(107)-1,
B422(1-103)-1, C18(131)-1, B351(245)-1,
D1(7-8)-1, D18(5/69-20)-1, C130(150)-1

F.222 Twin tandem engine high wing bomber -B
A3(8-7)-2, A6(13)-2, A10(92)-1,
C23(121)-1, B422(1-109)-1, C130(150)-1,
B18(1-248)-7, A7(248)-1, B73(10)-1,
C74(160)-2, A15(91)-0

F.223 (NC-223) Twin tandem engine high wing bomber, transport -B
A3(8-12)-2, A10(92)-1, B391(125)-1,
C23(163)-1, D23(102-101)-1, C80(229)-1,
B397(426)-1, B152(112c)-1, C130(154)-1,
A15(91)-0

F.223.4 (NC-223.4) Twin tandem engine high wing bomber, transport -C
A3(8-16)-2, D20(12/65-251)-3,
B391(127)-1, C23(164)-1, B73(43)-1,
D23(61-90)-2, B153(99c)-1, A15(91)-6,
C130(167)-1

F.224 Twin tandem engine high wing transport -B
B162(100)-7, B391(125)-1, C130(158)-1,
C25(219)-1, B57(59a)-1

F.420 Twin engine high wing fighter bomber -E
D16(3/76-40)-1, C18(120)-1,
B397(428)-1, C130(199)-1, D3(3-278)-1

F.460 Alize (F.480) High wing trainer -K
C78(341)-1, C130(205)-1

F.470 (NC-470) Twin engine high wing trainer -E
C23(169)-1, A15(91)-0, C130(203)-1

GERIN Jacques Gerin
V-6E Verivol Variable geometry wing -F
C87(62,P)-1, C18(286)-1, B279(176)-0,
D9(3/75-138)-0, B153(110c)-0

GOURDOU
G.11 C1 Variable wingspan fighter -J
C87(96)-6
G.50B Twin engine attack bomber -J
D14(4-54)-3
G-120HY Twin engine observation floatplane -E
A3(6-27)-2, D14(5-80)-3

GOURDOU-LESEURRE Societe Anonyme des Etablissements Gourdou-Leseurre
GL-22 High wing fighter -D
D7(18-68)-1, D9(11/80-234)-1,
D7(3-89)-1
GL-32 (LGL-32) High wing fighter -D
A10(107)-1, D7(3-90)-7,
D9(12/80-298)-2, B411(89)-1,
C78(212)-2, B422(1-72)-1,
B14(116,127)-7, C23(78)-1, B293(69)-6,
C24(72)-1
GL-432 High wing carrier bomber -E
B382(37)-1
GL-633 (LGL-633) High wing dive bomber -C
C112(3-41)-2, C78(258)-1, A10(108)-0,
B411(90)-0
GL-810 Observation floatplane -B
A3(6-23)-2, A15(91)-6, D23(61-46)-3,
B411(162)-0
GL-812 Observation floatplane -C
D23(61-128)-1, A3(6-24)-0, A15(91)-0
GL-832HY Observation floatplane -B
A3(6-25)-2, D25(3/62-41)-2,
D23(60-49)-1, A15(91)-0

GUERCHAIS-ROCHE Roche Aviation
T.30 Liaison -I
D10(2/67-51)-1, B279(262)-0,
B60(121c)-0
T.35 Tourer -L
B139(35)-2, D3(7-298)-2, B279(262)-0,
B60(120c)-1

HANRIOT Compagnie des Avions Hanriot (SNCAC)
H.16 High wing liaison -B
C18(253)-1, C23(94)-1, A15(92)-0
H.175 High wing naval observation -C
D23(60-50)-1, A15(92)-0
H.182 High wing trainer -B
C23(124)-1, B73(15)-1, C18(253)-1,
B279(185)-1, D3(5-208)-1, C112(3-43)-1,
C78(342)-6, A15(92)-0

H.185 High wing liaison -C
A15(92)-0

H.220 Twin engine fighter bomber -E
D9(2/82-88)-2, B152(113c)-1,
C24(106)-2, B397(430)-1, D3(4-110)-1,
A3(1-52)-0

H.230 Twin engine high wing trainer -E
D25(7/61-46)-1, B152(113c)-1,
D3(4-110)-1, A15(92)-0

H.231 Twin engine high wing trainer -E
D25(7/61-46)-1, C10(79)-1, A15(92)-0

H.232 Twin engine high wing trainer -B
D25(7/61-46)-2, C70(46)-2, C23(157)-1,
B397(432)-1, C121(1-67)-1, D26(192)-3,
A15(92)-0

H.433 Biplane trainer -B
C18(252)-1, C23(89)-1, A15(92)-0

H.436 Biplane trainer -B
C23(89)-1, C78(214)-1, A15(91)-0

H.437 Biplane ambulance -D
C18(252)-1, A15(92)-0

H.510 (NC-510) Twin engine
observation bomber -E
A3(8-30)-1, B153(99c)-1,
D25(10/57-45)-1, D3(4-110)-1,
C10(80)-1, C110(205)-1, C87(119)-6

NC-530 Twin engine observation
bomber -E
A3(8-30)-2, C25(184)-1,
D25(10/57-45)-1, B18(1-264)-7

NC-600 (H.220-2) Twin engine
fighter -E
D9(2/82-89)-2, A3(1-52)-2,
D25(10/60-46)-2, C24(123)-1,
B153(99c)-1, B18(1-259)-7

LATÉCOERE Societe Industrielle
d'Aviation Latécoere (Breguet)
Laté 29.0 High wing torpedo
floatplane -B
A3(6-29)-2, A10(95)-1, D25(3/62-47)-1,
B411(84)-1, D23(61-48)-2, B279(208)-1,
A15(93)-0

Laté 298 Reconnaissance bomber
floatplane -A
A3(6-31)-2, D20(8/68-460)-2, A10(95)-1,
B153(111c)-1, C74(163)-2, B411(85)-1,
B73(25)-1, B397(434)-1, B18(1-249)-7,
A15(93)-6

Laté 299 Carrier reconnaissance
bomber -E
A3(8-36)-2, D23(61-44)-1, C10(7)-1,
A10(96)-0

Laté 299A Tandem engine -F
A3(8-39)-2, C10(61)-1, A10(96)-0

Laté 302 Twin tandem engine high wing
patrol flying boat -C
A3(5-22)-2, B197(212)-1, C18(197)-1,
D3(4-291)-1, A15(93)-6, D23(61-51)-2,
C74(162)-2, B294(70)-6

Laté 381 Tandem engine high wing
flying boat -C
B73(14)-1, C74(162)-2, D3(4-291)-1

Laté 521 Six engine high wing
reconnaissance flying boat -I
A3(5-24)-1, D25(9/62-47)-2, B15(58)-7,
B391(145)-1, C74(163)-2, B404(97)-1,
B431(160)-1, B279(208)-1, B291(61)-1

Laté 523 Six engine high wing
reconnaissance flying boat -B
A3(5-24)-2, B73(14)-1, B197(212)-1,
D23(61-52)-2, A15(93)-6

Laté 550 Twin tandem engine torpedo
bomber floatplane -E
C110(205)-1

Laté 570 Twin engine bomber -E
D25(10/57-47)-1, D25(12/57-9)-3,
C10(61)-1, D14(6-86)-3

Laté 582 Three engine high wing
reconnaissance flying boat -E
B153(111c)-3, C110(206)-1, D3(4-303)-1

Laté 611 Achernar Four engine high
wing reconnaissance flying boat -E
A3(5-27)-2, D23(61-87)-1, B197(212)-1,
C10(76)-1, A15(94)-0

Laté 631 Six engine high wing transport
flying boat -I
D3(6-212)-2, B391(148)-1,

D25(3/60-9)-1, B16(193)-7, B139(150)-1,
C74(164)-2, B291(94)-1, B5(6)-1,
D18(5/69-24)-1

LEOPOLDOFF *Etablissements*
Aucouturier, Dugoua et Cie.
Colibri Biplane trainer -D
D3(4-303)-1, B153(112c)-0

LEVASSEUR *Etablissements*
P. Levasseur
P.L.7 Biplane carrier torpedo bomber -D
A10(103)-1, B411(149)-1, D23(61-42)-1,
B114(19-2120)-1, B279(211)-1,
B383(22)-1, C87(166,P)-1, A15(94)-0
P.L.14 Biplane torpedo floatplane -D
A10(103)-1, B411(150)-1, B279(211)-1,
A15(94)-0, B114(19-2120)-0
P.L.15 Biplane torpedo floatplane -B
A3(6-38)-2, A10(104)-1, D3(4-303)-1,
A15(94)-0, B114(19-2120)-0
P.L.101 Biplane carrier
reconnaissance -D
C18(200)-1, C110(206)-1, D3(4-303)-1,
A15(94)-0
P.L.201 High wing twin boom/float
torpedo bomber -E
C87(166,P)-1, D3(4-303)-1, D26(97)-3

LIORE ET OLIVIER *Etablissements*
Liore et Olivier (SNCASE)
LeO 201 (LeO 20) Twin engine biplane
parachute trainer -B
A10(98)-2, B411(87)-1, B159(129)-6,
B422(1-71)-1, B73(6)-1, B14(145,155)-7,
B279(213)-1, B289(52)-6, C25(56)-1,
C18(114)-1
LeO 206 Twin tandem engine biplane
bomber -B
B411(150)-1, B422(1-71)-1, C25(56)-1,
C23(85)-1, C18(115)-1, A10(99)-0,
A15(94)-0
LeO 213 Twin engine biplane transport,
parachute trainer -B
B391(157)-1, C23(156)-1, C25(128)-1,
C78(260)-1

LeO H-242 Twin tandem engine high
wing transport flying boat -L
D6(1/74-42)-1, B391(160)-1,
B162(128)-6, C15(82)-1, D3(5-3)-1
LeO H-246 Four engine high wing
reconnaissance flying boat -I
A3(5-44)-2, C12(106)-1, B391(164)-1,
B162(128)-2, C18(262)-1, B388(P)-1,
B152(115c)-2, D6(8/72-106)-1,
B431(161)-8, A15(94)-0
LeO 257 Twin engine biplane bomber -C
B422(1-99)-1, A10(99)-1, B411(88)-1,
C25(146)-1
LeO H-257bis Twin engine biplane
torpedo floatplane -B
A3(6-40)-2, A10(99)-1, B73(14)-1,
B114(16-1723)-1, C25(102)-1,
D23(61-72)-1, C87(74,P)-1, A15(94)-0
LeO H-258 Twin engine biplane torpedo
floatplane -B
D23(61-49)-2, A15(94)-6, A3(6-40)-0,
A10(100)-0
LeO H-259 Twin engine biplane torpedo
floatplane -E
D3(5-3)-1, A3(6-42)-0, A15(95)-0
LeO C.30 (**C.301,** version Cierva C.30)
Observation autogiro -B
B228(48)-1, B73(13)-1, C23(138)-1,
C18(207)-1, D3(5-3)-1, D23(60-58)-1
LeO C.34 Observation autogiro -C
B228(57)-1, C18(208)-1
LeO H-43 Observation floatplane -B
A3(6-43)-2, C110(207)-1, C87(166,P)-1,
D23(61-42)-1, D3(5-3)-1, A15(94)-0
LeO 45 Twin engine bomber -E
A3(8-67)-1, B71(173-4)-1, A10(100)-1,
B153(100c)-1, C25(171)-1, B397(436)-1,
A15(95)-0, D9(10/85-179)-1
LeO 451 Twin engine bomber -A
D9(10/85-179)-4, A3(8-67)-2, B71(173)-2,
D20(7/65-65)-2, A10(100)-2, A6(17)-2,
B252(92)-2, B18(1-254)-7, C23(139)-1,
B73(28)-1, A15(95)-6
LeO 453 Twin engine communications,
mapping -H

32

B71(173-10)-1, A3(8-67)-0, A15(95)-0,
D9(10/85-189)-6
LeO 455 Twin engine photographic,
engine test -M
A3(8-76)-1, B71(173-13)-1,
D9(10/85-189)-1, D20(8/65-39)-1,
A15(95)-0
LeO H-46 Twin engine torpedo
floatplane -E
D6(11/73-248)-1, C18(200)-1,
B153(101c)-3, B397(438)-1, D3(5-3)-1
LeO H-470 Twin tandem engine high
wing patrol flying boat -I
A3(5-46)-2, B391(162)-1, C18(265)-1,
B16(191)-7, C10(72)-1, D23(61-50)-2,
B152(115c)-2, A15(95)-6, B431(161)-8
LeO 48 Twin engine fighter -F
C10(80)-1, D9(4/85-204)-0

*LOIRE Ateliers et Chantiers de la Loire
(SNCAO)*
46 High wing fighter -B
D20(4/66-493)-2, D7(4-219)-2,
A10(106)-1, B411(89)-1, D9(5/85-254)-2,
B14(117,128)-7, C23(112)-1,
B422(1-102)-1, B293(56)-6, A15(95)-0
501 High wing pusher communications
flying boat -C
A3(5-30)-2, B197(210)-1, D18(4/70)-1
70 Three engine high wing
reconnaissance flying boat -B
A3(5-32)-2, B76(91)-1, B197(211)-1,
C110(208)-1, D3(5-27)-1, B397(442)-1
130 High wing pusher observation flying
boat -A
A3(5-35)-2, B153(91c)-1, C25(209)-1,
B197(211)-1, B73(15)-1, D23(61-41)-2,
B436(231)-1, C18(197)-1, A15(95)-0
210 Fighter floatplane -B
A3(6-45)-2, D7(4-221)-2, D20(6/61-54)-2,
A10(107)-1, D9(5/85-255)-2,
D23(61-43)-2, C18(202)-1, B153(89c)-1,
B397(444)-1, A15(96)-6

*LOIRE-NIEUPORT Groupe Loire-
Nieuport (SNCAO)*
LN 10 Twin engine torpedo
reconnaissance floatplane -E
A3(6-47)-2, D20(9/65-44)-2, C10(73)-3,
D26(69)-3
LN 140 (Ni-140) Carrier fighter
bomber -E
D25(10/59-9)-1, C87(68,P)-1,
C110(216)-1
LN 161 (Ni-161) Fighter -E
D7(4-223)-2, C18(158)-2,
D25(10/59-9)-1, C24(101)-1,
B152(103c)-1, D18(5/71-8)-2,
B436(234)-3, D9(5/85-255,6/85-332)-2
LN 40 Carrier dive bomber -C
A3(8-41)-1, D20(8/66-768)-1,
D25(7/60-9)-1, A10(105)-1, B382(90)-1,
A15(96)-0, B114(16-1763)-0
LN 401 Carrier dive bomber -B
A3(8-42)-2, D20(8/66-768)-2,
D25(5/59-46)-3, B383(47)-1,
C114(101)-1, A15(96)-0,
B114(16-1763)-0
LN 402 Carrier dive bomber -E
A3(8-42)-6, D20(8/66-768)-6, A15(96)-0
LN 411 Dive bomber -B
A3(8-44)-0, A15(96)-6, D23(60-79)-3,
D20(8/66-768)-0, B114(16-1763)-0
LN 42 Carrier dive bomber -E
A3(8-44)-2, D20(8/66-768)-2,
D25(5/59-46)-1, B289(63)-6, A15(96)-0

*MAILLET Societe Francaise de
Constructions Aeronautiques*
201 Liaison, trainer -I
B73(16)-1, B152(131c)-1, A15(96)-0,
B279(278)-0

MAKHONINE Ivan Makhonine
MAK-101 Variable wingspan -F
D9(3/75-135)-3, D3(8-261)-1,
C18(269)-1, C87(62,P)-1

MAUBOUSSIN *Avions Mauboussin*
(Etablissements Fouga et Cie)
M.123 Trainer -B
B152(129c)-1, B60(122c)-1, C18(173)-1,
D3(5-75)-1, B279(223)-0
M.124 Trainer -K
D3(7-116)-1
M.128 Light plane -K
D3(7-116)-1
M.129 Trainer -B
B60(123c)-1, C23(244)-1, B139(37)-2,
B279(223)-0
M.202 Trainer -L
B153(113c)-1, B60(123c)-1, D3(4-223)-3
M.300 Twin engine transport, trainer -H
D3(5-75)-1, D3(4-223)-3, B60(124c)-0
M.400 Twin engine biplane transport -E
D3(4-223)-2, D3(5-75)-1

MAX HOLSTE *Avions Max Holste*
M.H.52 Trainer -L
B60(124c)-1, B139(36)-2,
D3(7-116,295)-2, B279(193)-0

MORANE-SAULNIER *Aeroplanes*
Morane-Saulnier
M.S.225 High wing fighter, trainer -D
A10(109)-1, B411(151)-1, B73(5)-1,
C23(97)-1, B14(117,128)-2,
D11(11/66-47)-3, B293(71)-6, C24(99)-1,
B279(232)-1, A15(96)-0
M.S.226 High wing carrier fighter -D
D23(60-49)-1, D18(No.4)-1, A10(110)-0,
A15(96)-0
M.S.230 High wing trainer -A
B422(1-85)-1, B139(28)-1, C23(99)-1,
B14(150,159)-7, B73(15)-1,
C112(3-54)-2, B232(22)-1, C18(74)-1,
B380(21)-1
M.S.315 High wing trainer -A
B422(1-84)-1, B139(28)-1, C23(143)-1,
C18(172)-1, D3(4-29)-1
M.S.405 Fighter -C
D6(9/73-130)-1, B71(147)-1, A3(1-54)-1,

A10(110)-1, B61(38)-1, B397(446)-1,
A15(96)-0
M.S.406 Fighter -A
D6(9/73-130,10/73-183)-4, B71(147)-2,
A3(1-54)-2, B148(88)-4, A6(14)-4,
B61(38)-2, A10(110)-2, B164(17)-2,
B252(121)-2, A15(96)-6, A7(253)-1
M.S.410 Fighter -B
D6(10/73-185)-1, B71(147-4)-1,
D20(5/69-73)-1, B370(38)-1,
C121(1-58)-1
M.S.435 Trainer -C
D20(10/69-73)-1
M.S.450 Fighter -E
A3(1-58)-2, D25(9/62-43)-2, C24(116)-1,
B61(49)-1, C27(26)-1
M.S.470 Trainer -E
B60(125c)-1, D3(9-20)-1,
B114(23-2554)-0
M.S.472 Vanneau Trainer -M
B60(125c)-2, C23(278)-1, B139(61)-3,
D3(7-295)-2, C10(81)-1, B422(2-82)-1,
B114(23-2554)-0
M.S.500 Criquet (Fieseler Fi 156)
High wing observation -B
B71(228-136)-1, B139(16)-3, C23(248)-1,
C93(40)-1
M.S.502 Criquet High wing
observation -H
B71(228-136)-1, B139(16)-1, C23(248)-1,
C93(40)-1, B387(18)-1, D3(7-315)-1
M.S.506
See Switzerland: EFW D-3801
M.S.540
See Switzerland: Doflug D-3802

MUREAUX *Les Ateliers de Construction*
du Nord de la France et des Mureaux
(SNCAN)
ANF 113 High wing observation,
fighter -C
A10(112)-1, C24(110)-1, B279(233)-1,
A15(97)-0, B411(10)-0, B152(31b)-1
ANF 114 High wing night fighter -E
B422(1-76)-1, A15(97)-0, B411(10)-0

FRANCE

ANF 115 High wing reconnaissance
bomber -B
B411(10)-1, B422(1-95)-1, A15(97)-6,
C23(123)-1, C18(88)-1, C25(221)-1,
B14(158)-3
ANF 117 High wing reconnaissance
bomber -B
B422(1-119)-1, B73(23)-1, C23(123)-1,
B114(2-117)-1, C25(109)-1, B387(4)-1,
B14(149,158)-6, A15(97)-0

NIEUPORT-DELAGE *Societe
Anonyme Nieuport-Delage*
Ni-D 622 Sesquiplane fighter, trainer -B
D29(8/80-15)-1, A10(118)-2,
B422(1-100)-1, C23(95)-1, D1(3-30)-1,
B73(5)-1, B293(52)-6, C24(67)-1,
A15(97)-0
Ni-D 629 Sesquiplane fighter, trainer -C
D29(8/80-49)-1, B411(103)-1,
C24(111)-1, B279(238)-1, B387(8)-1,
A10(118)-0, A15(97)-0

NORD *Societe Nationale de Constructions
Aeronautiques du Nord (SNCAN)*
**1001 Pingouin (Messerschmitt
Bf 108)** Liaison -B
B139(63)-2, C23(250)-1, B387(36)-1,
B279(239)-0
**1101 Noralpha (Messerschmitt
Me 208)** Liaison -H
D9(1/79-45)-2, D3(7-117)-2, B139(63)-2
B60(129c)-1, C23(251)-1, B307(14)-1,
B279(279)-1

PAYEN *Societe Co-operative d'Etudes et
Productions Aeronautiques*
PA 22 Flechair Tandem wing -F
D20(2/67-396)-1,
D9(11/77-256,12/83-286)-1, C10(8,81)-1,
B380(24)-1, C107(166)-1, D3(4-222)-1,
D18(11/69-4)-1, B42(269)-1
PA 112 Flechair Tandem wing
fighter -J
D9(11/77-256)-2, D20(2/67-396)-3,
D18(11/69-6)-2, D9(12/83-289)-0

POTEZ *Societe des Avions et Moteurs
Henri Potez (SNCAN)*
25 (TOE) (Japan **CXP**) Sesquiplane
reconnaissance bomber -B
B421(142,170)-2, C83(175)-2,
B411(111)-1, B422(1-74)-1, C23(91)-1,
D7(25-23)-1, B391(177)-1, B279(256)-1,
C18(276)-2, A15(97)-6
29 (TOE) Sesquiplane reconnaissance
bomber, ambulance -B
B422(1-75)-1, B391(178)-1, C23(100)-1,
D23(102-89)-1, C25(268)-1, A15(97)-0
33 High wing liaison -B
C25(88)-1, C23(101)-1, A15(98)-0,
C131(105)-1
39 High wing observation -B
B411(152)-1, B73(23)-1, C18(278)-2,
C23(119)-1, C25(74)-1, C113(2-154)-1,
A15(98)-0
402 Three engine transport -C
A15(98)-0
438 High wing liaison -C
C23(110)-1, C112(3-61)-1, A15(98)-0
452 High wing observation flying boat -C
A3(5-39)-2, B197(210)-1, D3(5-291)-1,
A15(98)-0
453 High wing fighter flying boat -E
D7(4-218)-2, D3(5-291)-1, C87(111,P)-1,
D18(6/70)-1
540 Twin engine high wing bomber,
transport -B
A10(119)-1, B411(112)-1, B422(1-88)-1,
B167(35)-1, B14(145,155)-7, C78(270)-2,
B73(9)-1, B289(68)-6, C23(125)-1,
A15(98)-0
56 Twin engine transport -B
B391(181)-1, B16(186)-7, C25(144)-1,
C23(147)-1, B152(108c)-1, C78(304)-1,
C112(3-62)-2, A15(99)-0
585 High wing liaison -B
C23(165)-1, C78(303)-1, C112(3-67)-1,
D3(5-279)-1, A15(99)-0
62 Twin engine high wing transport -I
B391(182)-1, B15(56)-7, B284(4-196)-1,

35

B162(95)-2, B445(253)-1,
D23(102-103)-1

630 Twin engine fighter -B
A3(8-47)-1, B71(195-148)-1,
B421(214)-2, A10(120)-1, C23(148)-1,
B61(60)-2, B18(1-252)-7, B164(29)-1,
B397(450)-1, A15(99)-6

631 Twin engine fighter -A
A3(1-62)-2, B71(195)-2, A10(120)-3,
B88(1-78)-2, C23(149)-1, B422(1-112)-1,
B73(31)-1, B164(29)-3, C24(145)-1,
A15(99)-0

633 Twin engine bomber -B
A3(8-51)-2, A10(121)-1, A6(17)-3,
B422(1-112)-1, C25(233)-1, A15(99)-0

637 Twin engine reconnaissance
bomber -B
A3(8-55)-1, B71(195-152)-1,
B422(1-123)-1, A15(98)-6

63.11 Twin engine reconnaissance
bomber -A
D9(8/83-72)-4, A3(8-56)-2, B252(133)-2,
B71(195-153)-1, A7(254)-1, D3(1-190)-2,
C23(150)-1, B422(1-118)-1, A10(120)-1,
A15(99)-0, B88(2-87)-2

650 Twin engine high wing transport -B
B397(452)-1, B73(16)-1, C25(142)-1,
C23(170)-1, B422(1-97)-1, A15(99)-0

661 (662) Four engine transport -E
B391(185)-1, B153(97c)-1, C15(100)-1,
D3(5-291)-1, A15(99)-0

671 Twin engine fighter -E
A3(1-65)-2, B61(64)-1, C24(125)-1,
C10(52)-1

220 Twin engine reconnaissance
bomber -E
A3(8-64)-2, D14(2-21)-3, C10(66)-1

221 Twin engine reconnaissance
bomber -J
D14(4-59)-3, A3(8-66)-0

230 Fighter -E
A3(1-60)-2, C24(120)-1, C10(50)-1,
B18(1-267)-6

POTEZ-C.A.M.S. *(SNCAN)*
141 Antares Four engine high wing
reconnaissance flying boat -E
A3(5-42)-2, B153(97c)-1, D23(61-51)-2,
B197(212)-1, B73(45)-6, A15(98)-6,
B279(256)-0
160 $\frac{1}{3}$rd scale model 161 -F
B153(98c)-1, D3(5-279)-1, D6(2/73-88)-0,
B279(256)-0
161 Six engine high wing transport flying
boat -E
D6(2/73-88)-1, D3(4-147)-2,
D25(9/57-70)-1

ROMANO *Chantiers Aeronavals Etienne
Romano (SNCASE)*
R-82 Biplane trainer -B
B73(38)-1, B422(2-9)-1, C23(171)-1,
B152(116c)-3, D3(6-15)-1, C78(355)-6,
C112(3-69)-6
R-90 Biplane fighter floatplane -E
D7(4-218)-2, B397(454)-1, C110(210)-1,
D3(6-27)-1
R-110 Twin engine fighter -E
C18(188)-1, C24(107)-1, B152(117c)-3,
D26(71)-3, D3(6-27)-1
R-120 Three engine high wing
transport -K
C18(75)-1

ROUSSEL *M. Roussel*
R.30 Fighter -E
A3(1-67)-2, C24(123)-1, C18(163)-1,
D25(11/58-11)-1, C10(53)-1

S.A.F.R.A. *Societe Anonyme Francais de
Recherches Aeronautiques*
Delanne 190 P-2 Tandem wing glider -F
D25(9/56-31)-1
Delanne 20 (20T) Tandem wing -F
D18(12/70-8)-2, D9(12/83-286)-1,
D25(9/56-28)-1, C36(304)-1, A3(1-24)-0,
B42(32)-0, B279(142)-0

SALMSON *Societe des Moteurs Salmson*
(Compagnie Francais d'Aviation)
D.6 Cri-Cri High wing trainer -B
D20(6/64-71)-1, B153(115c)-1,
C18(184)-1, D9(10/75-194)-1,
D3(6-63)-1, C100(6-154)-1
D.7 Cri-Cri Major High wing
trainer -L
D20(6/64-71)-1, B139(25)-1,
B153(115c)-0
Phrygane High wing liaison -I
C18(184)-1, C23(156)-1

S.C.A.N. *Societe de Constructions Aero*
Navales du Pont-Neuf
20 High wing pusher flying boat
trainer -H
D9(3/80-141)-1, B60(131c)-3,
B139(150)-1, B401(64)-1, D3(6-312)-1

SCHRECK *Hydravions Louis Schreck*
(Franco-British Aviation)
FBA-17 Biplane pusher reconnaissance
amphibian-D
C83(393)-2, B391(189)-1, A9(439)-1,
C131(103)-1, B230(199)-1, B226(229)-1,
C75(137)-1, B279(269)-0

S.E.C.A.T. *Societe d'Etudes et de*
Constructions d'Avions Tourisme
RG-75 High wing liaison-I
B60(132c)-1, B279(278)-1

S.I.P.A. *Societe Industrielle Pour*
L'Aeronautique
S10 (Arado Ar 396) Trainer-C
B60(133c)-1, D3(6-40)-2, C23(279)-1,
A10(122)-0, B139(67)-0, B279(279)-0

STARK
A.S.20 Tandem wing -F
D3 (4-222)-2
A.S. 30 Tandem wing -F
D3 (4-223)-3

SUD-EST *Societe Nationale de*
Constructions Aeronautiques du Sud Est
(SNCASE)
S.E. 100 (Le0 50) Twin engine fighter -E
D9(4/85-204)-2, D16(11/81-38)-2,
A3(1-69)-2, D25(2/62-47)-2, C24(125)-2,
C10(54)-2, C18(188)-1, C87(99, P)-1
S.E.161 Languedoc (Bloch 161)
Four engine transport -H
B162(132)-2, B60(136c)-2, D3(7-201)-2,
B391(192)-1, C74(174)-2, B139(140)-2,
B16(194)-7, B176(114)-1, D24(1-77)-1,
C23(284)-1, C134(197)-1
S.E.200 (Le0 H-49) Six engine high
wing transport flying boat -I
D6(3/74-145)-1, B60(135c)-2,
D3(3-279)-2, B279(280)-1, A15(99)-0
S.E.400 Twin engine reconnaissance
floatplane -E
A3(6-49)-2, C10(75)-1
S.E.700 Postal helicopter -E
B60(137c)-1, B228(58)-1, D3(5-288)-1,
C10(82)-1, B161(46)-6

SUD-OUEST *Societe Nationale de*
Constructions Aeronautiques du Sud Ouest
(SNCASO)
S.O.30N Bellatrix Twin engine
transport -E
D9(11/77-256)-1, B60(141c)-1,
D3(6-72)-1
S.O.30R Bellatrix Twin engine
transport -H
D9(11/77-256)-1, B60(141c)-1,
D3(7-77)-2
S.O.80 Twin engine transport -E
D3(6-147)-1, D3(5-110)-3, B162(141)-0
S.O.90 Cassiopee (Bloch 800) Twin
engine transport -E
B60(140c)-1, B162(141)-1, D3(6-12)-1,
D25(9/57-69)-1, D3(7-294)-2
S.O.94 Corse Twin engine transport -H
B162(141)-2, D3(8-9)-2, C10(83)-3,
B139(121)-1

37

S.O.3020
See Centre NC-3021
S.O.6000 Triton Single jet trainer -H
D20(9/67-876)-2, B138(62)-2,
D25(5/58-42)-2, B60(143c)-1,
B405(230)-1, D3(7-294)-2, B410(126)-1

WIBAULT *Chantiers Aeronautiques*
Wibault-Panhoet
73C High wing fighter -D
C24(56)-1, D7(2-208)-6, A10(134)-0,
B411(159)-0, A1(119)-0, C131(106)-1

282T (283T) Three engine transport -I
D9(4/82-204)-2, B162(92)-2,
B391(214)-1, B15(48)-7, C23(156)-1,
D29(2/82-50)-1, B279(305)-1,
B291(48)-1, A15(99)-0

YOUNANOFF
HM-8 'Chevade No.1' High wing
sport -I
D23(102-43, 104)-1

GERMANY

AACHEN *Flugtechnische Fachgruppe an*
der Technischen Hochschule Aachen
FVA 9 High wing training gilder -L
C117(278)-1
FVA 10b Rheinland Training
sailplane -L
C117(279)-1
FVA 11 Eifel Training sailplane -L
C117(280)-1
FVA 13 High wing asymmetrical
sailplane -F
C117(281)-1

AEG *Allgemeine Elektrizitats Gesellschaft*
AEG Tethered electric observation
helicopter -E
C45(69)-1, C91(7)-1, B381(585)-0,
C16(84)-0, C142(142)-1, C139(31)-1

AGO *AGO Flugzeugwerke GmbH (Aktien*
Gesellschaft Otto)
Ao 192 Kurier Twin engine liaison -C
D9(6/77-305)-2, D20(1/68-53)-1,
D3(3-130)-2, B100(11)-1, B152(133c)-1,
C66(38,903)-1, C77(123)-1, C139(32)-2
Ao 225 Twin propeller fighter
bomber -J

C66(655)-0, A4(177)-0, B381(526)-0,
C139(33)-0

ALBATROS *Albatros Werke GmbH*
(Focke-Wulf)
A1 101 (L 101) High wing trainer, glider
tug -I
C66(40,903)-1, C113(1-9,2-15,3-7,4-7)-1,
B340(35)-1, C125(38)-1, C77(134)-1,
B232(93)-1, B305(18)-1, C41(78)-1,
C114(22)-1, C139(36)-1, C140(190)-1
Al 102 (L 102, Fw 55) High wing trainer,
also floatplane -I
B376(34)-1, C66(40,903)-1, C113(3-7)-1,
B305(19)-1, C125(38)-2, B339(63)-1,
C41(80)-1, C139(36)-1, C140(198)-1
A1 103 (L 103) High wing research -F
C41(84)-1, C125(47)-2, C139(36)-1

ARADO *Arado Flugzeugwerke GmbH*
Ar 65 Biplane fighter, trainer -B
A4(26)-2, D6(12/71-391)-2, B437(121)-1,
B340(88)-1, B429(216)-1, C66(42,904)-1,
B167(33)-1, C139(39)-1, C140(198)-1
Ar 66 Biplane trainer, bomber, also
floatplane -A
D9(7/78-42)-2, B381(17)-1, B437(121)-1,

C66(42,904)-1, B280(12)-1, B295(16)-1,
A15(100)-6, C77(138)-1, C74(83)-2,
C112(2-5)-2, C139(39)-2, C140(224)-1

Ar 67 Biplane fighter -E
A4(27)-2, D6(1/72-38)-2, C66(43,905)-1,
B437(123)-3, B429(218)-1, C14(36)-1,
C77(139)-1, C139(41)-1, C140(224)-1

Ar 68 Biplane fighter, trainer -A
A4(28)-2, B381(19)-2, D20(2/66-379)-1,
C66(44,905)-1, B429(218)-1,
D6(1/72-38)-2, A10(138)-1, B280(13)-1,
B437(122)-7, A15(100)-6, C139(41)-2

Ar 69 Biplane trainer -C
C66(45,906)-1, C14(42)-1, C117(19)-1,
C139(43)-2, D3(5-30)-1, C140(238)-1

Ar 76 High wing fighter, trainer -B
A4(31)-2, C66(46,907)-1, B340(51)-1,
B437(123)-3, C14(44)-1, B397(458)-1,
C139(44)-1, C125(53)-1, C140(240)-1

Ar 77 Twin engine trainer -E
C66(47,907)-1, B340(59)-1, C14(46)-1,
C117(21)-1, D3(5-30)-1, C139(44)-1

Ar 79 Liaison -I
D9(11/83-256)-2, C66(47,907)-1,
C117(22)-2, B340(177)-1, C14(48)-1,
C76(317)-1, B153(116c)-1, C139(46)-2,
C113(4-120)-1, B420(69)-1, A15(101)-0

Ar 80 Fighter -E
A4(32)-2, D20(2/67-396)-2, C139(48)-1,
D6(1/72-38)-2, C66(48,908)-1,
C14(50)-1, B437(123)-3, B429(220)-1,
B307(16)-1, B381(469)-1, B31(4)-6

Ar 81 Biplane dive bomber -E
A4(33)-2, C66(49,908)-1, B429(204)-1,
C14(52)-1, C77(141)-1, B437(123)-3,
B382(74)-1, C139(48)-2, B381(379)-1

Ar 95 Biplane reconnaissance bomber
floatplane -B
A4(35)-2, D20(6/67-678)-2, B381(23)-2,
A3(6-52)-2, B429(346)-1, A15(101)-6,
C66(51,909)-1, D3(2-178)-2, C139(50)-2,
B437(124)-3, B279(82)-1, B88(2-54)-2

Ar 96 Trainer -A
B381(27)-2, A6(18)-1, B437(124)-1,
C139(53)-2, D9(4/85-203)-2, A7(170)-1,

A4(25)-1, B293(92)-6, D3(3-66)-2,
A15(101)-6, B280(14)-1

Ar 195 Biplane carrier reconnaissance
bomber -E
A4(37)-2, C66(52,911)-1, B429(362)-1,
B437(125)-3, B295(18)-1, D3(5-30)-1,
C77(145)-1, C14(64)-1, C139(55)-1

Ar 196 Reconnaissance floatplane -A
D9(1/79-25)-4, A4(38)-2, B381(29)-2,
A3(6-54)-2, A6(18)-2, C66(55,912)-2,
A10(139)-1, B437(126)-2, D24(4-589)-2,
A15(101)-6, A7(24)-1, B18(1-110)-7

Ar 197 Biplane carrier fighter -E
A4(42)-2, D6(1/72-39)-2, C66(57,914)-1,
B381(22)-1, B280(17)-1, B429(362)-1,
B437(127)-3, B340(155)-1, B295(16)-1,
B187(57)-1, C139(59)-1

Ar 198 High wing reconnaissance -E
A4(44)-2, D25(9/61-67)-1,
C66(58,915)-1, B429(197)-1, C14(72)-1,
B437(127)-3, C87(118,P)-1, B408(344)-1,
C77(148)-1, C139(59)-1, B381(67)-1

Ar 199 Trainer floatplane -C
A3(6-58)-2, B381(34)-1, C66(58,915)-1,
C117(38)-2, B340(54)-1, B437(127)-3,
C14(74)-1, C77(148)-1, C139(61)-2

Ar 231 High wing sub-borne observation
floatplane -E
A4(45)-2, A3(6-60)-2, B381(35)-1,
C66(59,916)-1, B42(230)-1, B437(130)-3,
B18(1-137)-7, B429(356)-1, B364(156)-2,
B408(344)-1, C139(62)-2

Ar 232 Twin or four engine high wing
transport -B
A4(46)-2, B381(36)-2, B437(130)-2,
C66(60,916)-1, B280(17)-1, A7(170)-1,
B59(97c)-2, B18(1-145)-7, B66(1-9)-1,
B88(6-67)-2, A15(101)-0, C139(64)-2

Ar 233 (Ar 430) Twin engine high wing
liaison amphibian -J
C48(286)-3, C66(62)-3, C14(104)-3,
B59(98c)-0, C139(75)-3

Ar 234 Blitz Twin jet high wing
reconnaissance bomber -A
A4(49)-4, B64(92)-4, B71(215)-2,

39

A3(8-83)-2, B134(2-127)-2, B446-2,
B381(40)-2, B437(128)-4, C72-4,
B379(79)-2, A6(20)-2, A10(140)-2,
B280(18)-1, B429(375)-1, C139(66)-2,
A15(101)-6, A7(171)-1, B18(1-170)-7

Ar 240 Twin engine reconnaissance
bomber -B
A4(58)-2, B381(49)-2, A3(1-72,8-83)-2,
C139(72)-2, B59(100c)-2, A7(171)-1,
B437(131)-2, D6(1/72-39)-3, A10(140)-1,
B429(259)-1, A15(101)-6, B18(1-135)-7

Ar 340 Twin engine twin boom
bomber -J
D25(9/55-28)-3, C66(73)-3, B364(102)-3,
C14(109)-3, C139(74)-3

Ar 396 Trainer -H
B381(54)-1, C66(54,912)-2, B437(124)-1,
D25(7/63-51)-1, B364(161)-1,
D3(8-136)-1, C14(92)-1, C107(129)-1,
A15(101)-0, C139(55)-1

Ar 440 Twin engine fighter bomber -E
A4(63)-3, C66(72)-3, C139(75)-2,
C14(94)-3, B295(24)-6, B437(131)-0

ARGUS *Argus Motoren GmbH*
As 292 Fernfeuer Reconnaissance
drone -K
D24(16-2511)-2

AVA *Aerodynamische Versuchsanstalt,
Gottingen*
AF1 High wing endurance -F
C66(491)-0, C77(123)-1
AF2 Absauge Storch Blown wing
version Fieseler Fi 156 -F
D24(6-843)-2, C66(491)-0, C77(123)-1,
B71(228-134)-0, C139(86)-3

BACHEM *Bachem-Werke GmbH*
Ba 349 Natter Rocket-propelled
interceptor -C
A4(64)-4, D6(9/71-203)-4, B381(55)-2,
B437(132)-4, B138(55)-2, A3(1-76)-2,
C66(79,917)-2, B50(214)-5, C34(31)-5,
B18(1-178)-7, B429(382)-1, B244(P)-2,
B295(27)-1, A10(39)-1, C139(87)-2

BAUMGARTL
See Austria.

BERLIN *Flugtechnische Fachgruppe an
der Technischen Hochschule Berlin*
B5 Training sailplane -L
C117(282)-1, B232(82)-0
B6 Training glider -L
C117(283)-1, B232(82)-0
B8 High wing training glider -L
C117(284)-1, B232(82)-0
B9 (8-341) Twin engine prone pilot -F
A4(402)-1, C66(83,921)-2, C139(90)-2,
D24(12-1823)-1, B232(82)-1, C77(125)-1,
D25(11/60-9)-1, D14(6-85)-3,
B66(2-95)-1

BEUTH *Flugtechnische
Arbeitsgemeinschaft an der Ingenieurschule
Beuth*
FAB 3 Training glider -L
C117(272)-2

BLESSING *G. Blessing*
Kolibri-B Training sailplane -L
C117(260)-2

BLEY *Bley Flugzeugbau GmbH (Heini
Dittmar)*
Condor HD1 High wing training
sailplane -I
C117(262)-1, B284(4-179)-0
M-Condor High wing pusher motor
sailplane -L
C117(40)-1, C77(154)-1

BLOHM & VOSS *Blohm & Voss
Schiffswert, Abteilung Flugzeugbau*
BV 40 High wing interceptor glider -C
A4(100)-4, D25(7/60-30)-4, B381(84)-2,
D6(12/73-296)-2, B429(381)-1,
B437(138)-8, C66(103,927)-2,
B286(53)-2, D24(6-921)-2, C111(163)-2,
B295(28)-1, C139(119)-2
Ha 135 Biplane trainer -K
C111(91)-2, D9(1/82-45)-1, C139(92)-1,
C66(85,921)-1, D29(8/83-18)-1

Ha 137 Dive bomber -E
A4(70)-2, D25(4/61-51)-2, C111(94)-2,
C66(87,922)-1, B340(144)-1, C139(94)-2,
B437(133)-3, B429(203)-1, C29(108)-1,
D29(8/83-18)-1, C77(154)-1, B381(380)-1

BV 138 Three engine high wing twin
boom patrol flying boat -A
D9(11/79-229)-4, A4(71)-2, A3(5-49)-2,
B381(59)-2, A6(20)-2, B437(134)-2,
D29(8/83-10)-2, B280(22)-1, A10(142)-1,
A15(101)-6, A7(31)-1, C139(95)-2

Ha 139 Four engine reconnaissance
floatplane -B
A4(78)-2, B381(63)-2, A3(6-62)-2,
B437(133)-2, C139(100)-2, B429(358)-1,
B16(237)-7, B391(226)-1,
D29(8/83-48)-1, A15(102)-6

Ha 140 Twin engine reconnaissance
bomber floatplane -E
A4(80)-2, D25(9/63-43)-2, C139(102)-2,
C66(90,925)-1, B429(343)-1,
B437(133)-3, D9(8/83-51)-1,
C111(113)-2, C107(151)-1, B88(2-63)-2,
B397(462)-1, C29(132)-1, B381(269)-1

BV 141 Asymmetrical reconnaissance -C
A4(81)-2, D20(8/64-52,9/64-40)-2,
A3(8-118)-2, B381(66)-2, A7(259)-1,
C66(91,926)-2, B437(135)-2,
C139(102)-2, B18(1-136)-7, C111(116)-2,
B429(197)-1

BV 142 Four engine reconnaissance -C
A4(86)-2, A3(8-131)-2, B381(71)-1,
C66(94,927)-2, B437(136)-3,
C111(111)-2, B429(304)-1, B88(2-65)-2,
C77(158)-1, A15(102)-0, C139(105)-2

BV 143 Glide torpedo -E
B381(663)-3, B163(105)-3, C124(153)-5,
D24(6-815,7-1101)-4, C66(543,1058)-1,
B306(191)-1, C111(193)-1, C77(645)-1

BV 144 (Breguet) Twin engine variable
incidence high wing transport -G
D3(8-88)-2, B162(143)-2, C111(153)-2,
C66(94,928)-2, B295(32)-6, B437(136)-1,
D25(3/62-41)-1, C139(108)-2,
B59(102c)-3, B364(177)-3, B381(73)-2

BV 155 (Me 155) High altitude
fighter -E
A4(88)-2, C111(158)-2, B187(96)-1,
B381(88)-2, A3(1-80)-2, B437(136)-2,
B307(104)-2, B429(246)-1, C139(109)-2,
C66(96,928)-2, D3(8-124)-2

BV 222 Wiking Six engine high wing
reconnaissance flying boat -B
D9(4/81-180)-4, A4(91)-2, A3(5-56)-2,
B381(75)-2, C48(30)-2, C96-2,
B437(137)-2, C139(111)-2, D1(6-22)-2,
A15(102)-6, A7(178)-1, B18(1-152)-7

BV 237 Asymmetrical attack bomber -J
C139(115)-3, C364(67)-3, C124(151)-3

BV 238 Six engine high wing transport
flying boat -E
A4(97)-2, A3(5-63)-2, C111(139)-2,
B381(81)-1, C66(101,929)-2, C48(37)-2,
B437(139)-2, C96(40)-2, B429(360)-1,
B279(111)-1, C139(116)-2, C124(129)-2

BV 246 Hagelcorn (BV 226) Glide
bomb -C
B381(664)-3, B163(106)-1,
C66(544,1059)-1, C111(199)-3,
B325(89)-6, B306(196)-1, C88(201,P)-1,
B223(24)-6, B114(11-1198)-0

BV 250 Six engine high wing bomber -J
A4(98)-6, D25(8/57-36)-3, C139(118)-3,
C111(147)-6, C96(46)-3, B364(105)-3

BV 950 Friedensengel (L 10) Glide
torpedo -B
B163(105)-1, C66(543,1058)-1,
C111(195)-6, C77(645)-1, C88(201)-6,
B306(192)-1, C124(155)-6

L11 Schneewitchen Glide torpedo-C
C124(155)-6, B163(105)-0, C111(197)-0

BRANDIS
Circular wing -F
D9(3/79-156)-1, D6(6/73-288)-1,
C77(616)-1, D25(4/63-41)-1

*BRAUNSCHWEIG Institut für
Flugzeugbau an der Technischen
Hochschule Braunschweig (Prof. Hermann
Winter)*

LF 1 Zaunkönig High wing trainer -E
D9(12/76-282)-2, D9(5/82-229)-1,
B200(1-445)-1, B139(29)-1, B420(72)-2,
D3(9-62)-1, B433(17)-1, C93(3)-1,
C66(497)-0, B66(2-160)-1

BÜCKER Bücker Flugzeugbau GmbH
Bü 131 Jungmann (Japan **KXBu**)
Biplane trainer, attack -A
B71(222)-2, B381(91)-1, B421(210)-2,
C66(119,930)-2, B437(139)-1,
B14(334,339)-7, C74(86)-2, B293(57)-6,
B88(1-47)-2, B280(28)-1, C139(149)-2
Bü 133 Jungmeister Biplane
trainer -A
B381(92)-1, B421(212)-2,
C66(120,930)-2, D11(8/63-60)-2,
B310(P)-2, C107(130)-1, B437(140)-1,
B397(466)-1, C77(167)-1, C117(50)-2,
A15(102)-0, C139(150)-2
Bü 134 High wing club trainer -E
D9(10/77-204)-2, D24(6-825)-2,
D11(8/63-68)-1, C139(151)-3
Bü 180 Student Trainer -B
B59(102c)-1, C66(121,931)-2,
C117(52)-2, B340(35)-1, D3(5-84)-1,
B139(44)-1, B22(A-215)-1, C107(131)-1,
C77(168)-1, C139(152)-2
Bü 181 Bestmann (Sweden **Sk 25**)
Trainer -A
B381(94)-2, D3(4-188)-4, B421(254)-2,
C66(121,931)-2, B219(98)-2, B139(31)-2,
B437(140)-1, B59(104c)-1, B280(29)-1,
B279(109)-1, B88(3-44)-2, C139(153)-2
Bü 182 Kornett Trainer -C
D9(10/77-204)-2, B59(105c)-2,
C66(122,931)-1, D3(5-27)-2,
D11(8/63-68)-1, C107(132)-1,
B364(160)-1, C139(154)-1

*CHEMNITZ Flugtechnische
Arbeitsgemeinschaft an der Staatl.
Akademie für Technik, Chemnitz*
C10 Mid-engine powered glider -L
C117(92)-1, C77(260)-1

C11 High wing training glider -L
C117(274)-2

*DARMSTADT Akademische
Fliegergruppe an der Technischen
Hochschule Darmstadt*
D 22 Tandem wing trainer -K
C117(102)-2, B339(110)-1, C77(127)-1,
B420(46)-1, C66(488)-0, C139(33)-2
D 28 Windspiel High wing training
glider -L
C117(285)-1
D 29 Experimental -K
B152(140c)-1, C117(104)-2, D3(3-110)-1,
C66(488,697)-3, C77(127)-1, C139(34)-2
D 30 Cirrus High wing training
sailplane -L
C117(286)-1, D3(7-30)-3, C137(105)-1
D 31 High wing training sailplane -L
C117(287)-1

*DFS Deutsches Forschunginstitut für
Segelflug E.V.*
DFS 14
See Schneider ESG 38
DFS 30 Kranich (Karl Schweyer)
Training glider -I
B82(99)-2, C117(266)-2, D3(7-31,155)-2,
C113(4-21)-1, D11(6/63-26)-1, B69(27)-1,
B380(25)-1
DFS 39 Delta IV Tailless -F
D6(9/72-136)-2, B235(36)-2,
D20(5/69-73)-2, B71(225-51)-1,
C117(57)-1, C77(178)-1, C139(159)-1
DFS 40 Delta V Tailless pusher -F
B106(37)-1, B235(42)-2, C139(160)-2,
B71(225-50)-1, D3(7-258)-1, B381(509)-1
DFS 49
See Schneider Grunau Baby
DFS 54 High altitude sailplane -J
B381(96)-0
DFS 70 Meise (Olympia) High wing
training glider -L
B82(49)-2, B341(4-28)-1, B69(56)-1,
C117(268)-1, D3(7-30)-3

DFS 194 Rocket-propelled tailless -F
A4(594)-2, B106(41)-1, B235(45)-2,
B71(225-50)-1, C66(127)-3,
D6(9/72-136)-2, B439(73)-1,
B429(368)-1, B253(43)-6, C139(161)-2
DFS 203 Twin fuselage high wing
transport glider -J
C139(166)-3
DFS 228 Rocket-propelled
reconnaissance -E
A4(103)-2, A3(8-135)-2, B381(97)-2,
D3(7-129)-2, B253(45)-1, B437(142)-1,
B433(20)-1, C66(128)-3, B364(145)-3,
B279(144)-0, C139(163)-2
DFS 230 High wing transport glider -A
A4(104)-2, C104(7)-2, B381(100)-1,
C66(131,932)-1, A6(23)-2, B437(141)-2,
B88(4-72)-2, A7(190)-1, B280(38)-1,
A15(102)-6, B286(30)-3, C139(165)-2
DFS 230V7 High wing transport
glider -E
A4(107)-2, C66(133,932)-2, C104(113)-1,
C90(20)-1, B381(103)-3, B286(30)-3
DFS 331 High wing transport glider -E
A4(108)-2, C66(133,933)-2, B381(104)-1,
D6(4/72-210)-2, C104(141)-1,
B437(142)-3, B364(181)-1, C40(116)-1,
C77(181)-1, B286(46)-2, C139(167)-1
DFS 332 Rocket-propelled twin fuselage
research -G
D24(7-1029)-3, B381(105)-0,
C139(168)-3, B253(105)-0, B59(106c)-0
DFS 346 (Heinkel P.1068) Rocket-
propelled supersonic research -H
B381(636)-3, B332(68)-1, C139(169)-2,
D3(9-138,172)-7, B253(46)-6,
C66(130)-3, B279(144)-0
D-Sao Paulo Training sailplane -L
C117(271)-1, B106(33)-1
Fafnir II Training sailplane -L
C117(263)-1
Habicht Training glider-L
C117(264)-2, C118(81)-2, C49(209)-1,
C77(181)-1
Prasident High wing training

sailplane -L
C117(269)-1
Reiher Training sailplane -L
C117(270)-1
SG 5005 Schleppgerat Towed fuel
glider-E
D24 (14-2121)-1, D3(7-272)-1,
C66(651,1052)-1, B332(54)-1
Stummel Habicht Training glider for
Me 163-B
C118(82)-2, B196(178)-1, B106(71)-0,
C78(65)-0

DOBLHOFF
See Austria.

DORNIER Dornier Werke GmbH
Do B Merkur High wing transport, also
floatplane -I
B162(35)-2, B391(244)-1, C74(91)-2,
B340(52)-1, B381(3)-1, B339(65)-5,
B313(21)-1, C114(17)-1
Do 11 (Do F) Twin engine high wing
bomber -D
A4(110)-2, B437(142)-2, A10(143)-1,
B391(253)-1, B429(275)-1, C139(174)-2,
B313(32)-1, B381(6)-1, B340(119)-1,
C92(22)-1, A15(102)-0
Do 14 Twin engine high wing pusher
flying boat -F
C48(132)-2, C66(155,936)-1, B313(34)-1,
B42(121)-1, C28(90)-1, C139(175)-2
Do 15 Militar Wal 33 (Do J, Denmark
F.M.I) Tandem engine high wing patrol
flying boat -D
A4(112)-2, C48(92)-2, B429(340)-1,
B437(146)-3, C139(178)-2, D7(26-3)-1,
C92(169)-2, A15(102)-0
Do 17 Twin engine high wing bomber,
night fighter -A
A4(113)-2, B71(164)-2, A3(1-83,8-138)-2,
B381(106)-1, A6(22)-2, A10(144)-1,
B437(144)-2, B280(39)-2, A7(54)-1,
C66(139,936)-2, A15(102)-6,
C139(179)-2

Do 18 Tandem engine high wing patrol
flying boat -A
D9(4/80-181)-4, A4(124)-4, B381(115)-2,
A3(5-68)-2, A6(22)-2, C48(135)-2,
B437(143)-2, B280(45)-2, A10(147)-1,
A15(105)-6, A7(190)-1, B18(1-105)-7

Do 19 Four engine bomber -E
A4(127)-2, B437(146)-2, C66(153,941)-1,
B429(303)-1, C74(94)-2, C28(100)-1,
B340(237)-1, B313(43)-1, C114(41)-1,
B364(115)-1, C139(191)-2, B381(7)-1

Do 22 High wing reconnaissance bomber
floatplane -B
A4(129)-2, A3(6-66)-2, B381(119)-1,
B437(146)-2, C66(160,941)-2,
A10(147)-1, B429(345)-1, C74(94)-2,
C121(1-95)-1, A15(105)-6, C139(193)-2

Do 23 (Do 13) Twin engine high wing
bomber -D
A4(130)-2, D20(1/66-317)-2,
B437(147)-2, A10(144)-1, B429(276)-1,
B339(134)-5, C139(195)-1,
B14(147,157)-2, C74(92)-2, A15(105)-0

Do 24 (Sweden **Tp 24**) Three engine high
wing rescue, patrol flying boat -A
D7(21-9)-4, A4(133)-2, A3(5-71)-2,
B381(121)-1, B437(147)-2, C48(145)-2,
A6(25)-2, A10(148)-1, B280(46)-1,
A7(191)-1, A15(105)-6, B18(1-144)-7

Do 26 Twin tandem engine high wing
reconnaissance flying boat -B
A4(138)-2, A3(5-75)-2, B381(124)-1,
B437(148)-3, C66(162,943)-1,
C48(154)-2, B16(241)-7, B429(352)-1,
D3(2-78)-2, A15(105)-0, C139(200)-2

Do 212 High wing pusher amphibian -F
D6(9/73-147)-2, C48(161)-2,
C66(155,944)-1, B313(46)-1, C28(108)-1,
C107(157)-1, D3(9-169)-1, C139(201)-2

Do 214 (Do 216) Eight engine high wing
transport flying boat -J
C48(302)-2, D3(8-100)-7, C66(164)-3,
B437(148)-6, B313(47)-1, B364(157)-6,
C28(110)-6, C139(203)-2

Do 215 Twin engine high wing bomber,
night fighter -A
A4(139)-4, A3(9-7)-2, B381(126)-1,
C66(143,945)-2, A10(145)-1,
B437(145)-1, B429(284)-1, B88((1-51)-2,
B313(38)-1, A15(105)-0, C139(204)-2

Do 217 Twin engine high wing bomber,
night fighter -A
A4(143)-2, B71(261)-4, B64(36)-4,
D9(9/75-129)-4, B381(127)-2,
A3(1-85,9-12)-2, B437(149)-4,
B331(2-11)-2, A10(146)-2, A6(26)-2,
B280(48)-2, B88(3-47,5-59,6-68)-2,
B313(39)-1, A15(105)-6, A7(55)-1

Do 317 Twin engine high wing
bomber -E
A4(155)-2, A3(9-36)-2, B381(136)-1,
B437(148)-2, B429(321)-1,
C66(152,948)-1, B295(47)-1, B313(41)-1,
C28(120)-1, A15(106)-0, C139(216)-2

Do 318 (Weserflug) Boundary layer
control version Do 24 -E
C48(307)-3, B313(45)-1, A4(135)-0,
C66(162)-0, C139(220)-3

Do 335 Pfeil Tandem engine
tractor/pusher fighter bomber -C
A4(156)-4, B64(69)-4, B381(137)-2,
B437(152)-4, A3(1-87)-2, B308-4,
B378-2, C139(220)-4, A6(28)-2,
D4(8/73-40)-1, B429(266)-1, A10(148)-1,
A7(259)-1, B280(51)-1, A15(106)-0

Do 417 Twin engine high wing bomber-J
C139(228)-3

Do 635 (Do 335Z) Twin fuselage twin
tandem engine reconnaissance -J
B378(29)-3, C66(171,784)-3, B313(48)-6,
B295(47)-6, B381(141)-0, C139(230)-0

ERLA *Erla Maschinenwerke*
(Nestler und Breitfeld)
5D Trainer -K
C66(176,951)-1, C117(80)-2, C77(257)-1,
D3(3-230)-1, B279(155)-0
6A High wing powered glider -L
C66(176,951)-1, C117(79)-1

ESSLINGEN *Flugtechnische Arbeitsgemeinschaft an der Staatl. Ingenieurschule Esslingen a.N.*
E3 High wing training sailplane -L
C117(276)-2

FIESELER *Gerhard Fieseler Werke GmbH*
Fi 5R Trainer -L
C66(178,952)-1, C117(82)-2, C77(262)-1, D3(3-302)-1, C133(78)-2
Fi 97 Tourer -L
C66(179,952)-1, C117(84)-2, C77(262)-1, D3(3-302)-1
Fi 98 Biplane dive bomber -E
A4(164)-2, B437(154)-2, C66(179,952)-1, D25(4/60-9)-1, B429(202)-1,. C77(262)-1
Fi 99 Jung Tiger Sport, glider tug -I
C66(180,953)-2, C117(86)-2, D3(3-314,8-272)-1, C77(263)-1
Fi 103 (V-1, FZG 76) Pulse-jet flying bomb -A
B442-4, B220-2, B86-4, B163(46)-5, B381(666)-2, C66(545,1060)-1, B408(351)-4, B59(147c)-8, B88(5-60)-2, A7(198)-1, C34(39)-4
Fi 103 Reichenberg Pulse-jet manned attack -C
A4(170)-2, B220(20)-1, B381(149)-2, B388(98)-2, B437(155)-2, D20(10/67-940)-2, B138(50)-2, B337(191,P)-1, B244(P)-2
Fi 156 Storch (Sweden **S 14**) High wing observation, liaison -A
A4(165)-2, D9(12/76-282)-4, B71(228)-2, B381(142)-2, A6(30)-2, B437(156)-4, C93-2, B280(62)-2, A7(76)-1, A15(106)-6
Fi 157 Target drone -E
D20(7/69-65)-0
Fi 158 Piloted target drone -E
D20(7/69-65)-2, C66(182,954)-1, D25(4/60-9)-1, C77(265)-1, D3(3-302)-1
Fi 167 Biplane carrier reconnaissance bomber -C
A4(168)-2, A3(9-40)-2, B381(147)-1,

C66(182,954)-1, B295(51)-1, B437(155)-2, B429(363)-1, B340(154)-1, C77(266)-1, A15(106)-0
FiSk 199 (Fieseler-Skoda) Fighter bomber version Messerschmitt Bf 109G-2/R1 -E
B187(62)-1, A4(559)-1, B133(90)-1, B381(484)-1
Fi 253 Spatz High wing sport -L
C77(266)-1, C66(183)-0
Fi 256 (Morane-Saulnier) High wing observation, liaison -E
B381(146)-1, C93(32)-2, C66(182,955)-2, B326(52)-1, B295(51)-1, D3(7-12)-1, C91(36)-1, A4(168)-0, B437(157)-0
Fi 333 Twin engine high wing transport -E
D9(4/76-204)-3, B381(154)-3, C66(183)-3, B364(178)-3, B59(112c)-0
P 21A High wing towed stability research glider -F
D3(8-272)-1

FLETTNER *Anton Flettner GmbH*
Fl 184 Reconnaissance autogiro -E
B381(589)-1, B326(46)-1, C66(185,955)-1, C91(8)-1, C45(29)-1
Fl 185 Reconnaissance helicopter/autogiro -E
B381(590)-1, B326(47)-1, D25(9/56-75)-1, B364(184)-1, C45(29)-2, C66(185,955)-1, C91(8)-1, C77(267)-1, C16(68)-1, B161(20)-6
Fl 265 Twin rotor observation helicopter -C
D20(2/65-49)-1, B381(589)-1, B326(48)-1, D24(5-753)-1, C45(49)-2, C91(17)-1, C66(186,956)-1, B410(77)-1, B23(18)-6, C16(69)-1
Fl 282 Kolibri Twin rotor observation helicopter -B
D20(2/65-49)-2, B381(592)-1, B326(50)-1, D3(7-212)-2, C45(52)-2, B437(158)-1, B53(146)-1, B296(31)-6, C16(70)-1, B161(27)-1

Fl 285 Observation helicopter -J
B326(53)-0, C16(72)-0, C45(60)-0
Fl 339 Observation helicopter -J
B326(53)-6, C66(187)-6, B161(29)-6,
C45(60)-3

FOCKE ACHGELIS *Focke, Achgelis &*
Co. GmbH
Fa 61
See Focke-Wulf Fw 61
Fa 223 Drache (Fa 266 Hornisse)
Twin rotor helicopter -B
D9(5/84-245,6/84-291)-4, B381(598)-1,
D3(7-188)-2, C45(39)-4, C91(19)-2,
B437(159)-1, B376(98)-1, B296(30)-6,
B326(56)-1
Fa 225 Rotary wing conversion DFS 230
glider -E
B381(603)-1, A4(106)-1, B326(58)-1,
B376(102)-1, C91(37)-1, C90(23)-1,
C66(190,957)-1, C77(311)-1, B161(30)-6,
C45(46)-1
Fa 269 Twin pusher convertiplane
fighter -J
D9(1/75-47)-6, B381(604)-3, C66(191)-3,
B53(176)-3, C45(47)-7
Fa 284 Twin engine twin rotor transport
helicopter -J
B381(605)-3, B326(59)-6,
C66(192,711)-3, C91(40)-3, C45(48)-3
Fa 330 Bachstelze Submarine-borne
observation giro kite -A
B381(606)-1, B326(61)-1, C91(38)-2,
B228(94)-1, B376(103)-1, B310(P)-1,
C66(192,957)-1, B161(29)-1, B433(29)-1,
C45(73)-2, A15(107)-0

FOCKE-WULF *Focke-Wulf Flugzeugbau*
GmbH
Fw 44 Steiglitz (Sweden **Sk 12**) Biplane
trainer -A
B381(155)-1, A6(30)-2, B376(29)-1,
C125(44)-2, B280(64)-1, C70(84)-2,
B295(53)-1, C66(195,958)-1, B219(80)-2,
A15(107)-6

Fw 47 High wing weather
reconnaissance -B
B376(32)-1, C66(196,959)-1, C125(43)-1,
B305(19)-1, C41(60)-1, B381(8)-1
Fw 55 (Albatros Al 102) High wing
trainer, also floatplane -B
B376(34)-1, C66(196,959)-1, B305(19)-1,
C41(64)-1, C77(281)-1
Fw 56 Stösser High wing trainer -A
A4(173)-2, B381(158)-1, B437(158)-2,
B376(35)-1, C125(49)-2, C66(197,959)-1,
B295(54)-1, B280(65)-1, B293(75)-6,
A15(108)-0

Fw 57 Twin engine fighter bomber -E
A4(176)-2, D9(6/79-304)-2, B437(159)-2,
C125(55)-2, B376(37)-1, B429(295)-1,
C66(193,960)-1, B295(55)-1, B454(4)-6,
B305(21)-1, B381(394)-1
Fw 58 Weihe (Sweden **P 6**) Twin engine
trainer, general purpose -A
B381(160)-1, C115-1, D25(11/61-57)-2,
B437(160)-2, B376(38)-1, C125(57)-2,
D9(3/84-152)-2, C66(193,960)-1,
B340(59)-5, A15(108)-6
Fw 61 Twin rotor helicopter -F
B381(596)-1, B326(54)-1, B228(92)-1,
C91(11)-2, B376(94)-1, B408(213)-2,
B296(28)-6, C16(73)-1, C45(31)-2,
C66(189,956)-1
Fw 62 Biplane reconnaissance
floatplane -E
A4(178)-2, C125(63)-2, B376(41)-1,
B437(160)-3, B429(353)-1,
C66(199,961)-1, C41(76)-1, B305(22)-1,
C77(288)-1
Fw 159 High wing fighter -E
A4(179)-2, D9(6/79-304)-2, C125(66)-2,
B376(42)-1, B437(159)-3, B429(220)-1,
C66(200,961)-1, C41(86)-1, B305(22)-1,
B31(4)-6, B381(468)-1
Fw 186 Liaison autogiro -E
B376(97)-1, D24(15-2261)-1,
B381(143)-1, B326(63)-1, C45(25)-1,
B437(160)-1, C66(853,1049)-1,
B305(22)-1, C41(88)-1, C91(6)-1

Fw 187 Falke Twin engine fighter -C
A4(182)-2, A3(1-90)-2, B381(162)-2,
D9(6/79-305)-2, B376(44)-1,
B437(161)-2, C125(69)-2,
C66(201,962)-1, B429(252)-1,
A15(108)-0
Fw 189 Uhu Twin engine twin boom
reconnaissance -A
A4(188)-2, B64(113)-4, A3(9-45)-2,
B381(166)-2, B437(161)-4, A6(31)-2,
C125(76)-2, A10(149)-1, C66(202,963)-1,
A15(108)-6, A7(77)-1
Fw 190 Fighter -A
A4(194)-4, B71(3,94)-2, B64(78)-4,
B140-4, A3(1-93)-2, A6(32)-4,
B437(164)-4, B148(128)-4, B164(82)-4,
A10(150)-2, B248(46)-4, C125(87)-2,
B135(1-63)-2, B305-4, B376(51)-1,
A15(108)-6, A7(80)-1, B18(1-140)-7
Fw 191 Twin engine bomber -E
A4(220)-2, A3(9-59)-2, B381(197)-1,
C125(80)-4, C66(217,967)-2,
B437(169)-2, B429(321)-1, B376(70)-1,
B295(65)-1, B305(26)-1
Fw 200 Condor Four engine bomber,
transport -A
A4(223)-2, B64(7)-4, A3(9-65)-2,
B71(99)-2, B381(200)-2, A6(35)-2,
D6(1/73-22)-4, B437(170)-4, A10(152)-2,
B280(73)-2, A15(109)-6, C125(199)-2
Fw 300 Four engine reconnaissance
bomber -J
C66(222)-3, C125(236)-3, B364(178)-3,
B376(105)-0
P.VII Flitzer Single jet twin boom
fighter -J
B253(56)-1, C66(228)-3, B376(91)-6,
D24(11-1725,17-2679)-2, B379(234)-1
Ta 152 Fighter -B
A4(232)-4, D7(1-97)-4, B71(94)-2,
B64(78)-4, B381(207)-2, A3(1-110)-2,
B437(166)-5, B140(77)-4, B305(103)-2,
A15(110)-6, A7(197)-1, B18(1-176)-7
Ta 153 Fighter -E
A4(240)-1, B376(82)-1, B381(210)-0,

C66(727)-0, B305(110)-0
Ta 154 'Moskito' Twin engine high
wing night fighter -C
A4(241)-2, D29(2/78-38)-5, B386-2,
B299-4, B381(211)-2, A6(172)-2,
A3(1-115)-2, B437(172)-2, B376(87)-1,
C125(193)-2, C66(225,969)-2
Ta 183 Huckebein Single jet fighter -J
B381(626)-3, C66(227)-3, B253(57)-1,
B379(236)-7, C125(231)-3
Ta 283 Twin ramjet fighter -J
B381(633)-3, B253(61)-6, C66(231)-3,
B364(69)-3, B376(105)-0
Ta 400 Six engine high wing bomber -J
D25(7/61-50)-3, C66(223)-3, B253(62)-6,
B364(104)-3, B376(106)-1, C125(238)-3,
D26(193,194)-3, B429(314)-0
Triebflügel Pulse-jet rotary wing
VTOL interceptor -J
B381(609)-3, B253(60)-6, C66(234)-8,
B161(41)-6, B207(101)-6, C125(248)-3,
D16(1/86-46)-6

GÖPPINGEN *Sportflugzeugbau
Schempp-Hirth*
Gö 1 Wolf High wing training
sailplane-L
C118(15)-2, C117(321)-1, B232(90)-1,
B226(463)-1
Gö 2 High wing training glider -L
C118(20)-2, C117(322)-1
Gö 3 Minimoa Training sailplane -I
B82(74)-2, C118(22)-2, C117(323)-1,
D3(7-207)-1, B150(18)-1, C76(217)-1,
B286(4-178)-0
Gö 4 Goevier Training glider -A
C118(37,48,76)-2, C117(324)-2,
B69(56)-1
Gö 5 (Hütter 17) High wing training
glider -L
C118(31)-2, C117(326)-1, B69(27)-1
Gö 6 Minimoa 2a Training
sailplane -L
C118(35)-2
Gö 7 Sport -J

C118(45)-7

Gö 8 Glider model Dornier Do 214 flying boat -F

C118(53)-2, C48(178)-1, D3(8-100)-1, C66(164,944)-1, C77(397)-1, C139(205)-1

Gö 9 Pusher -F

D25(1/61-44)-2, C118(67)-2, A4(157)-1, C66(167,949)-1, B378(2)-1, B308(P)-1, D18(4/70)-1, C36(168)-1, C139(221)-2

GOTHA Gothaer Waggonfabrik AG

Go 145 Biplane trainer, attack -A

D9(7/81-32)-2, B381(215)-1, C66(240,970)-2, C40(98,102)-1, A6(36)-1, B437(172)-1, B280(76)-1, B295(68)-1, A15(110)-0

Go 146 Twin engine liaison -K

B153(133c)-1, C66(241,971)-2, D3(3-130,5-106)-2, C117(130)-1, C40(100)-1, B20(A-226)-1, C77(315)-1

Go 147 High wing tailless observation -E

A4(247)-2, C66(242,971)-1, B437(173)-2, B429(195)-1, C40(104)-1, C77(315)-1

Go 149 Trainer -E

D20(9/68-110)-1, B153(134c)-1, C40(106)-1, C66(243,971)-2, B397(480)-1, C117(108)-1, C77(315)-1

Go 150 Twin engine liaison -K

B153(134c)-1, C66(243,972)-2, C117(132)-2, D3(5-106,8-24)-1, B385(68)-1, B20(A-227)-1, C77(315)-1, C40(108)-1, B420(68)-1, B381(9)-1

Go 229

See Horten Ho 229

Go 241 Twin engine liaison -K

C66(243,972)-1, C40(112)-1

Go 242 High wing twin boom transport glider-A

A4(251)-2, C105(7)-2, B381(216)-1, B437(174)-2, C66(244,973)-1, A6(36)-3, B280(77)-1, C90(37)-1, A7(199)-1, A15(110)-0, B286(32)-2, B18(1-154)-7

Go 242A-2 High wing transport glider -F

A4(257)-1, C105(137)-1, B381(218)-1,

C66(245,973)-1, C40(122)-1

Go 244 Twin engine twin boom high wing transport -B

A4(254)-2, C105(102)-2, B381(219)-1, B252(58)-2, A6(36)-2, B437(174)-2, C66(246,973)-1, C40(118)-1, B248(64)-1, A15(110)-6

Go 345 High wing transport glider, also twin pulse-jet -E

A4(256)-3, C105(151)-3, B286(48)-7, B381(219,613)-3, B437(173)-7, C90(38)-3, B59(119c)-3, B364(182)-3, C40(126)-3, B253(71)-6, C66(246)-3

GOTHA-KALKERT Mitteldeutsche Metallwerke

Ka 430 High wing transport glider -C

A4(257)-3, D6(4/72-211,7/72-48)-2, B286(49)-3, C105(138)-3, B437(174)-7, C66(248)-3, B364(182)-3, C88(225)-6, A15(110)-0

HAMBURG Flugtechnische Arbeitsgemeinschaft an der H.T.L. Hamburg

Kobold Sport -L

C117(94)-2, C66(491)-0

Werk Nr.1 Tourer -L

B20(A-221)-1, C117(93)-1, C66(491)-0

HANNOVER Flugtechnische Fachgruppe an der Technischen Hochschule Hannover

AFH 4 Training sailplane -L

C117(288)-2

AFH 10 Training sailplane -L

C117(290)-2

HEINKEL Ernst Heinkel AG

HE 5 (Sweden **S 5**) Reconnaissance floatplane -D

B417(18)-1, B429(332)-1, B340(159)-1, C122(25)-1, C31(8)-1, C138(60)-1

HE 8 (Denmark **H.M.II**) Reconnaissance floatplane -B

B417(18)-1, B429(334)-1, C95(53,187)-2,

C73(15)-1, C140(166)-2, B408(337)-1,
B159(114)-6, A15(110)-0, C138(83)-1

HD 36 (Sweden **Sk 6**) Biplane trainer -D
B417(33)-1, C95(68,200)-1, C122(24)-1,
B436(58)-2, B219(58)-2, C140(152)-1

He 42 (HD 42) Biplane floatplane
trainer -B
B417(40)-1, C95(71,206)2, C140(206)-1,
C66(254,974)-1, B339(68)-1,
B340(160)-1, C114(31)-1, C77(339)-1,
A15(111)-0

He 45 Biplane reconnaissance bomber,
trainer -A
A4(259)-2, B381(220)-1, C95(73,206)-2,
B437(175)-2, B429(189)-1, B280(78)-1,
C66(254,974)-1, B417(41)-1, C92(168)-1,
A15(111)-6, C140(216)-1

He 46 High wing reconnaissance, ground
attack -A
A4(261)-2, A3(9-88)-2, B381(221)-2,
B437(175)-2, C95(74,207)-2,
B429(189)-1, B417(43)-1, B280(79)-1,
B295(70)-1, A15(111)-6, C138(97)-2

He 50 (He 66) Biplane reconnaissance
bomber, trainer -B
A4(264)-2, B381(224)-1, B437(175)-3,
C74(107)-2, C66(257,976)-1,
B429(201,337)-1, B417(46)-1,
B340(138)-1, C138(102)-1, A15(111)-0

He 51 Biplane fighter, trainer -B
A4(267)-2, B148(70)-4, D9(5/76-232)-5,
B437(176)-1, A6(37)-7, A10(164)-1,
B429(216)-1, C66(258,977)-1,
B411(75)-1, A15(111)-6, C138(98)-2

He 55 (**HD 55**, USSR **KR-1**) Biplane
reconnaissance flying boat -K
C48(201)-2, B417(38)-1, B309(122)-1,
B429(336)-1, C86(354,P)-1, C138(82)-1

He 59 Twin engine biplane patrol, rescue
floatplane -A
A4(273)-2, A3(6-68)-2, B381(226)-2,
B437(176)-2, C66(259,978)-2, A6(37)-2,
B252(70)-2, A10(165)-1, B280(81)-1,
A15(112)-6, C138(98)-2

He 60 Biplane reconnaissance

floatplane -B
A4(277)-2, A3(6-71)-2, B381(229)-2,
B437(178)-2, C66(260,979)-1,
B429(340)-1, B280(82)-1, B88(2-56)-2,
B411(166)-1, A15(112)-6, C138(101)-2

He 70 Blitz (Japan **LXHe**) Liaison -B
D9(2/75-76)-4, A4(280)-2, B381(232)-2,
B162(78)-2, B437(178)-3, A10(165)-1,
B429(192)-1, C74(110)-2, B306(14)-2,
A15(112)-6, C138(104)-2

He 72 Kadett, Seekadett Biplane
trainer, also floatplane -A
D24(10-1569)-2, B381(236)-2,
C66(265,983)-1, B437(179)-1,
B280(83)-1, B417(70)-1, C74(111)-2,
B339(127)-1, A15(112)-0, C138(95)-2

He 74 (Japan **KXHe**) Biplane fighter,
trainer -C
A4(285)-2, C95(98,223)-2, B437(180)-2,
B417(73)-1, C100(6-141)-1, C138(133)-2,
D16(9/84-13)-1, C66(266,984)-1,
C125(51)-1, C77(359)-1, C140(234)-1

He 100 (**He 112U**, '**He 113**', Japan
AXHe) Fighter, speed record -C
A4(331)-2, A3(1-122)-2, B381(238)-2,
D20(2/63-34)-2, A7(260)-1, B182-2,
B435(2-36)-2, B437(181)-2, C138(139)-2,
D9(10/82-202)-2, A15(112)-0

He 111 Twin engine bomber,
transport -A
A4(287)-4, A3(9-93)-2, B64(122)-4,
B71(15)-2, D9(6/79-296)-5, B437(180)-4,
B381(243)-2, A6(38)-4, B306-4,
B248(26)-4, B280(83)-2, A10(166)-1,
B429(282)-1, A15(113)-6, B134(1-5)-2

He 111Z Zwilling Five engine twin
fuselage glider tug -B
A4(303)-2, D20(6/64-69)-2, B306(180)-2,
B381(258)-1, B437(182)-3, B429(294)-1,
C66(274,991)-1, B417(84)-1, B42(151)-1,
B408(348)-1, B286(39)-2, C138(125)-2

He 112 (Japan **A7He 'Jerry'**) Fighter -B
A4(309)-2, D20(2/67-387)-2,
A3(1-119)-2, B381(261)-2, B182-1,
B437(185)-2, D9(10/82-201)-2,

49

B153(137c)-5, A10(167)-1, A15(114)-6

He 114 (Sweden **S 12**) Sesquiplane
reconnaissance floatplane -B
A4(315)-2, A3(6-74)-2, B381(265)-2,
B437(185)-2, B429(346)-1,
C66(278,995)-2, B417(87)-1, B295(78)-1,
C74(113)-2, A15(114)-0, C138(127)-1

He 115 (Sweden **T 2**) Twin engine patrol
bomber floatplane -A
A4(318)-2, A3(6-77)-2, B381(269)-2,
B437(186)-2, B252(72)-2, A6(41)-2,
B280(90)-2, C66(279,995)-2, A10(168)-1,
A15(114)-6, A7(96)-1, B18(1-121)-7

He 116 Four engine photo
reconnaissance -B
A4(324)-2, A3(9-135)-2, B381(274)-1,
D20(12/63-59)-2, C92(48)-1,
C66(280,997)-1, B437(187)-3,
C74(114)-2, C100(6-157)-2, B417(88)-1

He 118 (Japan **DXHe**) Dive bomber -C
A4(325)-2, D20(10/63-60)-2,
B381(380)-1, C66(280,998)-1,
B417(90)-1, B382(75)-1, C95(109,233)-2,
B437(187)-3, B429(204)-1,
D24(17-2609)-2

He 119 Mid-engine reconnaissance, also
floatplane -E
A4(328)-2, D25(1/61-23)-2,
C66(281,998)-2, B417(91)-1,
B364(106)-2, C95(110,233)-2,
B437(187)-3, B429(195)-1, B381(12)-1,
C107(81,154)-1, C138(185)-2

He 162 Spatz (Salamander) Single jet
high wing fighter -B
A4(366)-2, B64(19)-4, B379(238)-2,
B381(307)-2, B71(203)-2, A3(1-128)-2,
B437(194)-4, B164(128)-2, A6(42)-2,
B253(72)-1, A10(169)-2, A15(115)-6

He 170 Reconnaissance -B
A4(283)-2, A3(9-138)-2, B437(178)-2,
B306(24)-2, C66(264,981)-1, A10(166)-1,
B417(64)-1, B429(170)-1, C77(356)-1,
A15(115)-0, B381(235)-1, C138(111)-1

He 172 Biplane trainer, also floatplane -E
D24(10-1569)-2, B381(237)-1,

C66(266,1000)-1, B417(70)-1,
C77(359)-1, A15(112)-0, B437(179)-0

He 176 Rocket-propelled -F
B295(82)-3, B437(187)-6, B137(24)-6,
D24(23-2653)-3, B253(75)-6, D3(9-46)-6,
C66(288)-0, C138(150)-2

He 177 Greif Twin engine bomber -A
A4(336)-2, B64(46)-4, A3(9-142)-2,
B71(234)-2, B381(279)-2, B183-2,
B437(188)-8, B331(2-32)-2, A6(41)-2,
A10(169)-2, B280(95)-2, A15(115)-6

He 178 Single jet -F
D6(8/72-78)-2, B379(12)-2, B381(290)-2,
B138(40)-2, B222(96)-2, A10(37)-1,
B429(366)-1, B52(36)-1, B437(192)-3,
C66(291,1001)-1, C138(163)-2

He 219 Uhu Twin engine high wing
night fighter -A
A4(348)-4, B64(140)-4, B71(219)-2,
D29(8/79-10)-1, B381(298)-2,
A3(1-131)-2, B437(190)-4, A6(43)-2,
C99-2, A10(170)-2, B280(96)-2

He 270 Reconnaissance bomber -E
A4(285)-1, B381(235)-1, C66(265,982)-1,
B417(68)-1, B429(193)-1, B306(24)-1,
D20(10/65-119)-1, B437(178)-6,
B397(490)-1, C138(111)-1

He 274 (Farman) Four engine
bomber -H
A4(358)-2, A3(9-164)-2, B381(304)-1,
D3(7-140)-2, B437(192)-2, C138(184)-2,
C66(297,1002)-2, B429(310)-1,
B417(110)-1, B364(107)-2, B59(123c)-3

He 277 (He 177B) Four engine
bomber -E
A4(359)-2, A3(9-168)-2, B381(305)-1,
C66(298,1001)-1, B183(P)-1,
B437(193)-3, B429(310)-1, B417(109)-1,
C107(85)-1, C77(388)-1, C138(183)-1

He 280 Twin jet fighter -E
A4(361)-2, B379(18)-2, D6(4/72-184)-2,
D24(7-1071)-2, A3(1-125)-2, B138(41)-2,
B381(293)-2, B437(193)-2,
D9(10/82-202)-2, C138(192)-2,
B50(219)-1

He 343 Four jet bomber -J
B379(221)-7, D25(3/59-53)-7,
B417(118)-3, C66(304)-3, B184(14)-3,
C95(125)-3, B253(80)-6, C138(204)-2

He 419 Twin engine high wing high
altitude fighter -C
C66(779)-3, D9(12/82-246)-0, A4(356)-0,
C99(46)-3, B381(303)-0

P.1077 Julia Rocket-propelled high
wing fighter -J
D6(9/72-155)-3, D25(10/57-9)-6,
C66(308)-3, B364(208)-3, B253(82)-6,
C95(133)-3, D24(1-111)-7, C138(220)-7

HENSCHEL *Henschel Flugzeugwerke
AG*

Hs 117 Schmetterling (Hs 297) Anti-
aircraft missile -C
B381(688)-2, B163(148)-1,
C66(557,1060)-1, B325(58)-5,
C77(645)-1, B364(120)-1, B223(33)-6,
B116(144)-1, C34(10)-1,
B114(13-1371)-6

Hs 121 High wing fighter trainer -E
A4(375)-2, C66(313,1003)-1,
C140(236)-1, C117(164)-2, B437(196)-3,
B152(157c)-1

Hs 122 High wing reconnaissance -C
A4(376)-2, C66(313,1003)-1,
B381(321)-1, C117(166)-2, B429(194)-1,
D24(18-2857)-1, B437(196)-3,
B397(492)-1, B152(157c)-1

Hs 123 Biplane dive bomber -A
D9(8/78-72)-4, A4(377)-2, A3(9-172)-2,
B381(317)-2, B437(197)-2, A6(44)-2,
B429(202)-1, D24(2-163,3-413)-4,
B252(75)-2, A15(116)-6, A10(171)-1

Hs 124 Twin engine fighter bomber -E
A4(383)-2, D24(15-2361)-2, B381(494)-1,
C66(315,1005)-1, B429(295)-1,
C125(57)-1, B437(196)-3, C117(172)-2,
B153(140c)-1, B340(130)-1, B454(4)-6

Hs 125 Fighter trainer -E
A4(384)-2, C66(316,1006)-1, B340(51)-1,
C117(170)-2, B437(198)-3, C125(52)-1,

C77(393)-1, D3(5-173)-1, C140(244)-1

Hs 126 High wing reconnaissance -A
A4(385)-4, A3(9-183)-2, B381(321)-2,
B437(199)-2, A6(44)-2, D3(1-165)-4,
B252(76)-2, B280(99)-1, C74(117)-2,
A15(116)-6, A7(206)-1, B18(1-109)-7

Hs 127 Twin engine bomber -E
A4(389)-2, B381(395)-1, B429(295)-1,
B437(198)-3, C66(801)-3

Hs 128 Twin engine high altitude -F
A4(398)-2, D20(11/67-1005)-2,
B232(99)-1, D3(8-234)-1, B429(322)-1,
C87(65,P)-1, B381(327)-1, C66(320)-3

Hs 129 Twin engine ground attack -A
D9(12/80-277)-4, A4(390)-2, A3(10-7)-2,
B71(69)-2, B381(330)-2, A6(61)-2,
B437(200)-2, B280(101)-2, B252(77)-2,
B248(38)-2, A10(172)-1, A15(116)-6

Hs 130 Twin engine high altitude
reconnaissance bomber -E
A4(398)-2, A3(10-29)-2, B381(327)-1,
D25(12/57-9)-2, B437(201)-2,
C66(320,1007)-2, D3(8-235)-1,
B295(93)-1, B429(322)-1, B433(58)-1

Hs 132 Single jet dive bomber -G
B379(229)-7, A4(402)-7, A3(10-29)-7,
B381(339)-7, D20(7/65-57)-7,
B437(198)-7, B295(96)-3, C66(323)-3,
B253(87)-6

Hs 293 Rocket-boosted glide bomb -A
B163(108)-1, B381(673)-3, B189(23)-1,
B295(97)-2, D20(7/64-54)-3, B87(112)-6,
C66(561,1061)-1, B379(195)-1,
B388(P)-1, B114(13-1375)-1

Hs 294 Rocket-boosted glide bomb -C
B381(678)-3, B189(25)-6, B163(108)-6,
B379(23)-6, B114(13-1376)-6

Hs 295 Rocket-boosted glide bomb -C
B381(683)-3, C66(563,1059)-1,
B189(26)-0, B114(13-1377)-0

Hs 296 Rocket-boosted glide bomb -E
B381(685)-3, B189(26)-0, C66(563)-0,
B114(13-1377)-0

Hs 297
See Hs 117

Hs 298 Air-to-air missile -C
B381(692)-3, B163(212)-6, B189(26)-1,
B325(66)-6, B223(25)-6
B114(13-1376)-6
GT-1200 Anti-ship missile -E
B381(685)-3, B189(21)-6, B163(106)-3
P.75 Canard pusher fighter -J
D9(12/83-289)-3, B231(51)-3,
C66(326,809)-3, D25(7/56-30)-3,
D26(77)-3
Zitteroschen Supersonic air-to-ground
missile -E
B381(687)-3, B163(106)-3

HIRTH Wolf Hirth Flugzeugbau GmbH
Grunau 7 Moazagotl High wing
training sailplane -L
C118(16)-1, C117(304)-1
Hi 20 Mo Se Motor glider -L
C118(70)-2
Hi 21 Training sailplane -L
C118(88)-2
Hi 24 Twin boom pusher
reconnaissance -J
C118(103)-2
Stummel Habicht
See DFS

*HORTEN Gebruder Reimar und Walter
Horten*
Ho 2 (H II) Flying wing sailplane, also
powered -F
B381(342)-2, B300(12)-1, B439(35)-1,
B42(43)-1, D3(8-66)-1, C36(208)-1,
C117(306)-1, C137(36)-2
Ho 3 (H III) Flying wing sailplane, also
powered ammunition transport -F
A4(248)-1, B381(344)-2, B439(36)-1,
D3(8-66)-1, C36(208)-1, C137(59,76)-2
Ho 4 (H IV) Flying wing sailplane -F
D24(12-1847)-2, B381(345)-2,
D3(8-66,7-32)-2, A4(248)-1, B439(66)-1,
C117(308)-2, B66(1-145)-1, B433(58)-1,
C36(209)-1, C137(94)-2
Ho 5 (H V) Twin engine pusher flying
wing -F

C137(45,117)-2, B381(346)-3,
C66(329,1008)-2, B439(67)-1,
C36(209)-1, D3(8-67)-1
Ho 6 (H VI) Flying wing sailplane -F
B439(67)-1, D24(12-1847)-1,
B381(348)-0, C137(94)-2
Ho 8 (H VIII) Six engine pusher flying
wing transport, wind tunnel -J
C137(128)-2, C66(331)-3, B381(349)-0,
B439(69)-0, D25(10/61-47)-0,
B405(120)-0
Ho 10 (H X) Glider model single jet
flying wing fighter -G
C137(150)-2
Ho 11 (H XI) Flying wing glider -G
B381(353)-0
Ho 12 (H XII) Pusher flying wing
trainer, also glider -E
C137(155)-2, B381(353)-0
Ho 13 (H XIII) Glider model single jet
delta wing supersonic fighter -E
C137(150,158)-2
Ho 226 (Ho 254, Ho 7, H VII) Twin
engine pusher flying wing trainer -E
D24(15-2243)-2, B381(349)-1, A4(248)-1,
B439(68)-1, B300(24)-1, C137(122)-2,
C66(330,1008)-1, D3(8-67)-1, C77(398)-1
Ho 229 (H IX, 'Gotha Go 229') Twin
jet flying wing fighter -E
B300-2, A4(247)-2, D3(8-52)-2,
C137(134)-2, A3(1-117)-2, B381(350)-2,
B379(209)-2, D9(10/80-194)-2,
B437(173)-1, B439(70)-1, B138(54)-2,
C66(331,972)-2

*HÜTTER Dipl.-Ing. Wolfgang und
Ulrich Hütter*
H 28 III Training glider -L
C117(310)-1
Hü 211 (He 219E) Reconnaissance
version Heinkel He 219 -J
C118(99)-1, C66(302,815)-3, C99(47)-3,
A4(357)-0

*JACOBS-SCHWEYER Jacobs-
Schweyer Flugzeugbau GmbH*

Rhonsperber (USAAF **TG-19**)
Training glider -I
B82(98)-2, C117(311)-1, B10(170)-0
Weihe High wing training sailplane -L
B82(50)-2, C117(312)-2, B69(78)-1

*JUNKERS Junkers Flugzeug und
Motorenwerke AG*
F13 (Sweden **Tp 1**) Transport, also
floatplane -I
D7(16-66)-4, B162(18)-2, B418(17)-1,
B391(294)-1, B408(161)-2, C70(48)-1,
C74(119)-2, B15(118)-7, B222(53)-1,
A15(116)-0, C135(51)-2
A20 Transport, reconnaissance -D
B418(26)-1, B429(182)-1, B391(301)-1,
C65(1-34)-1, C29(50)-1, C135(65)-1
G24 Three engine transport, also
floatplane -I
D7(16-32)-1, B391(303)-1, B418(30)-1,
B15(124)-7, C74(120)-2, C65(1-46)-1,
C49(88)-1, B339(64)-1, D24(10-1517)-1,
B291(11)-1, C135(66)-2, B381(2)-1
G31 Three engine transport -I
B162(40)-2, B391(308)-1, B418(36)-1,
B122(49)-1, C65(1-58)-1, C74(122)-2,
C29(70)-1, C135(75)-1, A15(116)-0
W33 (USSR **PS-4**) Transport, also
floatplane -I
B418(39)-1, B391(312)-1, C74(120)-2,
B15(128)-7, C65(1-62)-1, B404(57)-1,
D7(26-8)-1, B291(15)-1, C114(14)-1,
C77(421)-1, C135(76)-1, C140(134)-1
W34 (Sweden **Tp 2**) Transport, trainer,
also floatplane -A
B162(36)-2, B381(354)-1, B437(212)-2,
D3(2-186)-2, A10(174)-1, B391(312)-1,
B280(132)-1, B418(41)-1, B291(15)-1,
A15(116)-0, C135(77)-1, C140(136)-1
A35 (**K53**) Reconnaissance -D
A10(175)-1, B429(183)-1, B418(42)-1,
C49(171)-1, C65(1-66)-1, C140(138)-1
G38 'Hindenburg' Four engine
transport -I
D7(24-31)-4, B162(62)-2, B381(356)-1,

C94(3)-2, D10(9/66-346)-2, B408(220)-2,
B418(50)-1, C114(122)-1, B295(99)-1,
A15(117)-0, C135(99)-2
R42 (**K30**) Three engine bomber, also
floatplane -D
A10(175)-1, B429(270)-1, B418(34)-1,
B411(167)-1, C65(1-78)-1, B381(13)-1
K43 'Vaquita' Reconnaissance bomber,
also floatplane -B
D20(12/68-72)-2, B418(48)-1,
A10(174)-1, B429(184)-1, C70(48)-1,
B411(79)-1, B370(48)-1, C65(1-80)-1,
A15(117)-0, C140(136)-1
A50 Junior (Japan **KXJ**) Trainer, also
floatplane -D
B418(55)-1, B200(2-370)-1, C69(134)-1,
C65(1-90)-1, B139(46)-1, B339(107)-1,
C100(6-115)-1, C29(80)-1, B420(34)-1,
C66(343)-0, C135(89)-1, C140(188)-0
K51 (**Mitsubishi Ki-20**) Four engine
bomber version G38-C
C114(11)-2, C66(344,1009)-1,
A10(245)-1, B411(169)-1, B429(273)-1,
B418(77)-1, C65(1-92)-1, D7(24-78)-3
Ju 52 Transport, also floatplane -L
B418(58)-1, B391(322)-1,
D25(1/63-49)-1, C65(1-94)-1, C29(86)-1,
D9(8/74-77)-1, C77(441)-1, C66(344)-0
Ju 52/3m (Sweden **Tp 5**, USAAF **C-79**)
Three engine transport, bomber, also
floatplane -A
A4(405)-2, B64(132)-4, B71(177)-2,
B381(357)-2, D9(8/74-76)-4, A3(6-83)-2,
B437(202)-8, A6(62)-2, B280(103)-2,
A15(117)-6, B456-2, A7(100)-1
Ju 60 Transport, liaison -I
D9(3/77-139)-2, B418(73)-1,
B391(332)-1, C66(349,1011)-1,
C65(2-4)-1, C77(456)-1
EF 61 Twin engine high wing high
altitude bomber -E
A4(446)-2, D25(10/61-49)-2, B418(84)-1,
B437(212)-3, C29(124)-1, B381(13)-1,
C66(350,1011)-1, B364(190)-3,
C77(458)-1

Ju 86 (Sweden **B 3, T 3**) Twin engine bomber, reconnaissance, transport -A
A4(414)-4, A3(10-31)-2, B381(370)-2, D6(1/72-25)-4, D7(20-15)-4, B437(204)-2, A6(63)-2, A10(176)-1, B280(109)-1, A15(118)-6, A7(207)-1

Ju 87 'Stuka' Dive bomber, ground attack -A
A4(428)-4, A3(10-52)-2, B423-4, D9(10/84-191)-4, B64(27)-4, B71(76,211)-2, A6(64)-4, B381(378)-2, B437(205)-4, B280(111)-2, B248(52)-4, A10(177)-2, B252(83)-2, A7(101)-1, A15(118)-6, B18(1-106)-7

Ju 88 Twin engine bomber, night fighter -A
A4(448)-4, A3(1-136,10-81)-2, D7(29-43)-4, B71(29,148)-2, B64(103)-4, B381(394)-2, B437(208)-4, B248(34)-4, B280(118)-2, A6(67)-4, A10(178)-2, B252(84)-2, B429(253,296)-1, A7(102)-1, A15(118)-6

Ju 88 Mistel Composite control aircraft/pilotless bomb Ju 88 -A
A4(477)-2, B381(570)-2, B388(111)-2, B307(106)-2, A3(10-110)-2, B331(2-54)-2, B437(241)-6, B418(121)-1, B163(109)-1, A15(119)-6, B18(1-172)-7

Ju 89 Four engine bomber -E
A4(483)-2, B437(212)-2, B381(418)-1, B418(109)-1, B429(303)-1, C66(388,1022)-1, C94(13)-2, C29(126)-1, B340(238)-1, A15(119)-0

Ju 90 Four engine transport -B
A4(504)-1, A3(10-151)-1, B381(418)-1, C94(18)-2, C66(388,1022)-1, B162(125)-2, B16(242)-7, B429(310)-1, B418(110)-1, D24(7-963)-1, C135(146)-2

Ju 160 (Japan **LXJ**) Communications, transport -I
D9(3/77-139)-2, B381(422)-1, B162(104)-2, C66(350,1011)-1, B418(74)-1, B16(234)-7, C29(98)-1, B152(160c)-1, A15(121)-0, C135(135)-2

Ju 187 Dive bomber -J

C65(2-54)-3, B423(25)-6, A4(442)-0, A3(10-73)-0, B429(208)-0

Ju 188 Racher Twin engine bomber -A
D9(4/82-179)-4, A4(485)-2, A7(104)-1, A3(10-123)-2, B381(424)-2, A6(70)-2, B437(213)-2, B331(2-48)-2, B280(128)-2, B252(85)-2, A15(120)-6, B66(2-51)-1

Ju 248
See Messerschmitt Me 263

Ju 252 Three engine transport -B
A4(491)-2, B381(429)-1, B437(214)-2, C66(347,1023)-1, C114(191)-1, B418(115)-1, B364(130,168)-2, C107(136)-1, A15(121)-0, B456(44)-1

Ju 287 Four jet bomber -E
A4(493)-2, B184-2, A3(10-133)-2, B381(431)-2, B138(52)-2, C72(41)-2, B379(220)-2, B437(214)-2, C66(361,1024)-2, B253(101)-1, A7(261)-1

Ju 288 Twin engine high wing bomber -E
A4(497)-2, B185-2, A3(10-138)-2, B381(437)-2, C66(381,1024)-2, B437(215)-2, B429(318)-1, B418(102)-1, A15(121)-0. B87(121)-6

Ju 290 Four engine bomber, transport -B
A4(504)-2, B186-2, A3(10-151)-2, B381(442)-1, D20(6/66-640)-2, D7(9-76)-1, B437(216)-2, B66(2-55)-1, A6(70)-2, A10(180)-1, A15(121)-6

Ju 322 Mammut Transport glider -E
A4(510)-2, B381(446)-1, D7(24-79)-2, B437(217)-2, C66(394,825)-3, D6(4/72-211)-2, B418(117)-3, B286(42)-2, B150(37)-6, C77(492)-1, C88(253)-3, C135(188)-2

Ju 352 Herkules Three engine transport -B
A4(512)-2, B381(448)-2, B437(217)-2, C66(348,1026)-2, B418(115)-1, D3(6-208)-2, B18(1-162)-7, B364(166)-2, B351(268)-1, A15(121)-6

Ju 388 Twin engine bomber, reconnaissance, night fighter -C
A4(514)-2, A3(1-142,10-164)-2

B381(450)-2, B429(256,324)-1,
B437(218)-2, D9(6/83-317)-1,
B280(131)-1, A10(180)-1, A15(121)-0
Ju 390 Six engine bomber,
reconnaissance -C
A4(519)-2, A3(10-170)-2, B381(455)-1,
B429(313)-1, B437(218)-3,
C66(392,1027)-1, B418(118)-1,
C94(45)-1, C29(182)-1, A15(121)-0
Ju 488 Four engine bomber -G
A4(520)-7, A3(10-173)-3, C66(386)-3,
B437(218)-3, B295(118)-3, B381(457)-0,
B429(314)-0, B364(111)-3
EF 126 Elli Pulse-jet fighter, ground
attack -H
B381(616)-3, B253(97)-6, C66(398)-3,
C65(2-59)-3, B59(134c)-0
EF 127 Walli Rocket-propelled
interceptor -J
B253(97)-6, C66(399)-3, B364(210)-3,
C113(4-34)-1, C65(2-59)-3
EF 128 Single jet tailless fighter -J
B381(621)-3, B253(98)-6, C66(400)-3,
D24(4-543)-4, C125(233)-3, C65(2-60)-3,
C113(4-34)-1

KIEL *Flugzeugbau Kiel GmbH*
FK166 Biplane trainer -K
C66(408,951)-1, C117(108)-1

KLEMM *Leichtflugzeugbau Klemm
GmbH*
L20 Trainer -K
B420(22)-2, B340(29)-1, B339(107)-1,
C114(16)-1, C77(496)-1, C140(108)-1
L25 (Kl 25) Trainer, liaison, also
floatplane -B
B381(459)-1, B340(29)-1, B200(2-102)-2,
C74(126)-2, B139(47)-1, B339(108)-1,
C112(1-58)-2, B152(163c)-1, B420(31)-1,
A15(122)-0, C140(108)-1
L26 Trainer -K
D19(4/62-293)-1, C77(502)-1,
C140(108)-1
L27 Trainer -K

B200(2-102)-1, D3(5-203)-1
Kl 31 Liaison -I
C117(204)-2, C77(505)-1, C66(403)-0,
A15(122)-0
Kl 32 Liaison -I
B381(459)-1, C74(127)-2,
C66(404,1027)-1, B139(47)-1,
B200(2-102)-1, B420(46)-1,
B152(163c)-1, B408(188)-3, C117(206)-2,
A15(122)-0
Kl 35 (Sweden **Sk 15**) Trainer, liaison,
also floatplane -A
B381(459)-1, B219(88)-2, B280(149)-1,
D6(11/71-334)-1, B295(119)-1,
C66(405,1028)-2, B279(206)-1,
B420(62)-1, B153(144c)-1, A15(122)-0
Kl 36 Liaison -K
C66(406,828)-3, C117(218)-2,
C77(510)-1
Kl 104
See Siebel Fh 104
Kl 105 Tourer -K
C66(407,829)-3, B153(145c)-1,
C117(218)-2, D3(4-279)-1, C77(512)-1
Kl 106 Trainer -K
C66(407,1028)-1, B112(42)-1,
C77(512)-1
Kl 107 Tourer -K
C66(407,1028)-2, B113(13)-1,
C76(350)-1, C117(220)-2, C77(513)-1

LIPPISCH *Prof. Dr. Alexander Lippisch*
DM-1 Delta wing glider -G
B381(461)-1, D3(8-32)-2, B235(85)-2,
B42(58)-1, B439(73)-1, C66(410,1029)-2,
B253(104)-6, B408(345)-1,
D25(4/56-13)-1
LP-12 Delta wing ramjet fighter -J
B235(81)-2, B439(73)-1, B253(106)-6
LP-13a Delta wing coal-fuel ramjet
fighter -J
B381(631)-3, D3(8-32)-3, B235(81)-3,
D25(4/56-13)-3, B253(107)-6, B439(73)-0

MESSERSCHMITT *Messerschmitt AG
(Bayerische Flugzeugwerke AG)*

M18 High wing survey, transport -B
B421(154,198)-2, B391(350)-1,
B196(29)-5, D25(11/62-37)-1,
B377(16)-1, B307(10)-1, C29(68)-1,
C81(28)-1, D3(4-271)-1

M20 High wing transport -I
B162(33)-2, B391(352)-1, B377(20)-1,
B196(47)-5, C74(130)-2, B381(14)-1,
D25(11/62-37)-1, B307(11)-1, C81(34)-1,
C29(74)-1, D3(4-270)-1

M23 Sport, trainer -K
B196(52)-5, B420(35)-2, B377(23)-1,
C29(78)-1, B307(11)-1, D3(4-270)-1,
C77(527)-1, C81(44)-1

M35 Aerobatic trainer -K
B377(33)-1, B196(76)-2, C112(2-18)-2,
B339(110)-1, C29(100)-1, C81(62)-1,
C114(221)-1, D3(4-270)-1, C78(348)-6,
C66(413)-0

M36
See Romania I.A.R.36

**Bf 108 Taifun (M37, RAF Aldon,
USAAF XC-44)** Liaison -A
B188-2, B381(464)-2, B421(216)-2,
D3(2-149)-4, B133(11)-1, A7(216)-1,
B307(13)-2, B280(160)-1, B437(219)-1,
D24(17-2563)-2, B377(35)-1

Bf 109 Fighter -A
A4(524)-4, B187-2, B307-4,
B71(40,113,184)-2, B381(467)-2, B133-4,
B64(149)-4, B148(84)-4, A3(1-144)-2,
B437(219)-4, B164(2)-4, A6(46)-4,
B280(161)-2, A10(182)-2, B31-2,
A7(118)-1, A15(122)-6, B18(1-124)-7

Bf 109Z Zwilling Twin engine twin
fuselage fighter -G
B187(59)-3, A4(572)-3, B133(118)-3,
B307(99)-3, B381(491)-0

Bf 110 Twin engine fighter -A
A4(573)-4, B71(23,207)-2, B381(493)-2,
B64(158)-4, B148(100)-4, A3(1-164)-2,
B437(224)-4, A6(58)-4, B248(16)-4,
B280(174)-2, B454-2, A10(184)-2,
B429(249)-1, A7(120)-1, A15(123)-6,
B135(1-37)-2, D9(5/86-240)-2

Me 155
See Blohm & Voss BV 155

Bf 161 Twin engine reconnaissance -E
A4(592)-1, D20(8/67-812)-1,
B381(506)-1, B377(81)-1, C92(140)-1,
B437(236)-6, B295(128)-1, C81(80)-1,
C77(551)-1, C66(445)-0

Bf 162 Jaguar Twin engine bomber -E
A4(592)-2, D20(8/67-812)-2,
B381(506)-1, B437(236)-2, B377(82)-1,
C66(445,1037)-1, B429(296)-1,
C81(82)-1, C77(551)-1, B454(5)-1

Bf 163 (Weserflug) Variable incidence
high wing observation -E
A4(669)-3, C66(446,888)-1, B196(91)-1,
C93(4)-1, B377(82)-0

Me 163 Komet Rocket-propelled tailless
interceptor -A
A4(594)-2, B106-4, D6(9/72-129)-4,
B71(225)-2, B64(167)-4, B246-2,
B381(508)-2, A3(1-171)-2, B437(227)-4,
B148(146)-4, B280(181)-2, B248(75)-2,
B429(368)-1, A7(121)-1, A15(124)-6,
B164(124)-2, B18(1-164)-7

**Me 164 (Messerschmitt-Caudron
MeC 164)** Twin engine high wing
transport -J
B364(179)-3, C66(451)-6, B377(143)-0

Me 208 (Nord 1100) Liaison -E
D9(1/79-45)-1, B377(91)-1,
C66(414,1038)-1, B364(179)-1,
C81(86)-1, A15(122)-0

Me 209 ('Me 109R') Fighter, speed
record -E
A4(606)-2, B187(98)-2, B381(520)-2,
A3(1-160)-2, D25(11/61-51)-2,
B307(99)-2, B437(227)-3,
C66(429,1038)-2, B429(231,245)-1

Me 210 Twin engine fighter bomber -A
A4(610)-4, D9(10/81-181)-2, B71(161)-1,
B381(526)-1, A3(1-177)-2, B437(230)-2,
D3(4-41)-4, A6(72)-3, A10(186)-1,
D29(2/83-10)-1, A15(124)-0

Me 261 Adolfine Twin engine long
range reconnaissance -C

A4(617)-2, A3(10-176)-2, B381(530)-1,
B437(236)-2, D25(12/59-39)-4,
B429(312)-1, C66(452,1040)-2,
C29(156)-1, B59(141c)-1, A15(124)-0

Me 262 Schwalbe (Sturmvogel) Twin
jet fighter, bomber -A
A4(619)-4, B51-4, B71(130)-2,
B381(531)-2, B64(58)-4, A6(74)-2,
A3(1-184)-2, B437(231)-4, B148(154)-4,
B164(126)-4, B379(27)-2, B248(70)-4,
B280(186)-2, B429(370)-1, B252(110)-2,
A15(125)-6, A7(123)-1, B18(1-166)-7

Me 263 (Junkers Ju 248) Rocket-
propelled tailless interceptor -E
A4(638)-2, B106(103)-1, B381(547)-2,
A3(1-175)-2, B235(78)-2, B437(236)-3,
C66(450,1043)-2, D9(7/83-40)-1,
B138(53)-2, B253(120)-1

Me 264 Four engine high wing
reconnaissance bomber -E
A4(640)-2, A3(10-178)-2, B381(549)-1,
D25(2/59-45)-4, C29(178)-1,
B437(237)-2, C66(462,1043)-2,
B429(312)-1, B59(142c)-1, A15(126)-0

Me 265 (Lippisch P.10) Twin engine
pusher tailless fighter -J
B235(62)-7, D25(4/56-13,3/57-11)-7,
C81(113)-3, C66(463)-0

Me 309 Fighter -E
A4(642)-2, A3(1-190)-2, B187(102)-1,
D25(10/61-37)-2, C29(172)-1,
B307(103)-2, B437(237)-3, B377(113)-1,
B429(245)-1, B381(553)-0

Me 310 Twin engine fighter bomber -J
A4(644)-1, B377(124)-1, D29(2/83-12)-1,
B381(566)-0, C66(443)-0

Me 321 Gigant High wing transport
glider -B
A4(645)-2, C103(7)-2, B381(555)-1,
D6(4/72-212)-2, D9(5/83-233)-1,
B437(238)-1, B377(114)-1, A6(74)-1,
C90(39)-1, B150(37)-7, B286(37)-2

Me 323 Gigant Six engine high wing
transport -A
D9(5/83-233)-4, A4(649)-2, B381(557)-2,

B437(238)-2, B280(190)-2, A6(74)-2,
C103(167)-2, D16(3/81-38)-1, A7(124)-1,
C66(465,1044)-2, A15(126)-6

Me 328 Twin pulse-jet attack bomber -E
A4(656)-2, A3(10-184)-2, B381(561)-2,
B437(237)-2, B337(191,P)-1,
B429(382)-1, B138(51)-2, B253(123)-6,
B295(142)-1, B377(121)-1

Me 329 Twin engine pusher tailless
fighter bomber -J
B235(62)-2, D25(10/55-11)-3,
B364(76)-3, C81(115)-3, C66(470)-0

Me 410 Hornisse Twin engine fighter
bomber -A
D9(10/81-181,11/81-229)-4, A4(658)-2,
B71(161)-2, B381(566)-2, B437(230)-2,
A3(1-180)-2, D29(2/83-10)-1, A6(72)-2,
B280(184)-2, A15(127)-6, B66(2-66)-1

P 1101 Single jet variable sweep wing
fighter -G
A4(665)-2, B381(622)-2, D3(9-80)-2,
B437(238)-2, B379(229)-2, B253(127)-1,
C66(471,1046)-2, B268(57)-1,
B395(79)-1, B429(381)-1

Enzian Anti-aircraft missile -E
B381(693)-2, B163(151)-1, B189(14)-5,
B377(130)-1, B116(148)-1, B224(86)-1,
C66(564,1060)-1, B223(34)-1, C34(16)-5,
B114(8-849)-1

MÖLLER Ing. Hans Günter Möller,
Flugzeugbau

Stomo 3 V-3 Sport -L
B420(63)-2, D11(9/67-26)-1,
B153(146c)-1, B20(A-241)-1, C77(570)-1

Stomo 3 V-11 (Sturmer) Sport -L
D11(9/67-27)-1, B153(146c)-1,
B20(A-242)-1, C117(234)-2, C77(570)-1,
B279(231)-0

Stromer Trainer, liaison -E
B420(69)-1, D11(9/67-28)-1, C77(570)-1,
C66(494)-0

MÜNCHEN Akademische Fliegergruppe
an der Technischen Hochschule München

Mü 10 Milan High wing training glider -L
C117(292)-2
Mü 13 Merlin (Atalante). High wing training glider -L
B82(44)-2, C117(106,294,342)-2, B69(78)-1
Mü 15 High wing training glider -L
C117(296)-2
Mü 17 Merle High wing training glider -L
C117(298)-2

NAGLER-ROLZ
See Austria.

NSFK Nationalsozialistischen Fliegerkorps
D-Helios (Ortsgruppe Berlin) High wing training sailplane -L
C117(316)-1
Gottingen IV (Ortsgruppe Gottingen) High wing training sailplane -L
C117(318)-2
Mowe (Ortsgruppe Bielefeld) High wing training glider -L
C117(317)-1

PEENEMÜNDE Heeresversuchsanstalt Peenemünde (HVP)
A4 (V-2) Ballistic missile -A
B381(647)-1, B163(48)-5, B224(23)-5, B26(43)-5, B428(106)-5, B325(12)-5, B116(36)-5, B59(148c)-8, B408(351)-1, C66(551)-6, B460-5
A5 Ballistic rocket -F
B381(647)-1, B224(24)-5, B26(40)-1, B116(48)-1, B306(88)-1
A9 Winged ballistic missile -J
B381(653)-6, B163(49)-0, B224(91)-6, B223(42)-8, C66(554)-6

PEENEMÜNDE Elektromechanische Werke (EMW)
C2 Wasserfall Anti-aircraft missile -C
B381(656)-1, B163(150)-5, B224(65)-5, B189(35)-6, B325(56)-5, C66(555)-6, B223(32)-6, B281(375)-1, B116(152)-1, B114(24-2588)-0
Taifun Anti-aircraft missile -C
B381(661)-0, B224(81)-1, B223(31)-6, C34(7)-6, B163(151)-0

RAAB Raab-Katzenstein Flugzeugwerke GmbH (Rheinische Luftfahrt Industrie, Rheinland)
R2 High wing training glider -L
C117(320)-1
R.K. 26 Tigerschwalbe (Sweden **Sk 10**) Biplane trainer -B
C49(201)-1, D20(12/69-51)-0
Schwalbe Biplane trainer -B
C66(886)-3, B339(102)-1, C114(18)-1, C77(577)-1, B397(364)-1, B279(258)-0, D24(19-2919)-1

RHEINMETALL
Rheinmetall-Borsig AG
F55 Feuerlilie (F25) Anti-aircraft missile -E
B381(705)-3, B163(148)-3, B189(19)-3, B116(142)-3, C34(28)-3
Hecht Anti-aircraft missile -E
B381(704)-3, B116(144)-6, C34(28)-8, C66(568)-0
Rheinbote (V-4) Ballistic missile -B
B163(22)-1, B381(707)-6, B116(145)-1, B223(43)-6, C34(134)-1, C66(571)-6, B114(20-2210)-0
Rheintochter Anti-aircraft missile -E
B381(709)-2, B163(149)-1, B189(32)-6, B325(68)-1, B223(35)-1, B116(138)-1, B408(353)-1, C34(22)-2, C66(569,1061)-1, B114(20-2212)-6

RHON-ROSSITTEN Rhon-Rossitten Gesellschaft (RRG, Kassel)
Falke (RVA) Training glider -L
B106(18)-1, C49(210)-1
Prufling High wing training glider -I
A9(473)-1, B339(30)-1, B284(4-180)-0

Zogling High wing training glider -I
B339(32)-1, B106(16)-1, B284(4-180)-0

RIESELER Walter Rieseler
RI, RII Coaxial rotor helicopter -F
C16(66)-1, C45(27)-1

RUHRSTAHL Ruhrstahl AG (Dr. Max Kramer)
X-1 (Fritz X, SD1400X) Glide bomb -B
B163(106)-5, B381(696)-2,
D20(2/68-102)-1, B189(77)-6, B388(P)-1,
B379(195)-1, C88(202,P)-1, C77(646)-1,
C66(566)-0, B114(10-1037)-8
X-4 (8-344) Air-to-air missile -E
B381(700)-2, B163(212)-5, B189(36)-1,
B325(61)-5, B379(151)-1, B223(26)-6,
C66(567)-6, C77(646)-1,
B114(24-2602)-0
X-7 Rotkappchen Anti-tank missile -B
B381(702)-3, B163(240)-3, C66(568)-0,
B114(24-2603)-0

SCHLEICHER Alexander Schleicher Flugzeugbau
Condor III High wing training sailplane -L
B82(82)-2, C117(327)-1, B232(79)-0
OBS High wing weather observation glider -F
B286(24)-1
Rhonadler High wing training sailplane -L
B82(83)-2, C117(328)-1
Rhonbussard High wing training sailplane -I
B82(84)-2, B232(79)-1, B69(78)-1,
C117(329)-1, B284(4-180)-0
Seeadler High wing flying boat glider -L
B337(105,P)-1, C117(340)-2

SCHNEIDER Flugzeugbau Edmund Schneider
Commodore High wing training sailplane -L
C117(336)-2

ESG 29 High wing training glider -L
B232(71)-1
ESG 38 (DFS 14 Schulgleiter) High wing training glider -L
C117(340)-2, C76(220)-1
ESM 5 High wing motor glider -L
C117(250)-2
Grunau Baby (DFS 49) High wing training glider -I
B82(97)-2, C117(333)-2, B341(4-29)-1,
C76(223)-1, B380(16)-1, B168(62)-1,
B337(45,P)-1, C77(585)-1, B284(4-180)-0
Grunau 8 High wing training glider -L
C117(338)-2
Motor Baby High wing pusher motor glider -L
C117(248)-2

SCHRIEVER Rudolf Schriever
Jet-propelled circular wing -K
B253(135)-6

SEGELFLIEGERGRUPPE
Segelfliegergruppe Des. I/K.G.
Schwalbe II Training sailplane -L
C117(314)-2

SIEBEL Siebel Flugzeugwerke KG
Fh 104 Hallore (Klemm Kl 104) Twin engine light transport -B
B381(578)-1, C74(137)-2,
C66(479,1046)-1, C29(122)-1,
B416(35)-1, D20(1/69-68)-1,
B153(147c)-1, B340(177)-1, C117(238)-2,
A15(127)-0
Si 201 High wing pusher observation -E
A4(668)-2, B437(240)-2,
C66(479,1046)-1, C93(4)-1, C29(144)-1,
B364(125)-1, C87(122,P)-1, C77(588)-1
Si 202 Hummel Communications, trainer -I
D6(9/73-148)-1, C74(138)-2,
C66(480,1047)-1, D24(11-1663)-2,
B340(175)-1, B153(147c)-1, C29(136)-1,
B420(66)-1, A15(127)-0

Si 204 Twin engine trainer, liaison -A
B381(578)-2, B421(266)-2, C74(138)-2,
B437(240)-1, B14(338,342)-7, A7(152)-1,
B280(243)-1, B59(146c)-2, B88(7-60)-2,
A15(127)-6

STUTTGART Flugtechnische
Fachgruppe an der Technischen Hochschule
Stuttgart
FS 16 Wippsterz High wing training
glider -L
C117(300)-1
FS 17 Training glider -L
C117(301)-1
FS 18 High wing training sailplane -L
C117(302)-1
Fl-D Fledermaus High wing training
sailplane -L
C117(345)-1

UDET Udet Flugzeugbau GmbH (also
Bayerische Flugzeugwerke)
U-12 Flamingo Biplane trainer -I
B71(257)-2, C74(139)-2, B133(9)-1,
B196(37)-1, B339(56)-1, C29(62)-1,
B420(23)-1, C81(18)-1, C49(190)-1,
C77(595)-1

WEBER Ing. Ernst Weber
EW 1 Training sailplane -L
C117(343)-1
EW 2 Training sailplane -L
C117(344)-1

EW 3 High wing training glider -L
C117(345)-1

WEIMAR Sportflugzeugbau Weimar
(Schmidt & Klaus)
Condor HD II High wing training
sailplane -L
C117(332)-1

WELTENSEGLER 'Weltensegler'
Segelflugzeugwerke
Hols-der-Teufel High wing training
sailplane -I
B235(2)-1, B284(4-182)-0

WESERFLUG Weser Flugzeugbau
GmbH (Rohrbach)
We 271 Twin engine high wing
amphibian -E
C48(277)-2, B429(351)-1, C77(599)-1,
C66(889)-6

ZEPPELIN Luftschiffbau Zeppelin
GmbH
LZ 130 Graf Zeppelin Electronic
surveillance rigid airship -I
B211(62)-1, B391(388)-1, B425(132)-1,
B332(8)-1, B426(77)-1, B431(98)-1,
B115(64)-1, C76(68)-1, C77(606)-1,
B114(24-2617)-0

GREAT BRITAIN

AERONCA Aeronautical Corporation of
Great Britain Ltd
Aeronca 100, 300 (C-3) High wing light
plane -I
B200(1-14)-2, B384(39)-1, B284(1-20)-0,
D3(8-116)-1, B139(23)-1, B279(68)-0

AIRSPEED Airspeed Ltd.

AS.4 Ferry Three engine biplane
transport -I
B399(33)-2, B200(1-17)-2, D3(5-191)-1,
B359(2-84)-2, B279(75)-1, B408(178)-1
AS.5 Courier Light transport,
communications -B
B399(41)-2, B200(1-20)-2, A11(470)-1,
D3(2-27)-2, B284(1-20)-1, B291(51)-1,

B278(8)-1, B16(79)-7, A15(127)-0

AS.6 Envoy (Japan **LXM**) Twin engine communciations -B
B399(54)-2, B162(114)-2, B200(1-23)-2, A11(470)-1, A12(334)-1, D3(1-199)2, B153(20c)-1, B16(81)-7, B278(9)-1, A15(127)-0

AS.8 Viceroy ('Gonzalez Gil') Twin engine light transport -K
B399(71)-1, B200(1-23)-1, C78(284)-1

AS.10 Oxford Twin engine trainer, communications -A
B399(73)-2, B71(227)-2, A11(18)-2, B59(7c)-2, D3(1-189)-4, A6(76)-2, B88(1-20,6-16)-2, A12(335)-1, B278(10)-2, A15(127)-6, A7(23)-1

AS.30 Queen Wasp Biplane target drone, also floatplane -C
B399(89)-2, A11(471)-1, B278(12)-2, B152(16c)-1, B408(203)-1, B359(2-118)-2, D3(2-50)-1, B21(A-166)-1

AS.39 Fleet Shadower Four engine high wing observation -E
B399(94)-2, D6(7/73-48)-2, D3(6-124)-2, B59(8c)-1, C3(138,154)-2, C87(130,P)-1, B114(9-958)-1

AS.45 Cambridge Trainer -E
B399(98)-2, D3(7-51)-2, B278(13)-1, B59(9c)-1, C3(141)-1

AS.49 (T.24/40) Fighter trainer -J
B399(163)-3

AS.51 Horsa High wing transport glider -A
B399(101)-2, D6(4/72-213)-5, B59(9c)-2, B278(14)-2, B286(70)-4, A8(537)-1, D3(5-125)-4, A6(76)-7, A7(169)-1, A15(128)-6, B18(1-76)-7

ARMSTRONG WHITWORTH *Sir W. G. Armstrong Whitworth Aircraft Ltd*
Atlas Biplane trainer, cooperation -B
B398(152)-2, A11(24)-2, A10(309)-2, B155(3,19)-1, B411(13)-1, D21(1/1-30)-1, B45(60)-1, B103(38)-1, B15(82)-7, A15(128)-0, B469(26)-1

Siskin Biplane fighter -D
B398(117)-2, A11(22)-1, A10(309)-2, B155(3,23)-1, D6(2/72-103)-2, B411(14)-1, D7(18-63)-1, B45(60)-1, B103(28)-1, B14(118,128)-7

A.W.XV Atalanta Four engine high wing transport -I
B398(219)-2, B162(74)-2, B200(1-44)-2, B284(4-157)-1, B291(42)-1, D7(28-7)-1, B408(227,233)-5, B15(100)-7, B431(107)-8, A15(128)-0

A.W.XVI Biplane fighter -D
B398(176)-2, D6(3/72-160)-2, A10(310)-1, B234(188)-1, B411(174)-0

A.W.19 Biplane general purpose, engine test -E
B398(193)-2, B233(247)-1

A.W.23 (C.26/31) Twin engine bomber, fuel tanker -E
B398(198)-2, B233(257)-1, D7(25-36)-1, B440(150)-1, B132(1-32)-1, D3(5-299)-1, B411(174)-0

A.W.27 Ensign Four engine high wing transport -I
D6(2/72-75)-4, B398(235)-2, B162(120)-4, B200(1-47)-2, B59(12c)-1, D3(2-221)-4, B153(22c)-1, B408(233)-1, B16(90)-7, A15(128)-0

A.W.35 Scimitar Biplane fighter trainer -B
B398(184)-2, D6(3/72-160)-2, C74(186)-2, B234(219)-1, A15(128)-0, B114(21-2279)-0

A.W.38 Whitley Twin engine bomber, transport -A
D7(9-10)-4, B143(1-3)-4, B398(255)-2, B71(153)-2, A11(26)-2, B134(2-27)-2, B278(16)-2, A6(77)-2, A10(310)-2, A15(128)-6, A7(25)-1, B18(1-48)-7

A.W.41 Albemarle Twin engine bomber, glider tug -A
B143(1-16)-2, B47(61)-1, B398(276)-2, D3(5-149)-4, A11(32)-2, B132(1-82)-2, A6(78)-2, B252(8)-2, B278(21)-7, B59(10c)-2, A15(128)-6, A7(172)-1

61

A.W.52 Twin jet research flying wing -H
D7(17-1)-4, B398(287)-2, D3(9-18)-4,
B138(73)-2, B439(81)-1, B139(92)-1,
B60(12c)-1, B405(10)-1, B410(36)-1,
B207(53)-1, D9(11/85-237)-1
A.W.52G Flying wing glider -F
D7(17-1)-4, B398(287)-2, D3(7-112)-2,
B60(12c)-1, B439(80)-1

ARPIN *M. B. Arpin & Co.*
A-1 Twin boom pusher light tourer -L
B200(1-407)-1, B153(23c)-1,
D6(4/73-204)-1, B279(83)-0, B55(1)-3

AUSTER
See Taylorcraft.

AVRO *A. V. Roe & Co., Ltd*
504 Biplane trainer -B
B198(179,197)-2, A11(42)-2, B177(29)-1,
D7(18-62)-1, A10(311)-1, B359(2-16)-1,
B222(42)-2, B170(14)-1, B103(37)-1,
B45(61)-1, B469(16)-1
594 Avian Biplane trainer -I
B198(243)-2, B177(98)-1, B170(33)-1,
B276(521)-1, B408(188)-1
616 Avian IV M Biplane trainer -B
B198(263)-2, B177(98)-1, B276(521)-1,
B170(34)-1, B155(4,28)-1, D7(18-69)-1,
B139(152)-1
618 Ten (Fokker F.VII) Three engine
high wing transport -I
B198(273)-2, B177(104)-1, B170(36)-1,
B287(58,143)-6, B281(259)-1,
B291(14)-1, D3(2-98)-1
621 Tutor (Denmark **L.B.IV**) Biplane
trainer -A
B198(283)-2, A11(46)-2, D3(3-27)-2,
B177(108)-1, B155(4,29)-1, B170(38)-1,
B278(22)-1, B293(27)-6, B45(61)-1,
A15(128)-0, B459(88)-1, B469(18)-1
624 Six Three engine high wing trainer -I
B198(277)-1, B177(106)-1, B170(37)-1
626 Prefect Biplane trainer -A
B198(292)-1, B177(110)-1, D3(3-183)-2,
A11(475)-1, B170(38)-1, B278(23)-1,

B155(4,29)-1, C49(194)-1, B152(21c)-1,
A15(128)-0, C131(132)-1
631 Cadet Biplane trainer -B
B198(302)-2, B177(116)-1, B170(39)-1,
B323(43)-1, B359(2-22)-2
636 (667) Biplane fighter trainer -B
B198(308)-2, B177(120)-1, B170(42)-1,
D3(2-110)-1
637 Biplane patrol version 626 -D
B198(295)-1, B177(110)-1, B170(39)-1
638 Club Cadet Biplane trainer -I
B198(311)-2, B177(117)-1, B170(41)-1,
B139(152)-1, B408(187)-1
641 Commodore Biplane liaison -I
B198(316)-2, B177(121)-1, B170(41)-1,
D9(5/82-217)-1, A15(129)-0
642/2m Twin engine high wing
transport -L
B198(278)-1, B177(122)-1, B170(42)-1,
B291(50)-1, D3(2-110)-1
642/4m 'Star of India' Four engine
high wing transport -I
B198(278)-1, B177(123)-1, B170(42)-1,
D3(2-110)-1, A15(129)-0
643 Mk II Cadet Biplane trainer -B
B198(203)-1, B177(116)-1, B170(40)-1,
B323(43)-1, C112(4-11)-2
652A Anson Twin engine
reconnaissance, trainer -A
B198(319,364)-2, B166-2, A11(48)-2,
B177(125)-1, D3(1-87)-4, A6(78)-2,
A10(312)-2, B278(24)-2, B252(10)-2,
A15(129)-6, A7(29)-1, B18(1-13)-7
671 Rota (Cierva C.30A) Radar
calibration autogiro -B
B198(437)-1, B326(69)-1, A11(476)-1,
B200(1-237)-2, B177(125)-1,
D6(4/75-20)-1, B284(1-28)-1, B296(20)-6,
C73(37)-1, A15(130)-6
674 (Hawker Audax) Biplane army
cooperation -B
B198(439)-1, D9(5/82-216)-1,
B177(192)-0
679 Manchester Twin engine
bomber -B

B143(1-19)-2, B198(334)-2, B71(260)-2,
A11(54)-2, B344(9)-2, A6(79)-2,
B285(1-5)-2, B278(27)-7, A10(313)-1,
A15(130)-6

683 Lancaster Four engine bomber -A
B143(1-26)-4, D9(12/81-281)-4,
B71(65,235)-2, B198(339)-2, B344-4,
A11(56)-2, A6(79)-4, B123-2, A10(314)-2,
B278(28)-2, B134(1-124)-2, B252(11)-2,
B177(142)-1, A7(26)-1, B170(50)-1,
A15(130)-6, B457-2, B18(1-72)-7

685 York Four engine high wing
transport -B
B198(357)-2, B71(168)-2, A11(62)-2,
D3(5-197)-4, B162(136)-2, B344(107)-2,
B278(33)-7, B177(149)-1, B59(15c)-2,
A15(130)-6, A7(173)-1, B18(1-88)-7

688 Tudor I Four engine transport -M
B198(373)-2, B59(13c)-2, D3(6-152)-2,
B177(152)-1, B291(93)-1, B170(56)-1,
B66(1-19)-1, D7(26-73)-1, B162(150)-3,
B200(1-124)-2

691 Lancastrian Four engine
transport -B
B198(385)-2, B344(106)-2, B59(13c)-2,
D3(7-33)-2, A11(476)-1, B177(157)-1,
B88(6-10)-2, B16(100)-7, B170(53)-1,
B123(58)-1

694 Lincoln Four engine bomber -M
B143(1-44)-2, B198(393)-2, B344(101)-4,
A11(64)-2, B132(2-120)-2, D3(7-17)-4,
A10(315)-1, B177(160)-1, B278(34)-7,
B233(341)-2

*B.A.C. British Aircraft Co.
(Kronfeld Ltd)*
Drone High wing pusher motor glider -I
B200(1-141)-2, D9(8/83-79)-1,
B139(24)-1, B284(1-27)-1, B408(182)-1
Primary High wing training glider -I
B284(4-180)-0

*BAYNES L. E. Baynes
(Alan Muntz & Co.)*
Bat (Slingsby) ⅓rd scale model carrier
wing glider -F

D3(7-308)-2, D6(10/71-277)-1, B69(74)-0
Heliplane Twin tilt rotor convertiplane
bomber -J
B161(22)-8, B53(174)-6, B207(100)-0

BLACKBURN
The Blackburn Aircraft Ltd
T.5 Ripon Biplane carrier torpedo
bomber, also floatplane -B
B199(215)-2, A3(7-68)-2, A12(50)-2,
B233(153)-2, A10(320)-1, B411(21)-1,
B14(142,153)-7, D17(2-28)-1,
B297(40)-1, A15(130)-0

B-2 Biplane trainer -I
B199(330)-2, B200(1-171)-2, D3(2-3)-2,
B359(2-24)-2, B139(152)-1, D3(8-244)-1,
B293(58)-6

B-5 Baffin Biplane reconnaissance -B
B199(349)-2, A12(52)-2, B233(220)-2,
B92(26)-1, A10(321)-1, B411(20)-1,
B14(142,153)-7, B45(64)-1, D17(2-29)-1,
A15(130)-6

B-6 Shark Biplane carrier
reconnaissance bomber, also floatplane -B
B199(364)-2, A12(54,342)-2, B427-2,
A3(6-86)-2, B276(108)-1, A10(322)-1,
B278(35)-2, B155(6,46)-1, D3(2-102)-2,
A15(131)-6

B-20 (R.1/36) Twin engine retractable
hull flying boat -E
B199(394)-2, A3(5-79)-2, B99(220)-2,
B59(19c)-1, B440(190)-1, D3(6-172)-2,
B42(229)-1, B294(84)-6, B88(6-16)-2,
B76(110)-6

B-24 Skua Carrier fighter, dive bomber,
target tug -A
B65(29)-4, B199(399)-2, A12(56)-2,
A10(322)-2, B278(36)-2, A6(83)-2,
B252(15)-2, D29(8/73-38)-1,
D3(1-103)-4, A7(177)-1, B234(252)-2

B-25 Roc Carrier turret fighter, also
floatplane -B
B199(411)-2, A12(58)-2, A3(2-4,6-88)-2,
B65(29)-1, B278(37)-2, A6(83)-1,
A10(323)-1, B234(259)-2, A7(177)-1,

A15(131)-0, B18(1-54)-7

B-26 Botha Twin engine high wing
torpedo bomber, trainer -A
B199(421)-2, A11(78)-2, B56(11c)-2,
B278(38)-2, B233(302)-2, B88(2-16)-2,
A10(323)-1, A7(176)-1, B45(99)-1,
A15(131)-0

B-29 (S.24/37) High wing carrier
bomber -J
B199(524)-1, B233(317)-0

B-37 Firebrand (B-45, 46) Carrier
torpedo strike fighter -M
B65(157)-4, B199(439)-2, A3(2-6)-2,
A12(60,343)-2, A10(324)-1, B278(39)-2,
D4(7/82-48)-2, B234(283)-2,
B59(Add.2)-2, B88(7-2)-2

B-44 (N.2/43) Retractable float fighter -J
B199(397,525)-3, D25(12/56-9)-3,
B462(6)-0, D3(6-172)-3, D14(1-8)-3,
B234(283)-0

B-48 Firecrest Carrier strike fighter -H
B199(452)-2, D20(12/63-57)-2,
D3(8-101)-2, D4(7/82-64)-1, B65(166)-1,
D17(2-31)-1, B234(323)-1

*BOULTON PAUL Boulton Paul
Aircraft Ltd.*
P.75 Overstrand Twin engine biplane
bomber, trainer -B
A11(90)-2, B233(238)-2, A10(325)-1,
B411(135)-1, B45(65)-1, B279(103)-1,
B408(276)-2, C74(197)-2, B103(59)-1,
B289(47)-6

P.82 Defiant Turret fighter, target
tug -A
D7(5-44)-4, B144(1-3)-4, B135(2-26)-2,
B71(117)-2, A3(2-11)-2, A11(92)-2,
A6(84)-2, B157(62)-4, B164(28)-2,
B278(40)-2, A10(326)-2, A15(132)-6

P.92 Twin engine high wing turret
fighter -J
D25(2/62-45)-3, D3(7-152)-3, C3(64)-3,
C88(99)-3, B234(274)-0

P.92/2 (Heston) Twin engine half-scale
flying model P.92 -F

D3(7-152)-2, D25(2/62-45)-1,
B234(274)-1, B60(25c)-1, C3(17)-1,
B212(59,P)-1

P.108 Balliol Trainer -H
D3(8-185)-2, A11(94)-2, B139(52)-2,
B406(68)-1, B103(128)-1, B334(277)-1,
B351(221)-1

BRISTOL
The Bristol Aeroplane Co., Ltd
105 Bulldog (Denmark **I J**,
Sweden **J 7**) Biplane fighter -A
D6(1/73-30,2/73-91)-4, B27(211)-2,
B71(6)-2, B148(54)-4, A11(100)-2,
C70(80)-2, A10(330)-2, B278(43)-2,
B297(34)-1, A15(132)-6, B458(40)-2

130 Bombay Twin engine high wing
bomber transport -B
D7(18-1)-4, B27(249)-2, A11(108)-2,
D3(1-119)-4, B57(18c)-2, B88(1-56)-2,
A10(332)-1, B278(46)-1, A7(181)-1,
A15(132)-6, B18(1-50)-7

142 Britain First Twin engine
transport -F
B27(257)-2, B357(114)-2, B143(1-47)-1,
B316(62)-1, B132(1-68)-1, B44(6)-1,
D7(28-8)-1, B402(451)-1, B359(1-135)-1,
D3(4-196)-1

142M Blenheim (149) Twin engine
bomber, night fighter -A
D7(28-8)-4, B143(1-46)-4, B144(1-12)-2,
B27(266)-2, B71(93,218)-2, D7(16-55)-5,
B44-5, A11(104)-2, A6(90)-2, B278(47)-2,
A10(330)-2, B164(21)-2, B134(2-7)-2,
B252(25)-2, A7(37)-1, A15(132)-6,
A3(2-15)-2, B18(1-22)-7, B316(64)-1

148B Army cooperation, engine test -E
B27(263)-2, B357(124)-2, B316(73)-1,
D25(5/58-11)-1, C3(154)-2

152 Beaufort Twin engine torpedo
bomber -A
D9(11/78-225)-4, B343-2, B27(283)-2,
A11(110)-2, A6(88)-2, A10(332)-2,
B278(57)-2, B252(24)-2, A7(36)-1,
A15(133)-6, B18(1-46)-7

156 Beaufighter Twin engine fighter -A
D6(1/74-25,3/74-124)-4, B144(1-15)-4,
B71(137)-2, B27(290)-2, A11(112)-2,
A6(85)-4, A3(2-17)-2, B148(130)-4,
B157(65)-4, B278(61)-2, B252(23)-2,
A7(35)-1, A15(133)-6, B135(1-57)-2
159 'Beaubomber' (B.1/39) Four
engine bomber -J
B27(308)-3, B132(1-91)-3, B316(114)-1,
B233(313)-0
160 Blenheim V (Bisley) Twin engine
bomber, ground attack -A
B27(277)-2, B143(1-55)-2, A11(118)-2,
B357(132)-2, B316(70)-1, B44(28)-1,
B134(2-18)-1, D3(4-6,4-51)-2,
D7(28-21)-2, B278(56)-6, A15(133)-6
163 Buckingham Twin engine bomber,
transport -B
B143(1-61)-2, B27(312)-1, A11(120)-2,
B132(2-88)-2, B278(68)-2, B59(Add.4)-2,
A7(182)-1, B316(84)-1, B88(7-22)-2,
A15(134)-0
164 Brigand Twin engine torpedo
bomber -M
B27(312)-2, A11(124)-2, D9(4/75-203)-2,
B278(69)-2, A10(335)-1, B59(Add.5)-2,
B88(7-21)-2, D3(7-51)-2, B316(85)-1,
B17(130)-7
166 Buckmaster Twin engine
trainer -M
B27(312)-1, A11(122)-1, B59(Add.6)-2,
B88(7-23)-2, A7(182)-1, B278(70)-2,
B316(85)-1, B139(126)-1, B334(279)-1
170 Freighter Twin engine high wing
transport -H
B27(330)-2, B162(156)-2, D3(7-5,40)-4,
B60(26c)-2, B316(89)-1, B200(1-204)-2,
B16(112)-7, C74(199)-2, B408(367)-1,
B279(107)-1

BRITISH AIRCRAFT *British Aircraft*
Manufacturing Co., Ltd. (British Klemm)
B.A. IV Double Eagle Twin engine
high wing liaison -I
D3(2-159)-2, B200(1-418)-1, B329(25)-1,

B359(1-172)-1
C.40 Rota II (Cierva C.40)
Observation autogiro -C
B55(12)-2, B359(2-159)-2,
B200(1-240)-1, D3(4-238)-2, B355(82)-1,
B447(25)-1, D29(2/78-12)-1,
B281(343)-1, B23(12)-6, B228(107)-0
Eagle (British Klemm B.K.1)
Communications -I
B200(1-137)-2, D3(2-111)-2,
B359(1-70)-3, C112(4-16)-2,
C100(6-136)-1, C78(286)-6, A15(134)-0
Swallow (British Klemm L.25)
Communications -I
B200(1-133)-2, C112(4-14)-2,
B459(71)-1, B279(90)-1, B139(44)-1,
B408(415)-1, B420(50)-1, D3(8-258)-1,
A15(134)-0

CHRISLEA *Chrislea Aircraft Co., Ltd*
L.C.1 Airguard Trainer -L
B200(1-449)-1, B153(32c)-1, D3(3-38)-1,
B279(124)-0

CIERVA *Cierva Autogiro Co., Ltd.*
C.30 (Denmark **I M**)
See Avro 671 Rota
C.40
See British Aircraft C.40
C.L.20
See Westland C.L.20
W.9 (Cierva-Weir) Experimental
helicopter -H
B60(30c)-1, B326(76)-1, B228(109)-1,
B405(52)-1, B23(21)-6, D25(12/55-46)-1,
D3(7-146)-1, B161(38)-6, B279(125)-0

COMPER *Comper Aircraft Ltd (Heston)*
C.L.A.7 Swift High wing sports -I
B200(1-246)-2, D10(1/67-16)-2,
B420(37)-2, B279(128)-1, B139(25)-1,
D3(3-38)-1, B459(194)-1, C134(132)-1

COSSOR *A. C. Cossor Ltd.*
Brakemine Anti-aircraft missile -E
B163(164)-1

CUNLIFFE-OWEN *Cunliffe-Owen Aircraft Ltd.*

OA-1 (British Burnelli) Twin engine twin boom transport -I
D25(3/61-11)-2, D23(102-24)-2, B200(1-443)-1, B359(1-175)-2, B154(14c)-1, B284(1-30)-1, B42(222)-1, B408(252)-1, A15(134)-0, C135(238)-4

DART *Dart Aircraft Ltd*
Totternhoe Training sailplane -I
B284(4-180)-0

De HAVILLAND *The de Havilland Aircraft Co., Ltd*
D.H. 50 Biplane transport -I
B201(183)-2, B200(1-290)-2, B408(262)-2, B172(21)-1, B323(47)-1
D.H. 60 Cirrus Moth Biplane trainer -B
B201(216)-2, B200(1-298)-2, C69(119)-2, A11(486)-1, C70(76)-1, B222(69)-2, B408(186)-2, B172(24)-1, B102(82)-1, A15(134)-0
D.H. 60G Gipsy Moth (Denmark **L.B. III**) Biplane trainer -B
B201(230)-2, A11(148)-2, B200(1-303)-2, D3(1-235)-2, B172(25)-1, B321(12)-1, D21(1/1-25)-1, C112(4-34)-2, C74(202)-3, A15(134)-0
D.H. 60G III Moth Major Biplane trainer -I
B201(250)-2, B200(1-309)-2, B172(25)-1, B139(153)-1, C49(181)-1, D3(3-122)-1, A15(134)-0
D.H. 60M Moth Biplane trainer -A
B201(242)-1, D3(1-146)-2, B172(25)-1, B155(9,93)-1, B208(20)-1, C49(180)-1, B359(2-30)-3, B411(176)-0
D.H. 60T Moth Trainer (Sweden **Sk 9**) Biplane trainer -B
B201(255)-1, B200(1-323)-1, B219(68)-2, B172(26)-1, B191(31)-1, C131(42,118)-1
D.H. 66 Hercules Three engine biplane transport -B
B201(269)-2, B162(39)-2, B200(1-315)-2,

B172(27)-1, B408(191)-1, B15(78)-7, B291(12)-1
D.H. 80A Puss Moth High wing communications -B
B201(292)-2, A11(487)-1, B200(1-318)-2, D3(1-115)-2, B172(29)-1, B284(2-45)-1, B139(26)-1, C112(4-37)-2, B191(28)-1, A15(134)-0
D.H. 82A Tiger Moth (Denmark **I S**, Sweden **Sk 11**, USAAF **PT-24**) Biplane trainer -A
B201(303)-2, B71(132)-2, A11(150)-2, A12(356)-1, B200(1-323)-2, A6(92)-2, D9(8/82-74)-5, B208-5, B278(72)-2, D3(2-183)-2, B59(32c)-2, A7(189)-1, A15(135)-6, B219(76)-2, C131(48)-1
D.H. 82B Queen Bee Biplane target drone, also floatplane -A
B201(318)-1, A11(487)-1, A12(356)-1, B408(204,496)-2, B152(29c)-1, B172(30)-1, B409(20)-1, C3(168)-1, C87(80,P)-1, B208(13)-0
D.H. 83 Fox Moth Biplane light transport, also floatplane -I
B201(322)-2, B200(1-327)-2, B323(79)-1, B172(32)-1, B102(85)-1, B284(2-73)-1, D3(2-75)-2, C112(4-42)-2, B191(37)-1, A15(135)-0, C131(49)-1
D.H. 84 Dragon (Denmark **II S**) Twin engine biplane transport -B
D9(3/84-129)-4, B201(328)-2, B162(88)-2, B200(1-331)-2, B323(53)-1, B284(2-74)-1, B172(32)-1, D3(1-59)-2, B15(105)-7, A15(135)-0, C131(54)-1
D.H. 85 Leopard Moth High wing communications -B
B201(336)-2, B200(1-335)-2, B284(2-75,4-164)-1, D3(1-107)-2, B172(32)-1, C112(4-48)-2, C60(1-P)-1, A15(135)-0
D.H. 86 Four engine biplane communications trainer -B
B201(341)-2, B162(89)-2, A11(488)-1, B200(1-338)-2, B323(59)-1, D3(1-99)-2, B172(33)-1, B15(107)-7, B88(2-20)-2,

D.H. 87 Hornet Moth Biplane
communications -B
B201(351)-2, B200(1-342)-2,
D9(2/78-99)-2, B284(2-81)-1, B172(34)-1,
B152(31c)-2, B420(55)-2, D3(2-15)-2,
B191(57)-1, A15(135)-0

D.H. 89 Dragon Rapide (Dominie)
Twin engine biplane trainer -A
B201(351)-2, B71(144)-2, A11(152)-2,
B162(90)-2, B200(1-348)-2, B278(74)-7,
B59(31c)-2, B172(35)-1, A7(189)-1,
A15(135)-6, B18(1-51)-7

D.H. 90 Dragonfly (Denmark **III S,**
Sweden **Tp 3**) Twin engine biplane
communications -B
B201(374)-2, B162(91)-2, B200(1-355)-2,
B284(3-101)-1, B172(36)-1,
B359(2-80)-2, C78(338)-1, B191(51)-1,
C112(4-58)-2, A15(135)-0

D.H. 91 Albatross Four engine
transport -I
D6(5/73-234)-4, B201(380)-2,
B162(113)-2, B200(1-355)-2, B16(88)-7,
D3(2-101)-4, B278(75)-3, B431(130)-8,
B172(36)-1, A15(135)-0

D.H. 93 Don Communications,
trainer -B
B201(388)-2, D6(2/74-84)-2, A11(488)-1,
D20(8/68-463)-1, B172(37)-1,
B359(1-56)-2, A15(135)-0

D.H. 94 Moth Minor
Communications -I
B201(392)-2, B200(1-358)-2, A8(548)-1,
B284(3-103)-1, B172(37)-1, D3(2-231)-2,
B152(34c)-1, B88(2-30)-2, B323(84)-1,
A15(136)-0

D.H. 95 Flamingo (Hertfordshire)
Twin engine high wing transport -B
B201(399)-2, D3(2-161)-4, B162(127)-2,
A11(489)-1, B200(1-361)-2, B278(76)-2,
B153(36c)-5, A7(188)-1, B16(92)-7,
A15(136)-0, B88(1-32)-2

D.H. 98 Mosquito Twin engine
bomber, fighter, reconnaissance -A

B143(1-64)-4, B144(1-31)-4,
D9(1/83-22,2/83-78, 3/83-138)-4, B34-1,
B369-2, B201(405)-2, B71(52,209)-2,
A11(154)-2, A6(93)-4, B148(142)-4,
A10(345)-2, B278(77)-2, B252(31)-2,
A4(2-26)-2, B164(72)-4, A15(136)-6

D.H. 98 Sea Mosquito TR.33 Twin
engine carrier reconnaissance bomber -M
D9(6/84-284)-5, A12(86)-2, B88(7-6)-2,
B201(415)-1, A10(345)-1, B34(159)-1,
B172(41)-1, B369(399)-1, B60(39c)-1,
A3(2-33)-0

D.H. 100 Vampire (Sweden **J 28**) Single
jet twin boom fighter -M
B144(1-51)-2, B201(423)-2, B148(168)-4,
A3(2-35)-2, A11(172)-2, A10(345)-2,
D3(6-306)-5, B138(46)-2, B88(7-7)-2,
B157(79)-2

D.H. 102 (B.4/42) Twin engine night
bomber -J
B201(522)-0, B233(340)-0, B369(71)-0

D.H. 103 Hornet (Sea Hornet) Twin
engine fighter -M
B144(1-52)-2, B201(433)-2, B71(174)-2,
A3(2-37)-2, A12(88)-2, D3(7-20)-4,
A11(170)-2, B278(85)-2, B164(134)-2,
A10(347)-1, B60(34c)-2

D.H. 104 Dove (Devon) Twin engine
transport -H
B201(443)-2, B162(158)-2,
B200(1-367)-2, D3(6-272)-2, B172(47)-1,
B60(33c)-2, B176(48)-1, B16(108)-7,
B139(109)-2

D.H. 108 Swallow Single jet tailless
research -H
D7(10-1)-4, B201(465)-2,
D20(10/66-156)-2, B138(61)-2,
B172(52)-1, B405(69)-1, B439(83)-1,
B408(193,384)-2, D3(7-135)-2,
B60(32c)-1

T.K.2 Racer, communications -L
D3(2-135)-2, B201(526)-1, B172(58)-1,
B153(70c)-1, B359(1-73)-1,
B200(2-450)-1

DESOUTTER *Desoutter Aircraft Co.,*
Ltd
Desoutter I (Koolhoven F.K.41) High
wing liaison -I
B200(1-385)-2, B279(143)-1, C126(63)-1,
B408(187)-1, A15(180)-0
Desoutter II High wing liaison -I
B200(1-385)-1, C126(64)-1,
B284(3-109)-1, C70(88)-1, D3(6-35)-1,
C121(1-52)-1, A15(180)-0

FAIREY *The Fairey Aviation Co., Ltd*
III F Biplane general purpose, also
floatplane -B
B400(144)-2, B71(44)-2, A12(114)-2,
A11(208)-2, A10(354)-2, B233(164)-2,
B411(44)-1, B45(69)-1, B101(70)-1,
B103(39)-1, B469(29)-1
Albacore Biplane carrier torpedo
bomber, also floatplane -A
B65(60)-4, B400(288)-2, A12(136)-2,
A3(6-94)-2, A6(96)-2, A7(62)-1,
B278(100)-2, B252(44)-2, B58(30c)-2,
A10(358)-1, A15(139)-6, B18(1-56)-7
Barracuda High wing carrier
bomber -A
B65(99)-4, B400(312)-2, B71(240)-2,
A12(148,162)-2, B278(104)-2,
A10(360)-2, A6(96)-2, B252(45)-2,
B88(5-13,7-8)-2, A15(140)-6, A7(63)-1
Battle Light bomber, trainer, engine
test -A
D9(3/81-127)-4, B143(2-3)-4,
B400(264)-2, B71(34)-2, A11(216)-2,
A6(97)-2, D3(5-214,226)-2, B278(96)-2,
B285(1-55)-2, A10(357)-2, B252(46)-2,
A7(194)-1, A15(139)-6, B233(286)-2
Fantome
See Belgium: Avions Fairey Feroce
F.C.1 Four engine transport -J
B400(296)-2, D6(9/72-144)-2,
B153(38c)-1, D3(4-95)-1, B359(1-188)-1
Firefly II M
See Belgium: Avions Fairey

Firefly Carrier reconnaissance fighter -A
B65(145)-4, D6(3/72-139,6/72-309)-4,
B400(326)-2, A12(154,164)-2,
A3(2-42)-2, B148(150)-4, A6(98)-2,
B278(106)-2, A10(359)-2, A15(141)-6
Fox
See Belgium: Avions Fairey
Fulmar Carrier fighter -A
B65(69)-4, B400(303)-2, B71(254)-2,
A12(142)-2, A3(2-39)-2, A6(98)-2,
B164(26)-4, B278(102)-2, B252(50)-2,
A10(359)-1, A15(140)-6, A7(65)-1
Gordon Biplane general purpose, also
floatplane -D
B400(217)-2, A12(212)-2, B233(191)-2,
A10(355)-1, B411(48)-1, B45(69)-1,
B15(104)-7, B359(2-38)-2, B103(46)-1,
B278(88)-0, C131(44)-1
Hendon Twin engine bomber -D
B400(208)-2, A11(214)-2, B132(1-15)-2,
B233(203)-2, B152(38c)-1, B411(143)-1,
A10(355)-1, B103(64)-1, B45(70)-1,
C74(206)-2, B469(60)-1
O.21/44 Tandem engine carrier torpedo
bomber -J
B400(354)-1, D3(8-244)-1
P.4/34 (Denmark **L.M.I**) Light
bomber -E
B400(303)-2, D9(12/77-309)-2,
B132(1-27)-2, B233(297)-1,
B65(69)-1, B153(39c)-1, B359(1-50)-1
Primer
See Belgium: Tipsey M
Seafox Biplane reconnaissance
floatplane -B
B400(283)-2, A12(134)-2, A3(6-92)-2,
D3(2-89)-4, A7(195)-1, B278(87)-2,
B56(24c)-2, B88(1-11)-2, B233(264)-2,
A15(139)-6, B18(1-19)-7, B469(40)-1
Seal Biplane carrier reconnaissance, also
floatplane -B
B400(221)-2, A12(120)-2, B233(200)-2,
B359(2-40)-2, B45(69)-1, A15(138)-6,
B114(21-2296)-0, B469(31)-1

Spearfish Carrier bomber -E

D9(1/78-20)-4, B400(351)-2, B88(7-24)-2,
A12(363)-1, D17(2-30)-1, D3(7-27,40)-4,
B233(346)-1, B59(Add.11)-1,
B66(1-99)-1, C3(126)-1, B60(42c)-2

Stooge Experimental anti-aircraft
missile -H
B400(45)-1, B163(188)-1, B428(90)-1,
D3(8-211)-1, B114(22-2404)-0

Swordfish Biplane carrier torpedo
bomber, also floatplane -A
B65(7)-4, B400(236)-2, B178-1,
B71(212)-2, A12(122)-2, A6(99)-2,
B278(88)-2, A3(6-90)-2, A10(356)-2,
B252(47)-2, A7(68)-1, A15(138)-6,
D16(1/86-8)-1, B18(1-14)-7

FANE *Fane Aircraft Co., Ltd*
F.1/40 Flying Observation Post High
wing pusher observation, version
Comper Scamp -E
D3(5-200)-2, D20(9/66-78)-1,
B200(2-472)-1, C3(138,155)-1

FOLLAND *Folland Aircraft Ltd*
43/37 (FO.108) Engine test -B
D9(12/79-304)-1, B58(32c)-1,
D3(5-228,7-225,8-224)-1, C3(187)-1
E.28/40 (FO.116) Carrier torpedo
bomber -J
B233(328)-0, D3(8-244)-1

FOSTER WIKNER *Foster Wikner
Aircraft Co., Ltd*
Warferry (Wicko G.M.1) High wing
liaison -I
B88(4-9)-2, B200(2-43)-2, B56(47c)-1,
D6(5/73-255)-1, B92(35)-1, D3(1-187)-2,
A15(141)-0, B139(26)-1, B279(169)-0

GENERAL AIRCRAFT *General
Aircraft Ltd (Monospar Co.)*
Monospar (ST-4, ST-6, ST-10, ST-12)
Twin engine liaison -I
B200(2-46)-2, B162(103)-2,
B284(3-113)-1, D3(9-149)-1, C78(296)-1,
A15(141)-0

Monospar ST-25 Universal, Jubilee
Twin engine liaison -I
B200(2-52)-2, D3(2-39,51)-2,
B359(1-133)-2, C78(296)-1, B139(126)-1,
D3(9-149)-1, B153(42c)-1, C112(4-64)-2,
A15(141)-0

G.A.L. 33 Cagnet Twin boom pusher
trainer -E
D3(9-150)-1, D3(4-62)-1, B130(63)-3,
B284(3-115)-0

G.A.L. 35 High wing target drone flying
boat -J
D26(99)-3, D3(9-150)-6

G.A.L. 38 Fleet Shadower Four engine
high wing observation -E
D6(7/73-48)-2, B59(38c)-1, D3(6-100)-2,
C3(9,156)-2, D25(5/59-9)-1, D3(9-151)-1,
B114(9-958)-0

G.A.L. 41 Twin engine pressure cabin
version Monospar ST-25 -F
D3(9-150)-1, C3(187)-1, D3(5-71)-1

G.A.L. 42 Cygnet (Chronander-
Waddington) Trainer,
communications -I
B200(2-56)-2, B56(25c)-1, D3(3-315)-2,
B284(3-116)-1, B420(69)-2,
B359(1-104)-2, B22(A-164)-5, C3(162)-1,
A15(141)-0

G.A.L. 45 Owlet Trainer -I
B200(2-343)-1, B57(28c)-2, B88(2-10)-2,
D3(2-207)-2, B408(189)-1,
D9(6/75-309)-1, B359(1-104)-2

G.A.L. 46 Twin engine high wing high
altitude fighter bomber -J
D9(8/76-76)-8, D3(9-151)-6, B234(288)-0

G.A.L. 47 Flying Observation Post
High wing twin boom pusher
observation -E
D3(5-200)-2, B200(2-473)-1, C3(156)-1,
D3(9-151)-1, D26(68)-3

G.A.L. 48 Hotspur Training transport
glider -A
D6(4/72-208)-1, B58(33c)-2, D3(3-183)-2,
B286(77)-2, A7(199)-1, B88(3-5)-2,
B278(108)-1, C3(146,183)-2

G.A.L. 48B Twin Hotspur Twin
fuselage transport glider -E
D6(4/72-208)-2, B286(81)-2, D3(7-10)-2,
B59(Add.13)-1, C3(183)-1, B278(108)-3,
C88(262,P)-1, B150(49)-3
G.A.L. 49 Hamilcar High wing
transport glider -A
B286(60)-4, D3(5-199,296)-4,
D6(4/72-208)-1, A6(100)-2, B59(37c)-2,
B88(5-18)-2, B278(109)-1, B18(1-77)-7,
B150(111)-7, A15(141)-6
G.A.L. 50 (X.27/40) Half-scale
G.A.L.49 Hamilcar -F
D6(3/72-128)-1, D3(9-151)-1
G.A.L. 55 Training glider -E
D3(7-285)-2, D3(9-151)-1, B69(74)-0
G.A.L. 56 Flying wing glider -F
D3(7-285)-2, B60(45c)-1, B439(78)-1,
B66(1-106)-1, D3(9-151)-1
G.A.L. 58 Hamilcar X Twin engine
high wing powered glider -B
B88(7-25)-2, B59(Add.12)-2,
D3(6-281)-2, A7(198)-1, B279(175)-1

GLOSTER Gloster Aircraft Co., Ltd
AS.31 Survey (D.H.67) Twin engine
biplane photographic -B
B205(189)-2, B200(2-348)-1,
B201(275)-2, B329(23)-1, A15(141)-0
E.28/39 Pioneer Single jet -F
B205(237)-2, B138(42)-2, B52(11)-5,
B278(118)-1, B88(6-25)-2, B408(333)-2,
A7(262)-1, A10(37)-1, B59(40c)-1,
B66(1-111)-1, B367(6)-1
E.1/44 Ace Single jet fighter -H
B205(227)-2, D9(9/80-149)-2,
B138(80)-2, D3(9-112)-2, B234(324)-1
F.5/34 Fighter -E
B205(227)-2, D9(8/80-104)-2,
B234(241)-2, D25(1/62-43)-1, B49(34)-1,
D9(1/83-43)-1, B152(43c)-1,
B359(1-46)-1, B22(A-167)-1
F.9/37 Twin engine fighter -E
B144(1-61)-2, B205(231)-2,
D4(4/76-16)-2, A3(2-51)-2, B278(117)-2,

D9(8/80-104)-2, D3(5-119,7-273)-2,
B49(158)-2, B59(40c)-1, B157(19)-1
F.18/37 Twin boom pusher fighter -J
B205(407)-3
F.9/40 Meteor Twin jet fighter -A
B144(1-63)-4, B367-2, B205(245)-2,
A3(2-53)-2, B148(162)-4, A6(102)-2,
A11(230)-2, B278(78)-2, A10(369)-2,
B164(125)-2, A15(141)-6, A7(83)-1
F.18/40 Twin engine fighter -J
B205(409)-0, B234(263)-0
Gambet
See Japan: Nakajima A1N
Gamecock
See Finland: V.L. Kukko
Gauntlet Denmark **II J**) Biplane
fighter -A
D7(2-163)-4, B205(167)-2, B71(10)-2,
B144(1-53)-2, A11(226)-2,
D9(8/80-103)-2, B14(119,129)-2,
B249(22)-1, A10(367)-1, A15(141)-6
Gladiator (Sweden **J 8**) Biplane
fighter -A
D6(3/73-125)-4, B144(1-54)-4, B249-2,
B71(98)-2, B205(204)-2, A3(2-47)-2,
B148(76)-4, A6(100)-2, A11(228)-2,
B164(24)-2, D23(74-30)-2, A10(368)-2,
B278(113)-1, B458(44)-2, A15(141)-6
Mars VI Nighthawk (Nieuport) Biplane
fighter trainer -D
B205(84)-2, D9(6/80-307)-2,
B234(158)-2, A11(342)-2, A10(400)-1,
B293(22)-6, B411(177)-0, B469(6)-1
Sea Gladiator Biplane carrier fighter -A
A12(186)-2, B205(214)-1, B249(97)-2,
D6(3/73-133)-1, B334(94)-1,
B234(236)-3, B135(2-19)-1, A3(2-48)-1

*GOLDFINCH-ROLT Bill Goldfinch
and Tony Rolt*
Colditz Cock High wing escape
glider -G
B336(564)-3, D20(9/66-73)-1

*HAFNER Raoul Hafner (A.R. III
Construction Co.)*

70

A.R.III Gyroplane Experimental autogiro -I
B200(2-352)-1, B152(43c)-1, C142(45)-1, D3(4-238)-2, B359(2-161)-1, B23(13)-6
A.R.IV Gyroplane (Short-Hafner) Observation autogiro -J
B29(455)-3, B152(44c)-0, D6(5/73-255)-0
PD.6 (Short-Hafner EA-115) Experimental helicopter -J
D6(5/73-255)-6, B29(455)-0, B228(120)-0

HAFNER Raoul Hafner (Airborne Forces Experimental Establishment)
Rotabuggy 10/42 (Rotajeep) Rotary wing Jeep conversion -E
D6(5/72-273)-2, D20(12/63-45)-2, B326(87)-6, D29(2/78-18)-1, B211(297)-1, B161(31)-6, B207(80)-1, C88(267,P)-1, B23(17)-6, C142(48)-2
Rotachute 11/42 (Rotaplane) Rotary wing parachute -E
D20(12/63-44)-2, D3(7-308)-2, B326(88)-1, B228(130)-1, B23(17)-6, D29(2/78-12)-1, B161(30)-6, C88(267,P)-1, B150(100)-6, C142(46)-1
Rotatank Rotary wing tank transport -G
B326(90)-0, B161(31)-0, D6(5/72-273)-0, C142(49)-0

HANDLEY PAGE Handley Page Ltd
H.P.42 Four engine biplane transport -I
B28(306)-2, B200(2-72)-2, B162(71)-2, B79(61)-1, B222(70)-1, B408(167)-4, B284(3-117)-1, B15(94)-7, B431(104)-5, A15(141)-0
H.P.50 Heyford Twin engine biplane bomber trainer -D
B28(287)-2, B71(182)-2, A11(248)-2, B233(189)-2, A10(375)-2, B79(58)-1, B411(65)-1, B45(73)-1, B15(102)-7, B103(54)-1, B469(62)-1
H.P.51 Twin engine high wing transport -E
B28(347)-1, B233(257)-1, B117(61)-1, B79(66)-1

H.P.52 Hampden (Hereford, Sweden **P 5)** Twin engine bomber-A
D9(11/84-244)-4, B143(2-11)-4, B46-2, B71(58)-2, A6(102)-2, B28(351)-2, D7(14-47)-5, B285(2-26)-2, A11(252)-2, A10(376)-2, B134(2-35)-2, B278(122)-2, B252(64)-2, A7(89)-1, A15(141)-6, B79(67)-1
H.P.54 Harrow (Sparrow) Twin engine high wing bomber transport -B
B28(372)-2, A11(250,501)-2, B233(270)-2, A10(376)-1, B278(125)-1, A7(202)-1, D3(5-3)-2, B117(72)-1, B103(64)-1, A15(141)-0, B88(1-25)-2, B79(72)-1
H.P.57 Halifax Four engine bomber, transport -A
D7(15-11)-4, B143(2-21)-4, B28(381)-2, B71(11)-2, A11(256)-2, B134(2-83)-2, B285(2-35)-2, B363-2, A6(104)-2, D3(3-101)-4, B278(127)-2, B252(63)-2, B79(75)-1, A10(377)-1, A15(142)-6
H.P.67 Hastings (H.P.68 Hermes) Four engine transport -H
B28(435)-2, B60(49c)-2, A11(264)-2, B88(7-26)-2, D3(7-123)-2, B79(85)-1, B45(170)-1, B17(138)-7, B103(120)-1, B334(218)-1
H.P.75 Manx Twin engine pusher tailless -F
B28(423)-2, D3(6-256)-2, B405(107)-1, B79(84)-1, B59(Add.14)-1, B439(78)-1

HAWKER Hawker Aircraft Ltd
Audax Biplane army cooperation, glider tug -B
B250(202)-2, B71(140)-2, A11(282)-2, B149(69)-1, B206(58)-1, A7(203)-1, B278(136)-1, D9(5/82-216)-1, B173(34)-1, A15(142)-0
Danecock (Denmark **L.B.II Dankok**) Biplane fighter -D
B250(98)-2, A10(64)-1, C73(13)-1, B234(154)-2, B206(17)-1, B173(16)-1,

D4(3/82,-152)-1, D25(12/61-27)-1,
B293(25)-6

Dantorp (Denmark **H.B.III**) Biplane
torpedo bomber, also floatplane -C
B250(112)-2, C73(17)-1, A10(380)-1,
B206(25)-1, D11(2/63-80)-3,
B233(223)-1, B173(18)-1, B152(27b)-1,
B289(41)-6

Demon Biplane fighter, glider tug -B
B250(191)-2, A11(280)-2,
D9(5/82-256)-2, A10(382)-1,
B278(135)-1, B234(208)-2, B411(67)-1,
B152(50c)-1, B206(52)-1, B122(9)-1

Fury Biplane fighter -B
D7(3-1)-4, B250(168)-2, B71(18)-2,
B148(56)-4, A11(278)-2, D9(6/80-285)-5,
B278(141)-2, A10(381)-2, C78(214)-2,
A15(142)-6, B469(15)-1

Fury (F.2/43) Fighter -E
B144(2-53)-2, B250(303)-2, A3(2-83)-2,
B71(126-3)-1, B335(166)-2, B234(306)-1,
D9(7/82-48)-1, B206(94)-1, A10(391)-1,
B49(131)-1, B60(53c)-2

Hardy Biplane general purpose -B
B250(208)-2, A11(286)-2, B71(140)-1,
B233(233)-2, B206(61)-1, A10(384)-1,
B278(138)-1, B173(35)-1, B45(79)-1,
A15(142)-6

Hart (Sweden **B 4, S 7**) Biplane light
bomber, also floatplane -B
B250(127)-2, B71(57)-2, A11(276)-2,
B278(132)-1, B155(14,141)-1,
B411(68)-1, B149(64)-8, B222(64)-2,
A10(380)-1, B206(31)-1, B469(36)-1

Hartbees Biplane ground support -B
B250(218)-2, A10(384)-1, B233(240)-2,
B278(137)-1, B329(24)-1, B206(64)-1,
B173(36)-1, B297(58)-1, B114(12-1244)-1

Hector Biplane army cooperation,
glider tug -B
B250(230)-2, A11(292)-2, B233(288)-2,
B278(140)-1, A7(203)-1, B239(91)-2,
B206(68)-1, B45(79)-1, B173(39)-1,
A15(143)-0, B469(37)-1

Henley Target tug, engine test -A
B250(266)-2, A11(302)-2, B88(2-7)-2,
D3(2-29)-4, B132(1-27)-1, A7(204)-1,
B206(80)-1, B173(46)-1, B153(48c)-1,
B278(145)-2

Hind Biplane light bomber, trainer -B
B250(221)-2, A11(288,502)-2,
B421(208)-2, B92(50)-1, A10(385)-1,
B411(69)-1, B88(1-15)-2, B206(65)-1,
B278(139)-1, A15(143)-0

Horsley Biplane light bomber, target
tug, engine test -B
B250(104)-2, A11(272)-2, B88(2-76)-2,
B233(140)-2, A10(380)-1, B411(70)-1,
B206(22)-1, B45(74)-1, B173(17)-1,
B103(36)-1, B469(39)-1

Hotspur Turret fighter -E
B250(271)-2, B234(256)-2,
D9(6/82-296)-2, B206(82)-1, B173(47)-1,
D3(3-204)-1, D25(2/58-42)-1, B251(31)-1

Hurricane Fighter -A
B144(2-3)-4, B250(234)-2, B251-2,
A3(2-57)-2, B71(24,111)-2, A11(294)-2,
B148(92)-4, A6(105)-4, B349-2,
B164(8)-4, A7(90)-1, B135(1-17)-2,
B278(146)-2, B157(5)-4, A10(386)-2,
A15(143)-6, B18(1-28)-7

Nimrod (Denmark **L.B.V.
Nimrodderne,** Japan **AXH**) Biplane
carrier fighter, also floatplane -D
B250(184)-2, A12(210)-2,
D9(4/82-207)-2, B278(144)-1,
A10(383)-1, B234(205)-2, B411(72)-1,
B206(49)-1, C73(18)-1, A15(142)-6

Nisr (Persian Audax) Biplane general
purpose -B
B250(204)-1, B88(2-79)-2, B206(59)-1,
B173(34)-1, B359(2-50)-1

Osprey (Sweden **S 9**) Biplane carrier
reconnaissance, target tug, also
floatplane -B
B250(196)-2, A12(212)-2, C89(191)-1,
B234(193)-2, B411(73)-1, B206(53)-1,
C31(14)-1, A10(383)-1, B173(32)-1,
A15(142)-0, B469(38)-1

P.1005 (B.11/41) Twin engine
bomber -J
B132(2-108)-3, B250(417)-0, B233(239)-0

Sea Fury Carrier fighter -M
D9(2/80-82)-4, B250(303)-2, B71(126)-2,
B148(174)-4, A12(220)-2, B88(7-12)-2,
A10(391)-2, B278(166)-2, B206(94)-1,
B17(140)-7

Sea Hurricane Carrier fighter -A
B65(108)-4, B250(255)-1, B251(115)-2,
A12(214)-2, B234(279)-2, B206(72)-1,
A10(388)-1, B278(154)-7, B157(52)-1,
A15(144)-0

Tempest Fighter -A
B144(2-44)-4, D9(2/81-91)-4,
B250(290)-2, B71(197)-2, A11(308)-2,
A3(2-76)-2, B335(102)-4, B278(161)-2,
B157(38)-4, B164(118)-2, A6(110)-2,
A10(390)-1, B252(68)-2, B206(88)-1,
A15(144)-6, B49(101)-1, A7(93)-1

Tomtit Biplane trainer -B
B250(149)-2, A11(274)-2, B200(2-89)-2,
B155(14,140)-1, B173(23)-1, D3(4-75)-2,
B206(37)-1, D10(8/83-313)-1 B227(36)-1,
B334(53)-6, B459(83)-1, B469(19)-1

Tornado Fighter -E
B144(2-33)-2, B250(274)-2, A3(2-68)-2,
B88(5-1)-2, B234(264)-2, B206(82)-1,
B278(165)-2, B335(13)-1,
D9(6/82-296)-1, B49(46)-1

Typhoon Fighter -A
B144(2-33)-4, B250(279)-2, B71(81)-2,
A3(2-72)-2, A11(304)-2, D6(8/72-91)-5,
B148(132)-4, B278(155)-2, B157(30)-4,
B335(12)-5, A6(109)-2, A10(389)-2,
B252(69)-2, B206(84)-1, A15(144)-6,
B49(46)-1, A7(94)-1, B18(1-66)-7

*HELMY S. Helmy (Aerogypt High Speed
Development Co., Ltd)*
Aerogypt Three or two engine transport
model, tourer -E
B200(2-359,360)-1, D3(6-304)-1

HESTON Heston Aircraft Co., Ltd
A.2/45 (JC6) Twin boom pusher
observation -H
D3(8-225)-2, D25(1/58-41)-1,
B279(190)-1

Phoenix (JA1) High wing
communications -I
B200(2-93)-1, D3(1-211)-2, B152(52c)-1,
B359(1-110)-2, B139(27)-1, B279(190)-1,
A15(145)-0

P.92/2
See Boulton Paul

Racer (JA5) Speed record -F
D9(7/75-49)-2, D3(4-94)-4,
D20(9/66-77)-2, B200(2-365)-1,
B359(1-44)-1, B408(245)-1, B395(59)-1,
B16(98)-7

T.1/37 (JA3) Trainer -E
D9(7/75-49)-1, B2(106)-3, D3(4-194)-1

T.7/37 (JA4) Trainer -J
D9(7/75-49)-6

HILLSON F. Hills and Sons, Ltd
Bi-Mono Jettisonable upper wing
biplane -F
D3(5-140)-2, D7(23-68)-1, B42(162)-1,
D25(1/57-15)-1, C3(186)-3, B279(191)-1,
C88(77,P)-1

F.H.40 Slip Wing Hurricane
Jettisonable upper wing Hawker
Hurricane -E
B250(261)-1, D25(1/59-42)-2,
D3(6-292)-2, B251(102)-2, B42(163)-1,
D7(23-67)-1, B135(1-24)-1, B234(277)-1,
B157(18)-1, B173(44)-1

Helvellyn Trainer, communications -L
B200(2-366)-1

Praga (Praga E.114 Air Baby) High
wing tourer -L
B200(2-96)-2, B420(51)-4,
D3(4-194,7-124,7-175)-1, C74(68)-2,
B279(125)-1, C85(168,P)-2

73

I.M.A. International Model Aircraft Ltd
T.G.Mk.I Towed target glider -A
D3(7-118)-2
T.G.Mk.II Towed target glider -H
D3(7-118)-2

MARENDAZ Marendaz Aircraft Ltd
Marendaz Trainer Trainer -I
B200(2-379)-1, B20(A-154)-1,
B279(220)-0

MARTIN BAKER Martin Baker
Aircraft Co., Ltd
M.B.2 (F.5/34) Fighter -E
D6(12/72-298)-2, B234(244)-2,
D25(9/57-45)-2, B200(2-490)-1,
B279(223)-1, B153(50c)-1, B212(60,P)-2,
B160(60)-1, B49(34)-1, D9(11/85-256)-2
M.B.3 (F.18/39) Fighter -E
B144(2-55)-2, D9(2/79-73,11/85-256)-2,
B234(285)-2, A3(2-86)-2, B279(222)-1,
B212(66,P)-1, D20(2/66-364)-2,
D29(12/84-30)-1, B49(93)-1
M.B.5 (F.18/39) Fighter -E
B144(2-57)-4, D9(2/79-73)-4, A4(2-88)-2,
B88(7-13)-2, B234(302)-1, B212(67,P)-1,
D29(12/84-30)-1, B157(76)-1,
B66(1-150)-1, B49(124)-1,
D9(11/85-256)-2

MILES Miles Aircraft Ltd (Phillips &
Powis Aircraft Ltd)
M.2 Hawk Trainer, sport -I
B63(56)-2, B200(2-137)-2, B238(26)-2,
B359(1-86)-1, B213(8)-1, B408(186)-1,
B402(431)-1, B420(48)-1, B284(3-122)-0,
A15(145)-0
M.2F Hawk Major (M.2H) Trainer,
sport -I
B63(64)-2, B200(2-142)-2, B238(28)-2,
B213(9)-1, C112(4-76)-2, B329(23)-1,
A15(145)-0
M.2Y Hawk Trainer Trainer -B
B63(66)-1, B359(1-88)-1, B284(3-123)-0,
A15(145)-0

M.3A Falcon Major (Sweden **Tp 7**)
Liaison -B
B63(77-2), B200(2-147)-2, B359(1-90)-1,
C78(351)-6, C112(4-79)-2. B279(230)-1,
A15(145)-0
M.3B Falcon Six (Gillette Falcon)
Liaison, M.52 wing research -I
B63(81)-1, B238(30)-2, B200(3-123)-1,
D9(7/76-46)-1, B321(30)-1, D3(7-244)-2,
B139(47)-1, B66(1-161)-1, B278(167)-0,
A15(145)-0, B60(63c)-1
M.4 Merlin Communications -I
B63(87)-2, B200(2-382)-1, B238(32)-2,
B323(65)-1, B359(1-91)-1, A15(145)-0
M.5 Sparrowhawk Wing flap
research -F
B63(89)-2, B200(2-151)-2, B238(34)-2,
D3(5-123)-1
M.6 Hawcon Airfoil research -F
B63(95)-2, B238(36)-2, D9(11/85-235)-1
M.7 Nighthawk Trainer,
communications -I
B63(98)-2, A11(505)-1, B200(2-283)-1,
B139(48)-1, D3(5-123)-1, A15(145)-0
M.8 Peregrine Twin engine boundary
layer research -F
B63(102)-2, B238(38)-2, B359(1-129)-1,
D3(5-123)-1
M.9 Kestrel (R.R. Trainer) Trainer -E
B63(107)-2, B200(2-490)-1, B238(40)-2,
D3(6-22)-2, B152(59c)-1
M.9A Master I Trainer -A
B63(114)-2, A11(338)-2, D3(2-65)-4,
B58(42c)-2, A12(373)-1, B88(1-17)-2,
B153(55c)-5, B278(176)-6, B292(57)-6,
A15(145)-0, B18(1-52)-7
M.11 Whitney Straight
Communications -I
B63(121)-2, B200(2-154)-2, B278(167)-1,
B238(44)-2, B139(48)-1, B284(3-124)-1,
B420(60)-1, D3(8-259)-1, A15(145)-0
M.12 Mohawk Communications -I
B63(130)-2, D19(1/81-53)-4,
B200(2-384)-1, B238(46)-2, B152(58c)-1,
B420(60)-5, B279(251)-1, A15(145)-0

M.13 Hobby Racer, wind tunnel
research -F
B63(133)-2, B238(48)-2

**M.14 Magister (Hawk Trainer
Mk III)** Trainer -A
B63(135)-2, A11(336)-2, A12(373)-1,
B200(2-158)-2, B88(1-16)-2,
B278(168)-1, A7(217)-1, B213-4,
B238(50)-2, B45(129)-1, A15(145)-0

M.15 'Pup' (T.1/37) Trainer -E
B63(147)-2, B238(52)-2

M.16 Mentor Trainer,
communications -B
B63(149)-2, B88(2-11)-2, D3(1-75)-2,
A11(506)-1, A7(218)-1, B200(2-491)-1,
B238(54)-2, B278(169)-0, A15(145)-0

M.17 Monarch Communications -I
B63(151)-2, B200(2-161)-2, B152(60c)-2,
B284(3-128)-1, B238(56)-2, B278(169)-0,
A15(145)-0

M.18 Trainer, research -E
B63(156)-2, B57(36c)-2, B88(4-6)-2,
B200(2-385)-1, B139(47)-1, B238(58)-2,
B359(1-98)-2, D3(4-39)-2,
D9(11/82-240)-1

M.19 Master II Trainer, glider tug -A
B63(163)-1, B59(56c)-2, B88(2-6)-2,
A11(338)-0, B200(2-491)-1, D3(6-34)-2,
B359(1-60)-2, B329(29)-1, B279(230)-1,
A15(145)-0

M.20 Fighter -E
B144(3-3)-2, B63(172)-2, A3(2-90)-2,
B88(5-8)-2, D3(5-164)-2, B49(57)-1,
B278(170)-2, B157(28)-1, B212(51,P)-1,
B66(1-154)-1, D6(12/71-388)-1

M.24 Master Fighter Fighter -E
B63(114)-1, D3(8-8)-1, B49(57)-0,
B234(276)-0

M.25 Martinet Target tug -A
B63(189)-2, A11(340)-2, B59(55c)-2,
B88(4-15)-2, D20(12/66-277)-2,
A12(374)-1, B278(171)-1, A6(111)-3,
A7(217)-1, A15(145)-0

M.27 Master III Trainer -A
B63(163)-2, B59(54c)-2, B278(176)-2,

B88(3-4)-2, B200(2-492)-1, D3(3-186)-2,
A11(338)-1, A6(111)-1, A7(218)-1,
A15(145)-0

M.28 Communications -C
B63(194)-2, B57(37c)-2, B278(172)-2,
B88(4-7,6-20)-2, B238(68)-2,
B200(2-387)-1, D3(4-27)-2, A7(219)-1,
B59(54c)-1

M.29 Trainer -J
B63(201)-6

M.30X Minor Twin engine faired
wing -F
B63(202)-2, D3(6-256)-2, B238(70)-2,
D25(3/58-11)-1, C3(189)-1

M.33 Monitor Twin engine high wing
target tug -C
B63(207)-2, A12(232)-2, B59(53c)-2,
B88(7-27)-2, B238(72)-2, D25(4/61-47)-1,
B278(173)-2

M.35 Libellula Tandem wing pusher -F
B63(213)-2, D7(5-59)-2, D25(3/58-52)-2,
B238(74)-2, D9(12/83-288)-1,
B59(52c)-1, B42(12)-1, B278(174)-3,
B231(59)-3, C3(190)-1

M.37 Martinet Trainer Trainer -H
B63(222)-2, D20(12/66-277)-1,
D3(7-263)-1, A15(145)-0, B60(65c)-1

M.38 Messenger Observation,
liaison -B
B63(224)-2, B59(52c)-2, D3(6-92)-4,
B88(6-19)-2, B200(2-164)-2, A11(506)-1,
B278(174)-2, B238(76)-2, D24(5-763)-1,
A15(145)-6

M.39B Libellula Twin engine tandem
wing -F
B63(239)-2, D7(5-58)-2, B238(78)-2,
B278(175)-3, B231(60)-2, B132(2-127)-1,
B66(1-157)-1, B42(12)-1, B59(51c)-1,
D9(12/83-287)-3

M.45 Trainer -J
B63(252)-6

M.48 Messenger 3 Communications -E
B63(230)-1, B200(2-164)-1, B59(51c)-1

M.50 Queen Martinet (Q.10/43)
Target drone -B

B63(190)-1, D20(12/66-277)-0,
D3(7-162)-1, A11(340)-0, B60(64c)-1

M.52 (E.24/43) Single jet supersonic
research -J
D7(13-35)-4, B63(268)-2, D3(7-244)-2,
B395(91)-1, B405(153)-1, B408(381)-3

M.57 Aerovan Twin engine high wing
transport -M
B63(289)-2, B200(2-168)-2, B59(50c)-2,
D3(6-140)-2, B238(80)-2, B16(107)-7,
B408(370)-1, B279(230)-1, B139(127)-1,
B176(100)-1

M.60 Marathon (18/44) Four engine
high wing transport -H
B63(301)-2, D3(7-141)-2, B60(62c)-2,
B162(184)-2, B238(84)-2, B200(2-85)-2,
D7(26-77)-1, B291(115)-1

M.64 (L.R.5) Tourer -E
B63(314)-1, D3(8-15)-1

M.65 Gemini Twin engine tourer -H
B63(316)-2, B200(2-173)-2, D3(7-44)-2,
B238(82)-2, B60(61c)-1, B139(127)-1,
D24(4-563)-1

Hoopla High wing radio controlled
pilotless bomber -J
B63(178)-1, B163(30)-1, C88(204,P)-1,
D24(17-2715)-1

MOSSCRAFT *Moss Bros Aircraft Ltd*
M.A.2 Trainer -L
B200(2-394)-1, B153(56c)-1, B139(48)-1,
B22(A-176)-1, B279(233)-0

PARNALL *Parnall Aircraft Ltd*
Heck 2 (Hendy Heck II)
Communications -I
B200(2-178)-2, D3(2-123)-2,
B359(1-77)-1, B239(90)-2, B139(49)-1,
D3(9-72)-1, A15(145)-0, B279(248)-0
382 (Heck 3) Trainer -E
B200(2-179)-1, B153(57c)-1,
B359(1-78)-1, D3(5-243)-1,
B284(3-128)-0

PERCIVAL *Percival Aircraft Ltd*
P.1 Gull Four Communications -I
B200(2-182)-2, B102(86)-1, D3(9-30)-1
P.3 Gull Six Communications -I
B200(2-183)-1, B153(59c)-1,
B284(3-129)-1, B16(80)-7, B408(209)-1,
D3(9-30)-1, C112(4-81)-2, B459(73)-1
P.10 Vega Gull Communications -B
B200(2-190)-2, B153(59c)-1, D3(1-67)-2,
A11(508)-1, B92(32)-1, B408(248)-2,
B319(110)-1, B284(3-129)-1, C78(303)-6
P.16 Petrel (Q.6) Twin engine
communications -B
B200(2-194)-2, D3(3-41)-4, B88(2-13)-2,
B154(34c)-1, B152(62c)-4, A11(509)-1,
B278(179)-1, A7(226)-1, B284(3-132)-1,
A15(145)-0
P.28 Proctor I Communications -A
B88(2-12)-2, A11(354)-0, B57(39c)-1,
D3(9-31)-1, B279(250)-1, C3(160)-3,
A15(145)-0, B278(178)-0
P.30 Proctor II Wireless trainer -A
A12(380)-1, A11(354)-0, C3(140)-1,
A15(145)-0, B278(178)-0
P.31 Proctor IV (T.9/41 Preceptor)
Wireless trainer -A
B88(5-22)-2, D3(5-53)-4, B278(178)-2,
A11(354)-1, B200(2-200)-1, B59(58c)-1,
A15(145)-0
P.32 Mew Gull Ground attack version
P.6 Mew Gull -J
D3(9-32)-0. B284(3-133)-0
P.34 Proctor III Wireless trainer -A
A11(354)-3, B200(2-197)-2, A7(227)-1,
D3(6-252)-1, A15(145)-0
P.40 Prentice (T.23/43) Trainer -H
B88(7-14)-2, D3(7-99)-2, A11(356)-2,
B200(2-204)-2, B139(39)-2,
D9(3/82-148)-1, B60(69c)-1, B17(134)-7,
B45(194)-1, B334(276)-1

REID AND SIGRIST *Reid and
Sigrist Ltd*
R.S.1 Snargasher Twin engine trainer,
communications -E

D9(9/75-153)-2, B153(60c)-1, B55(80)-2,
D20(4/67-516)-1, B200(2-411)-1,
B397(262)-1, B279(259)-0, B20(A-163)-1
R.S.3 Desford Twin engine trainer -E
D3(6-303)-2, B60(71c)-1, B66(2-91)-1,
D20(4/67-516)-1, B200(2-411)-1,
B139(128)-1, B279(259)-0

R.F.D *R.F. Dagnell Ltd*
Type A. T. Dagling High wing training
glider -I
B284(4-181)-0, B88(7-15)-0

SARO *Saunders-Roe Ltd*
A.17 Cutty Sark Twin engine high wing
amphibian trainer -I
B200(2-221)-2, B99(148)-2, B281(257)-1,
B291(21)-1, B284(3-135)-0
A.19 Cloud Twin engine high wing
amphibian trainer -B
A11(360)-2, B99(152)-2, B200(2-416)-1,
B103(52)-1, B45(81)-1, B359(2-98)-1,
B408(273)-1, B397(264)-1, B411(179)-0
A.27 London Twin engine biplane
reconnaissance flying boat -B
A3(5-82)-2, A11(362)-2, B99(184)-2,
B88(1-52)-2, B278(180)-2, A10(407)-1,
A7(231)-1, B103(63)-1, B45(81)-1,
A15(146)-6
A.33 (R.2/33) Four engine high wing
reconnaissance flying boat -E
B99(211)-2, B89(258)-1, D17(1-48)-1
S.36 Lerwick Twin engine high wing
reconnaissance flying boat -B
A3(5-84)-2, B99(213)-2, A11(364)-2,
B88(1-54)-2, D20(3/68-165)-2,
A10(408)-1, B278(181)-2, A7(231)-1,
B45(132)-1, A15(146)-0
A.37 Shrimp Four engine high wing
model R.5/39 flying boat -F
A3(5-88)-2, B47(110)-2, B99(218)-2,
B200(2-418)-1, B154(36c)-1,
B284(3-135)-1
SR.A/1 (E.6/44) Twin jet high wing
fighter flying boat -H

B462-2, D20(5/67-584)-2, B99(236)-2,
B138(72)-2, A10(38)-1, B234(324)-1,
D29(8/83-40)-1, D3(8-185)-2,
B405(207)-1, B17(142)-7, B66(2-97)-1

SCOTT *Scott Light Aircraft Co. (Zander
& Scott)*
Primary High wing training glider -I
B284(4-180)-0
Viking Training glider -I
B69(56)-1, B284(4-178)-0

SCOTTISH AVIATION *Scottish
Aviation Ltd*
A.4/45 Prestwick Pioneer High wing
observation -H
D3(8-225)-2, D7(10-22)-1, A11(366)-2,
B200(2-224)-2, B139(21)-2, B103(135)-1,
B334(239)-1, B16(132)-7

SHORT *Short Brothers Ltd*
S.16 Scion Twin engine high wing
transport -I
B29(286)-2, B162(79)-2, B200(2-240)-2,
B284(3-136)-1, B16(82)-7, D3(4-178)-2,
B174(31)-1, A15(146)-0
L.17 Scylla (S.17/L) Four engine
biplane transport -I
B29(272)-2, B162(85)-2, B200(2-426)-1,
B284(3-137)-1, B174(32)-1,
B359(2-90)-1, B291(46)-1, B408(227)-8,
B431(106)-8
S.19 Singapore III Twin tandem engine
biplane reconnaissance flying boat -B
B29(251)-2, A3(5-91)-2, A11(370)-2,
B99(181)-2, B278(182)-2, A10(411)-1,
B411(155)-1, A7(233)-1, B45(82)-1,
A15(146)-6, B469(50)-1
S.20 Mercury Four engine high wing
floatplane trainer -I
B29(301)-2, B99(203)-2, B200(2-427)-1,
B153(51c)-4, B404(101)-1, B174(33)-1,
B440(149)-1, B410(16)-1, B351(19)-1,
B284(3-137)-0

S.22 Scion Senior Four engine high wing transport, also floatplane -I,F
B29(296)-2, A3(5-93)-2, B200(2-428)-1, D3(4-178)-2, B174(34)-1, B359(2-102)-2, B152(26a)-1

S.23 Empire C (S.30, S.33) Four engine high wing transport flying boat -I
D7(11-71,15-33)-4, B29(312)-2, A3(5-102)-2, B71(84)-2, B99(190)-2, B408(234)-5, B174(35)-1, B284(3-138)-1, B431(162)-5, A15(146)-6

S.25 Sunderland Four engine high wing patrol flying boat -A
D9(9/81-125)-4, B29(345)-2, B71(189)-2, A3(5-95)-2, A11(372)-2, D3(1-39)-4, B278(183)-2, B99(196)-2, B327-5, B252(145)-2, A10(412)-2, A6(112)-2. A7(151)-1, A15(146)-6, B174(38)-1

S.25 Sandringham Transport version S.25 Sunderland -H
B29(398)-2, B162(151)-2, B99(230)-2, B200(2-248)-2, B60(74c)-2, D3(6-188)-8, B176(110)-1, B174(42)-1, B76(106)-1, B16(118)-7

S.26 Empire G Four engine high wing transport flying boat -I
B29(334)-2, A3(5-104)-2, B71(84)-1, B162(131)-2, D3(2-185)-4, B153(65c)-5, B278(188)-2, B284(3-139)-1, B99(215)-2, A15(146)-0

S.29 Stirling Four engine bomber, transport -A
D7(10-42)-4, B143(2-38)-4, B29(370)-2, B71(142)-2, A11(378)-2, B134(2-43)-2, B278(189)-2, A6(112)-2, B252(144)-2, A10(413)-2, D3(3-53)-4, B174(45)-1, A7(150)-1, A15(147)-6, B132(1-42)-2

S.31 Half-scale S.29 Stirling flying model -F
B29(372)-1, B143(2-38)-1, D7(10-43)-1, B174(47)-1, B212(57,P)-1, B66(2-101)-0

S.32 (14/38) Four engine transport -J
B29(341)-2, D6(9/72-144)-2, B153(66c)-1, D3(4-95)-1, B174(48)-6

S.35 Shetland Four engine high wing reconnaissance flying boat -E
B47(103)-2, B29(390)-2, A3(5-108)-2, B99(225)-2, B59(59c)-2, B200(2-429)-1, B88(6-23)-2, B174(48)-1, B16(122)-7, B76(117)-1

S.38 Sturgeon (S.11/43) Twin engine carrier bomber -H
B29(413)-2, A12(260)-2, D3(7-248)-5, B88(7-29)-2, B174(51)-1, B66(2-104)-1

S.45 Seaford (Sunderland IV, R.8/42) Four engine high wing reconnaissance flying boat -M
B29(360)-2, A3(5-106)-2, B99(228)-2, B88(7-28)-2, A11(513)-1, D3(7-3)-2, B278(187)-2, B174(49)-1, B59(Add.16)-1, B114(21-2289)-0

SLINGSBY *Slingsby Sailplanes Ltd*
Baynes Bat
See Baynes
T.1 Falcon I High wing training glider -I
B284(4-180)-0
T.3 Primary High wing training glider -I
B284(4-178)-1, D3(7-30)-3
T.4 Falcon III High wing training glider -I
D12(7/43-213)-2, D3(7-31)-3, B130(118)-3, B284(4-179)-0, B1(Sec.H)-3
T.5 Grunau Baby (Schneider) High wing training glider -I
D12(7/43-213)-2, D3(7-31)-3, B130(118)-3, B284(4-180)-0, B1(Sec.H)-3
T.6 Kirby Kite I High wing training glider -I
B284(4-179)-1, B69(49)-1
T.7 Kirby Cadet (Cadet TX.1) High wing training glider -A
B88(7-15)-2, D12(7/43-213)-2, D3(7-31)-3, B130(118)-3, B284(4-182)-0
T.8 Kirby Tutor (Cadet TX.2) High wing training glider -I
B342(5)-1, D3(7-234)-1, B69(49)-1, B284(4-182)-0, B82(143)-0

T.9 King Kite High wing training glider -I
B284(4-182)-0

T.12 Kirby Gull I High wing training sailplane -I
B69(27)-1, B284(4-182)-0

T.13 Petrel High wing training sailplane -K
B82(141)-2, B69(49)-1, D3(7-98)-1

T.15 Kirby Gull II High wing training sailplane -I
D3(7-31,207)-2, B284(4-182)-0

T.17 (X.10/40) High wing transport glider -J
D6(4/72-208)-3

T.18 Hengist (X.25/40) High wing transport glider -C
D6(4/72-209)-2, B88(7-30)-2, B286(65)-2, D3(7-39)-2, B279(275)-1

T.20 (TX.8/45) High wing training glider -H
D3(7-32)-3, D3(7-163)-1

T.21 Sedbergh High wing training glider -H
B82(142)-2, B69(27)-1, D3(8-213)-1

SPARTAN *Spartan Aircraft Ltd*
Clipper Communications -L
B200(2-435)-1, D3(2-2)-1, D3(6-147)-1
Cruiser Three engine transport -I
B200(2-281)-2, B279(282)-1, D3(1-194)-2, B287(85,172)-6, B359(1-182)-3, B284(3-141)-0

SUPERMARINE *Supermarine Works, Vickers-Armstrongs Ltd*
B.12/36 Four engine bomber -J
B12(319)-2, B132(1-45)-7, D9(7/79-50)-2, D25(1/62-45)-2, C3(116)-3, B233(294)-0
E.10/44 Attacker Single jet fighter -H
B12(268)-2, D9(5/82-233)-4, A12(312)-2, B138(61)-2, B60(79c)-1, A10(432)-2, B164(154)-2, B139(79)-2, B66(2-115)-1

F.18/37 (Type 327) Twin engine fighter -J
B49(156)-2, B12(331)-2

S.24/37 (Type 322 'Dumbo') Variable incidence high wing carrier torpedo bomber -E
B12(162)-2, D3(7-94)-2, D9(11/82-237)-2, D20(4/64-61)-2, B88(7-31)-2, B60(85c)-1, B233(317)-1, C3(127)-1, B95(68)-1, B66(2-120)-1

Scapa Twin engine biplane reconnaissance flying boat -D
B12(128)-2, A11(392)-2, B99(172)-2, A10(425)-1, B411(155)-1, B359(2-135)-1, B45(83)-1, B103(58)-1, B95(32)-1, B114(21-2274)-0

Seafang Carrier fighter -E
D9(3/80-140)-2, B12(263)-1, B88(7-20)-2, A12(398)-1, B346(200)-2, B60(80c)-2, B278(212)-3, A3(2-119)-0, B66(2-128)-1

Seafire Carrier fighter -A
B12(247)-2, B65(126)-4, B71(221)-2, A3(2-114)-2, B346(77)-2, B278(210)-2, B88(6-14,7-18)-2, A10(430)-1, B157(52)-1, A7(153)-1, A15(148)-0

Seagull ASR.I (S.14/44, Type 381) Variable incidence high wing rescue amphibian -H
D9(11/82-237)-2, B12(156)-2, B99(242)-2, D3(8-297)-8, B66(2-132)-1

Sea Otter Biplane rescue amphibian -A
B12(156)-2, A3(5-116)-2, A11(414)-2, A12(296)-2, B278(196)-2, B88(6-8)-2, B99(208)-2, D3(5-211)-2, A7(235)-1, A15(148)-0, B18(1-89)-7

Southampton Twin engine biplane reconnaissance flying boat -B
B12(96)-2, B99(128)-2, A11(386)-2, B321(22)-1, A10(424)-1, B411(117)-1, B45(82)-1, B103(32)-1, B297(32)-1, B279(287)-1, B469(52)-1

Spiteful Fighter -M
B144(3-41)-2, B12(263)-1, A3(2-117)-2, D20(9/67-877)-2, A11(516)-1,

B346(198)-2, B88(7-19)-2, B49(127)-2,
B59(Add.20)-2, B278(212)-1
Spitfire Fighter, reconnaissance -A
B144(3-5)-4, B12(209)-2, B346-4,
D9(2/85-74,3/85-132,4/85-181)-4,
B71(41,166,206,246)-2, A3(2-92,6-95)-2,
A11(398)-2, D9(9/76-133)-5,
B135(1-25)-2, B333-4, A6(115)-4,
B148(96)-4, B278(197)-2, A7(154)-1,
B157(13)-4, B164(12)-2, A10(426)-2,
B252(149)-2, A15(148)-6, B18(1-38)-7,
B475(64)-1
Stranraer Twin engine biplane
reconnaissance flying boat -B
B12(134)-2, A3(5-111)-2, A11(396)-2,
B99(187)-2, B88(1-53)-2, A10(426)-1,
B278(193)-7, B276(438)-1, A7(235)-1,
A15(147)-6
Walrus (Seagull V) Biplane pusher
rescue amphibian -A
D7(17-13)-4, B12(141)-2, A3(5-113)-2,
B71(224)-2, A12(290)-2, A11(394)-2,
B278(194)-2, B303-5, B99(174)-2,
A6(114)-2, A15(147)-6, A7(157)-1

TAYLORCRAFT *Taylorcraft*
Aeroplanes (England) Ltd
Auster I (Model D/1) High wing
observation -A
D7(11-31)-1, D3(5-70)-2, D3(9-90)-1,
A11(128)-1, B45(103)-1, A15(134)-0
Auster II High wing observation -E
B88(4-8)-2, D7(11-33)-1, D3(5-70)-2,
D3(4-171)-2, A11(128)-0, A15(134)-0
Auster III (Model F) High wing
observation -A
D7(11-33)-1, D3(5-70,9-90)-2,
B58(56c)-1, B122(22)-1, A11(128)-0,
A15(134)-0
Auster IV (Model G) High wing
observation -A
D7(11-34)-1, B88(5-14)-2, D3(5-94)-4,
D3(9-90)-1, B58(57c)-1, B278(71)-1,
B351(107)-1, A11(128)-0, A15(134)-0

Auster V (Model J) High wing
observation -A
D7(11-34)-5, A11(128)-3, D3(9-90)-1,
B59(74c)-1, A7(183)-1, B278(71)-3,
A15(134)-0
Auster VI (A.O.P.6, Model K) High
wing observation -M
A11(36)-2, B88(7-1)-2, D7(11-41)-1,
D3(9-91)-1, B279(85)-1, B60(14c)-1
Model A High wing communications -I
D3(6-231)-1, B284(3-145)-0, D3(9-90)-0
Model H High wing training glider -E
B88(5-15)-2, B58(57c)-1, D3(5-70)-2,
D3(9-92)-1, A15(134)-0
Plus C (Model C) High wing
communications -I
B200(2-289)-1, D7(11-33)-1,
B284(3-145)-1, B154(45c)-1, D3(9-90)-1,
A15(134)-0
Plus D (Model D) High wing
communications -I
B88(2-9)-2, B200(2-289)-2,
D3(1-223,5-70)-2, B284(3-148)-1,
D7(11-33)-1, B279(289)-1, A15(134)-0

TIPSEY *Tipsey Aircraft Co., Ltd*
Tipsey BC (Belfair)
See Belgium: Tipsey
Tipsey M (Fairey Primer)
See Belgium: Tipsey
Tipsey Trainer (Tipsey B) Trainer -I
B200(2-296)-2, B400(40)-1, D3(4-159)-2,
B55(106)-2, B420(67)-1, B152(73c)-1,
B284(3-150)-0

VICKERS *Vickers-Armstrongs Ltd*
F.7/41 (Type 432 'Mayfly') Twin
engine high altitude fighter -E
B144(3-43)-2, B11(250)-2, A3(2-121)-2,
B88(7-32)-2, B60(88c)-1, D3(7-152)-2,
B234(288)-1
Valentia Twin engine biplane
transport -B
B11(163)-2, A11(432)-2, B233(232)-2,
D7(10-35)-1, A7(238)-1, B411(157)-1,

B278(215)-1, B45(85)-1, B408(168)-1,
A15(149)-0

Valparaiso (Vixen) Biplane general
purpose -D
B11(180)-1, D9(3/81-123)-1,
B411(179)-0, D7(27-43)-1

Vespa Biplane army cooperation -D
B11(198)-2, B233(142)-1, B70(32)-1,
B404(73)-1, B95(34)-1

Viking (Valetta) Twin engine
transport -M
D7(21-38)-4, B11(395)-2, D3(6-176)-2,
B59(75c)-2, B162(153)-2, A11(518)-1,
D3(7-198)-5, B200(2-307)-2, B16(114)-7,
B45(201)-1

Vildebeeste Biplane torpedo bomber -B
B11(272)-2, A11(428)-2, D4(2/69-22)-2,
A10(437)-2, B278(213)-2, A6(119)-1,
B233(213)-2, B411(123)-1, D3(3-116)-2,
A15(149)-6

Vincent Biplane general purpose -B
B11(287)-2, A11(430)-2, B233(262)-2,
B278(214)-1, A10(438)-1, B95(36)-1,
B359(2-68)-2, B411(125)-1, B45(88)-1,
A15(149)-0

Virginia Twin engine biplane parachute
trainer -B
B11(143)-2, A11(424)-2, B233(125)-2,
B95(18)-1, B411(126)-1, A10(436)-1,
B45(84)-1, B103(30)-1, B334(42)-1,
B150(13)-6, B469(56)-1

Warwick Twin engine bomber,
transport -A
B143(2-69)-2, B11(364)-2, B71(229)-2,
A11(444)-2, B59(76c)-2, A6(123)-2,
B278(222)-2, B132(1-36)-1, A7(238)-1,
A15(150)-6, A10(441)-1

Wellesley Bomber -B
D9(7/80-25)-4, B143(2-49)-2, B11(299)-2,
B71(256)-2, A11(434)-2, B278(216)-7,
B285(2-58)-2, D16(3/81-11)-1, A6(119)-1,
A15(149)-0, D3(2-77)-4, A10(438)-1

Wellington Twin engine bomber -A
B143(2-53)-4, B11(309)-2, B71(125)-2,
D7(13-63)-5, A11(436)-2, B240-2,

A6(120)-4, B134(1-60)-2, B278(217)-2,
A10(439)-2, B252(154)-2, A7(159)-1,
A15(149)-6, B132(1-20)-2, B233(278)-2

Windsor Four engine bomber -E
B143(2-74)-2, B11(386)-2,
D25(10/67-940)-2, B132(2-112)-2,
B278(224)-2, B88(7-34)-2, D3(6-268)-2,
A7(263)-1, B59(Add.21)-1, B66(2-139)-1

WEIR G. & J. Weir Ltd
W.5 Twin rotor helicopter -F
B23(13)-1, D25(12/55-45)-1,
B228(138)-0, B161(21)-0

W.6 Twin rotor helicopter -F
D25(12/55-46)-1, C3(192)-3, B23(13)-0,
B228(139)-0, B161(21)-0

W.9
See Cierva W.9

WESTLAND Westland Aircraft Ltd
C.L. 20 Autogiro -F
B239(74)-2, B407(74,182)-2,
B228(141)-1, B200(1-239)-1,
B282(109)-1, B408(214)-1

Lysander High wing army
cooperation -A
D9(1/84-21,2/84-80)-4, B71(159)-2,
B345-5, A11(460,521)-2, D3(1-153)-4,
B278(227)-1, B233(290)-2, B149(66)-8,
B252(156)-2, B282(104)-1, A10(443)-1,
B276(449)-1, A6(124)-1, A15(150)-6

P.12 Tandem wing tail turret version
Lysander -F
D9(2/84-80)-2, B71(159-11)-1,
B345(17)-1, B212(55,P)-1, B42(34)-1,
B407(78)-1, B282(106)-1, D6(1/72-37)-2,
D3(9-116)-1

Wallace Biplane general purpose -D
A11(458)-2, B233(217)-2, B407(180)-2,
B239(62)-2, B278(226)-1, B282(94)-1,
A10(443)-1, A7(263)-1, B411(128)-1,
A15(150)-6

Wapiti Biplane general purpose -B
B71(32)-2, A11(456)-2, D21(1/1-4)-2,
B407(176)-2, B278(225)-1, B282(78)-1,

B233(180)-1, B329(20)-1, A10(442)-1,
A15(150)-0, B469(42)-1

Welkin Twin engine high altitude
fighter -C
D9(8/76-76)-4, B144(3-53)-4,
A3(2-126)-2, B278(235)-2, B88(6-15)-2,
A11(521)-1, B59(80c)-1, D3(7-269)-2,
B282(115)-1, B60(89c)-1, B66(2-148)-1

Wessex Three engine high wing
transport -I
B200(2-327)-2, B407(178)-2,
D3(1-110)-2, B239(52)-2, B282(85)-1,
B281(258)-1, B291(26)-1, B284(3-150)-0,
D17(1-30)-1, B411(180)-0

Whirlwind Twin engine fighter -A
B144(3-45)-4, D6(7/73-30)-4, B71(191)-2,
B348-4, A3(2-123)-2, A11(462)-2,
B278(230)-2, B247(59)-2, A6(124)-2,
A10(444)-2, B49(153)-1, A15(151)-6

Widgeon High wing communications -L
B200(2-322)-2, B407(174)-2, B239(46)-2,
B282(70)-1

Wyvern (N.11/44) Carrier torpedo
strike fighter -H
D7(1-20)-4, D3(8-160)-2, A12(410)-1,
B407(99)-1, B234(314)-1, B282(118)-1,
B17(158)-7, B114(24-2601)-6,
B138(92)-2, B139(69)-2, B66(2-156)-1

HUNGARY

MANFRED WEISS *Weiss Manfred*
Repulogep es Motorgyar Reszvenytarsasag
W.M.10 Biplane trainer -L
D3(7-15)-1, D11(8/63-72)-6
W.M.13 Biplane trainer -L
B152(168c)-1
W.M.16 Budapest Biplane trainer,
reconnaissance -B
D20(10/69-56)-1, A15(151)-0
W.M.21 Solyom Biplane
reconnaissance -A
D20(9/64-46)-2, B280(247)-1,
C10(224)-1, B159(223)-6, A15(151)-6,
B114(22-2363)-0
W.M.23 Ezustnyil Fighter -E
D20(5/66-579)-2, D10(8/66-292)-1,
D14(2-29)-3, B114(24-2599)-0
W.M.23 II Fighter -J
D14(3-37)-3, D10(8/66-293)-0

M.A.V.A.G. *Magyar Allami Vaggon es*
Gepgyar
Heja (Reggiane Re.2000) Fighter -A
D20(7/66-707)-6, A13(237)-1,

A3(2-173)-6, C33(215)-1, B330(10)-1,
B71(123-8)-1, D9(7/75-46)-0

M.S.E. *Muegyetemi Sportrepulo Egyesulet*
M.19 Tourer -L
B152(167c)-1, D3(5-171)-1, B279(233)-0
M.21 Biplane trainer -B
B152(167c)-1, D3(5-171)-1, B279(233)-0
M.24 Nebulo (M.25) Trainer -B
B153(149c)-1, B139(48)-1,
D20(6/63-49)-1, D3(5-171)-1
M.29 Tourer -L
D3(5-171)-1

REPULO MUSZAKI INTEZET
Laszlo Varga
X/H Twin turboprop fighter bomber -G
D6(6/71-53)-3

RUBIK *Erno Rubik*
R-18 Kanya High wing glider tug -H
B139(29)-1
R-21 High wing twin boom transport
glider -J
D6(3/72-130)-3

SZEKESFEHERVAR *Sandor Loczy*
Hungaria (Version Udet U-12) Biplane
trainer -B
B71(257-115)-1

B280(235)-1, D20(7/63-51)-1,
B139(26)-1, B338(86)-1,
D9(11/78-238)-1, A15(151)-0

UHRI *Uhri Testverek Repulogepgyar*
(Andras Fabian)
Levente II High wing trainer, liaison -A

VARGA *Ludvig Varga*
Kaplar High wing trainer -H
B139(27)-1

INDIA

H.A.L. *Hindustan Aircraft Ltd*
G-1 High wing transport glider -E
B286(187)-1, D6(5/72-250)-1,
D9(1/75-12)-1, B149(25)-1

PC-5A (Harlow PC-5) Trainer,
communications -B
B149(25)-1, D9(1/75-10)-1,
D6(3/73-140)-1, B284(4-172)-1

ITALY

ALLIEVO
Pavullo High wing training glider -K
D3(7-30)-3

AMBROSINI *Societa Aeronautica*
Italiana Ing. A. Ambrosini
S.A.I. 2S Liaison -I
A13(7)-1, C13(175)-2, B153(171c)-1,
B139(49)-1, A15(152)-0, B20(A-281)-1
S.A.I. 3 Liaison -I
A13(8)-1, B152(192c)-1, D3(6-51)-1,
B20(A-282)-0
S.A.I. 7 Trainer -M
A13(11)-1, C20(10-113)-2, B401(4)-2,
D20(5/64-63)-1, B17(261)-7,
B153(171c)-1, D3(7-282)-1, C13(260)-0
S.A.I. 10 Griffone High wing trainer,
also floatplane -I
C20(11-19)-2, A13(9)-1, B20(A-282)-1,
D3(6-63)-1, C13(261)-0

S.A.I. 11 High wing trainer -E
C20(11-24)-1

S.A.I. 107 Fighter -E
A13(13)-1, D6(10/71-261)-1,
C20(2-73)-1, D25(2/56-43)-1, A15(152)-0

S.A.I. 207 Fighter -B
A13(13)-2, A3(2-188)-2,
D6(10/71-261)-2, C20(2-71)-2,
C13(242)-2, B18(1-238)-7, A15(152)-6,
B279(78)-0

S.A.I. 403 Dardo Fighter -E
A3(2-190)-2, D6(10/71-262)-2,
A13(15)-1, C20(2-72)-1, C13(242)-1,
C88(108)-6, A15(152)-0, B114(7-694)-0

S.S.4 Canard pusher fighter -E
A13(17)-2, A3(2-186)-2,
D9(12/83-288)-2, C20(2-21)-2, B42(9)-1,
C39(102-54)-2, D6(10/71-261)-2,
B231(48)-3, C36(153)-1, C43(2-93)-1

ANSALDO *Aeronautica Ansaldo S.A. (Fiat)*
A.120 High wing reconnaissance bomber -B
C13(67)-2, C17(88)-2, D20(12/69-55)-1, C33(162)-1, C49(168)-1, A15(152)-0
A.300 Biplane general purpose, trainer -D
A10(196)-1, C13(56)-2, C17(74)-2, C83(164)-2, B411(11)-1, C44(119)-1, B391(392)-1, B279(310)-1, B412(70)-1, B114(1-16)-0

A.V.I.A. *Azionaria Vercellese Industrie Aeronautiche (Francis Lombardi)*
L.3 (F.L.3) Trainer, also floatplane -B
C20(11-5)-2, A13(292)-1, C13(205)-2, C17(155)-1, B139(38)-2, B338(70)-1, C32(114)-1, B279(217)-1, A15(152)-0, B420(72)-1
L.4 Twin engine trainer -E
C20(11-15)-1
LM.02 Dive bomber glider -E
C20(6-63)-2, C88(186,P)-1, A13(292)-0

BESTETTI *Aeronautica Bestetti*
Bestetti-Bazzocchi E.B.4 Canard pusher -F
C36(308)-1
Bestetti-Colombo C.3 Twin engine trainer -E
C20(11-93)-2, D3(7-282)-1, A13(193)-0, C13(263)-0
Bestetti-Nardi BN.1 Twin engine twin fuselage trainer -E
C20(11-87)-2, C36(306)-1

BREDA *Societa Italiana Ernesto Breda*
Ba.25 Biplane trainer, also floatplane -A
A13(20)-2, C20(10-17)-2, C13(107)-2, B152(171c)-1, B293(43)-6, B14(150,159)-2, D9(5/75-242)-1, C17(103)-2, C74(260)-2, A15(152)-0
Ba.27 Fighter -D
D9(8/74-90)-2, A10(198)-1, A13(25)-1,

D25(10/58-6)-1, C80(65)-1, C43(2-68,127)-1, C13(128)-0, B114(3-248)-0
Ba.28 Biplane trainer, also floatplane -B
A13(24)-1, C13(124)-2, C20(10-18)-1, C17(103)-1, B153(152c)-1, B58(112c)-1, B319(35)-1, C49(196)-1, C33(185)-1
Ba.39 Liaison -I
C13(108)-2, A13(27)-1, D3(2-182)-1, A15(152)-0
Ba.44 Twin engine biplane transport -I
C20(7-19)-2, A13(28)-1, B391(394)-1, B153(152c)-1, D7(2-213)-1, C80(119)-1, A15(152)-0, C13(129)-0
Ba.64 Fighter bomber -B
A13(30)-1, C13(136)-2, C17(107)-2, D29(8/81-30)-1, B152(172c)-1, C43(2-74)-1, C80(99)-1, B397(514)-1
Ba.65 Fighter bomber -A
A13(31)-2, C20(1-13)-2, C13(148)-2, D6(11/71-332)-2, B366(72)-2, A10(198)-2, A7(180)-1, B280(25)-1, D29(8/81-30)-1, B18(1-191)-7, A15(152)-6, B88(1-65)-2
Ba.75 Ground attack, reconnaissance -E
A13(36)-1, D25(12/61-47)-1, C13(260)-0
Ba.82 Twin engine bomber -E
A13(37)-1, D3(2-182)-1, B153(154c)-1, B397(518)-1, C13(259)-0
Ba.88 Lince Twin engine fighter bomber -B
A13(38)-2, C20(1-21)-2, B366(73)-2, C13(195)-2, D29(8/81-41)-1, B280(27)-1, A10(198)-1, A7(263)-1, B18(1-201)-7, A15(152)-0, D25(11/60-11)-2, B88(1-66)-2
Ba.201 Picchiatello Dive bomber -E
A13(42)-2, C20(6-55)-2, D9(6/84-307)-2, D6(6/71-53)-1, D3(7-284)-1, D25(5/58-6)-1, D26(14)-3, C13(263)-0
Ba.205 Biplane trainer -E
C20(11-73)-6
B.Z.303 Twin engine night fighter -J
C35(394)-3, A13(44)-0, D25(10/61-49)-0

CANT *Cantieri Riuniti dell'Adriatico (C.R.D.A.)*

18 Biplane trainer flying boat -D
A13(52)-0, D20(10/68-52)-0

21 Biplane pusher reconnaissance flying boat -D
C35(154)-1

25 Biplane pusher fighter flying boat -D
D9(5/75-259)-2, C13(98)-2, C17(101)-2,
C43(2-52)-1, C80(73)-1, C110(425)-1

Z.501 Gabbiano High wing reconnaissance bomber flying boat -A
A13(52)-2, A3(5-120)-2, C20(4-25)-2,
B58(114c)-2, C13(140)-2, A6(129)-1,
A10(199)-1, A7(183)-1, B280(30)-6,
B18(1-186)-7, B88(1-70)-2, A15(153)-0

Z.505 Three engine transport floatplane -I
A13(55)-1, C20(8-13)-1, C35(226,367)-2,
C80(89)-1

Z.506 Airone Three engine reconnaissance bomber, transport floatplane -A
A13(55)-2, A3(6-101)-2, C20(5-5,8-11)-2,
A6(129)-2, A10(199)-1, C13(172)-2,
B162(111)-2, B391(402)-1, B280(31)-6,
B18(1-194)-7, A7(39)-1, B88(1-71)-2

Z.508 Three engine high wing bomber, record flying boat -E
A13(60)-2, C35(242,371)-2, C80(112)-1,
D3(2-242)-1, C13(258)-0, C15(80)-1

Z.509 Three engine transport floatplane -I
A13(60)-1, C20(8-14)-1, C35(298)-1,
B153(156c)-1, C80(100)-1

Z.511 Four engine transport floatplane -E
A13(62)-2, A3(6-104)-2, C20(9-57)-2,
C13(238)-2, C35(327,385)-2, C10(142)-2,
B16(220)-7, A15(153)-0, C15(143)-1

Z.515 Twin engine reconnaissance bomber floatplane -E
A13(64)-2, A3(6-106)-2, C20(6-29)-2,
C35(303,385)-2, C13(262)-0, C15(79)-1

Z.516 Three engine floatplane version
Z.1007bis -E
C20(6-32)-1

Z.1007 Alcione Three engine bomber -A
A13(64)-2, C20(5-39)-2, B366(55)-4,
D16(5/82-8)-2, D6(5/72-272)-2,
A6(130)-2, A10(200)-2, B252(26)-2,
C13(189)-2, A15(153)-6, A7(40)-1

Z.1011 Twin engine bomber, transport -C
A13(69)-2, C35(316,381)-2, D3(2-242)-1,
A15(153)-0, C13(258)-0

Z.1012 Three engine transport, trainer -B
A13(71)-2, C20(10-69)-2,
C35(320,383)-2, B153(157c)-1,
B20(A-267)-1, A15(153)-0, C13(259)-0

Z.1014 Four engine bomber -J
D15(1-13)-3, B366(61)-0

Z.1015 Three engine bomber, mail plane -E
C35(331,389)-3, D16(5/82-15)-1,
C21(G5-32)-1, A13(73)-0

Z.1018 Leone Twin engine bomber -B
A13(73)-2, C20(6-5)-2, C13(210)-2,
C35(332,387)-2, A10(201)-1,
D29(4/85-43)-1, B18(1-239)-7,
C88(142)-6, A15(153)-0

CAPRONI *Societa Italiana Caproni*
Ca.100 (Version D.H.60 Moth) Biplane trainer, also floatplane -A
A13(79)-2, C20(10-5)-2, C13(88)-2,
B280(34)-1, D9(10/77-202)-1,
C17(102)-1, C1(1-17)-1, C49(179)-1,
A15(153)-0

Ca.101 Three engine high wing bomber, transport -B
A13(81)-2, C13(96)-2, B14(146,156)-2,
C17(111)-2, B391(407)-1, B153(158c)-1,
C74(260)-2, B411(137)-1, B289(83)-6,
A10(204)-1

Ca.102 Two or four engine high wing bomber, transport -C

A10(205)-1, C17(112)-1, A13(84)-0,
C13(128)-0
Ca.111 High wing reconnaissance,
transport, also floatplane -B
C20(7-5)-2, A13(84)-1, C13(112)-2,
C17(112)-2, A10(205)-1, B411(138)-1,
B152(178c)-1, B397(524)-1,
B114(5-503)-5, A15(154)-0
Ca.113 Biplane trainer -K
A13(85)-1, C13(105)-2, B153(158c)-1,
D9(3/81-139)-1, B139(153)-1,
C113(3-189)-1, A15(154)-0
Ca.114 Biplane fighter -B
D9(6/75-306)-2, C43(1-90,2-128)-1,
A13(86)-0, C13(129)-0
Ca.123 Twin engine transport -I
A13(86,303)-1, C33(94)-1, C15(54)-1,
D3(3-2)-1
Ca.124 Reconnaissance bomber
floatplane -E
B152(179c)-1, B85(178)-1, D3(3-2)-1,
A13(86)-0
Ca.133 Three engine high wing
transport, bomber -A
A13(87)-2, C20(7-43)-2, C13(150)-2,
B88(2-71)-2, B391(409)-1, B280(34)-1,
A10(205)-1, A6(130)-6, B15(178)-7,
A15(154)-6
Ca.134 Biplane reconnaissance -E
A13(89)-2, B153(159c)-1, B397(526)-1,
D3(3-2)-1, C110(426)-1
Ca.140 High wing transport, version
Ca.111 -E
C20(7-17)-1
Ca.142 Three engine high wing
transport, version Ca.133 -E
C20(7-48)-1
Ca.148 Three engine high wing
transport, version Ca.133 -B
A13(92)-1, C20(7-58)-1, C17(115)-1,
B391(410)-1, B139(130)-1, C80(198)-1,
A15(154)-0, C13(150)-0
Ca.161 Biplane altitude record version
Ca.113, also floatplane -F
A13(92)-1, C13(171)-2, B153(158c)-1,

B404(84)-1, B403(322)-1
Ca.163 Biplane aerobatic -K
C20(10-99)-1
Ca.164 Biplane trainer -B
C20(10-97)-2, C13(181)-2, A13(93)-1,
C23(158)-1, C17(153)-1,
D9(10/77-202)-1, B139(153)-1,
B422(1-122)-1, A15(154)-0
Ca.165 Biplane fighter -E
D9(6/75-307)-2, D20(6/69-100)-2,
A13(94)-6, C43(2-86)-1, D3(3-14)-1
Ca.183 Tandem piston/jet engine high
altitude fighter -J
A13(94)-3
Ca.225 Twin engine bomber -J
A13(94)-0, C10(136)-0
Ca.405
See Reggiane
Ca.602 Biplane trainer -E
C20(10-110)-2, A13(94)-0, B58(122c)-0
Ca.603 Biplane trainer -E
C20(10-107)-2, A13(94)-0, B58(122c)-0,
C13(262)-0
Campini N.1 Single jet -F
A13(95)-2, B138(41)-2, D25(4/56-15)-2,
D3(8-262)-1, C13(227)-2, B58(117c)-1,
B42(126)-1, B5(42)-1, B408(342)-1,
B16(218)-7, C10(147)-2

CAPRONI-AV.I.S. *Avio Industrie*
Stabiensi
C.4 Trainer -E
C20(11-45)-2, C13(262)-0

CAPRONI BERGAMASCHI *Caproni*
Aeronautica Bergamasca
AP.1 (Ca.301) Attack, reconnaissance,
also floatplane -D
A13(99)-2, C1(1-39)-2, C13(118)-2,
C17(106)-2, D9(6/75-307)-2, A10(201)-1,
B411(31)-1, B397(512)-1, C43(2-73)-1
Ca.135 Twin engine bomber -B
A13(102)-2, C20(4-69)-2, C1(1-104)-4,
C13(184)-2, B88(2-68)-2, A10(206)-1,

B280(35)-1, A6(131)-6, C17(131)-1,
A15(154)-6

Ca.166 Liaison -I
C1(1-92)-2

Ca.169 Twin engine bomber, version
Ca.135 -E
C1(1-153)-2, A13(105)-1, C20(4-74)-1,
D25(6/60-50)-1

Ca.308 Borea Twin engine transport -I
C1(2-11)-2, A13(105)-1, C13(144)-2,
B391(411)-1, B153(151c)-1, D3(3-2)-1,
A15(155)-0

Ca.309 Ghibli Twin engine bomber,
transport -B
A13(106)-2, C1(2-25)-4, C20(5-23)-2,
C13(176)-2, B153(151c)-1, B372(38)-1,
D25(9/62-39)-1, B280(36)-1,
B351(227)-1, A15(155)-0

Ca.310 Libeccio Twin engine bomber,
transport, also floatplane -A
C1(2-75,125,139)-4, C20(5-29)-2,
A13(108)-1, C13(183)-2, A6(131)-1,
B14(146,156)-2, A10(206)-1,
B153(151c)-1, B88(1-67)-2, A15(155)-6

Ca.311 Twin engine reconnaissance
bomber -B
C1(2-151)-4, C20(5-53)-2, A13(109)-1,
C13(206)-2, D6(7/71-98)-1, C17(160)-2,
B88(2-74)-2, A7(184)-1, B18(1-212)-7,
A15(155)-0

Ca.312 Twin engine bomber, transport,
also floatplane -B
C1(2-185)-4, C20(5-38)-1, A13(112)-6,
B88(2-75)-2, A6(131)-1, C13(206)-1,
A15(155)-0

Ca.313 (Sweden **B 16, S 16**) Twin
engine reconnaissance bomber, trainer -A
A13(112)-1, D6(7/71-98)-1, C20(5-65)-2,
C13(209)-3, A10(207)-1, C31(21)-1,
D25(9/62-40)-1, B88(3-54)-2,
B59(151c)-3, A15(155)-0

Ca.314 Twin engine reconnaissance
bomber -A
D6(7/71-99)-4, C20(5-63)-2, A13(113)-1,
C17(161)-2, B280(37)-1, A10(207)-1,

C13(208)-2, B366(79)-1, B372(16)-1,
A15(155)-0, C80(200)-1

Ca.315 Twin engine liaison, trainer -E
C1(2-211)-8, A13(113)-0, A15(155)-0

Ca.316 Twin engine reconnaissance
floatplane -B
C1(2-133)-2, C20(6-33)-2, A3(6-99)-2,
D3(4-118)-2, A13(113)-1, A15(155)-0,
C13(262)-0

Ca.331 Raffica Twin engine night
fighter, bomber -E
A13(114)-2, C20(2-61)-2, A3(2-129)-2,
D9(7/75-46)-2, C13(230)-2,
D25(3/57-54)-1

Ca.335 Maestrale (SABCA S.47)
Reconnaissance fighter -E
A13(117)-1, C20(2-11)-2, C33(166)-1,
C10(125)-1

Ca.355 Dive bomber -E
C20(2-12)-2, A13(117)-1, D25(8/61-40)-1

Ca.380 Corsaro Twin engine twin
fuselage high altitude fighter bomber -J
A13(118)-3, D25(6/60-50)-3, C88(107)-6

*CAPRONI VIZZOLA Caproni Vizzola
S.A.*

F.4 Fighter -E
A3(2-131)-2, D9(7/75-48)-2, C20(2-26)-2,
A13(119)-1, C10(95)-1, C13(263)-0

F.5 Fighter -B
A3(2-133)-2, A13(119)-2, C20(1-67)-2,
D9(7/75-48)-2, C13(226)-2, A10(207)-1,
A7(264)-1, B154(118c)-1, B372(14)-1,
A15(155)-6

F.6M Fighter -E
A3(2-135)-2, C20(2-25)-1, D9(8/75-84)-1,
A13(121)-1, D3(7-284)-1, A15(155)-0

F.6Z Fighter -E
D6(8/72-107)-2, C20(2-29)-1,
D9(8/75-84)-3, A13(122)-6, A15(155)-0

*C.N.A. Compagnia Nazionale
Aeronautica (Caproni)*
PM.1 High wing trainer -C
C20(11-31)-2, A13(133)-2, B20(A-272)-1,
C13(261)-0, B279(126)-0

FIAT *Societa Anonima Aeronautica d'Italia*
BR.3 Biplane bomber, trainer -D
C13(58)-2, C17(104)-2, A10(208)-1,
B411(53)-1, C80(74)-1, A13(137)-0
BR.20 Cicogna (Japan **'Ruth'**) Twin
engine bomber -A
D9(6/82-290)-4, A13(138)-2, B71(110)-2,
C20(4-75)-2, B366(51)-4, A10(208)-2,
B252(51)-2, A7(69)-1, B280(52)-6,
A6(132)-6, A15(155)-6, B18(1-196)-7
CR.20 Asso Biplane fighter, also
floatplane -D
A13(143)-2, D9(2/79-69)-2, C13(84)-2,
A10(210)-1, B411(54)-1, B15(162)-7,
B293(33)-6, C49(163)-1, D9(1/85-50)-1,
A15(155)-0, D7(29-61)-1
CR.23 Twin engine fighter bomber -J
A13(160)-0, C10(136)-0
CR.25 Twin engine reconnaissance
fighter -B
A13(157)-2, C20(2-5)-2, A3(2-151)-2,
D9(4/79-204)-2, C13(202)-2, C17(110)-2,
A10(213)-1, B366(75)-1, B372(61)-1,
A15(156)-6
CR.30 Biplane fighter, trainer, also
floatplane -B
B424(4)-2, A13(147)-1,
D9(2/79-69,3/79-144)-1, C13(106)-2,
A10(210)-1, B411(55)-1, C49(164)-1,
B297(48)-1, A15(155)-0
CR.32 Freccia Biplane fighter,
trainer -A
D7(22-52)-4, B71(22)-2, B148(66)-4,
B424(12)-2, A13(148)-2, C20(1-5)-2,
A3(2-137)-2, A10(211)-2, B366(7)-2,
B167(38)-2, D16(11/83-38)-2,
B280(54)-1, A6(132)-1, B411(56)-1,
A15(155)-6, D9(3/79-144)-2
CR.33 Biplane fighter -E
B424(26)-2, D9(3/79-144)-1, A13(151)-1,
C43(2-65)-1
CR.42 Falco (Sweden **J 11**) Biplane
fighter -A
D7(20-1)-4, A13(153)-2, B424(28)-2,

B71(16)-2, C20(1-55)-2, B148(112)-4,
A3(2-139)-2, B366(9)-4, A10(212)-2,
B164(34)-4, B280(56)-2, A6(133)-1,
D23(74-32)-2, C13(199)-2, A15(156)-6,
B458(52)-2, D16(7/86-44)-2
G.2 Three engine transport -I
C13(111)-2, A13(161)-1, B391(412)-1,
D3(3-290)-1
G.5bis Trainer -L
A13(162)-1, B139(46)-1, D3(3-290)-1
G.12 Three engine transport -B
A13(162)-2, C20(9-37)-2, C13(213)-2,
B391(417)-1, B60(145c)-1, A7(195)-1,
D3(4-111)-2, B18(1-221)-7, B5(71)-1,
A15(157)-0, C15(141)-1
G.18 Twin engine transport -I
C20(8-39)-2, A13(165)-1, C13(164)-2,
D16(11/85-48)-1, B391(414)-1,
B153(162c)-1, B16(210)-7,
D29(4/85-39)-1, C10(137)-1, A15(156)-0
G.50 Freccia Fighter -A
A13(166)-2, B424(41)-2, C20(1-31)-2,
B71(188)-2, B366(13)-4, A3(2-142)-2,
B252(53)-2, B280(59)-1, B164(42)-2,
C13(192)-2, A10(214)-1, A6(133)-6,
B18(1-208)-7, A7(73)-1, A15(156)-6
G.55 Centauro Fighter -B
D6(5/74-233)-4, A13(171)-2, B424(56)-2,
C20(3-15)-2, A3(2-147)-2, B366(36)-2,
B164(43)-2, A10(214)-2, C13(247)-2,
B280(60)-1, B18(1-234)-7, A6(133)-3,
A7(196)-1, A15(157)-6, B60(147c)-1
G.56 Fighter -E
A3(2-149)-2, B424(61)-2, A13(173)-1,
D9(4/79-205)-1, C20(3-22)-1,
A15(157)-0, B60(147c)-1

FIAT-C.A.N.S.A. *Construzione
Aeronautiche Navaresi S.A.*
C.4 Trainer -E
A13(47)-1
C.5 Biplane trainer -B
C20(11-25)-2, A13(45)-1, C17(154)-1,
B153(155c)-1, B20(A-264)-1, C10(145)-1,
C13(260)-0

C.6 Falchetto Biplane trainer -E
A13(46)-1, C20(11-73)-1
FC.12 Ground attack, trainer -E
A13(47)-2, C20(11-63)-2, C13(262)-0
FC.20 Twin engine reconnaissance
bomber, ground attack -C
A13(47)-2, C20(2-65)-2, C13(241)-2,
B25(P)-1, B18(1-220)-7, D3(7-284)-1,
C10(126)-1, C88(227,P)-1, A15(152)-0

*FIAT-C.M.A.S.A. Construzione
Meccaniche Aeronautiche S.A.*
AS.14 Twin engine land base attack
version RS.14 -E
A13(128)-1, B366(77)-6, C20(5-80)-0,
B280(62)-0, A15(156)-0
G.8 Biplane trainer -B
C20(10-33)-2, A13(124)-1, C13(119)-2,
C17(152)-1, A15(155)-0
G.50B Trainer version Fiat G.50 -B
C20(11-57)-2, B424(50)-2, A13(129)-1,
C80(186)-1, A15(156)-0
G.50V Daimler Benz engine version Fiat
G.50 -E
A13(129)-1, B424(49)-1, A3(2-143)-6,
A15(156)-0
ICR.42 Floatplane fighter version Fiat
CR.42 -E
A3(6-110)-2, A13(128)-1, B424(38)-1,
C20(1-66)-6, B164(35)-1, D7(20-3)-6,
A15(156)-0, D16(7/86-51)-1
RS.14 Twin engine reconnaissance
bomber floatplane -A
A13(125)-2, A3(6-108)-2, C20(5-73)-2,
B366(75)-2, B58(119c)-2, C13(224)-2,
A10(213)-1, B280(61)-1, B18(1-228)-7,
A15(156)-0, A7(196)-1, B88(3-50)-2

I.M.A.M.
See Meridionali.

JONA Ing. Alberto Jona (Magni)
J.6/S Sesquiplane trainer -E
B154(122c)-1, A13(195)-1, B85(197)-1,
B22(A-252)-1, D3(4-231)-1, B411(168)-0,
B279(220)-0

*LOMBARDA Aeronautica Lombarda
S.A.*
AL.12P High wing transport glider -C
A13(18)-2, C20(9-73)-2, B286(189)-2,
D6(5/72-250)-1, B25(P)-1, D3(7-284)-1,
C88(267,P)-1
A.R. Radio controlled flying bomb -C
C20(6-67)-2, A13(18)-1,
D20(2/68-108)-1, C10(150)-1,
C88(205,P)-1, C110(435)-1
R.S.1 Canguro High wing training
glider -B
C17(243)-1, B25(P)-1

MACCHI Aeronautica Macchi S.A.
M.41 Biplane pusher fighter, trainer
flying boat -D
A13(177)-1, B14(124,134)-2, C13(97)-2,
C17(100)-2, C49(28)-1, C43(2-50)-1,
C2(P)-1, D9(8/85-83)-2
C.3
See Bestetti-Colombo C.3
C.77 High wing pusher reconnaissance
flying boat -E
C13(143)-2, A13(178)-1, B152(184c)-1,
C110(427)-1, C2(P)-1, D3(5-39)-1,
B19(1055)-0
C.94 Twin engine high wing transport
flying boat -I
C20(8-29)-2, A13(180)-1, B391(426)-1,
C13(182)-2, C74(255)-2, B153(164c)-1,
B16(208)-7, C2(P)-1, A15(157)-0
C.99 Twin engine high wing
reconnaissance bomber flying boat -E
A13(181)-1, B152(185c)-1, C2(P)-1,
D3(5-51)-1, A15(157)-0, C110(427)-1
C.100 Three engine high wing transport
flying boat -I
C20(8-35)-2, A13(182)-1, B391(429)-1,
B154(123c)-1, B16(216)-7, C2(P)-1,
A15(157)-0, C13(260)-0
C.200 Saetta Fighter-A
D9(12/77-284)-4, A13(183)-2,
C20(1-45)-2, B71(64)-2, A3(2-157)-2,
B148(110)-4, A6(134)-2, B164(44)-2,

B366(19)-2, B135(2-49)-1, A10(218)-2,
B252(97)-2, B280(153)-1, A7(115)-1,
A15(157)-6, D9(9/85-154)-2

C.200 bis (Breda) Piaggio engine version
C.200 -E
D9(9/85-154)-1, B71(64-9)-1,
D9(12/77-291)-6

C.201 Fighter -E
A3(2-161)-2, A13(186)-1,
D9(9/85-154)-1, C2(P)-1, B135(2-54)-6,
A15(157)-0

C.202 Folgore Fighter -A
D6(1/72-17)-4, A13(187)-2, C20(2-41)-2,
B71(28)-2, B366(25)-4, A3(2-163)-2,
B135(2-54)-2, B128-2, B280(155)-2,
B164(45)-2, B252(98)-3, B18(1-218)-7,
A10(219)-1, A6(135)-1, A15(157)-6,
D9(9/85-155)-2

C.205V Veltro Fighter -A
D7(24-11)-4, A3(2-166)-2, C20(3-5)-2,
B366(30)-4, A13(191)-1, A6(135)-2,
B128(33)-1, B280(157)-1, A10(219)-1,
C13(244)-2, B135(2-57)-1,
D9(9/85-155)-1

C.205N Orione Fighter -E
D7(24-13)-2, A3(2-168)-2, A13(192)-1,
B135(2-58)-1, B366(30)-1, B128(36)-1,
B252(100)-1, B280(158)-1, B279(219)-1,
A15(158)-0, D9(10/85-208)-2

C.206 Fighter -G
B128(6,50)-6, A13(192)-0, A15(158)-0

C.207 Fighter -J
B128(6,50)-6, A13(192)-0, A15(158)-0

MAGNI *Piero Magni Aviazione S.A.I.*
PM.3-4 Vale High wing aerobatic
trainer -L
A13(194)-1, C13(120)-2, B153(166c)-1,
D3(5-51)-1, B279(220)-0, B20(A-277)-1

PM.4-1 Supervale High wing trainer -E
A13(195)-0, B153(166c)-0, B279(220)-0

MANTELLI *Ing. Adriano Mantelli*
AM.6 Twin boom pusher light plane -L
A13(293)-0

MERIDIONALI *S.A. Industrie*
Meccaniche e Aeronautiche Meridionali
(I.M.A.M., Romeo)

Ro.1 (Version Fokker C.V) Biplane
reconnaissance, trainer -D
A13(196)-1, C13(76)-2, C14(86)-2,
B71(87-8)-1, D19(4/71-256)-1,
B289(29)-6, B62(64)-1, C80(60)-1,
C127(49)-1, C33(1)-1, C10(146)-1

Ro.30 Biplane reconnaissance, trainer -B
A13(197)-1, C17(102)-1, C80(69)-1,
B105(95)-6, C13(128)-0

Ro.37 Biplane reconnaissance -A
A13(198)-2, C20(4-5)-2, D9(6/76-306)-2,
C13(145)-2, B153(166c)-1, A10(216)-1,
B280(159)-1, A7(215)-1, B18(1-190)-7,
A15(158)-6

Ro.41 Biplane fighter, trainer -B
C20(10-39)-2, A13(201)-1, C13(158)-2,
D9(2/83-99,3/83-152)-2, B153(167c)-1,
B139(155)-1, C33(67)-1, C17(138)-2,
A15(158)-0

Ro.43 Biplane reconnaissance fighter
floatplane -A
A13(203)-2, C20(4-17)-2, A3(6-111)-2,
C13(166)-2, B58(120c)-1, A10(216)-1,
B280(159)-1, B18(1-193)-7, C17(140)-2,
A15(158)-6

Ro.44 Biplane fighter floatplane -B
C20(1-27)-2, A13(205)-1, A3(6-111)-1,
D9(3/83-152)-2, A10(217)-1, C17(140)-1,
A15(158)-0, B280(160)-0, C13(258)-0,
B114(20-2217)-0

Ro.45 Biplane reconnaissance -E
A13(206)-1

Ro.51 Fighter, also floatplane -E
A13(206)-2, C20(1-41)-2,
D9(3/83-152)-2, B153(168c)-1,
B167(38)-1, B397(546)-1, B22(A-254)-1,
C43(2-82)-1, C13(259)-0

Ro.57 Twin engine fighter, fighter-
bomber -B
A13(209)-2, C20(2-15)-2, A3(2-153)-2,
D9(3/83-152)-2, C13(212)-2, A10(217)-1,

B18(1-229)-7, B279(226)-1, C17(165)-2,
A15(158)-6
Ro.58 Twin engine fighter -E
A13(211)-2, C20(3-31)-2, A3(2-155)-2,
D9(3/83-153)-2, C88(106)-6
Ro.63 High wing observation -B
C20(11-51)-2, A13(213)-1,
D6(3/72-150)-1, C17(175)-1,
C88(234,P)-1, A15(158)-0

NARDI Ing. Fratelli Nardi
FN.305 Trainer -A
A13(214)-2, C20(10-53)-2, C13(161)-2,
B153(168c)-1, B16(215)-7,
D10(8/83-300)-1, C17(139)-1,
C23(154)-1, A15(158)-0, B279(235)-0
FN.310 Tourer, ambulance -L
A13(217)-1, B153(169c)-1, C20(10-51)-0,
A15(158)-0, C13(259)-0
FN.315 Trainer -A
D25(1/63-49)-2, B421(262)-2,
A13(217)-1, C20(10-54)-1, C13(161)-1,
B153(169c)-1, B139(74)-1, A15(158)-0,
B279(235)-0
FN.316 Trainer -E
C20(10-67)-1

PIAGGIO Societa Anonima Piaggio & C.
P.23R (P.123) Three engine speed
record -F
A13(221)-1, D29(12/79-18)-1,
D20(1/67-333)-1, D25(9/61-65)-1
P.32 Twin engine bomber -E
A13(222)-2, C20(4-89)-2, C13(157)-2,
D4(12/79-16)-1, B153(170c)-1,
C21(E4-46)-1, B88(2-69)-2, C74(268)-2,
C80(87)-1, C49(83)-1
P.32bis
See Reggiane
P.50 Four engine bomber -E
A13(224)-2, D29(12/79-21,50)-1,
D25(9/61-65)-1, C87(48,P)-1, C42(5)-1,
C13(259)-0
P.108 Four engine bomber -A
A13(227)-2, C20(6-17)-2, B366(61)-4,

C42(6)-2, D29(12/79-10)-1, A10(220)-2,
D6(3/73-141)-5, A6(136)-1, B280(231)-1,
B58(121c)-2, C13(215)-2, B18(1-226)-7,
A7(145)-1, B297(93)-1, A15(158)-0
P.108C, P.108T Four engine
transport -B
C20(9-65)-2, A13(229)-1, C42(41)-1,
B16(221)-7, D29(12/79-54)-1, B388(P)-1,
B366(62)-6, A15(158)-0, C15(145)-1
P.111 Twin engine high altitude -F
A13(232)-1, D3(7-284)-1, C10(149)-1
P.114 (P.108 Idro) Floatplane version
P.108 -J
C42(47)-1, B366(62)-6
P.119 Mid-engine fighter -E
A13(232)-2, C20(3-37)-2, A3(2-170)-2,
D25(7/57-43)-2, C10(108)-3,
C88(122,P)-1, C13(263)-0
P.133 Four engine bomber -G
C42(48)-1, A13(234)-0, A15(158)-0

*REGGIANE Officine Meccaniche
'Reggiane' S.A. (Caproni)*
Ca.405 Procellaria Twin engine long
range -F
B330(5)-2, A13(235)-1, C20(4-92)-1,
C21(E4-48)-1, B153(171c)-1
P.32bis Twin engine bomber -E
B330(4)-2, A13(235)-1, D7(2-215)-1
Re.2000 Falco I (Sweden **J 20**)
Fighter -A
B330(7)-2, A13(236)-2, C20(1-75)-2,
B71(123)-2, D9(7/75-46)-2, A3(2-172)-2,
D20(7/66-703)-1, A6(138)-2, C13(218)-2,
A10(222)-2, B280(232)-2, B252(136)-2,
B164(46)-2, A7(229)-1, A15(158)-6,
B458(46)-2
Re.2001 Falco II Fighter -A
D7(2-214)-5, B330(17)-2, C20(2-31)-2,
B148(138)-4, B71(244)-2, A3(2-175)-2,
A13(240)-1, D9(7/75-46)-2, B366(21)-2,
C13(231)-2, B164(47)-2, A10(222)-1,
A6(138)-1, A7(230)-1, A15(159)-6
Re.2002 Ariete Fighter bomber -B
B330(28)-2, C20(2-53)-2, A3(2-178)-2,

B71(244)-1, D9(7/75-47)-2, A13(242)-1,
C13(237)-2, B366(44)-1, A10(223)-1,
A15(159)-0, B18(1-230)-7
Re.2003 Reconnaissance bomber -E
B330(39)-2, C20(6-59)-2, A13(243)-1,
B71(244)-1, D29(4/85-51)-1,
D20(10/67-939)-1, A15(159)-0.
C13(263)-0
Re.2004 Fighter -J
B330(41)-3, A13(244)-0, B71(244-236)-0
Re.2005 Sagittario Fighter -B
B330(42)-2, A13(245)-2, C20(3-23)-2,
B366(39)-4, A3(2-180)-2, D9(7/75-47)-2,
B71(244)-1, A6(138)-2, A10(223)-2,
A15(159)-6, B18(1-236)-7
Re.2006 Fighter -G
B330(54)-2, D7(2-222)-3,
B71(244-239)-0, A13(246)-0
Re.2007 Single jet fighter -J
D7(2-220)-8, B330(58)-6,
D20(5/66-580)-3, B71(244-239)-6

SAIMAN *Societa Anonima Industrie*
Meccaniche Aeronautiche Navali
200 Biplane trainer -A
C20(10-89)-2, A13(248)-1, C13(204)-1,
C17(153)-1, B153(172c)-1,
C33(40)-1, A15(160)-0, B20(A-282)-1
202 Trainer, liaison -A
C20(10-73)-2, A13(248)-2, C13(203)-2,
B18(1-192)-7, C17(155)-1, B153(172c)-1,
B139(49)-1, C10(139)-1, A15(160)-0
204 Trainer, liaison -I
A13(249)-1, C20(10-78)-1, B153(173c)-1,
B20(A-283)-1, B13(2-178)-1
205 Biplane trainer -E
C20(10-92)-0
208 Biplane trainer -E
C20(11-73)-6
303 Liaison -H
C20(10-86)-0
V.A.L. Ground attack -E
C20(3-45)-0

SAVOIA-MARCHETTI *Societa*
Idrovolanti Alta Italia 'Savoia-Marchetti'
S.55 Tandem engine twin hull flying
boat -D
A13(251)-2, B391(436)-1, C13(78)-2,
B32(46)-2, B15(158)-7, B411(168)-1,
B294(52)-6, B222(56)-1, B431(144)-1,
B279(276)-1
S.56 Biplane liaison amphibian -I
A13(250)-1, B32(57)-2, C13(92)-2,
D19(3/58-192)-1, B25(P)-1
S.62 (USSR **MBR-4**) Biplane pusher
bomber flying boat -B
B32(69)-2, B309(123,244)-2,
B391(439)-1, C74(272)-2, C80(62)-1,
C84(III-113)-1, B218(9-156)-1,
C17(99)-2, A15(161)-0, A13(250)-0
S.66 Three engine pusher twin hull
flying boat -I
C20(8-5)-2, A13(256)-1, B162(65)-2,
B391(440)-1, B32(84)-2, B15(168)-7,
C13(110)-2, B294(53)-6, B431(144)-1,
B281(241)-1
S.71 Three engine high wing transport -I
B32(89)-2, A13(257)-1, B391(442)-1,
B15(170)-7, D3(6-75)-1, C13(114)-2,
A15(161)-0, B471(46)-1
S.72 Three engine high wing bomber -D
B32(93)-2, A13(257)-1, A10(224)-1,
B279(276)-1, B471(83)-1
SM.73 Three engine transport -I
C20(7-25)-2, B162(96)-2, A13(258)-1,
B391(444)-1, B32(96)-2, B15(174)-7,
D7(13-73)-1, C74(272)-2, B431(119)-1,
B374(61)-1
SM.74 Four engine high wing
transport -I
A13(259)-2, C20(7-37)-2, B162(97)-2,
B391(447)-1, B15(180)-7, B32(102)-2,
C13(125)-2, B373(29)-1, B374(64)-1,
A15(161)-0, C15(83)-1
SM.75 Marsupiale Three engine
transport -A
C20(8-47)-2, A13(260)-1, B391(449)-1,
B32(102)-2, C13(186)-2, B18(1-207)-7,

B153(173c)-1, B374(66)-1, C17(148)-2, A15(161)-0

SM.76 Three engine transport -L
C20(8-61)-1, B32(106)-0

SM.77 Three engine twin hull flying boat -I
C20(8-8)-1, B32(112)-1

SM.78 Biplane pusher reconnaissance flying boat -D
B32(114)-2, C17(105)-1, D3(6-75)-1, A13(262)-0, A15(161)-0

SM.79 Sparviero Three engine bomber -A
D9(7/84-26,8/84-76)-4, A13(262)-2, B134(1-17)-2, C20(4-47)-2, B71(89)-2, B366(45)-4, C19-4, B280(236)-2, A6(137)-2, A10(224)-2, B32(118)-2, B252(140)-2, B18(1-198)-7, A7(148)-1, A15(161)-6, B474-2

SM.81 Pipistrello Three engine bomber transport -A
A13(270)-2, C20(4-35)-2, B71(146)-2, B366(67)-4, B280(240)-2, B252(141)-2, C13(168)-2, A6(140)-1, A10(225)-1, A15(162)-6, A7(149)-1, B18(1-188)-7

SM.82 Canguru Three engine bomber transport -A
A13(273)-2, C20(9-5)-2, B366(71)-2, B280(242)-2, A6(140)-2, C13(221)-2, B18(1-216)-7, B88(2-73)-2, A7(232)-1, A15(162)-6

SM.83 Three engine transport -I
A13(276)-1, C20(7-61)-2, B162(98)-2, B391(451)-1, B153(175c)-1, B16(214)-7, B374(86)-1, D3(3-267)-2, A15(162)-0

SM.84 Three engine bomber -A
A13(278)-2, D20(7/66-709)-2, C20(5-81)-2, B366(59)-2, C13(228)-2, B88(3-49)-2, B372(15)-1, A10(226)-1, B18(1-224)-7, A15(162)-0, A7(232)-1

SM.85 Twin engine dive bomber -B
A13(281)-2, C20(5-17)-2, C13(185)-2, B373(61)-1, A10(226)-1, C10(134)-2, B372(13)-1, B371(36)-1, B382(93)-1, A15(162)-0

SM.86 Twin engine dive bomber -E
D6(10/71-278)-2, C20(5-18)-1, A13(283)-1, B373(65)-1, B382(94)-1, A15(162)-0, C13(261)-0

SM.87 Three engine transport floatplane -I
C20(8-85)-2, A13(283)-1, B391(450)-1, B16(212)-7, D3(6-87)-1, A15(161)-0, C13(261)-0, C15(79)-1

SM.89 Twin engine attack bomber -E
D20(10/69-73)-2, C20(2-77)-2, A13(284)-1, C13(240)-2, C10(136)-1, C88(227,P)-1

SM.90 Three engine transport -E
C20(8-50,84)-1, C15(144)-1, A13(285)-0, C80(152)-1, C13(188)-0

SM.91 Twin engine twin boom fighter -E
A13(285)-2, C20(3-41)-2, A3(2-182)-2, D25(11/59-46)-2, C13(252)-2, B373(83)-1, D3(8-296)-1, C88(106,P)-1

SM.92 Twin engine twin fuselage fighter -E
A13(285)-2, A3(2-184)-2, C20(3-43)-1, D25(11/59-46)-2, B373(83)-1, D3(7-10)-2, C13(252)-1, B25(P)-1, C88(106,P)-1

SM.93 Dive bomber -E
D20(10/69-73)-2, D9(8/82-98)-2, C20(6-85)-2, A13(288)-1, B373(69)-1, C13(252)-1, D3(7-284)-1, C88(185,P)-1

SM.95 Four engine transport, bomber -M
D9(2/76-83)-2, A13(288)-2, C20(9-89)-2, B162(164)-2, C13(255)-2, B391(453)-1, D3(6-304)-2, B16(222)-7, C74(274)-2, A15(162)-0, B60(149c)-1, C15(195)-1

S.C.A. Stabilimento Construzione Aeronautiche (Sergio Stefanutti)
S.S.2 Canard pusher light plane -F
A13(294)-1, C36(151)-1, B231(46)-3, D9(12/83-286)-0

S.S.3 Anitra Canard pusher light
plane -F
D9(12/83-286)-2, A13(294)-1,
C20(2-23)-1, C39(102-55)-0, C36(152)-1,
D3(6-87)-1, D20(12/69-75)-1, B231(46)-0
S.S.4
See Ambrosini

*TALIEDO Construzione Aeronautiche
Taliedo (C.A.T.)*
QR.14 (Marinavia Farina) Twin engine
liaison -H
C20(11-99)-2, B139(121)-1, D3(7-283)-1,
B279(220)-0, C13(310)-0

TM.2 High wing transport glider -E
C20(9-85)-2, B286(191)-2,
D6(5/72-250)-1, A13(98)-3, B150(55)-3

*UMBRA Aeronautica Umbra S.A.
Construzione Aeronautiche e Meccaniche*
MB.902 Twin engine fighter -G
A13(290)-3, D14(1-15)-3
T.18 (AUT.18) Fighter -E
D20(8/66-767)-2, C20(1-71)-2,
D6(7/71-110)-2, A13(290)-2,
B154(110c)-1, C43(2-90)-1, B397(510)-1,
C13(260)-0

JAPAN

---

*AERONAUTICAL RESEARCH
INSTITUTE Imperial University, Tokyo*
I-Go I-C Radio controlled air to ground
missile -E
B163(113)-0, A2(533)-0

AICHI Aichi Kokuki K.K.
B7A Ryusei 'Grace' (AM-23) Carrier
torpedo bomber -B
A2(288)-2, C6(73)-2, C109(74)-2,
A10(230)-1, D25(9/59-61)-1, A6(142)-1,
B280(8)-1, B18(2-203)-7, A7(167)-1,
A15(163)-6
D1A 'Susie' (Heinkel He 50, AB-9)
Biplane carrier dive bomber -B
A2(268)-2, C109(76)-2, C95(76,211)-2,
C100(2-56)-2, A10(228)-1, C6(66)-1,
B411(8)-1, B279(72)-1, B382(36)-1,
A15(162)-0, C140(210)-1
D3A 'Val' (AM-17) Carrier dive
bomber -A
A2(271)-2, B71(241)-2, C6(67)-2,
C109(78)-2, B280(9)-2, A7(22)-1,
A10(228)-2, A6(141)-2, B119(20)-2,
B252(6)-2, A15(162)-6, B18(2-142)-7

E3A (Heinkel He 56) Biplane
reconnaissance floatplane -D
C95(78,214)-2, C100(2-6,36)-2,
B226(355)-1, C140(230)-1
E8A (AB-7) Biplane reconnaissance
floatplane -E
C100(2-49)-3, A2(552)-0
E10A 'Hank' (AB-12) Biplane pusher
reconnaissance flying boat -B
C109(120)-2, C100(2-8,62)-2, B68(10)-1,
A15(162)-0, B411(169)-0
E11A 'Laura' (AB-14) Biplane pusher
reconnaissance flying boat -B
A3(5-124)-2, C6(210)-2, C109(121)-2,
A2(489)-1, C100(2-9,68)-2, B68(14)-1,
A15(163)-6
E12A (AM-18) Reconnaissance
floatplane -E
C109(134)-2, C6(174)-2,
C100(2-10,81)-2, C63(140)-1, A2(277)-0
E13A 'Jake' (AM-19) Reconnaissance
floatplane -A
A2(277)-2, A3(6-114)-2, C109(124)-2,
C6(176)-2, B18(2-158)-7, A6(143)-2,

B59(156c)-2, B280(10)-1, A7(168)-1,
A15(163)-6

E16A Zuiun 'Paul' (AM-22)
Reconnaissance floatplane -A
A2(284)-2, A3(6-116)-2, C6(181)-2,
C109(130)-2, B18(2-198)-7, A6(142)-2,
A10(230)-1, B280(11)-1, B88(6-50)-2,
A7(168)-1, A15(163)-0

F1A (AB-13) Biplane reconnaissance
floatplane -E
C100(2-66)-2, C6(172)-3, A2(553)-0

H9A (AM-21) Twin engine high wing
training flying boat -B
A2(281)-2, A3(5-122)-2, C6(212)-2,
C109(147)-2, C100(2-87)-3, A10(229)-1,
A15(163)-0, B83(62)-0, B114(11-1188)-0

M6A Seiran (AM-24) Sub-borne attack
bomber floatplane -B
B264-2, A2(291)-2, A3(6-118)-2,
C6(145)-2, C109(110)-2, A10(231)-1,
C100(2-96)-2, D29(2/84-47)-1,
B408(324)-1, B193(224)-3, A15(164)-0

M6A1-K Nanzan Land-based trainer
version M6A -E
B264(8)-2, C109(112)-2, A2(294)-1,
A3(6-119)-1, C100(2-12,97)-2, C6(145)-1,
A10(231)-1, D29(2/84-47)-1, B279(72)-1,
A15(164)-0

S1A Denko (AM-25) Twin engine night
fighter -G
A2(295)-2, C6(6)-2, C100(2-98)-2,
B193(63,216)-2, C129(369)-2

FUKUDA Fukuda Keihikoki K.K.
Hikari Ken 2 Motor glider -K
C100(8-182)-2, B226(582)-1
Hikari 8-1 Lightplane -L
C100(8-184)-2
HT-3 Glider version Hitachi HT-3 -F
C100(8-184)-1
Ki-23 (Hikari 6-I) High wing training
sailplane -B
C4(216)-1, C11(IV-94)-1, A2(535)-0
Ku-9 Transport glider -E
D6(5/72-250)-0, A2(539)-0

HIROSHO Hiro Naval Air Arsenal
G2H Twin engine bomber -D
D6(10/71-276)-2, C109(88)-2,
C100(3-20,167)-2, A10(231)-1,
C6(107)-1, B226(473)-1, C87(56,P)-1,
B279(192)-0, B114(10-1069)-0
H1H Twin engine biplane
reconnaissance flying boat -D
C100(3-17,150)-2, B226(279)-1,
A2(553)-0, B413(50)-1
H2H Twin engine biplane
reconnaissance flying boat -D
C100(3-18,155)-2, B226(332)-1,
A2(553)-0
H3H Three engine high wing
reconnaissance flying boat -E
C100(3-19,158)-2, B226(354)-1,
C84(III-97)-1, A2(553)-0
H4H Twin engine high wing
reconnaissance flying boat -D
C100(3-19,161)-2, B226(367)-1,
B413(154)-1, C84(III-99)-1

HITACHI Hitachi Kokuki K.K.
1 (Gasuden Model 2) Biplane trainer -E
C100(8-54)-2, B226(564)-1
2 Biplane trainer -E
B226(563)-1, B279(192)-0
A6M2-K Trainer version Mitsubishi
A6M -A
C109(161)-2, A2(397)-2, B135(1-51)-1,
B304(45)-1, C129(278)-1
HT-3 Twin engine transport -J
C100(8-63)-3
LXG1
See Tokyo Gasu Denki KR-2

KAWANISHI Kawanishi Kokuki K.K.
A8K Carrier fighter -J
D14(5-84)-3
Baika Pulse-jet suicide attack -J
A2(490)-6, B270(216)-3, C100(3-142)-6,
B315(189)-6, B244(P)-6, C6(276)-6,
C88(192)-6

E5K (E5Y) Biplane reconnaissance
floatplane -D
C100(3-67)-3, B226(358)-1, A2(552)-0
E7K 'Alf' Biplane reconnaissance
floatplane -A
A2(297)-2, A3(6-121)-2, C6(186)-2,
C109(115)-2, C100(3-11,70)-2,
B193(71,255)-2, B280(133)-1,
A15(164)-0, B83(63)-0
E8K Reconnaissance floatplane -E
C100(3-11,82)-2, B226(453)-1, A2(552)-0
E10K Biplane reconnaissance flying
boat -E
C100(3-11,84)-2, B226(450)-1, A2(552)-0
E11K High wing pusher reconnaissance,
transport flying boat -B
A3(5-129)-2, C6(215)-2, C100(3-12,86)-2,
C109(187)-1, C63(156)-1, A15(164)-0
E13K Reconnaissance floatplane -E
C6(190)-3, C100(3-92)-2, C63(140)-1,
A2(277)-0
E15K Shiun 'Norm' Reconnaissance
floatplane -B
A2(314)-2, A3(6-126)-2, C6(192)-2,
C109(128)-2, B193(49,162)-2,
C100(3-15,117)-2
H3K 'Belle' (Short-Kawanishi K.F.1)
Three engine biplane flying boat -D
B29(263)-2, C100(3-10,64)-2,
B226(353)-1, B68(6)-1, B365(P)-1
H6K 'Mavis' Four engine high wing
reconnaissance, transport flying boat -A
D9(12/85-293)-4, A2(301)-2,
A3(5-126)-2, C6(217)-2, B71(233)-2,
A6(143)-2, A7(208)-1, B280(134)-2,
B252(86)-2, A10(232)-1, B18(2-144)-7,
A15(164)-6
H8K 'Emily' Four engine high wing
reconnaissance, transport flying boat -A
D9(4/83-179)-4, A2(307)-2, A3(5-131)-2,
B71(233)-2, C6(223)-2, C39(68)-4,
C109(148)-4, A6(144)-2, A10(232)-1,
B252(136)-1, A15(164)-6, A7(209)-1
H11K Soku Four engine high wing
transport flying boat -J

C109(167)-2, C6(275)-3, C100(3-140)-2,
C39(68-55)-1, A2(554)-0
J6K Jinpu (J3K) Fighter -J
C6(272)-3, A2(490)-6, B193(259)-3,
C129(391)-3, C100(3-135)-3
K6K Biplane trainer floatplane -E
C6(242)-2, C100(3-90)-2, B226(485)-1,
A2(555)-0
K8K Biplane trainer floatplane -B
C6(244)-2, C109(157)-2, C63(174)-1,
C100(3-94)-0, A2(555)-0
N1K Kyofu 'Rex' Fighter floatplane -B
A2(317)-2, A3(6-123)-2, D9(7/83-40)-2,
B71(213)-1, C6(8)-2, B280(137)-1,
A10(233)-1, B18(2-180)-7, C129(323)-2,
A15(165)-0, A7(209)-1
N1K-J Shiden 'George' Fighter -A
D6(4/73-178)-4, A2(320)-2, A3(3-4)-2,
B71(213)-2, D9(7/83-41)-2,
B135(1-111)-2, A6(144)-2, B280(138)-2,
B164(98)-2, C109(46)-4, C129(323)-2,
A10(234)-1, A7(106)-1, B18(2-171)-7,
A15(165)-6
P1Y2-S Kyokko Twin engine night
fighter version Yokasuka P1Y -B
A3(3-10)-2, A10(235)-1, C6(111)-1,
C100(3-137)-3, A2(465)-0

*KAWASAKI Kawasaki Kokuki Kogyo
K.K.*
Type B1 Otsu-Shiki (Salmson 2A.2)
Biplane reconnaissance, trainer -D
C100(4-22)-2, D11(3/68-37)-1,
B226(137)-1, C5(7,53)-2, B279(268)-1
Type 88-II (KDA-2) Biplane
reconnaissance bomber, also
floatplane -D
C62(112)-2, C108(73)-2, A10(236)-2,
C100(4-30)-2, B15(188)-7, B411(82)-1,
C124(66)-1, B289(22)-6, B281(173)-1,
A15(166)-0, C140(158)-2
Type 92 (KDA-5) Biplane fighter -D
C62(36)-2, D20(11/69-79)-2,
D9(8/83-90)-2, C108(16)-2, A10(236)-1,
C124(72)-1, B411(80)-1, B293(38)-6,

C100(4-58)-2, C74(280)-2, C140(210)-1

Ki-3 Biplane light bomber -D
C108(50)-2, C100(4-64)-2, C5(99)-2,
A10(236)-1, C62(86)-2, B411(81)-1,
A15(166)-0, C140(220)-1

Ki-5 Fighter -E
C108(17)-2, D9(8/83-90)-3,
C100(4-71)-2, C39(76-4)-2, C124(79)-1

Ki-10 'Perry' Biplane fighter, trainer -B
A2(86)-2, D9(8/83-91)-2, C108(14)-2,
C5(104)-2, C100(4-72)-2, A10(236)-1,
B411(82)-1, B15(192)-7, B412(116)-1,
A15(166)-6, C140(236)-2

Ki-28 'Bob' Fighter -E
C4(6)-2, D9(8/83-91, 9/83-154)-2,
C108(18)-2, C129(47)-2, C5(123)-3,
C39(76-21)-2, C100(4-80)-2, C62(154)-1,
C101(256)-1, A2(197)-0

Ki-32 'Mary' Light bomber -A
A2(90)-2, C4(81)-2, C108(58)-2,
A10(237)-1, B18(2-124)-7, B280(140)-1,
B289(60)-6, B193(23,90)-2, B412(57)-1,
A15(166)-6

Ki-45 Toryu 'Nick' Twin engine
fighter -A
B141(1-3)-4, A2(93)-2, B71(105)-2,
A3(3-12)-2, B164(94)-4, C4(8)-2,
D9(9/83-154)-2,
D6(11/73-225, 12/73-276)-4,
B280(141)-2, C129(111)-2, B252(88)-2,
A6(146)-2, A10(238)-2, C100(4-88)-2,
A15(166)-6, A7(107)-1, B18(2-160)-7

Ki-48 'Lily' Twin engine bomber -A
A2(102)-2, C4(85)-2, C108(60)-2,
A6(146)-2, A10(239)-1, A7(210)-1,
C62(94)-4, B280(143)-1, B18(2-162)-7,
C100(4-99)-2, A15(167)-6

Ki-56 'Thalia' (Version Lockheed 14)
Twin engine transport -A
A2(108)-2, C62(136)-2, C4(168)-2,
C108(91)-2, B18(2-159)-7, A7(210)-1,
B412(38)-1, B193(112)-3, C100(4-104)-2,
A15(167)-0

Ki-60 Fighter -E
B141(1-18)-2, A2(110)-2, A3(3-17)-2,

C129(147)-2, C4(15)-2, D9(9/83-155)-2,
B193(54,182)-2, C108(34)-2,
C100(4-107)-2

Ki-61 Hien 'Tony' Fighter -A
B141(1-21)-4, D9(8/75-75)-4, A2(112)-2,
B71(118)-2, A3(3-19)-2, B148(148)-4,
C129(153)-2, B280(144)-2, C4(17)-2,
A6(148)-2, A10(240)-2, B252(89)-2,
B135(1-106)-2, B164(96)-2, A15(167)-6

Ki-64 'Rob' Tandem engine fighter -E
D9(2/78-77)-4, B141(1-34)-4, A2(121)-2,
A3(3-25)-2, C4(23)-2, C129(185)-2,
B193(54,183)-2, D9(10/83-190)-2,
C100(4-120)-2

Ki-66 Twin engine dive bomber -E
A2(123)-2, C4(91)-2, B193(57,181)-1,
C108(59)-2, C5(171)-2,
C100(4-18,123)-2, C62(161)-1,
C101(316)-1, B114(15-1611)-0

Ki-78 (KEN III) High speed -F
A2(125)-2, C4(203)-2, C129(189)-2,
B193(52,190)-2, C62(140)-2,
C108(104)-2, C100(4-126)-2,
D25(12/59-46)-1, D3(9-169)-1

Ki-88 Mid-engine fighter -J
C4(224)-2, C100(4-129)-2, C39(76-38)-2,
A2(483)-1, C129(231)-3, B193(257)-1,
D25(3/56-11)-3, C108(88)-3, D14(1-1)-3,
C11(V-52)-1

Ki-91 Four engine bomber -J
C4(225)-2, A2(484)-1, D29(6/81-50)-6,
B193(196,258)-2, C62(162)-1,
C100(4-130)-2

Ki-96 Twin engine fighter -E
B141(1-37)-2, A2(127)-2, A3(3-27)-2,
D9(10/83-190)-2, C4(25)-2, C129(135)-1,
A10(241)-1, B193(59,202)-2,
C100(4-134)-2, C108(41)-2

Ki-100 Fighter -A
D9(10/76-185)-4, B141(1-39)-4,
A2(129)-2, A3(3-29)-2, C4(27)-2,
D9(10/83-190)-2, C108(36)-2,
C100(4-136)-2, B280(147)-1, A7(211)-1,
C129(180)-1, A10(240)-1, B18(2-204)-7,
A15(167)-6

Ki-102 'Randy' Twin engine fighter -A
B141(1-46)-2, A2(134)-2, A3(3-33)-2,
D9(10/83-191)-2, A6(147)-2,
C129(136)-2, B280(148)-1, A10(241)-1,
C100(4-20,142)-2, A7(211)-1, C4(31)-2,
B18(2-196)-7, B193(59,204)-2,
A15(168)-6

Ki-108 Twin engine high altitude
fighter -E
B141(1-49)-2, A2(138)-2, A3(3-36)-7,
D9(10/83-191,11/83-242)-2, C4(201)-2,
C62(144)-2, C129(142)-1, C100(4-146)-3,
B193(208)-3

Ki-119 Light bomber -J
A2(141)-3, C4(228)-3, C100(4-150)-3,
C5(200)-3

Ki-148 (I-Go I-B) Radio controlled air to
ground missile -C
C4(231)-2, B163(113)-1, A2(532)-6,
C100(4-152)-3, C88(204)-6

KAYABA *Kayaba Seisakusho K.K.*
HK-1 (Dr Hidemasa Kimura) Tailless
glider -F
B439(85)-1, B226(Page 184 -45)-1
Ka-1 Ka-Go (Version Kellett KD-1A)
Observation autogiro -A
A2(143)-2, C4(139)-2, C100(8-88)-2,
C108(90)-2, B193(65,240)-2,
B326(103)-1, C62(128)-2, B280(149)-0,
A15(168)-0, B83(92)-0, B467(119)-3
Ka-2 (Version Kellett KD-1A)
Observation autogiro -E
C4(140)-1, C100(8-89)-1, B326(103)-1,
A2(143)-0, A15(168)-0
Katsuodori Single ram-jet tailless
fighter -J
C100(8-87)-3
Ku-2 Tailless glider -F
B439(85)-1, C4(217)-1,
B226(Page 184 -46)-1, A2(539)-0
Ku-3 Tailless glider -F
B439(85)-1, C4(217)-1,
B226(Page 188 -54)-1, A2(539)-0

Ku-4 Tailless pusher -J
C100(8-86)-3, B439(86)-0, A2(539)-0

KOBE *Kobe Seikosho K.K. (Osaka*
University)
Te-Go High wing observation -E
C4(160)-2, C108(89)-2, C100(8-96,P)-2,
B226(626)-1, B193(241)-3

KOKUSAI *Nippon Kokusai Koku Kogyo*
K.K. (Nikkoku)
Ki-59 'Theresa' (TK-3) Twin engine
high wing transport -B
A2(145)-2, C4(170)-2, C108(95)-2,
B193(65,242)-2, B226(603)-1,
C100(7-154)-2, C62(131)-2,
B114(15-1608)-0, A15(168)-0
Ki-76 'Stella' High wing liaison, anti-
submarine -A
A2(147)-2, C4(141)-2, C108(84)-2,
C100(7-159)-2, B193(33,108)-2,
B226(627)-1, B68(20)-1, B18(2-170)-7,
C62(127)-2, A15(168)-6
Ki-86 'Cypress' (Bücker Bü 131)
Biplane trainer -A
A2(503)-2, C4(185)-2, C108(100)-2,
C62(149)-2, B193(27,114)-2,
C100(7-161)-2, B71(222-263)-1,
A15(102)-0, B280(28)-0
Ki-105 Ohtori 'Buzzard' (Ku-7-II)
Twin engine twin boom high wing fuel
tanker -C
C4(172)-2, C62(138)-2, C108(96)-2,
C100(7-168,P)-2, A2(485)-1,
B226(661)-1, B193(244)-3, B83(94)-0,
B114(15-1618)-0, B286(89)-1
Ku-7 Manazuru 'Buzzard' High wing
twin boom transport glider -E
D6(5/72-250)-2, B286(87)-2, A2(485)-1,
C100(7-165)-2, C4(218)-1, B193(231)-1,
C88(268,P)-1, B150(127)-6, C11(V-92)-1,
B83(94)-0
Ku-8-II 'Gander' High wing transport
glider -A
B286(89)-2, C4(218)-2, A2(484)-1,

D6(5/72-251)-1, C100(7-163)-2,
A7(224)-1, B193(230)-1, B150(126)-1,
D3(6-207)-2, A15(168)-0
Ta-Go Suicide attack -E
C100(7-36,171)-1

KYUSHU Kyushu Hikoki K.K.
A5M4-K Trainer version **Mitsubishi A5M** -B
C100(8-38)-1, C129(260)-1, D7(19-39)-1,
C6(31)-1, A2(346)-6
J7W Shinden Canard pusher fighter -E
C39(102)-4, D25(7/56-30)-4, A2(335)-2,
A3(3-38)-2, C100(8-45)-2,
D9(12/83-288,1/84-41)-2,
B193(61,214)-4, C6(22)-2, C109(58)-4,
B231(63)-4, C129(355)-2, A7(265)-1,
B50(111)-1, B18(2-200)-7
K9W Momiji 'Cypress' (Bücker Bü 131) Biplane trainer -A
A2(503)-2, C109(158)-2, C100(8-36)-1,
C6(253)-1, A15(102)-0
K10W 'Oak' (Version North American NA-16, JNAF KXA) Trainer -A
C6(255)-2, C100(8-34)-2, B68(17)-1,
D19(2/79-102)-1, A2(506)-3,
C109(159)-1, C63(178)-1, A15(168)-0,
B114(14-1537)-0
K11W Shiragiku Trainer, utility -A
A2(330)-2, C6(257)-2, C100(8-39)-2,
C109(160)-2, B193(45,175)-2, A6(148)-1,
B280(150)-1, B226(656)-1, B18(2-186)-7,
A15(168)-0
Q1W Tokai 'Lorna' Twin engine anti-submarine, trainer -A
A2(332)-2, C6(115)-2, C100(8-42)-2,
B193(45,156)-2, A10(243)-1, A6(149)-1,
B280(151)-1, A7(212)-1, B18(2-197)-7,
A15(169)-0
Q3W Nankai Anti-submarine version K11W -E
A2(332)-0, A15(168)-0, C100(8-39)-0

MAEDA Maeda Koku Kenkyujo
Ku-1-I High wing twin boom transport glider -C
D6(5/72-251)-1, B286(84)-2,
C100(8-92)-2, C4(217)-1, A2(539)-0
Ku-6 Sora-Sha (Toku-3) Tank carrier glider -E
C100(8-94)-6, B286(87)-0,
D6(3/72-130)-0, A2(539)-0
Ku-10 Training glider -B
C4(219)-3, A2(539)-0

MANSYU Mansyu Hikoki Seizo K.K. (Manko, Manpi)
Ki-65 Fighter -J
C100(7-151)-0, A2(537)-0
Ki-71 'Edna' Reconnaissance version Mitsubishi Ki-51 -E
C4(145)-7, B68(8)-6, A2(180)-0,
A15(171)-0, C100(7-148)-0
Ki-79 Trainer version Nakajima Ki-27 -A
C4(187)-2, C62(151)-2, C108(101)-2,
C100(7-149)-2, A2(486)-6, D7(2-155)-1,
C129(44)-1, C60(3-P)-1, A15(169)-0,
B114(15-1613)-0
Ki-98 Twin boom pusher attack -J
C4(227)-3, A2(486)-6, D25(3/56-13)-3,
B193(236)-3, C88(228)-6, C100(7-151)-3,
C39(76-40)-7, C129(234)-3
Ki-116 Light weight version Nakajima Ki-84 -E
A2(235)-0, C100(7-153)-0, C4(76)-0,
A15(175)-0
MT-1 Hayabusa Light transport -B
C100(7-144)-2, B153(184c)-1,
B226(521)-1, D3(5-51)-1, A15(169)-0
MT-2 Light transport -L
C100(7-146)-1

MITSUBISHI Mitsubishi Jukogyo K.K.
Type 92 (2MR8) High wing reconnaissance -D
C62(114)-2, C108(86)-2, C100(1-36)-2,
C5(92)-2, B365(P)-1, C4(221)-1,
C87(166,P)-1

A5M 'Claude' Carrier fighter -A
D7(19-26)-4, A2(342)-2, B148(78)-4,
A3(3-40)-2, C6(24)-2, A10(247)-2,
A6(149)-2, C129(249)-2, B280(192)-1,
A7(125)-1, B18(2-126)-7, C100(1-131)-2,
B293(80)-6, A15(169)-6

A6M Reisen 'Zero' ('Zeke', 'Hamp')
Carrier fighter -A
B267-4, B148(126)-4, A2(362)-2,
B71(129,190,236)-2, A3(3-43)-2,
B135(1-50)-2, C109(36)-4, B304-2,
B280(194)-2, B164(76)-2, A6(150)-2,
A10(252)-2, C129(265)-2, B252(115)-2,
A15(170)-6, A7(126)-1, B18(2-138)-7

A7M Reppu 'Sam' Carrier fighter -C
A2(399)-2, D20(5/65-41)-2, C129(349)-2,
C6(42)-2, C109(40)-2, B413(17)-1,
B267(45)-7, C100(1-182)-3,
B18(2-210)-7, A3(3-51)-7

B1M (3MT) Biplane carrier attack
bomber -D
C100(1-10,108)-2, A10(244)-1,
B411(94)-1, B226(259)-1, B75(45)-6

B2M (3MR, Blackburn T.7B) Biplane
carrier attack bomber -D
C100(1-11,108)-2, A10(246)-1,
B411(95)-1, B226(335)-1, B289(23)-6,
B15(190)-7, B114(3-239)-6, B199(295)-1

B5M Carrier attack bomber -B
C6(87)-2, C109(70)-2, A2(491)-1,
A10(251)-1, B411(169)-1, C100(1-148)-2,
A15(170)-0, B83(100)-0, B114(3-242)-0

C1M (2MR1) Biplane carrier
reconnaissance -D
C100(1-9,92)-2, B226(210)-1,
C84(II-32)-1, A2(551)-0

C5M 'Babs' Reconnaissance -B
C6(158)-2, C109(137)-2, C100(1-152)-2,
A2(149)-3, B18(2-134)-7, B193(154)-3,
A15(169)-0, B466(20)-1

F1M 'Pete' Biplane observation
floatplane -A
A2(358)-2, A3(6-129)-2,
D25(10/62-49)-2, C6(200)-2, A6(152)-2,

B280(198)-1, A10(249)-1, C109(132)-2,
B18(2-150)-7, A15(169)-0, A7(220)-1

G1M Twin engine reconnaissance -E
C100(1-124)-2, B226(435)-1, C109(89)-1,
C63(98)-1, C84(III-39)-1

G3M 'Nell' Twin engine bomber -A
A2(350)-2, B71(160)-2, C6(119)-2,
C109(90)-2, A6(152)-2, A7(128)-1,
A10(248)-2, B119(41)-2, B280(199)-1,
B18(2-122)-7, A15(169)-6

G4M 1-Rikko 'Betty' Twin engine
bomber -A
D9(12/84-298)-4, A2(378)-2, B71(210)-2,
B134(2-52)-2, C6(128)-2, A6(153)-2,
B280(200)-2, B119(46)-2, B252(118)-2,
A10(253)-2, C100(1-168)-2,
B18(2-152)-7, A7(129)-1, A15(170)-6

G6M Escort fighter version G4M -B
C6(128)-1, C109(175)-1, C63(103)-1,
D9(12/84-302)-6, A2(380)-0,
B134(2-54)-6, C100(1-172)-6,
D26(188)-3, A15(170)-0, B83(105)-0

J2M Raiden 'Jack' Fighter -A
D6(7/71-67)-4, A2(388)-2, A3(3-53)-2,
B280(203)-2, C129(309)-2, B252(113)-2,
B164(99)-2, A10(255)-1, A6(154)-7,
A15(172)-6, C6(45)-2, C109(53)-4,
C100(1-176)-2, B18(2-182)-7, A7(220)-1

J4M Senden 'Luke' Twin boom pusher
fighter -J
C6(277)-2, C129(388)-3, C100(1-190)-3,
B226(684)-1, A2(491)-6

**J8M Shusui (Ki-200, Messerschmitt
Me 163)** Rocket-propelled tailless
interceptor -C
D9(6/76-283)-5, A2(404)-2, A3(3-62)-2,
C129(379)-2, B71(225-71)-1,
C100(1-187)-2, B193(61,218)-2,
B246(P)-1, B18(2-206)-7, C6(52)-2

K3M 'Pine' (Ki-7) High wing trainer -A
A2(339)-2, C6(260)-2, C109(152)-2,
C100(1-13,114)-2, A7(221)-1,
C63(180)-1, B18(2-130)-7, A15(169)-0,
B83(108)-0

K7M Twin engine high wing trainer -E
C6(264)-2, C100(1-154)-2, C109(191)-1,
C63(180)-1, A2(555)-0

L4M
See Ki-57

Q2M Taiyo Twin engine patrol
bomber -J
C6(278)-3, C100(1-191)-3, B193(261)-3,
C109(190)-0, A2(557)-0

Hinazuru (Airspeed AS.6) Twin
engine light transport -L
C100(1-200)-2, B399(59)-1,
B154(133c)-1, B226(439)-1, B16(250)-7

Ka-14 (9-shi) Fighter -E
C100(1-129)-2, A2(342)-1, D7(19-27)-1,
C129(249)-1, B226(481)-1

Ki-1 Twin engine bomber -D
C108(55)-2, C5(94)-2, C100(1-14,40)-2,
C62(88)-2, B226(427)-1, B365(P)-1,
B412(187)-1, C101(219)-1, C87(55,P)-1,
A15(169)-0, A2(47)-1

Ki-2 'Louise' Twin engine bomber -D
C108(54)-2, C5(98)-2, C100(1-14,44)-2,
A10(246)-1, B411(97)-1, B412(187)-1,
B15(191)-7, B289(78)-6, A15(169)-0,
B114(15-1592)-6, A2(56)-1, C140(155)-1

Ki-7
See K3M

Ki-15 'Babs' Reconnaissance -A
C4(147)-2, C108(76)-2, C100(1-18,52)-2,
A2(149)-1, B280(205)-1, C5(110)-2,
B412(36)-1, B83(109)-1, A6(154)-6,
A15(169)-0

Ki-18 Fighter -E
C4(35)-2, C100(1-19,51)-2, A2(343)-1,
C129(252)-1, D7(19-31)-1, C39(76-24)-1,
C101(233)-1

Ki-20 (Junkers K51) Four engine
bomber -D
C5(88)-2, C100(1-38)-2, C94(11)-2,
A10(245)-1, B418(77)-1, B411(169)-1,
B226(402)-1, B429(273)-1, C62(160)-1,
D7(24-78)-3, C140(188)-1

Ki-21 'Sally' Twin engine bomber -A
A2(155)-2, B71(172)-2, B134(2-20)-2,

B280(266)-2, A10(250)-2, A6(155)-2,
B252(114)-2, C4(93)-2, B18(2-154)-7,
A15(170)-6, A7(130)-1

Ki-30 'Ann' Light bomber -A
A2(164)-2, C4(103)-2, C108(56)-2,
C100(1-63)-2, B193(22,88)-2,
A10(250)-1, C62(89)-2, A6(156)-1,
B412(41)-1, A15(170)-6

Ki-33 Fighter -E
C4(37)-2, C108(19)-2, C100(1-54)-2,
C129(252)-1, D7(19-31)-1, C39(76-25)-1,
C62(156)-1, A2(343)-0

Ki-46 'Dinah' Twin engine
reconnaissance, fighter -A
D9(11/80-277)-4, A2(168)-2, B71(82)-2,
B141(1-51)-2, B280(209)-2, B252(119)-2,
A6(156)-2, C4(152)-2, A10(257)-1,
A15(171)-6, A7(131)-1, A3(3-92)-2

Ki-51 'Sonia' Light bomber -A
A2(178)-2, C4(108,159)-2,
C100(1-19,65)-2, C108(78)-2, A7(221)-1,
A10(254)-1, B280(211)-1, B18(2-136)-7,
B293(77)-6, A15(171)-0

Ki-57 'Topsy' (MC-20, L4M) Twin
engine transport -A
A2(182)-2, C4(175)-2, B162(92)-2,
B193(28,110)-2, B280(212)-1, A7(222)-1,
B18(2-166)-7, C108(92)-2, C5(157)-2,
A15(171)-6

Ki-67 Hiryu 'Peggy' Twin engine
bomber -A
D9(7/83-25)-4, A2(186)-2, B134(2-120)-2,
A6(158)-2, B252(120)-2, C4(113)-2,
B193(24,98)-2, B280(213)-7, A7(132)-1,
B18(2-190)-7, A15(172)-6, A10(256)-1,
C39(50)-4, C100(1-78)-2

Ki-69 Escort fighter version Ki-67 -J
B141(1-57)-0, A2(190)-0

Ki-73 'Steve' Fighter -J
B68(21)-6, A2(192)-0

Ki-83 Twin engine high altitude
fighter -E
B141(1-53)-2, A2(192)-2, A3(3-58)-2,
C129(195)-2, B193(58,192)-2, C62(82)-2,

C4(39)-2, C100(1-86)-2, C39(76-51)-2,
B18(2-192)-7

Ki-95 Reconnaissance version Ki-83 -J
D26(101)-3, A2(190)-0

Ki-97 Transport version Ki-67 -J
C4(226)-3, C100(1-86)-3, A2(190)-0

Ki-103 Interceptor version Ki-83 -J
B141(1-56)-0, A2(193)-0

Ki-109 Interceptor version Ki-67 -B
B141(1-57)-2, C4(41)-2, C108(72)-2,
C100(1-83)-2, D9(7/83-31)-1,
A10(256)-1, B134(2-125)-1, A2(194)-1,
C5(172)-1, A15(172)-0

Ki-167 Flying bomb version Ki-67 -B
D9(7/83-32)-6, C39(50-40)-6

Ki-200
See Mitsubishi J8M

I-Go I-A (I-Go-1-Ko) Radio controlled
air to ground missile -C
C4(230)-2, B163(113)-1, C100(1-88)-3,
D9(7/83-31)-1, A2(532)-0, C88(204,P)-1,
C11(V-101)-1, B26(92)-0

MIZUNO

202 High wing training glider -K
B67(22)-1, D11 (Winter/60 -87)-1

Shinryu
See Yokasuka

NAKAJIMA *Nakajima Hikoki K.K.*

Avro 504 Biplane trainer -D
C100(5-119)-2, B226(140)-1,
D11(3/68-37)-0

**Ko-3 (Ko-Shiki 3, A3, Nieuport
24C.1)** Biplane trainer -D
C100(5-33)-2, B226(113)-1, C5(50)-2,
B365(P)-1, D11(3/68-36)-0, A10(115)-1,
B411(163)-0

**Ko-4 (Ko-Shiki 4, A4, Nieuport
29C.1)** Biplane trainer -D
C100(5-7,36)-2, B226(253)-1,
D11(3/68-36)-1, C5(65)-2, A10(116)-1,
B411(101,171)-1, B422(1-69)-1,
B293(29)-6

Type 91 High wing fighter -D
C62(34)-2, C108(13)-2, A10(258)-2,

C100(5-42)-2, B226(365)-1, B411(97)-1,
B365(P)-1, B15(189)-7, B293(70)-6,
A15(172)-0

NAF-2 Biplane carrier fighter -E
C100(5-17,148)-2, B365(P)-1,
B226(468)-1

LB-2 Akatsugi Twin engine bomber,
transport -E
C6(137)-2, C100(5-19,158)-2,
B226(511)-1

Douglas DC-2 'Tess' Twin engine
transport -I
A2(498)-1, C100(5-224)-1, B121(179)-0,
B226(474)-1, B465(17)-0

A1N (Gloster Gambet) Biplane carrier
fighter -D
B205(157)-2, C100(5-128)-2, A10(257)-1,
B226(319)-1, B365(P)-1

A2N Biplane carrier fighter -D
C109(30)-2, C100(5-9,136)-2,
A10(258)-1, B226(360)-1, B411(98)-1,
B167(31)-1, B293(41)-6

A3N Biplane carrier fighter -D
C100(5-138)-1, A2(549)-0

A4N Biplane carrier fighter -D
C100(5-124)-2, A10(258)-1, C109(32)-1,
B411(99)-1, B365(P)-1, A15(172)-0

A6M2-N 'Rufe' Floatplane fighter
version Mitsubishi A6M -A
A2(426)-2, A3(6-134)-2, B71(129-12)-2,
A6(150)-2, C129(274)-2, B280(214)-1,
B304(46)-1, A10(264)-1, B135(1-52)-1,
A15(174)-0, A7(219)-1, B18(2-164)-7

B5N 'Kate' Carrier torpedo bomber -A
A2(411)-2, B71(141)-2, B119(5)-2,
B280(215)-2, B252(122)-2, A10(260)-1,
A6(159)-2, C6(91)-2, B18(2-146)-7,
A15(173)-6, A7(222)-1

B6N Tenzan 'Jill' Carrier torpedo
bomber -A
A2(429)-2, B119(9)-2, A6(159)-2,
B280(217)-7, B252(124)-2, A10(265)-2,
C6(98)-2, B18(2-187)-7, B59(170c)-2,
A15(174)-0, A7(133)-1

C2N (Fokker Super Universal) High

wing reconnaissance -D
C100(5-11,148)-2, B226(438)-1,
B67(12)-1, C84(III-23)-1, A15(178)-0

C3N Carrier reconnaissance -E
C6(161)-2, C109(136)-1, C100(5-161)-1,
C63(134)-1, A2(551)-0

C6N Saiun 'Myrt' Carrier
reconnaissance -A
A2(434)-2, C6(163)-2, B193(134)-4,
B88(6-56)-2, B280(218)-1, A10(267)-1,
A6(160)-3, B18(2-193)-7, A7(134)-1,
A15(175)-6

D3N (DB) Carrier dive bomber -J
C63(198)-6, C100(5-168)-0, A2(551)-0

E2N 'Bob' (Heinkel HD 25) Biplane
reconnaissance floatplane -D
C100(5-8,124)-2, B226(280)-1, B68(5)-1,
A2(551)-0, C140(116)-1

E4N (Vought V-50/90 Corsair) Biplane
reconnaissance floatplane -D
C100(5-132)-2, C109(114)-1, C82(106)-1,
B283(54)-1, B226(356)-1, C84(III-55)-1,
A15(172)-0

E8N 'Dave' Biplane reconnaissance
floatplane -A
A2(408)-2, A3(6-132)-2, C6(205)-2,
C109(118)-2, C100(5-151)-2, A7(223)-1,
B403(370)-1, B18(2-121)-7, B289(96)-6,
A15(172)-0

E12N Reconnaissance floatplane -E
C63(189)-3, C6(175)-0, C100(5-169)-0,
A2(277)-0

G5N Shinzan 'Liz' Four engine
bomber, transport -B
A2(423)-2, D29(6/81-10)-1,
C39(90-11)-2, B193(62,220)-2,
C6(139)-2, C100(5-174)-2, B413(65)-1,
B18(2-127)-7, C109(98)-2, B59(172c)-3

G8N Renzan 'Rita' Four engine
bomber -E
A2(440)-2, D16(7/81-16)-2,
D9(2/76-84)-2, C39(90-35)-2, C6(141)-2,
B193(62,221)-2, C100(5-198)-2,
B18(2-194)-7, A7(265)-1, B413(27)-1

G10N Fugaku Six engine long range

bomber -J
D20(4/64-57)-3, C6(279)-3,
D16(7/81-34)-6, A2(493)-6, B193(260)-3,
C100(5-204)-3

J1N Gekko 'Irving' Twin engine
fighter, reconnaissance -A
B466-2, A2(417)-2, A3(3-84)-2,
C129(299)-2, B164(97)-2, A10(264)-2,
A6(160)-2, C109(50)-4, B280(219)-1,
B18(2-165)-7, A15(174)-6, A7(135)-1

J5N Tenrai Twin engine fighter -E
A3(3-88)-2, C129(363)-2,
B193(72,212)-2, C6(63)-2, C109(56)-2,
C100(5-195)-3, A2(492)-1

L1N
See Nakajima Ki-34

L2D
see Showa

Kikka Twin jet attack bomber -E
B266-2, D6(5/72-268)-2, A2(443)-2,
B138(56)-2, C100(5-202)-2, C129(373)-2,
B193(63,226)-2, B18(2-208)-7,
B408(323)-1, C6(150)-2

Ki-4 (Type 94) Biplane reconnaissance,
also floatplane -D
C62(116)-2, C108(107)-2,
C100(5-14,49)-2, B226(448)-1,
B279(234)-1, C101(221,223)-1,
A15(172)-0, B114(15-1592)-0

Ki-6 (Fokker Super Universal) High
wing trainer -D
C100(5-11,60)-2, B226(459)-1,
B365(P)-1, C11(IV-79)-1, A15(178)-0

Ki-8 Fighter -E
C100(5-15,54)-1, C39(76-5)-2,
B226(456)-1, B365(P)-1, C5(102)-1,
C101(229)-1, A2(535)-0

Ki-11 Fighter -E
C108(108)-2, C39(76-8)-2,
C100(5-17,57)-2, B365(P)-1, C101(230)-1

Ki-12 Fighter -E
D9(1/81-38)-3, C100(5-18,62)-1,
C39(76-19)-1, C101(237)-1, C62(154)-1,
D26(160)-3, A2(535)-0

Ki-19 Twin engine bomber -E

C4(120)-2, C100(5-19,65)-2, C5(114)-2,
A2(487)-1, C62(160)-1, B153(179c)-1
Ki-27 'Nate' Fighter -A
D7(6-81)-4, B141(2-3)-4, A2(196)-2,
A3(3-66)-2, B148(102)-4, C129(27)-2,
A6(161)-2, A10(259)-2, B280(220)-1,
A15(172)-6, C100(5-66)-2, A7(136)-1,
C4(43)-2, B18(2-128)-7
Ki-34 'Thora' (AT-2, L1N) Twin
engine transport -A
A2(204)-2, C4(180)-2, C100(5-74)-2,
C108(94)-2, B162(126)-2, C62(130)-2,
B153(179c)-1, B16(251)-7, A15(173)-0,
B58(132c)-2
Ki-43 Hayabusa 'Oscar' Fighter -A
B141(2-16)-4, D9(1/80-26)-4, A2(206)-2,
B71(46)-2, B135(2-70)-2, A3(3-70)-2,
B148(124)-4, A6(162)-4, B164(80)-2,
B280(222)-2, C129(53)-2, A10(261)-2,
B252(123)-2, C100(5-77)-2, B18(2-131)-7
Ki-44 Shoki 'Tojo' Fighter -A
B141(2-36)-4, A2(215)-2, B71(225)-2,
A3(3-76)-2, C129(83)-2, B164(92)-2,
A6(164)-2, B280(224)-1, A10(263)-1,
B18(2-188)-7, A15(173)-6, A7(223)-1
Ki-49 Donryu 'Helen' Twin engine
bomber -A
A2(223)-2, C4(122)-2, C100(5-22,94)-2,
A6(164)-2, B280(226)-2, B252(125)-2,
A10(262)-1, B18(2-168)-7, A7(224)-1,
A15(173)-6
Ki-58 Escort fighter version Ki-49 -E
A2(225)-0, C100(5-101)-0, A15(174)-0
Ki-62 Fighter -J
A2(487)-6, C108(112)-0
Ki-80 Engine test version Ki-49 -F
A2(225)-0, C100(5-101)-0, A15(174)-0
Ki-84 Hayate 'Frank' Fighter -A
D9(1/76-22)-4, B141(2-49)-4, A2(230)-2,
B71(70)-2, A3(3-79)-2, B148(164)-4,
B135(2-125)-2, A6(166)-4, B252(126)-2,
A10(266)-2, C129(199)-2, C4(66)-2,
C100(5-102)-2, B280(228)-7, A7(138)-1,
B18(2-176)-7, A15(174)-6
Ki-87 High altitude fighter -E

B141(2-62)-2, A2(238)-2, A3(3-90)-2,
C129(215)-2, B193(60,194)-2, C4(74)-2,
C100(5-106)-2, C39(76-52)-2, C62(66)-2,
C108(47)-2
Ki-106
See Tachikawa
Ki-113 Steel version Ki-84 -G
A2(235)-0, C100(5-110)-0, C4(76)-0,
A15(175)-0, B141(2-56)-0
Ki-115 Tsurugi (Showa Toka) Suicide
attack -C
A2(241)-2, C4(129)-2, B193(60,209)-2,
C108(70)-2, C62(110)-2, B280(230)-1,
A10(40)-1, A6(169)-1, C100(5-28,110)-2,
B50(226)-1
Ki-116
See Mansyu
Ki-201 Karyu Twin jet fighter -J
C4(229)-3, C129(235)-3, C39(76-42)-7,
B193(258)-3, C100(5-115)-3, C5(201)-3,
A2(488)-6, C62(159)-3

NIHON *Nihon Hikoki K.K. (Nippi)*
K8P (K8Ni) Biplane trainer floatplane -E
C6(266)-2, C100(8-74)-1, C109(156)-1,
C63(174)-1, A2(555)-0
L7P Twin engine high wing transport
amphibian -E
D6(1/72-36)-3, C6(234)-1, C109(165)-1,
C100(8-75)-3, A15(175)-0,
D19(1/84-16)-0
LB-2 (Tokyo University) High wing light
plane -L
C100(8-178)-2, B226(559)-1

NIHON KOGATA *Nihon Kogata
Hikoki K.K.*
Chikara (Yokasuka?) Training
glider -E
C63(172)-1, C102(235)-1, A2(564)-0
Hachi Motor glider -L
B226(565)-1, C100(8-95)-1
K-14 Kirigamine Training glider -B
A2(564)-0, C6(271)-0
K-16 Canard glider -F

C39(102-53)-2, C100(8-95)-0

Ku-11 (K-11) High wing transport
glider -E
D6(5/72-252)-2, B286(93)-2,
C100(8-95)-2, C4(220)-1, B226(588)-1

MXJ1 Wakakusa (K-15, 6-2) High
wing training glider -E
C102(233)-3, A2(556)-0, C6(271)-0

*NIPPON KOKUKI Nippon Kokuki
Kogyo*
D-1 Glider version Tachikawa Ki-54 -F
C100(8-128)-1

NOBORITO Noborito Research Institute
Fu-Go Weapon Balloon bomb -A
B265-2, D6(2/74-79)-1, B81(135)-1,
B87(108)-6

*NOZAWA Nozawa Aeronautical
Research Institute*
X-1 Light plane -L
C100(8-180)-2, B226(556)-1

Z-1 (Version Taylor Cub) High wing
light plane -L
C100(8-180)-2, B226(557)-1

*RIKUGAN Rikugan Kokugijutsu
Kenkyujo*
Ki-93 Giken Twin engine fighter,
ground attack -E
D9(5/77-251)-4, B141(2-65)-4, A2(244)-1,
A3(3-94)-2, C129(221)-2, C4(132)-2,
B193(58,200)-2, C100(7-140,P)-2,
C62(108)-2, B83(128)-0

Ki-202 Shusui-kai Version Mitsubishi
Ki-200 -J
C100(7-142)-3, C39(76-41)-3, A2(406)-0

SHOWA *Showa Hikoki K.K.*
L2D 'Tabby' (Douglas DC-3) Twin
engine transport -A
A2(499)-2, C6(236)-2, B121(253)-1,
B193(46,172)-2, D29(6/84-10)-1,
C100(5-178,8-66)-2, B465(18)-1,

C109(164)-2, A15(175,197)-0

Toka Version Nakajima Ki-115 -J
B315(269)-0, A2(243)-0

TACHIKAWA Tachikawa Hikoki K.K.
KKY Light Ambulance Biplane
ambulance -I
C100(7-58)-2, B226(421)-1,
B153(181c)-1, C11(IV-82)-1,
D3(6-219)-1, A15(175)-0

KKY-2 (KS-1) Biplane ambulance,
survey -K
C100(7-60)-1, B226(522)-1, C11(IV-82)-1

Ki-9 'Spruce' Biplane trainer -A
A2(246)-2, C4(189)-2, C62(146)-2,
C108(97)-2, C100(7-51)-2, C5(105)-2,
B153(180c)-1, B83(130)-1, A15(175)-0,
B114(15-1592)-0

Ki-17 'Cedar' Biplane trainer -A
A2(248)-2, C4(193)-2, C62(148)-2,
C5(106)-2, C100(7-55)-2, B153(180c)-1,
B83(130)-1, A15(175)-0,
B114(15-1593)-0

Ki-24 High wing training glider -B
C4(216)-1, C61(143)-1, C11(IV-95)-1,
A2(535)-0

Ki-25 High wing training sailplane -E
C4(216)-1, A2(535)-0

Ki-36 'Ida' Army cooperation -A
A2(250)-2, C4(161)-2, B193(29,104)-2,
C100(7-66)-2, C62(120)-2, A6(170)-2,
B280(245)-1, B412(14)-1, C108(74)-2,
A15(175)-6

Ki-54 'Hickory' Twin engine trainer,
transport -A
A2(254)-2, C4(195)-2, D9(9/76-149)-2,
B193(27,113)-2, A7(236)-1, B280(246)-1,
B18(2-149)-7, B292(81)-6, C100(7-72)-2,
A15(176)-6

Ki-55 'Ida' Trainer -A
C108(102)-2, C100(7-70)-2, A2(250)-1,
B412(69)-1, C4(198)-1, C5(157)-1,
A15(176)-0

Ki-70 'Clara' Twin engine
reconnaissance -E

A2(257)-2, C4(165)-2, B193(57,184)-2,
C100(7-83,P)-2, C108(87)-2, C62(126)-2,
C88(231)-6, B114(15-1612)-0
Ki-74 'Patsy' Twin engine high altitude
reconnaissance bomber -C
A2(259)-2, C4(134)-2, B193(56,186)-2,
C62(106)-2, C108(67)-2, C100(7-87)-2,
D25(6/60-38)-1, B412(202)-1,
A10(268)-1, B114(15-1612)-0
Ki-77 (A-26) Twin engine long range -F
D20(3/64-43)-2, D16(7/76-10)-1,
A2(262)-2, C4(206)-2, A10(268)-1,
D18(9/70-9)-2, C100(7-79)-2,
B193(64,188)-2, C108(106)-2
Ki-92 Twin engine transport -J
C4(182)-3, C100(7-89)-2, B193(198)-3,
C5(190)-3, A2(538)-0
Ki-94-I Tandem engine tractor/pusher
twin boom fighter -J
C100(7-93)-2, C39(76-53)-2,
C129(225)-2, A2(265)-1, C4(77)-1,
C11(V-48)-1, A3(3-96)-0
Ki-94-II High altitude fighter -G
A2(265)-2, A3(3-96)-2, C129(225)-2,
C39(76-53)-2, C100(7-93)-2,
D25(9/56-11)-3, C62(68)-2, C108(40)-2,
C4(77)-2, B193(201)-3
Ki-106 Wood version Nakajima Ki-84 -E
C108(39)-2, B193(206)-5, C100(7-96)-2,
C5(196)-2, A2(235)-1, B141(2-54)-1,
C4(79)-1, C62(157)-1, C101(320)-1,
A3(3-82)-1
Ki-110 Wood version Ki-54 -E
A2(256)-0, C100(7-98)-0, A15(176)-0
R-38 High wing trainer -E
C100(7-64)-2, B22(A-276)-1
SS-1 (Ro-Shiki B) Twin engine pressure
cabin -F
C100(7-76)-2, A2(508)-3, C4(209)-3,
B120(139)-0, C11(V-112)-1
Type LO Ro-Shiki 'Thelma'
(Lockheed Model 14) Twin engine
transport -A
C4(214)-2, A2(507)-1, C100(7-75)-1,
B120(139)-0, A15(176)-0

TOKYO GASU DENKI Tokyo Gasu
Denki Kogyo K.K. (Gasuden)
Koken Long range -F
D16(7/76-12)-1, D20(3/64-45)-1,
C100(8-59)-2, B152(204c)-1,
B226(539)-1, B16(253)-6, C87(P)-1
KR-2 Chidori-Go (Hitachi LXG1)
Biplane liaison -I
C100(8-52)-2, C6(333)-1, B226(476)-1,
C101(216)-1, C84(III-109)-1,
D11(8/63-74)-6, B201(325)-0, A15(164)-0
TR-1 Twin engine transport -L
C100(8-56)-1, B153(182c)-1,
B226(528)-1, D3(5-46)-1, B20(A-292)-1
TR-2 Twin engine transport -L
C100(8-56)-2, B226(530)-1

TOKYO KOKU Tokyo Koku K.K.
Aiba-Tsubame 8 Biplane trainer -L
C100(8-80)-2
Aiba 10 Biplane trainer -L
B226(560)-1, C100(8-82,P)-1
Aiba 11 Biplane light transport -L
C100(8-82,P)-2, B226(561)-1
Ki-107 Trainer -E
C4(200)-2, C108(103)-2, C100(8-84)-2,
C62(150)-2, A2(488)-1, B226(662)-1,
C5(198)-1, B193(246)-3

WATANABE Watanabe Tekkosho K.K.
E9W 'Slim' Biplane sub borne
reconnaissance floatplane -B
A3(6-137)-2, D25(2/62-45,3/62-47)-2,
C6(198)-2, C100(8-31)-1, C109(122)-1,
C63(144)-1, C87(129,P)-1,
D29(2/84-45)-0, A15(176)-0
E14W Sub borne reconnaissance
floatplane -E
A2(451)-0, A3(6-138)-0, D29(2/84-46)-0,
C6(196)-0
K6W Biplane trainer floatplane -E
C100(8-32)-1, C6(243)-0, A2(555)-0
K8W Biplane trainer floatplane -E
C100(8-33)-1, A2(555)-0

YOKASUKA *Dai-Ichi Kaigun Koku*
Gijitsusho (Kugisho)

B3Y Biplane carrier attack bomber -D
C100(2-18,140)-2, C109(66)-1,
B266(405)-1, A10(268)-1, B411(130)-1

B4Y 'Jean' Biplane carrier attack
bomber -B
A2(449)-2, C100(2-144)-2, C109(67)-2,
A10(269)-1, B411(159)-1, B413(112)-1,
B279(309)-1, B83(134)-0, A15(176)-0,
B114(3-241)-6

Chikara
See Nihon Kogata

D3Y Myojo Wood version Aichi D3A -C
A2(469)-2, C6(77)-2, C109(86)-2,
B119(28)-1, B413(17)-1, B226(685)-1

D4Y Suisei 'Judy' Carrier dive bomber,
reconnaissance -A
A2(454)-2, B71(241)-2, B119(26)-2,
B280(247)-2, B252(158)-2, A6(170)-2,
A10(269)-2, B18(2-184)-7, C6(79)-2,
C109(82)-2, C100(2-153)-2,
B88(6-63,7-69)-2, A7(164)-1, A15(177)-0

D5Y Myojo-Kai Suicide attack version
D3Y -J
A2(470)-0, B315(268)-0

E1Y Biplane reconnaissance
floatplane -D
C100(2-16,116)-2, B226(264)-1,
A2(551)-0

E5Y Biplane reconnaissance
floatplane -E
C100(2-16,130)-2, C84(III-79)-1,
A2(552)-0

E6Y Biplane sub borne reconnaissance
floatplane -D
C100(2-16,134)-2, B226(371)-1,
C109(172)-1, D29(2/84-45)-0, A2(552)-0

E14Y 'Glen' Sub borne reconnaissance
floatplane -A
A2(451)-2, A3(6-138)-2, C6(196)-2,
D9(7/65-242)-1, B18(2-148)-7,
D29(2/84-46)-3, C109(123)-2, A7(244)-1,
B59(175c)-3, A15(176)-6

Funryu 1 Radio-controlled air-to-ground
missile -E
B163(113)-0, A2(533)-0,
B114(10-1044)-0

Funryu 2 Anti-aircraft missile -E
B163(154)-6, A2(533)-6, B26(92)-0,
B114(10-1044)-0

Funryu 4 Anti-aircraft missile -E
B163(154)-6, A2(533)-6, B26(92)-0,
B114(10-1044)-0

H5Y 'Cherry' Twin engine high wing
reconnaissance flying boat -B
A3(5-136)-2, C6(230)-2, C109(146)-2,
B193(48,168)-2, A2(495)-1,
C100(2-148)-2, C84(IV-96)-1, A15(176)-0

H7Y 'Tillie' Four engine high wing
reconnaissance flying boat -E
D6(10/71-276)-0, C6(233)-0, B68(22)-6,
C100(2-181)-0, A2(553)-0

K1Y (Version Avro 504K) Biplane
trainer floatplane -D
C100(2-15,114)-2, A2(554)-0,
B198(185)-0

K2Y (Version Avro 504K) Biplane
trainer -A
C100(2-15,126)-2, A2(493)-1,
B226(320)-1, B198(185)-0

K4Y Biplane trainer floatplane -A
C6(246)-2, C100(2-17,129)-2,
C109(153)-1, B411(171)-1, A2(494)-1,
B266(362)-1, C84(III-101)-1, B83(137)-0

K5Y 'Willow' Biplane trainer, also
floatplane -A
A2(446)-2, C6(248)-2, C109(154)-2,
C100(2-18,142)-2, B280(249)-1,
B226(434)-1, B413(50)-1, B18(2-120)-7,
B68(24)-1, C60(3-P)-1

L3Y 'Tina' Transport conversion
Mitsubishi G3M -B
C109(165)-1, C100(1-144)-1, C6(122)-1,
B71(160-13)-1, A2(356)-0

MXY1 High wing aerodynamic
research -F
B226(472)-1, B264(28)-1,

107

C100(2-17,168)-1, C6(267)-1,
C109(192)-1

MXY3 Radio-controlled target glider -E
C6(268)-3, C100(2-170)-3, A2(556)-0

MXY4 Radio-controlled target drone
floatplane -B
C100(2-171)-3, C6(268)-3, C102(229)-1,
C109(192)-1, A2(556)-0

MXY5 High wing transport glider -C
D6(5/72-251)-2, B286(96)-2, C6(269)-2,
C100(2-173)-2, C109(168)-1,
D25(9/57-27)-1, B226(Page 193 -67)-1,
A2(556)-0

MXY6 Canard glider -F
C39(102-40)-2, C100(2-174,8-45)-1,
C129(355)-2, C109(64)-1, A2(335)-1,
C63(67)-1

MXY7 Ohka 'Baka' Rocket-propelled
suicide attack -A
A2(476)-2, B71(210-115)-2, C6(147)-2,
B138(52)-2, D3(6-260)-5, A6(171)-2,
B280(250)-1, A10(271)-1, B50(223)-1,
B244(P)-2, A7(165)-1, A15(177)-0

MXY8 Akigusa Training glider for
Mitsubishi J8M -B
D9(6/76-283)-1, A2(405)-1, C6(270)-6,

C109(64)-1, C129(380)-1, C100(2-174)-1,
B193(232)-1, B439(86)-1, B246(P)-1,
A3(3-63)-1

MXY9 Shuka Single jet version
MXY8 -J
A2(406)-0, D9(6/76-288)-0

MXY9 Ground target decoy -B
C109(193)-1

P1Y Ginga 'Frances' Twin engine
bomber -A
A2(462)-2, C6(108)-2, C109(102)-2,
C100(2-20,160)-2, A6(171)-2,
B193(44,146)-2, B280(251)-1,
A10(270)-1, A7(166)-1, B18(2-199)-7

R2Y Keiun Mid-engine long range
reconnaissance -E
A2(472)-2, D25(3/59-27)-2, C6(155)-2,
C100(2-20,166)-2, C109(140)-2,
B193(61,256)-2

Shinryu (Mizuno) High wing suicide
attack glider -E
B270(217)-3

YOKOI Yokoi Koku K.K.
Ku-13 Shusui Training glider for
Mitsubishi Ki-200 -J
A2(406)-0

LATVIA

CUKURS Herbert Cukurs
C-6 Light plane -L
B226(498)-1, C101(247)-1

LKOD Liepaja Kara Ostas Darbnica
KOD-1 (Estonia **OGL PON-1**) Biplane
trainer, reconnaissance -B
B153(32b)-1, D7(18-70)-0

*V.E.F. Valsts Elektrotechniska Fabrika
(Karlis Irbitis)*
I-12 (J-12) Trainer, tourer -B
B153(183c)-1, D3(6-243,7-192)-1,

B420(66)-1, A15(177)-0, B279(295)-0
I-15 Trainer -E
D9(1/79-45)-1, D3(6-243)-1
I-16 Fighter -E
D9(4/83-200)-2, D15(1-20)-3,
C88(107)-6, B279(295)-0
I-17 Trainer -B
B279(295)-0
I-18 Trainer -C
B279(295)-0
I-19 Fighter -J
B279(295)-0

LITHUANIA

ANBO *Karo Aviacijos Tiekimo Skyrius*
Anbo VI High wing trainer -K
D7(29-64)-1
Anbo VIII Light bomber -E
D7(29-64)-2
Anbo 41 (Anbo IV) High wing
reconnaissance -B

D7(29-65)-2, B153(183c,32b)-1,
B397(562)-1, B342(65)-1, B20(A-293)-1,
C114(138)-1, A15(177)-0, B411(171)-0,
B279(203)-0
Anbo 51 High wing trainer -K
B153(183c)-0, B20(A-293)-0,
B279(203)-0, D7(29-66)-0

MEXICO

AZACARTE *Juan F. Azacarte S en C*
02U-4A (Vought Corsair) Biplane
military -D
B152(42b)-1, B283(54)-0, A14(125)-0,
C82(104)-0, B279(288)-0, C10(225)-0

LASCURIAN
Salinas Twin engine light transport -L
B22(A-280)-1

TNCA *Talleres Nacionales de
Construcciones Aeronauticas*
Tezuitlan (Antonio Sea) Trainer -C
B165(248)-2, C10(225)-1,
D9(11/81-248)-0, B21(A-362)-0,
B279(288)-0
TTS-5 Twin engine light transport -H
B139(128)-6, B60(151c)-0, B279(288)-0

NETHERLANDS

AVIOLANDA *Maatschappij Voor
Vliegtuigbouw N.V. 'Aviolanda'*
LVA High wing fighter -J
C52(224)-1

DeSCHELDE *Koninklijke Maatschappij
'DeSchelde'*
S.12 Tourer -L
C56(16)-2, B19(1031)-1, C127(93)-1,
D3(3-158)-1, C60(3-P)-1
S.20 Twin boom pusher tourer,
trainer -E
C56(80)-2, D9(7/74-47)-1,
D25(3/59-45)-1, C57(1-144,154)-1,
C127(121)-1, D3(3-158)-1

S.21 Twin boom pusher fighter -G
D6(2/74-74)-4, A3(3-98)-2, C56(96)-2,
D25(5/59-11)-2, C127(123)-1,
C57(1-155)-6, C87(93)-6

DIEPEN *Frits Diepen Vliegtuigen N.V.*
DIFOGA 421 Twin boom pusher light
transport -H
C127(123)-1, C36(217)-1, B60(152c)-1,
B328(142)-1, D3(7-160)-1

FOKKER *N.V. Nederlandische
Vliegtuigfabrik Fokker*
C.V. (Denmark **II R, III R;** Sweden **S 6**)
Biplane reconnaissance bomber -A
B71(87)-2, B421(138,etc)-2, A10(273)-1,

109

B328(69,119)-1, B411(56)-1,
C57(1-85)-1, C127(48)-1, C69(106)-2,
D23(79-58)-2, A15(178)-6

C.VII-W Biplane reconnaissance
floatplane -B
C58(1-117,127)-1, B328(76,123)-1,
C127(69)-1, B408(159)-1, D3(4-14)-1,
A15(178)-0, B411(171)-0

C.VIII High wing reconnaissance, also
floatplane **C.VIII-W** -B
C58(1-119,132)-1, C57(1-93,107)-1,
B328(76)-1, C127(75)-1, D3(4-14)-1,
A15(179)-0

C.IX Biplane reconnaissance -B
B421(184)-2, B328(85)-5,
C57(1-94,108)-1, C127(77)-1,
B411(171)-0

C.X Biplane reconnaissance bomber -B
A3(3-72)-2, A6(126)-2, B328(96)-5,
A10(275)-1, D23(79-60)-2, C70(39)-2,
C127(90)-1, A7(248)-1, B411(144)-1,
A15(179)-6

C.XI-W Biplane reconnaissance
floatplane -B
A3(6-143)-2, B88(3-75)-2,
B328(100,123)-1, C58(1-122,133)-1,
C127(96)-1, B436(247)-1, B153(189c)-1,
B397(566)-1, A15(179)-0

C.XIV-W Biplane reconnaissance,
trainer floatplane -B
A3(6-145)-2, C127(115)-2,
B328(106,123)-1, C58(1-141,135)-1,
B153(190c)-1, C10(229)-1, D23(79-50)-6,
A15(180)-6

C.XV-W Reconnaissance floatplane -J
B328(123)-1

D.XIII Biplane fighter, trainer -D
D9(3/80-149)-2, B339(87)-1,
C113(3-168)-1, A10(272)-1, C114(19)-1,
C127(54)-1, B293(40)-6, B14(126,135)-7,
B411(171)-0, B114(7-677)-1,
C140(100)-2

D.XVI Biplane fighter -D
D9(3/80-149)-2, A10(274)-2, B328(82)-1,
C127(73)-1, B167(35)-1,

C57(1-119,124)-1, C43(1-74)-1,
B114(7-677)-1, A15(179)-0

D.XVII Biplane fighter -B
D9(3/80-150)-2, D25(10/62-28)-2,
A10(274)-1, B328(88,122)-5,
B14(126,135)-7, B293(62)-6, C127(80)-1,
A15(179)-0

D.XIX Biplane fighter -J
C52(196)-3, B328(96)-6, D3(4-14)-6

D.XXI (Denmark **III J**) Fighter -A
D6(8/71-152)-4, D9(10/77-178)-4,
B71(63)-2, C52-4, A3(3-100)-2,
B148(94)-4, A6(126)-2, B252(56)-2,
A10(276)-1, A15(180)-6, A7(249)-1

D.XXIII Tandem engine tractor/pusher
twin boom fighter -E
D6(2/74-69)-4, A3(3-108)-2,
D9(4/80-200)-2, B328(114)-1,
C127(120)-1, C57(1-181,167)-1,
B18(1-275)-7, B153(187c)-1,
D23(79-68)-2

F.VII-3m Three engine high wing
transport, bomber -B
D7(12-24,13-43)-5, B162(26)-2,
B391(468,477)-1, C57(1-115,112)-1,
A10(275)-1, B328(76)-2, C78(316)-2,
B289(86)-6, A15(178)-6

F.VIII (Sweden **Tp 10**) Twin engine high
wing transport -B
B391(474)-1, B328(73,116)-1,
C127(66)-1, C57(1-123)-1, C70(56)-1,
B291(24)-1, B36(16)-1, C121(3-56)-1,
A15(178)-6, B431(71)-6

F.IX (Avia F39) Three engine high wing
transport, bomber -B
B391(483)-1, B328(80)-1, C127(74)-1,
D3(4-26)-1, A15(179)-0

F.XII Three engine high wing
transport -L
B162(52)-2, B391(487)-1, C112(3-83)-2,
B328(85)-1, C127(77)-1

F.XVIII Three engine high wing
transport, anti-submarine -I
B328(94, 98)-2, B391(490)-1,

C57(1-117,123)-1, C112(3-85)-2,
C127(82)-1, C60(2-P)-1, A15(180)-0

F.XXII (F.22) Four engine high wing
transport -I
D6(11/71-292)-4, D3(3-135)-2,
B200(2-37)-2, B391(494)-1, B328(129)-1,
C127(92)-1, B291(59)-1, C51(43)-1

F.XXXVI (F.36) Four engine high wing
transport -I
B162(93)-2, D6(11/71-292)-1,
B200(2-38)-1, B391(493)-1, B328(97)-1,
B15(204)-7, C127(88)-1, C51(9)-1,
B351(249)-1, D17(2-21)-1

G.1 Twin engine twin boom fighter,
reconnaissance -B
D9(10/74-178,11/74-239,12/74-286)-4,
B71(134)-2, A3(3-104)-2, C53-4,
B164(22)-4, A6(127)-2, A10(279)-2,
C127(105)-1, A7(250)-1, D9(4/80-200)-2,
D23(79-64)-2, B88(1-84)-2, B18(1-274)-7,
A15(180)-6

G.2 Twin engine bomber -J
C53(128)-1, D26(189)-3

S.IIA Biplane ambulance -B
C57(1-72,80)-1, B328(56)-1, A15(178)-0,
B411(172)-0

S.IV Biplane trainer -D
C57(1-73,81)-1, B328(60)-1,
D28(8/78-120)-1, C127(55)-1, C54(42)-1,
D3(9-102)-1, A15(178)-0

S.IX Biplane trainer -B
B153(190c)-1, B328(106)-1,
C57(1-150,163)-1, C58(1-144,139)-1,
C127(111)-1, C10(234)-1, D3(9-103)-1,
A15(180)-0

T.IV Twin engine reconnaissance
bomber floatplane -B
A3(6-141)-2, B88(3-77)-2, A10(277)-1,
B411(145)-1, C127(67)-1,
B328(101,130)-1, C58(1-113,125)-1,
B397(572)-1, A15(178)-0

T.V Twin engine bomber -B
D1(5-3)-4, C55-4, D25(7/63-55)-2,
A10(278)-2, D23(79-66)-2, A7(250)-1,

C74(305)-2, B88(3-78)-2, C127(109)-1,
A15(180)-0

T.VI Twin engine twin boom bomber -J
C55(71)-6

T.VII-W Twin engine bomber
floatplane -J
B328(113)-1, C55(69)-1

T.VIII-W Twin engine reconnaissance
bomber floatplane -B
D7(20-63)-4, B71(176)-2, A3(6-147)-2,
A6(128)-2, B18(1-276)-7, A10(278)-1,
A11(496)-1, C127(117)-1, B294(76)-6,
A15(180)-6

T.IX Twin engine bomber -E
C55(72)-2, B328(114)-1,
C57(1-176,166)-1, D25(4/56-11)-1,
B436(243)-1, C127(48,P)-1, C87(120)-1,
D14(1-12)-3, B114(22-2445)-0

KOOLHOVEN N.V. Koolhoven
Vliegtuigen

F.K.41 High wing liaison -I
C126(63)-1, C127(70)-1, B291(19)-1,
C51(42,87)-1, A15(180)-0

F.K.43 High wing liaison -I
C57(1-189)-1, C126(67)-1,
D19(2/81-124)-1, B279(206)-1,
B139(28)-1, C127(79)-1, C51(32,92)-1

F.K.46 Biplane trainer -B
B153(191c)-1, C126(77)-1,
C57(1-152,140)-1, C127(86)-1,
C51(28)-1, D3(4-279)-1, C60(2-P)-1,
A15(180)-0

F.K.49 Twin engine high wing survey,
also floatplane -B
C126(84)-2, B153(192c)-1,
C57(1-132,128)-1, D3(4-279)-1,
C127(89)-1, C60(1-P)-1, A15(181)-0

F.K.50 Twin engine high wing
transport -L
B162(108)-2, B153(192c)-1, B391(501)-1,
C127(98)-1, C51(147)-1, C126(88)-1,
C67(84)-1, D25(1/61-9)-1, C60(2-P)-1,
B16(255)-7

F.K.50B Twin engine high wing bomber -J
C126(90)-2, D25(1/61-9)-1

F.K.51 Biplane trainer, observation -B
A7(252)-1, B153(193c)-1, C126(92)-2, D6(2/72-104)-2, C127(94)-1, C112(3-91)-2, D23(79-71)-1, C78(347)-1, C57(1-134)-1, A15(181)-0, C134(163)-1

F.K.52 Biplane fighter, trainer, liaison -C
D9(12/83-307)-2, D4(6/76-44)-2, C126(104)-2, B88(1-32)-2, C70(43)-1, C57(1-138)-1, B153(193c)-1, C127(104)-1, A15(181)-0

F.K.55 Mid-engine high wing fighter -E
D6(3/72-148)-4, C126(113)-4, D9(12/83-307)-1, C57(1-157,145)-1, B153(195c)-1, C127(113)-1, C87(87,P)-1, D25(2/59-11)-2

F.K.56 Trainer, reconnaissance -B
D28(5/78-91,8/78-123)-5, C126(118)-1, B153(195c)-1, C127(112)-1, C58(1-148,146)-1, C10(234)-1, C60(1-P)-1, A15(181)-0

F.K.57 Twin engine transport -L
B152(217c)-1, C126(124)-1, C127(113)-1, B20(A-255)-1, D3(4-291)-1

F.K.58 Fighter -B
D9(1/84-40)-2, A3(3-110)-2, B164(1)-2, C126(126)-2, A10(280)-1, C74(306)-2, C57(1-158,146)-1, D9(4/76-185)-2, A15(181)-0

F.K.59 Twin engine torpedo floatplane -J
C126(137)-1

WALRAVEN *L. W. Walraven (Netherlands East Indies)*
W-2 Merbaboe I Twin engine light transport -L
C60(2-P)-1, D3(7-15)-1, B153(197c)-0
W-4 Trainer -L
B153(197c)-1, C60(2-P)-1, D3(7-15)-1, B279(302)-0

NORWAY

M.F. *Marinens Flyvebatfabrikk*
DT-2B (Douglas DT) Biplane torpedo bomber floatplane -D
B121(65)-2, A14(110)-1, B411(182)-1, A9(153)-2, B450(21)-1
M.F.10 Biplane trainer floatplane -B
B397(578)-1, B152(220c)-1, B153(198c)-1, B279(221)-0

M.F.11 (Høver) Biplane reconnaissance floatplane -B
A3(6-152)-2, B153(198c)-1, D29(2/81-29)-1, C70(53)-1, C10(236)-1, C121(2-58)-1, A15(181)-6, B279(221)-0
M.F.12 Biplane trainer -B
B153(198c)-0

PERU

FAUCETT *Cia. de Aviacion Faucett S.A.*
F.19 (Faucett-Stinson) High wing transport, also floatplane -B
B59(177c)-1, B153(199c)-1, B279(161)-1, D20(10/64-97)-1, B176(63)-1, B419(79)-1, D3(3-290)-1

POLAND

BARTEL *Wielpolska Wytwornia Samolotow 'Samolot' Sp Ake*
BM4 (M.4) Biplane trainer, liaison -B
A1(357)-2, C46(128)-2, C83(302)-2, B91(83)-1, C75(96)-6, A15(185)-0, B411(173)-0, C136(16)-1
BM5 (M.5) Biplane trainer -B
A1(363)-1, C46(132)-2, C83(309)-2, B91(83)-1, B411(173)-0, C136(16)-1
BM6 (M.6) Biplane trainer -E
A1(368)-1, C46(134)-2, C83(314)-2, C75(144)-1

LUBLIN *Zaklady Mechaniczne E. Plage & T. Laskiewicz*
R-VIII Biplane reconnaissance bomber, also floatplane -B
A1(278)-1, C46(141)-2, C83(189,396)-2, B91(82)-1, A15(182)-6
R-XIII High wing observation, also floatplane -A
B71(231)-2, A1(299)-2, C46(150)-2, C83(269,401)-2, A7(254)-1, C74(310)-2, D16(7/83-40)-1, B91(94,119)-1, A15(182)-6, C136(16)-1
R-XIV High wing trainer -B
A1(299)-1, C46(150)-2, C83(328)-2, B411(173)-0
R-XVI High wing transport, ambulance -B
A1(316)-1, C46(160)-2, C83(365)-2, C75(39)-1, A15(182)-0

L.W.D. *Lotnicze Warsztaty Doswiadczalne*
Szpak-2 Liaison -H
B139(42)-0, B91(239)-0, D3(9-99)-0, B60(156c)-0

L.W.L. *Lwowskie Warsztaty Lotnicze*
CW 5 High wing training sailplane -B
A1(693)-1, C46(386)-2, C136(24)-1

CW 7 High wing training sailplane -B
A1(698)-1, C46(390)-2
ITS-IV High wing sailplane -F
A1(700)-1, C46(404)-2
ITS-8 High wing twin boom pusher motor glider -C
A1(651)-1, C46(435)-2, C136(24)-1

L.W.S. *Lubelska Wytwornia Samolotow Sp Ake*
L.W.S.2 High wing ambulance -E
A1(331)-1, C46(169)-2, C83(370)-2, B152(222c)-1
L.W.S.3 Mewa High wing reconnaissance -B
A1(333)-2, B88(1-31)-2, C46(170)-2, C83(284)-2, B153(202c)-1, B91(112)-1, D16(7/83-50)-1, C75(89)-1, A15(182)-0, B114(17-1889)-0, C136(18)-1
L.W.S.4 Zubr (P.Z.L.30) Twin engine high wing bomber, trainer -B
A1(341)-2, C46(173)-2, C83(229)-2, B153(200c)-1, D20(6/65-43)-1, A10(281)-1, B91(146)-1, D16(7/83-45)-1, B279(217)-1, B87(83)-6, C136(18)-1
L.W.S.6 Zubr Twin engine high wing bomber -E
A1(341)-1, C83(233)-2, C46(173)-1, D20(6/65-43)-3, A10(282)-1
L.W.S.7 Mewa 2 High wing reconnaissance -J
C83(288)-6, A1(338)-0, C46(173)-0, A15(182)-0

NIKOL *Morski Dyon Lotniczy*
A-2 High wing pusher reconnaissance amphibian -E
A1(658)-1, C46(118)-2, C83(411)-2, D25(11/59-30)-6

P.W.S. *Podlaska Wytwornia Samolotow Sp Ake*

P.W.S. 10 High wing fighter, trainer -B
A1(402)-2, C46(190)-2, C83(97)-2, A10(282)-1, D16(7/83-32)-1, B411(153)-1, B293(76)-6, B279(255)-1, C112(4-84)-2, B91(87)-1, C136(18)-1

P.W.S.14 Biplane trainer -C
A1(413)-1, C83(339)-2, C46(195)-2, B411(173)-0, C136(18)-1

P.W.S.16 Biplane trainer -B
A1(419)-1, C46(197)-2, C83(341)-2, B411(173)-0

P.W.S.18 (Avro 621) Biplane trainer -B
A1(426)-2, C83(344)-2, B411(173)-0, A15(128)-0, C136(20)-1

P.W.S.24 High wing transport, survey -B
A1(444)-2, C46(206)-2, C83(374)-2, B391(508)-1, A15(183)-0, C136(18)-1

P.W.S.26 Biplane trainer, liaison -A
A1(419)-2, C46(198)-2, C83(348)-2, B153(200c)-1, D16(7/83-41)-1, A7(255)-1, C74(310)-2, B91(97)-1, C114(70)-1, A15(183)-0, C136(18)-1

P.W.S.33 Wyzel Twin engine trainer -C
A1(464)-2, C83(353)-2, C46(210)-2, B153(203c)-1, D16(7/83-51)-1

P.W.S.35 Ogar Biplane trainer -C
A1(468)-6, C83(357)-3, C46(212)-3, A15(183)-0

P.W.S.41 Trainer -J
A1(474)-0, C46(213)-0

P.W.S.42 Sokol Fighter -J
D26(178)-3, A1(475)-0

P.W.S.101 Training sailplane -B
A1(704)-1, C46(397)-2, C136(24)-1

P.W.S.102 Rekin High wing training sailplane -B
A1(706)-2, C46(400)-2, C136(24)-1

P.W.S.103 High wing training sailplane -C
A1(701)-0, C46(402)-3

P.Z.L. *Panstwowe Zaklady Lotnicze*

P.Z.L.4 Three engine high wing transport -E
A1(138)-1, C46(220)-2, B150(27)-6

P.Z.L.5 Biplane club trainer -B
A1(141)-1, C46(222)-2, C83(320)-1

P.7 High wing fighter -A
D7(28-37)-2, A1(147)-2, C83(113)-2, C46(225)-2, B408(279)-2, A10(284)-1, B411(113)-1, A7(255)-1, B15(289)-7, B293(73)-6, A15(183)-6

P.11 High wing fighter -A
D7(28-40)-4, A1(158)-2, B71(75)-2, B148(60)-4, C83(124)-2, A3(3-114)-2, A6(172)-2, B252(134)-2, A10(285)-1, A7(256)-1, A15(183)-6

P.23 Karas Reconnaissance bomber -A
A1(186)-2, B71(104)-2, C83(199)-2, A6(172)-2, D16(7/83-41)-1, B252(135)-2, A10(288)-1, A7(256)-1, B18(1-278)-7, A15(184)-0

P.24 High wing fighter -A
D7(28-45)-2, A1(201)-2, B71(170)-2, C83(140)-2, C46(252)-1, A3(3-117)-2, A10(286)-2, B88(1-24)-2, B18(1-277)-7, B411(153)-1, A15(184)-6

P.37 Łos Twin engine bomber -B
A1(222)-2, B71(258)-2, C83(239)-2, A6(287)-2, A10(289)-2, A7(257)-1, B88(1-80)-2, B279(247)-1, D16(7/83-30)-1, B18(1-279)-7, A15(184)-6

P.38 Wilk Twin engine fighter bomber -E
A1(236)-2, D25(10/60-11)-2, C83(155)-2, C46(269)-2, B153(203c)-1, C136(14)-1, D16(7/83-49)-1, B91(100)-1, B397(584)-1, C10(245)-1, C87(115,P)-1

P.42 Reconnaissance bomber -E
A1(192)-1, C83(208)-1, C46(246)-1, B71(104-6)-1, A15(184)-0

P.43 Tchaika Reconnaissance
bomber -B
A1(193)-1, C83(210)-2, C46(247)-1,
B71(104-6)-1, A10(288)-1, B152(224c)-1,
D16(7/83-44)-1, B397(582)-1, A15(184)-6

P.Z.L.44 Wicher Twin engine
transport -E
A1(244)-1, C83(376)-2, C46(271)-2,
C74(314)-2, B152(225c)-1, B16(270)-7,
C15(109)-1, B19(A-297)-1, C136(14)-1

P.45 Sokol Fighter -J
A1(250)-6, C83(455)-6, C46(274)-6,
D25(11/59-30)-6

P.46 Sum Reconnaissance bomber -C
A1(254)-2, C83(212)-2, C46(275)-2,
B88(1-30)-2, C74(315)-2, B153(202c)-1,
D16(7/83-51)-1, C10(247)-1,
C87(20,P)-1, A15(184)-0, C136(14)-1

P.48 Lampart Twin engine fighter
bomber -J
A1(240)-6, C83(462)-3, C46(277)-6,
D25(11/59-30)-6, C87(115)-6

P.49 Mis Twin engine bomber -J
A1(228)-6, C83(450)-6, C46(278)-6,
D25(11/59-30)-6, C87(57)-6, A15(184)-0

P.50 Jastrzab Fighter -E
A1(259)-2, C83(159)-2, C46(279)-2,
D16(7/83-50)-1, A3(3-120)-7, C136(14)-1

P.54 Rys Twin engine fighter bomber -J
A1(241)-0, C87(115)-0, C83(466)-0,
C46(277)-0

P.62 Dabrowski Fighter -J
A1(265)-7, C83(464)-3, D13(1-5)-3,
D25(11/59-30)-6, C46(31)-6

S-1 High wing liaison -H
B91(238)-1

R.W.D. *Doswiadczalne Warsztaty*
Lotnicze

RWD 8 High wing trainer -A
A1(510)-2, C83(331)-2, C46(299)-2,
C74(322)-2, B91(110)-1, B152(226c)-1,
D16(7/83-40)-1, C114(70)-1, A15(184)-0,
C10(248)-1, C136(6)-1

RWD 9 High wing STOL tourer -K
A1(520)-2, C46(304)-2, C18(143)-1,
D3(6-27)-1, C136(8)-1

RWD 10 High wing aerobatic trainer -B
A1(530)-2, C46(308)-2, C74(322)-2,
B152(226c)-1, D3(6-27)-1, C136(6)-1

RWD 11 Twin engine transport -I
A1(534)-1, C46(311)-2, B152(227c)-1,
B16(269)-6, D3(6-27)-1, C136(8)-1

RWD 13 High wing liaison,
ambulance -B
A1(539)-2, C83(337,367)-2, C46(313)-2,
B153(204c)-1, B16(268)-7, C74(323)-2,
C75(108)-6, C112(4-87)-1, D3(8-108)-1,
A15(184)-0, B19(A-298)-1, C136(8)-1

RWD 14 Czapla High wing
reconnaissance -B
A1(547)-2, C83(280)-2, C46(318)-2,
C74(323)-2, D16(7/83-50)-1, A7(253)-1,
A15(185)-6, C136(8)-1

RWD 15 High wing tourer, utility -B
A1(552)-1, C46(320)-2, B153(204c)-1,
D3(6-27)-1, B20(A-299)-1, C136(8)-1

RWD 16 Tourer -L
A1(556)-2, C46(322)-2, B153(205c)-1,
D3(6-27)-1, B20(A-299)-1

RWD 17 High wing trainer, also
floatplane -B
A1(561)-1, C46(323)-2, C83(409)-2,
B153(205c)-1, A15(185)-0, C136(8)-1

RWD 18 Twin engine high wing STOL
transport -G
A1(565)-6, C46(326)-6

RWD 19 Tourer -L
A1(567)-1, C46(327)-2, B153(206c)-1,
D3(6-46)-1

RWD 20 Tricycle gear version
RWD 9 -F
A1(526)-1, C46(328)-2

RWD 21 Tourer -L
A1(556)-1, C46(328)-2, B153(206c)-1,
D3(6-46)-1

RWD 22 Twin engine reconnaissance
bomber floatplane -J
A1(569)-7, C46(330)-2, C83(460)-6

RWD 23 Trainer -C
A1(572)-1, C46(332)-2, B153(207c)-1,
D3(6-46)-1
RWD 25 Sokol Fighter -J
A1(574)-3, C83(457)-3, D13(1-11)-3,
C46(333)-6, D25(11/59-30)-6

SCIBOR-RYLSKI *Slaskie Warsztaty Szybowcowe*
SR-3 (RS-III) High wing light plane -I
A1(663)-1, C46(119)-2

W.S. *Warsztaty Szybowcowe*
Bak Training motor glider -B
A1(576)-1, C46(437)-2, C136(24)-1
Czajka High training glider -A
A1(708)-1, C46(417)-2, C136(22)-1
Komar High wing training sailplane -A
A1(715)-1, C46(421)-2, C136(22)-1

Orlik (USAAF **XTG-7**) Training
sailplane -B
A1(721)-1, C46(428)-2, D20(1/67-332)-0,
B10(170)-0, C136(24)-1
SG-3 High wing training sailplane -B
A1(713)-1, C46(412)-2
Sroka High wing training sailplane -B
A1(717)-1, C46(425)-2
Wrona High wing training glider -A
A1(710)-1, C46(419)-2, C75(89)-1

W.W.S. *Wojskowe Warsztaty Szybowcowe*
W.W.S.1 Salamandra High wing
training glider -A
A1(725)-1, C46(392)-2, C83(500)-1
W.W.S.2 Zaba High wing training
glider -A
A1(727)-1, C46(394)-2, C83(500)-1
W.W.S.3 Delfin High wing training
sailplane -B
A1(728)-1, C46(395)-2, C136(22)-1

ROMANIA

I.A.R. *Regia Autonoma Industria Aeronautica Romana*
I.A.R.14 Fighter trainer -B
D6(12/73-299)-3, D9(1/83-44)-2,
C74(328)-6, B152(230c)-0
I.A.R.15 Fighter -C
D6(12/73-299)-2, D9(1/83-44)-2,
C74(328)-2, B152(230c)-1, B397(586)-1,
B22(A-281)-1
I.A.R.16 Fighter -E
D9(1/83-44)-2, D6(12/73-299)-1,
C110(283)-1, B22(A-281)-1
I.A.R.22 Trainer -B
B22(A-282)-1, D3(4-206)-1
I.A.R.23 Liaison -K
B152(231c)-1, B22(A-282)-1, B16(275)-7,
D3(4-219)-1

I.A.R.24 Liaison -K
B152(231c)-1, B22(A-283)-1,
B397(588)-1, D3(4-219)-1
I.A.R.27 Trainer -B
D10(8/83-300)-1
I.A.R.36 (Messerschmitt M36) High
wing transport -B
B196(74)-2, B391(510)-1, B377(34)-1,
B15(291)-7, B307(15)-1, C77(534)-1,
C81(66)-1, A15(185)-0
I.A.R.37 Biplane reconnaissance
bomber -B
B153(208c)-1, C74(328)-2, C10(249)-1,
D3(4-219)-1, A10(291)-0,
D20(11/69-79)-0, A15(185)-0
I.A.R.38 Biplane reconnaissance -B
A10(291)-0, D20(11/69-79)-0,

B114(13-1416)-0, A15(185)-0

I.A.R.39 Biplane army cooperation -A
D20(11/69-79)-2, A10(291)-1,
D10(8/83-301)-1, D6(6/71-34)-1,
B411(173)-1, B22(A-283)-1, A15(185)-6

I.A.R.80 Fighter -A
D9(7/76-32,1/83-44)-2, A3(3-123)-2,
B164(38)-2, B432(1-18)-2, B18(1-284)-7,
A10(291)-1, B153(208c)-1, B167(70)-1,
C10(249)-2

I.A.R. 81 Fighter, dive bomber -A
D9(7/76-32)-1, D25(11/62-16)-2,
B432(2-17)-2, D10(8/83-301)-1,
A10(291)-1, A15(185)-6, A3(3-124)-0,
D9(1/83-45)-0

**JRS-79B (Savoia-Marchetti
SM.79JR)** Twin engine bomber -B
D9(8/84-78)-1, B71(89-4)-1,
B134(1-20)-1, D10(8/83-300)-1,
C20(4-53)-1, A13(265)-6, A6(137)-6,
B280(237)-6

P.Z.L. P.11 High wing fighter -B
D7(28-43)-1, A1(163)-1, B71(75-7)-1,
A3(3-114)-1

P.Z.L. P.24 High wing fighter -B
D7(28-44)-1, B71(170-7)-1, A1(208)-0,
A3(3-118)-0

S.E.T. *Societatea Pentru Exploatari
Tehnice*

Fleet Model 10-G Biplane trainer -B
D6(4/72-219)-1, D10(7/83-262)-1,
B218(6-85)-1, B430(150)-1

S.E.T.7K Biplane observation -B
D10(8/83-300)-1, C74(335)-2,
B153(209c)-1, A15(186)-6, D3(6-99)-1,
B279(271)-0, B114(21-2308)-0

S.E.T.10 Biplane trainer -B
B153(210c)-1, D3(6-99)-1, B22(A-284)-0

S.E.T.X Biplane trainer -B
B397(590)-1, D3(6-99)-1, B279(271)-0

S.E.T.XV Biplane fighter -B
B153(209c)-1, A10(290)-1, B397(592)-1,
D3(6-99)-1, B411(173)-0, B279(271)-0

SOVIET UNION

ANTONOV *Oleg Konstantinovich
Antonov*

A-7 (RF-8) High wing transport
glider -A
A5(39)-2, B286(161)-2, D6(5/72-252)-1,
D3(7-80)-2, C74(351)-2, A7(169)-1,
C88(258,P)-1, C86(307,P)-1, C10(194)-1,
A15(213)-0

A-9 (RF-9) High wing training
sailplane -M
C74(351)-2, C116(183)-2, B6(518)-1,
A5(40)-0

KT (A-40) Biplane tank carrier glider -E
D6(7/72-48,3/72-129)-2, A5(40)-3,
B286(170)-6, C88(258,P)-1

N2 (OKA-38) Ambulance version ShS -C
B6(532)-6, A5(41)-0, C86(225)-0

ShS (OKA-38, version Fieseler Fi 156)
High wing liaison -C
B6(532)-1, C86(225,P)-1, A5(41)-0

U-s4 (A-1) High wing training glider -B
A5(39)-0, B6(517)-0

U-s6 (A-2) High wing training glider -B
A5(39)-0, B6(517)-0

ARKANGELSKII *Aleksandr
Aleksandrovich Arkangelskii*

Ar-2 (SB-RK) Twin engine dive bomber
version Tupolev SB-2 -B
A5(54)-2, A10(564)-1, B309(109)-1,

B129(2-6)-1, D25(6/58-53)-3,
B88(3-61)-2, D3(4-214)-2, C98(74)-1,
D29(12/82-31)-1, A15(218)-0
MMN Twin engine bomber -E
A5(55)-6
SBB Twin engine bomber -E
A5(55)-3

BAKSHAYEV *Grigorii Ivanovich*
Bakshayev (NIAI)
RK (LIG-7) Variable wing aspect ratio -F
D9(3/75-137)-2, A5(211)-3, C86(71,P)-1
RK-1 (RK-800) Tandem wing fighter -G
D9(3/75-137)-3, A5(212)-3, C86(72,P)-1,
C87(96,P)-1

BARTINI *Roberto L Bartini*
R-114 Rocket-propelled interceptor -J
A5(57)-0
STAL-7 Twin engine transport -E
D6(10/72-182)-2, C86(296,P)-1, A5(56)-3

BEDUNKOVICH *Anatolii Georgievich*
Bedunkovich (NIAI)
SKh-1 (LIG-10) Biplane agricultural,
ambulance -E
A5(214)-6, C86(336,P)-1

BELYAYEV *Viktor Nikolayevich*
Belyayev
DB-LK Twin engine twin fuselage
bomber -E
C87(61,P)-2, C86(167,P)-1, A5(57)-3
EI Twin boom pusher fighter -J
A5(58)-0

BEREZNYAK-ISAEV *Aleksandr*
Yakovlyevich Bereznyak, Aleksei
Mikhailovich Isaev
See Bolkhovitinov

BERIEV *Georgii Mikhailovich Beriev*
Be-2 (KOR-1) Biplane scout
floatplane -A
A5(61)-2, D20(6/67-681)-2, C74(359)-2,

C116(176)-2, A10(565)-1, B309(125)-1,
A3(6-155)-7, C121(3-76)-1, B18(2-223)-7,
A15(213)-0
Be-4 (KOR-2) High wing scout flying
boat -B
A5(63)-2, B6(54)-2, D20(6/67-682)-2,
B309(128)-1, C10(196)-2, C88(236,P)-1,
C86(355,P)-1, A15(213)-0
Be-6 (LL-143) Twin engine high wing
patrol flying boat -H
A5(64)-2, B6(56)-2, D20(6/67-682)-2,
C74(360)-2, C116(174)-2, A10(566)-1,
C86(352,P)-1, B17(210)-7,
B114(17-1815)-1, B142(90)-2
Be-8 High wing utility amphibian -H
A5(63)-2, D20(6/67-682)-2, B6(58)-1,
C86(353,P)-1, B142(94)-2, C110(468)-1
MBR-2 (MP-1, BU) High wing pusher
reconnaissance flying boat -A
A5(59)-2, D20(5/67-563)-2, A3(5-138)-2,
B88(3-63)-2, A6(174)-2, A10(565)-1,
C74(359)-2, B391(558)-1, A7(176)-1,
A15(213)-6, B18(2-216)-7
MBR-7 (MS-8) High wing pusher
reconnaissance flying boat -E
A5(62)-3, D20(5/67-564)-3, C86(351,P)-1
MDR-5 (MS-5) Twin engine high wing
patrol flying boat -E
A5(62)-2, D20(5/67-564,6/67-682)-2,
B309(128)-1, C86(349,P)-1

BISNOVAT *Matus Ruvinovich Bisnovat*
SK-1 High speed -F
D9(8/84-101)-2, A5(70)-6
SK-2 High speed -F
D9(8/84-101)-6, A5(70)-3

BOLKHOVITINOV *Prof. Viktor*
Fedorovich Bolkhovitinov
BI (Bereznyak-Isaev) Rocket-propelled
interceptor -E
B145(1-3)-4, D6(12/73-282)-4, B6(535)-2,
A3(3-125)-2, A5(58)-3, C116(77)-2,
C74(361)-2, C123(50)-2, C86(98,P)-1,
B160(110)-6, C141(48)-1

DB-A (DB-2A) Four engine bomber -B
A5(72)-2, D20(11/67-1004)-2,
B436(172)-2, C116(78)-2, C74(361)-2,
D9(9/75-153)-1, C86(166,P)-1,
C87(61,P)-1
I Tandem engine fighter -J
A5(74)-0
S Tandem engine attack bomber -E
D20(6/68-357)-1, B6(534)-1, A5(73)-3,
C86(222,P)-1, C87(25,P)-1

BOROVKOV-FLOROV *Aleksei*
Andreyevich Borovkov, Ilya Florentyevich
Florov
D High wing tandem piston/ramjet
engine fighter -J
A5(75)-0
I-207 Biplane fighter -C
A5(74)-2, D20(6/68-208)-2, C86(36,P)-1,
C141(40)-1

BRATUHKIN *Ivan Pavlovich*
Bratuhkin
2 MG Omega Twin engine twin rotor
helicopter -F
D20(2/65-17)-3, A5(75)-3, B6(68)-3,
B326(107)-3, C86(391,P)-1, B108(15)-3,
B23(17)-6
G-3 Omega (G-4) Twin engine twin
rotor helicopter -M
D20(2/65-16)-2, A5(76)-2, B6(71)-1,
B326(107)-1, B108(16,P)-2, B405(46)-1,
D3(7-50)-1, B228(428)-1, B309(158)-1,
B296(29)-6
Omega II (G-2) Twin engine twin rotor
helicopter -F
B447(54)-1, D20(2/65-18)-0, A5(76)-0,
B6(70)-0, B326(107)-0, B108(17)-0
TsAGI 11-EA PV Compound
helicopter -F
B326(143)-1, B309(86)-1, C86(383,P)-1,
C37(156)-6, A5(282)-0, B228(427)-0,
B108(12)-0

CHIZHEVSKII *Vladimir Antonovich*
Chizhevskii (BOK)
BOK-7 High altitude endurance version
Tupolev RD -F
A5(72)-0, C86(186)-0
BOK-11 (BOK-15) High altitude
reconnaissance version Tupolev RD -E
D10(4/66-133)-1, C86(187,P)-1,
A5(72)-0, C87(66,P)-1, B309(120)-0

CHYERANOVSKII *Boris Ivanovich*
Chyeranovskii
BiCH-21 (SG-1) Tailless racer -F
A5(79)-3, C86(268,P)-1

CHYETVERIKOV *Igor Vyacheslavovich*
Chyetverikov
ARK-3 Tandem engine high wing
reconnaissance flying boat -E
D20(8/67-803)-2, A5(81)-2, A3(5-143)-2,
B309(124)-1, C86(361,P)-1,
B153(213c)-1, B436(200)-1, B294(66)-6,
B18(2-217)-7, C10(199)-1
MDR-6 (Chye-2) Twin engine high
wing reconnaissance flying boat -B
D20(8/67-803)-2, A5(82)-2, B6(80)-2,
A3(5-141)-7, C74(428)-2, A7(185)-1,
A10(567)-1, B18(2-224)-7, B309(126)-1,
A15(213)-0, B142(97)-1

FLOROV *Ilya Florentyevich Florov*
No.4302 High wing rocket propelled
research -H
A5(85)-3

GORBUNOV *Vladimir Petrovich*
Gorbunov
105 (Samolet 105) Light weight version
LaGG-3 -E
D9(10/80-194)-3, A5(86)-3, B145(1-17)-0,
D9(1/81-41)-0

GRIBOVSKII *Vladimir Konstantinovich*
Gribovskii
G-22 Sport -K
A5(87)-3, D3(5-96)-6, C86(266)-6

G-27 Twin engine trainer -E
C86(252,P)-1, A5(88)-3, C38(125)-6
G-28 (TI-28) Racer, fighter trainer -E
A5(88)-3, C86(268)-0
G-29 (G-11) High wing transport
glider -B
A5(88)-3, D6(5/72-252)-0, B286(162)-0,
C88(257)-6
G-30 (G-11M) Powered version G-29 -E
A5(88)-6

*GRIGOROVICH Dmitri Pavlovich
Grigorovich*
IP-1 (DG-52) Fighter -D
D9(2/81-100)-2, A5(96)-2, A10(570)-1,
D20(6/66-626)-2, B309(95)-1,
C86(46,P)-1, C87(93,P)-1, B293(83)-6,
B114(19-2114)-0

GRUSHIN Pyetr Dmitriyevich Grushin
BB-MAI (BB-2) Tandem wing attack -E
A5(101)-0, C86(221)-0
Gr-1 (IS) Ground attack -G
A5(101)-0
Sh-tandem Tandem wing attack -E
C86(232,P)-1, C87(116,P)-1, A5(100)-3

*GST Gidro-Samolet Transportnyi
(Amtorg)*
GST (Consolidated PBY) Twin engine
high wing patrol flying boat -A
A5(38)-1, A7(201)-1, B309(128)-1,
C98(87)-1, C86(348,P)-1, B59(185c)-3

GUDKOV Mikhail Ivanovich Gudkov
Gu-1 Mid-engine fighter -E
A5(101)-0, B6(538)-0, D9(6/81-303)-0,
C86(80)-0
Gu-82 (LaGG-3/M-82) Radial engine
LaGG-3 conversion -E
D9(7/81-44)-2, A5(101)-3, B6(168)-0,
B145(1-16)-0, D9(1/81-41)-0
K-37 (LaGG-3K-37) Ground attack
version LaGG-3 -C
D9(1/81-30)-0, A5(101)-0, B145(1-16)-0,
B6(167)-0, C86(79)-0

ILYUSHIN Sergei Vladimirovich Ilyushin
DB-3 (TsKB-26, TsKB-30) Twin
engine bomber -A
A5(102)-2, D16(5/83-45)-4, A10(570)-2,
B88(3-62)-2, D25(4/63-43)-2, C70(61)-2,
A15(214)-6, B241(221,P)-2, C71(46)-2,
B6(86)-1, D9(2/86-81)-2
DB-4 (TsKB-56) Twin engine
bomber -E
A5(106)-3, C86(175,P)-1, C37(63)-6
DB-PT Torpedo floatplane version
DB-3 -E
B6(89)-1, C86(358,P)-1, C87(79,P)-1,
A5(103)-0, A15(214)-0, D9(2/86-85)-0
I-21 (TsKB-32) Fighter -E
A5(102)-3, D9(11/75-256)-3,
D9(2/83-99)-0, C86(63)-0
Il-1 Fighter version Il-2 -E
D9(2/83-99)-3, C86(91,P)-6, A5(110)-0,
B6(105)-0
Il-2 Shturmovik (TsKB-57, BSh-2)
Ground attack -A
D7(12-1)-4, B71(88)-2, A5(107)-2,
B6(94)-2, A6(175)-2, A10(571)-1,
D29(12/82-30)-2, B252(78)-2, A7(98)-1,
C116(87)-2, A15(213)-6, B309(112)-2
Il-4 (DB-3F) Twin engine bomber -A
D9(3/86-133)-4, A5(104)-2, B6(86)-2,
D25(4/63-43)-2, A6(178)-2,
B309(106,238)-2, A10(574)-1,
B252(79)-2, D16(5/83-48)-1, C71(72)-2,
A15(214)-6, A7(99)-1, B18(2-228)-7
Il-6 Twin engine bomber -E
A5(106)-3, B6(93)-0, C37(63)-6,
C86(166)-0
Il-8 Ground attack -E
D20(12/66-269)-2, D29(12/82-46)-2,
D7(13-26)-1, B309(143)-1, B6(99)-1,
A5(110)-3, C86(240,P)-1, A15(213)-0
Il-10 Shturmovik (Avia B-33) Ground
attack -A
D7(13-26)-4, A5(110)-2, B6(100)-1,
B139(59)-2, D29(12/82-44)-1,
A10(575)-1, B72(30)-2, B309(143)-1,
B371(99)-1, A15(214)-6, B18(2-251)-7

Il-12 Twin engine transport -H
B6(106)-2, B162(179)-2, B139(112)-2,
A5(111)-1, B391(536)-1, D3(8-189)-2,
C74(365)-2, B16(162)-7, B176(80)-1,
C116(45)-2

Il-16 Ground attack -E
D7(13-27)-1, C86(241,P)-1,
C88(221,P)-1, A5(111)-0, B6(104)-0

*KALININ Konstantin Alekseyevich
Kalinin*
K-5 High wing transport -A
B391(549)-1, C74(387)-2, B309(131)-1,
A5(128)-3, B16(157)-7, B162(49)-6,
B152(239c)-1, C86(284,P)-1, C116(57)-2,
A15(213)-0

KAMOV Nikolai Ilyich Kamov
A-7 (TsAGI-7) Observation autogiro -B
B326(146)-1, B108(7,P)-1, C74(444)-2,
D3(7-268)-1, C86(388,P)-1,
C87(123,P)-1, C38(309)-6, A5(283)-0,
A15(217)-0

AK Pusher observation autogiro -J
C86(389)-6, A5(131)-0, B326(149)-0,
B108(8)-0

*KOCHYERIGIN Sergei Aleksandrovich
Kochyerigin*
BSh-1 (PS-43, Vultee V-11) Attack,
liaison -B
C86(233,P)-1, A5(147)-0

DI-6 (TsKB-11, TsKB-38) Biplane
fighter, trainer -A
D9(7/75-50,11/83-242)-2, A5(144)-2,
A10(578)-1, C86(50,P)-1, C97(27)-2,
B309(104)-1, C141(14)-1, C98(37)-1,
A15(214)-0, D19(3/60-246)-1

OPB-41 (OPB) Dive-bomber -E
A5(146)-3, C88(186,P)-1, C86(184)-0

R-9 Reconnaissance bomber -E
D6(3/72-151)-6, A5(146)-0,
C86(217,P)-1, C87(119,P)-1

TsKB-27 (SR) Reconnaissance -E
A5(145)-2, D6(3/72-151)-1, C86(217,P)-1

*KOLYESNIKOV-TSYBIN Dmitri
Nikolayevich Kolyesnikov, Pavel
Vladimirovich Tsybin*
KTs-20 (KC-20) High wing transport
glider -C
D6(5/72-252,3/72-130)-1, B286(167)-3,
C88(258,P)-1, A5(147)-0

KOROLYEV Sergei Pavlovich Korolyev
RP-318 Rocket-propelled SK-9
sailplane -F
B98(101,248)-5, D6(12/73-283)-3,
B137(40)-1, B26(83)-1, C123(49)-6,
C86(97,P)-1, B131(P)-1, A5(148)-0

Type 212 Rocket-propelled flying
bomb -E
B98(100,253)-5, B163(24)-5, B137(84)-1,
B131(P)-1

*KRYLOV-RENTEL V. Ya. Krylov,
Vladimir Fedorovich Rentel*
MA-1 High wing transport amphibian -E
A5(150)-1, C86(364)-0

*KUZNETSOV Vyacheslav A. Kuznetsov
(with Mikhail Leontevich Mil)*
A-15 (TsAGI-15) Reconnaissance
autogiro -G
B108(9,P)-2, B326(148)-1, C86(390,P)-1,
A5(283)-0

LAVILLE Andre Laville
PS-89 (ZIG-1) Twin engine transport -B
A5(151)-3, B391,(559)-1, C74(419)-2,
C116(61)-2, C86(296,P)-1, D3(4-300)-1

*LAVOCHKIN Syemyen Alekseyevich
Lavochkin*
**LaGG-1 (Lavochkin, Gorbunov,
Gudkov I-22)** Fighter -B
D9(2/84-96)-3, A5(152)-0, B145(1-10)-0,
D13(1-13)-3, B6(163)-0

**LaGG-3 (Lavochkin, Gorbunov,
Gudkov I-301)** Fighter -A
D9(1/81-23)-4, B145(1-8)-4, A5(152)-2,

B6(163)-2, A3(3-127)-2, A10(578)-2,
B164(52)-2, A6(180)-2, B252(90)-2,
A15(214)-6, A7(109)-1, B18(2-236)-7
La-5 Fighter -A
B145(1-18)-4, B71(149)-2, A5(153)-2,
B6(168)-2, D7(2-113)-5, B148(152)-4,
A3(3-131)-2, A6(176)-4, B164(59)-4,
A10(580)-1, A15(214)-6, B18(2-242)-7
La-7 (La-120) Fighter -A
B145(1-36)-4, D9(11/76-241)-4,
A3(3-135)-2, A5(155)-2, B6(172)-1,
B71(149)-1, D1(1-22)-2, A10(580)-1,
A6(177)-1, A15(215)-6, A7(110)-1
La-9 (La-130) Fighter -H
A5(156)-2, D9(3/84-150)-2, A3(3-138)-2,
B6(175)-2, A10(581)-1, C74(395)-2,
B309(145)-1, C86(93,P)-1, C116(106)-2
La-11 (La-140) Fighter -H
D9(12/75-291,3/84-150)-2, A5(157)-2,
B164(144)-2, B6(178)-1, A10(582)-2,
C74(395)-2, B309(166)-1, A6(179)-7,
C86(93,P)-1, C141(156)-2
La-126 Fighter -E
D9(2/84-97)-1, A5(156)-1, B6(174)-1,
B142(49)-1, B145(1-41)-0
La-150 Single jet high wing fighter -H
B142(7,63)-2, A5(157)-2,
D20(4/68-220)-2, D9(3/84-150)-2,
B6(179)-1, B309(154)-1, C86(108,P)-1,
C98(134)-1, C37(134)-1

LISUNOV *Boris Pavlovich Lisunov*
Li-2 (PS-84, Douglas DC-3) Twin
engine transport -A
B121(254)-1, D9(8/79-88)-1, A5(165)-1,
C74(397)-2, A7(212)-1, B309(134)-1,
B129(2-35)-1, D29(6/84-11)-1,
A15(197)-6, B465(17)-1

MIKOYAN-GUREVICH *Artyem
Ivanovich Mikoyan, Mikhail Iosifovich
Gurevich*
DIS (MiG-5) Twin engine fighter -C
B145(1-55)-2, D9(10/77-184)-2,

D16(11/82-43)-2, C74(398)-2, A5(171)-1,
B6(202)-1, C86(73,P)-1, D6(9/71-219)-2
I-211 (MiG-5M, MiG-3/M-82, I-210)
Radial engine MiG-3 -C
B145(1-57)-2, A5(168)-2, C141(130)-2,
D9(10/77-185)-1, D7(18-14)-2,
C86(77-6), D16(11/82-44)-1,
B18(2-245)-1, A3(3-144)-7, B6(198)-0

I-220A (I-221[2A], MiG-11) High
altitude fighter -E
D7(18-17)-2, B145(1-59)-0, A5(169)-3,
D9(10/77-188)-1, B6(199)-1,
D16(11/82-44)-1, B114(17-1892)-0

I-224(4A) (I-222[3A], MiG-7) High
altitude fighter -E
D7(18-24)-2, B145(1-59)-2, A5(169)-2,
D9(1/75-47,10/77-189)-2,
D16(11/82-44)-2, A3(3-146)-7,
B18(2-250)-7, B6(199)-1, C86(90,P)-1
I-225(5A) High altitude fighter -E
D7(18-24)-2, A5(170)-2, D9(1/75-48)-1,
D16(11/82-46)-1, B6(199)-0, C141(48)-1,
B114(17-1892)-0, B145(1-59)-1
I-231(2D) (I-230(D), 'MiG-3D') High
altitude fighter -C
D7(18-15)-2, B145(1-61)-2, A5(171)-3,
D9(10/77-186,1/75-48)-2, C141(48)-1,
D16(11/82-44)-2, B6(199)-0
I-250(N) (MiG-13) Tandem piston/jet
engine fighter -M
B145(1-62)-2, D9(7/76-43)-2,
D16(11/82-46)-2, B6(203)-1, A5(172)-3,
C74(399)-2, A3(3-148)-7, B309(146)-1,
C86(104,P)-1, C98(116)-1, C141(132)-2
I-270(Zh) Rocket-propelled
interceptor -H
D20(2/68-43)-2, D9(1/80-41)-1,
B137(151)-2, B6(205)-1, A5(172)-3,
B309(153)-1, C86(101,P)-1, B142(16)-1
MiG-1 (I-61) Fighter -B
B145(1-43)-2, A3(3-140)-2, B6(193)-1,
B309(118,241)-2, A5(167)-0, A10(584)-2,
C116(115)-2, D16(11/82-41)-1,
B279(229)-1, A15(215)-6, B18(2-225)-7

MiG-3 (I-200) Fighter -A
B145(1-43)-4, D7(18-11)-4, A5(168)-2,
B6(194)-2, A3(3-142)-2, D6(10/71-252)-4,
B148(134)-4, A6(181)-2, B164(49)-4,
B252(112)-2, C74(398)-2, A10(583)-1,
D16(11/82-42)-1, A7(216)-1, A15(215)-6

MiG-8 (Tokaev Utka) High wing
canard pusher research -H
D9(11/77-257,12/83-290)-2, B231(57)-2,
C74(399)-2, B6(541)-1, D20(2/65-43)-2,
C37(130)-1, C86(374,P)-1, A5(172)-3

MiG-9 (I-300(F)) Twin jet fighter -H
A5(173)-2, B6(206)-2, D9(11/74-232)-2,
B142(59)-2, B164(142)-2, B138(60)-2,
A10(584)-1, B17(198)-7, C123(52)-2,
B159(151)-6, C141(134)-2

*MOSKALYEV Aleksandr Sergeyevich
Moskalyev*

SAM-5bis High wing ambulance -B
C86(291,P)-1, A5(204)-0

SAM-11bis High wing amphibian -E
C86(363,P)-1, A5(205)-0

SAM-12 Trainer -K
A5(206)-0

SAM-13 Tandem engine tractor/pusher
twin boom fighter -E
A5(206)-3, C86(62)-6, D20(6/68-356)-0,
C10(167)-0

SAM-14 High wing transport -E
A5(206)-0, C86(292)-0

SAM-16 Twin engine high wing
reconnaissance flying boat -J
A5(206)-0, C86(355)-0

SAM-23 High wing twin boom transport
glider -E
D6(3/72-130,5/72-252)-6, B286(168)-6,
A5(206)-0, C86(307)-0

SAM-24 Twin engine version SAM-23 -J
C86(292,308)-6, A5(206)-0, B6(539)-0

SAM-25 High wing transport -M
A5(206)-3, C86(292)-0

*MYASISHCHYEV Vladimir
Mikhailovich Myasishchyev*

DB-108 (VM-16,VM-17,VM-18) Twin
engine bomber, version Pe-2VI -E
A5(208)-0

DIS Twin engine fighter version Pe-2 -E
A5(208)-0

DVB-102 (M-2) Twin engine high wing
high altitude bomber -E
A5(207)-2, D20(5/66-581)-2, C74(409)-2,
B6(287)-1, B309(140)-1,
D10(4/66-135)-1, C86(189,P)-1,
C88(182,P)-1, C98(98)-1

DVB-202 Four engine bomber -J
A5(208)-0, C37(80)-6, C86(192)-0

MV Kombain Twin boom pusher
ground attack -J
A5(207)-0

SDB Twin engine bomber, version
Pe-2VI -J
A5(208)-0

VB-109 High altitude bomber version
Pe-2VI -E
B6(289)-1, A5(208)-0, C86(189,P)-1,
C88(183,P)-1

NIKITIN Vasilii Vasilyevich Nikitin

LSh (U-5/MG-31) Biplane liaison -E
A5(216)-0, C86(249)-0

U-5 (NV-5) Biplane trainer -C
C86(249,P)-1, A5(215)-0

UTI-5 (NV-2bis) Fighter trainer -E
D9(7/74-47)-1, A5(214)-3, C86(253,P)-1

UTI-6 (NV-6) Biplane fighter trainer -E
D9(7/74-47)-1, A5(216)-3, C86(254,P)-1

*NIKITIN-SHYEVCHYENKO Vasilii
Vasilyevich Nikitin, Vladimir Vasilyevich
Shyevchyenko*

IS-1 (I-220) Folding wing bi-monoplane
fighter -E
B145(1-64)-2, A5(216)-2, D7(2-186)-1,
A3(3-150)-2, C74(370)-2, C86(70,P)-1,
C10(167)-3

IS-2 (I-220bis) Folding wing bi-
monoplane fighter -E
B145(1-165)-2, A5(217)-2, D7(2-186)-1,
C86(71,P)-1, C141(43)-1, A3(3-150)-0
IS-4 Folding wing bi-monoplane
fighter -E
D7(2-168)-8, B145(1-66)-8, A5(217)-3,
C74(370)-6
IS-14 Folding wing bi-monoplane
fighter -J
D7(2-189)-6
IS-18 Folding wing bi-monoplane
fighter -J
D7(2-189)-6

***NYEMAN** Iosif Grigoryevich Nyeman
(Kharkov KhAI)*
KhAI-1 Light transport -B
C74(362)-7, B391(550)-1, B309(132)-1,
A5(139)-3, C116(44)-2, C86(217,P)-1,
D3(4-300)-1, A15(215)-0
R-10 (KhAI-5, Ivanov, PS-5)
Reconnaissance bomber, transport -A
A5(140)-2, D9(11/76-240)-2,
D25(2/62-43)-2, A10(590)-1,
B411(152)-1, B309(109)-1,
D29(12/82-31)-1, C87(119,P)-1,
A15(215)-0, B114(20-2173)-0

***PASHININ** Mikhail Mikhailovich
Pashinin*
I-21 (IP-21) Fighter -E
A5(220)-3

***PETLYAKOV** Vladimir Mikhailovich
Petlyakov*
Pe-2 Peshka (PB-100) Twin engine
bomber -A
D9(8/79-76)-4, B71(216)-2, A5(222)-2,
B6(295)-2, D20(12/64-50)-2, A6(182)-2,
A10(592)-2, B252(132)-2, C71(80)-2,
A15(215)-6, A7(143)-1, B18(2-234)-7
Pe-2VI (Pe-2I, Myasishchyev) High
altitude fighter version Pe-2 -E
B145(2-5)-2, A5(223)-2, D9(8/79-93)-2,

D20(3/67-453)-2, B6(301)-0,
D10(4/66-135)-1, C86(181,P)-1,
C88(102,P)-1, A15(216)-0, B142(28)-1
Pe-3 Fighter version Pe-2 -A
B145(2-3)-3, D9(8/79-81)-6, B60(160c)-1,
A5(223)-0, A15(216)-0, C141(116)-3
Pe-8 (ANT-42, TB-7) Four engine
bomber -B
D9(8/80-76)-4, A5(224)-2, B6(304)-2,
D20(4/64-57)-2, B18(2-230)-7, A6(184)-2,
A10(591)-1, B59(184c)-2, B158(25)-1,
A15(216)-6, A7(144)-1
VI-100 Sotka (Samolet 100) Twin
engine high altitude fighter -E
D9(8/79-76)-2, B145(2-3)-2, A5(224)-2,
B6(295)-1, B71(216)-1, C86(178,P)-1,
A15(216)-0, C141(116)-1

***POLIKARPOV** Nicolai Nicolayevich
Polikarpov*
BDP (S-1) High wing transport glider -C
D6(5/72-252)-1, B6(318)-1,
D20(8/68-456)-1, B286(162)-1,
A5(252)-6, C86(307,P)-1, C88(258,P)-1
I-5 (VT-11) Biplane fighter, trainer -D
D20(9/64-45)-2, A5(237)-2, A10(596)-1,
C74(414)-2, B411(105)-1, C141(106)-2,
B309(94,224)-2, B14(123,132)-7,
B293(46)-6, A15(216)-0
I-15 Chaika (TsKB-3) Biplane
fighter -B
D7(11-9)-2, A5(239)-2, A3(3-153)-2,
A10(597)-2, B88(2-81)-2, A6(184)-3,
B411(106)-1, C97(12)-2, B15(280)-7,
A15(216)-6, C141(108)-2
I-15bis Chato (I-152, TsKB-3ter)
Biplane fighter -A
D7(11-14)-4, A5(240)-2, A3(3-155)-2,
A10(600)-1, B309(98)-1, C141(110)-2
I-153 Chaika (I-15ter) Biplane
fighter -A
D7(11-22)-4, B145(2-7)-4, A5(241)-2,
A3(3-157)-2, B148(114)-4, A6(184)-1,
A10(600)-1, C116(86)-2, B411(109)-1,
A15(216)-6, C141(112)-2

I-16 Mosca (TsKB-12, UTI-4, Rata)
Fighter -A
B145(2-16)-4, B135(2-5)-2, B71(122)-2,
A5(243)-2, A3(3-161)-2, B148(74)-4,
A6(186)-4, A10(597)-2, C141(114)-2,
A15(216)-6, A7(228)-1, B18(2-220)-7

I-17 (TsKB-15,19,33) Fighter -E
A5(245)-2, D9(3/78-148)-2, A3(3-166)-2,
A10(599)-1, C74(417)-2, C97(42)-2,
B88(2-83)-2, C86(58,P)-1, B18(2-222)-7,
A15(216)-6

I-180 Fighter -C
B145(2-33)-2, A5(248)-2, D20(2/69-73)-2,
C86(58,P)-1, C79(26)-6, C141(42)-1

I-185 Fighter -C
B145(2-35)-2, B6(310)-2,
D20(8/68-455)-1, C74(418)-2, C79(29)-6,
C86(69,P)-1, C88(55,P)-1, C97(44)-2,
A15(216)-0, A5(249)-3, C141(43)-1

I-190 Biplane fighter -E
A5(250)-0, C86(36)-0, C79(30)-0

ITP(M) Fighter -E
B145(2-41)-2, B6(315)-1, D9(4/75-205)-2,
C97(44)-2, A5(251)-3, C86(81,P)-1,
C88(55,P)-1, B309(148)-1, C98(94)-1

Ivanov Reconnaissance bomber -E
A5(246)-2, D20(7/68-406)-2,
D29(12/82-33)-1, C86(218,P)-1

LNB Night bomber version Po-2 -A
C88(127,P)-1, C86(182,P)-1, A5(231)-1,
A6(189)-0

LSh (U-2VOM) Ground attack version
Po-2 -A
C88(222,P)-1, C86(242,P)-1, A5(231)-0

Malyutka Rocket-propelled
interceptor -J
D20(8/68-456)-1, B6(319)-1,
C86(99,P)-1, A5(253)-0, C123(165)-0

MP Twin engine version BDP -E
A5(253)-2, D20(8/68-456)-1,
C88(258,P)-1, B6(319)-0, B286(165)-0

NB(T) Twin engine high wing
bomber -E
A5(252)-2, D20(9/67-877)-2, B6(317)-1,

D20(8/68-455)-1, C86(182,P)-1.
D14(1-7)-3

Po-2 (U-2) Biplane general purpose -A
A5(229)-2, A10(602)-1, B309(77,221)-2,
C74(414)-2, B391(577)-1, A6(189)-3,
A7(229)-1, B269(94)-1, B289(28)-6,
A15(216)-6, B18(2-214)-7

R-5 Rasante (P-5) Biplane
reconnaissance bomber, transport -A
A5(234)-2, A10(595)-1, B309(74,220)-2,
C74(415)-2, B391(560)-1, B411(110)-1,
D29(12/82-31)-1, B15(276)-7,
C78(263)-2, A15(216)-0

R-Z Natacha (P-Z) Biplane
reconnaissance bomber, transport -B
D9(6/76-307)-2, A10(599)-1,
B411(110)-1, C78(265)-2, A5(237)-3,
B371(30)-1, C86(215,P)-1, C114(59)-1,
C74(415)-6, A15(216)-0

SPB(D) Twin engine dive bomber -E
B309(111)-1, C86(184,P)-1, A5(247)-3,
C98(55)-1

TIS Twin engine long range fighter -E
B145(2-38)-2, D20(8/68-455)-2,
B6(313)-1, C74(419)-2, A5(250)-3,
C86(73,P)-1, C88(101,P)-1, C116(127)-2

VIT (TsKB-44, TsKB-48) Twin engine
ground attack -E
D20(3/66-419)-2, C74(417)-2, A5(247)-1,
B309(111)-1, C86(233,P)-1,
D29(12/82-31)-2, D20(7/68-405)-1,
C87(117,P)-1, C116(128)-2

VP(K) High altitude interceptor -J
D9(4/75-206)-2, C86(90,P)-1, A5(251)-3

PUTILOV *Aleksandr Ivanovich Putilov*
(OOS)
STAL-2 High wing light transport -B
A5(218)-2, C74(420)-2, B391(564)-1,
B309(134)-1, C86(289,P)-1, C37(81)-1,
C116(63)-2
STAL-3 High wing light transport -B
C74(420)-2, B391(564)-1, B309(132)-1,
B153(215c)-1, A5(219)-3, C86(290,P)-1,
C116(64)-2

STAL-11 Light transport, reconnaissance -E
C86(295,P)-1, A5(219)-3

RAFAELYANTS Aram Nazarovich Rafaelyants
RAF-11 Twin engine transport -E
A5(254)-1, C86(300,P)-1, C37(82)-1, C38(115)-1

SAMSONOV Pyetr Dmitriyevich Samsonov
MDR-7 Twin engine high wing reconnaissance flying boat -E
A5(256)-0

SHAVROV Vadim Borisovich Shavrov
Sh-2 (S-2) Sesquiplane light transport amphibian -A
D9(4/82-205)-2, C116(179)-2, B391(562)-1, C70(55)-1, A5(257)-3, B309(127)-2, C86(364,P)-1, C121(2-90)-1, D3(9-89)-3, A15(217)-0
Sh-7 (S-7) High wing light transport amphibian -E
A5(258)-2, B391(563)-1, B309(127)-1, C86(364,P)-1, B22(A-296)-1

SHCHYERBAKOV Alexei Yakovlyevich Shchyerbakov
IVS Tandem mid-engine/ramjet fighter -J
A5(259)-0
Shchye-2 Shchuka (TS-1) Twin engine high wing transport -A
D20(7/69-65)-2, B6(539)-1, B72(44)-2, B401(47)-2, C74(422)-2, A5(259)-3, C10(29,193)-2, C86(306,P)-1, D3(9-89)-3, A15(217)-0

SUKHOI Pavel Osipovich Sukhoi
ShB (SB) Assault bomber version Su-2 -E
D20(2/66-374)-1, C86(221,P)-1, A5(262)-0, B6(324)-0

Su-1 (I-330) High altitude fighter -E
B145(2-43)-2, A5(262)-2, C141(44)-1, D20(2/66-373)-2, B6(330)-1, C86(68,P)-1
Su-2 (ANT-51, BB-1) Reconnaissance bomber -A
D20(4/65-43,2/66-373)-2, A5(261)-2, B6(322)-2, B18(2-226)-7, A6(189)-2, B252(148)-2, A10(608)-1, B371(72)-1, A15(217)-6
Su-3 (I-360) High altitude fighter -E
D20(2/66-373)-2, B145(2-43)-1, B6(332)-1, A5(262)-3, C86(77,P)-1
Su-4 Re-engined Su-2 -E
B6(324)-1, A5(262)-0, D20(2/66-375)-0, C86(221)-6, A15(217)-0
Su-5 (I-107) Tandem piston/jet engine fighter -E
D9(7/76-43)-4, B145(2-45)-4, A5(266)-2, D20(3/66-437)-2, B6(333)-1, C74(423)-2, B309(148)-1, C86(104,P)-5, C10(173)-1
Su-6 (OBSh, Samolet 81) Ground attack -E
D9(4/80-202)-2, D20(3/66-435)-2, A5(263)-2, D29(12/85-45)-2, C74(424)-2, B6(327)-1, A10(608)-1, C88(220,P)-1, A15(217)-0
Su-7 Rocket-boosted fighter -E
B145(2-47)-2, D20(3/66-436)-2, D9(4/80-203)-1, D16(11/82-48)-1, C74(424)-2, A5(265)-3, B131(P)-1, C86(91,P)-1, C98(127)-1
Su-8 (DDBSh) Twin engine ground attack -E
D20(3/66-437)-2, C74(425)-2, B6(334)-1, A5(264)-3, B309(147)-1, C86(242,P)-1, C88(222,P)-1, C116(137)-2
Su-9 Twin jet fighter -H
D18(4/66-490)-2, A5(266)-2, B142(61)-2, C74(425)-2, B6(336)-1, B309(154)-1, C86(109,P)-1, C116(138)-2, C98(135)-1

TIKHONRAVOV Prof. Mikhail Klavdiyevich Tikhonravov
I-302 Twin ramjet rocket-boosted interceptor -E

A5(281)-0, B6(541)-0, C86(99)-0,
C123(50)-0

TOMASHYEVICH *Dmitrii*
Lyudvigovich Tomashyevich
I-110 (Samolet 110, Type 110)
Fighter -E
B145(2-48)-2, B6(542)-1, A5(281)-3,
C86(82,P)-1, C88(55,P)-1
Pegas Twin engine ground attack -E
D20(8/69-69)-2, B6(544)-1, A5(281)-6,
C86(242,P)-1, C88(222,P)-1

TSYBIN *Pavel Vladimirovich Tsybin*
Ts-25 High wing transport glider -M
A5(284)-2, C86(308,P)-1, C74(445)-2,
B286(172)-1, B142(93)-1

TUPOLEV *Andrei Nicholayevich*
Tupolev
ANT-9 (PS-9) Three engine high wing
transport -B
B162(58)-2, C74(432)-2, A5(295)-1,
B391(531)-1, B15(277)-7, B309(81)-1,
D4(7/82-16)-1, B408(476)-1,
B152(237c)-1, A15(218)-0
ANT-14 Five engine high wing
transport -D
B162(69)-2, C74(432)-2, B309(82)-1,
D4(7/82-17)-1, C86(286,P)-1, A5(296)-3,
B15(274)-7, C116(67)-2
ANT-20bis (PS-124) Six engine
transport -C
D25(6/58-8)-2, C74(434)-2, A5(300)-2,
B391(534)-1, D4(7/82-76)-1,
B408(223)-1, B15(282)-7, B309(91)-1,
B269(49)-1, A15(218)-0
ANT-35 (PS-35) Twin engine
transport -B
A5(308)-2, B162(112)-2, C74(435)-2,
B391(535)-1, B16(159)-7, B153(214c)-1,
D3(4-207)-2, B309(131)-1, C86(297,P)-1,
A15(218)-0, C15(111)-1
ANT-37 (DB-2) Twin engine bomber -E
D16(5/83-45)-2, C74(436)-2,
C86(159,P)-1, C87(59,P)-1, A5(309)-3,

C37(86)-1, C116(148)-2, B309(93)-0
ANT-42
See Petlyakov Pe-8
ANT-44 (MTB-2, TsAGI-44) Four
engine high wing reconnaissance
amphibian -B
D20(11/68-71)-2, C74(437)-2, A5(312)-1,
B309(125)-1, B408(477)-1, D3(8-28)-1,
C86(351,P)-1, C87(76,P)-1, C98(67)-1,
A15(218)-0
ANT-51
See Sukhoi Su-2
Kr-6 (R-6, ANT-7, PS-7) Twin engine
reconnaissance fighter, transport, also
floatplane -D
C74(432)-2, A5(293)-1, A10(612)-1,
B411(120)-1, C86(52,P)-1, C116(145)-2,
C114(141)-1, A15(218)-0,
B114(20-2173)-0
MTB-1 (MDR-4, ANT-27) Three
engine high wing reconnaissance,
torpedo bomber flying boat -B
A10(616)-1, A5(305)-3, C86(347,P)-1,
C87(76,P)-1, B309(122)-0
PS-40, PS-41 Transport versions
SB-2 -B
C86(294,P)-1, D3(7-92)-1, A5(310)-6,
D25(6/58-53)-6, A15(218)-0
RD (ANT-25) Long range endurance,
bomber -D
A5(303)-2, C74(434)-2, A10(616)-1,
B309(92)-1, B411(185)-1, B222(82)-1,
B15(284)-7, C87(58,P)-1, C86(156,P)-1,
C116(147)-2
SB-2 Katiuska (ANT-40) Twin engine
bomber -A
A5(309)-2, D16(5/83-48)-4, D7(27-9)-5,
D20(3/67-448)-1, A6(190)-2,
B309(107,230)-2, D25(6/58-53)-2,
B252(152)-2, B241(245,P)-2, A10(617)-1,
A7(158)-1, C71(3)-2, A15(218)-6,
B18(2-218)-7
SB-3 (USB) Trainer, glider tug version
SB-2bis -A
A5(310)-6

127

TB-1 (G-1, ANT-4) Twin engine bomber -D
A5(287)-2, C74(430)-2, B309(69,216)-2, A10(611)-1, B411(121)-1, C86(142,P)-1, B279(293)-1, C116(142)-2, A15(218)-0

TB-3 (G-2, ANT-6) Four engine bomber, transport -A
A5(290)-2, D25(6/62-43)-2, A10(613)-1, B88(2-86)-2, B158(20)-1, B129(2-34)-1, A6(191)-3, A7(237)-1, B18(2-215)-7, A15(218)-6

Tu-1 (ANT-63P) Long range fighter version Tu-2 -H
D7(4-182)-1, A5(120)-1, C86(94,P)-1, B6(355)-0, A15(218)-0

Tu-2 (ANT-58,59,60,61,62,63) Twin engine bomber -A
D7(4-173)-4, A5(313)-2, B6(351)-2, D20(3/68-157)-2, B252(153)-2, A6(191)-2, A10(618)-1, B309(144)-2, A7(237)-1, A15(218)-6, B18(2-248)-7

Tu-4 (Boeing B-29) Four engine bomber -H
A5(323)-1, B6(357)-1, D6(7/71-104)-1, C74(438)-2, A10(620)-1, B142(29)-1

Tu-6 (Tu-2R, ANT-64) Reconnaissance version Tu-2 -B
D7(4-178)-1, A5(320)-1, B6(354)-1, C86(177)-0, B142(23)-1

Tu-8 (ANT-69) Twin engine bomber -H
A5(322)-2, C86(177)-0, D7(4-184)-2

Tu-10 (ANT-68) Twin engine bomber -M
A5(319)-1, C86(177)-0, D7(4-184)-1

Tu-70 Transport version Tu-4 -H
D6(8/71-160)-1, A5(324)-1, B6(359)-1, B309(193)-1, B298(89)-1, D3(9-5)-2, C86(310,P)-1, B401(52)-1, B142(38)-1, C98(136)-1

UTB-2 (Tu-2U, Sukhoi) Trainer version Tu-2 -H
A5(319)-2, C74(426)-2, D7(4-174)-1, B6(356)-1, C86(252,P)-1

TYROV *Vsyevolod Konstantinovich Tyrov*
OKO-1 Transport -E
D20(12/69-75)-2, A5(352)-3, B16(160)-7, C86(295,P)-1, C37(82)-1

Ta-1 (OKO-6) Twin engine fighter -E
A5(352)-3

VAKHMISTROV *Vladimir Sergeyevich Vakhmistrov*
Zvyeno-7 Tupolev TB-3 carrier plus two Polikarpov I-16SPB fighter bombers -B
D7(19-5)-1, A5(354)-1, B145(2-22)-1, B309(189)-1, B269(55)-1, C86(56,P)-1, C97(2)-1, C141(27)-1

YAKOVLEV *Aleksandr Sergeyevich Yakovlev*
UT-1 (AIR-14) Trainer, ground attack, also floatplane -A
A5(359)-2, D9(8/84-101)-2, C74(373)-2, B309(131)-1, C116(168)-2, C86(251,P)-1, C113(1-156)-1, A15(218)-0, C98(45)-1

UT-2 (Ya-20) Trainer, ground attack -A
A5(362)-2, A6(193)-2, B309(131)-1, C74(374)-2, B139(42)-2, B59(187c)-1, B72(58)-2, C86(250,P)-1, C98(44)-1, A15(219)-0

UT-2MV Trainer -E
B6(449)-1, D3(6-120)-1, C86(250,P)-1, A5(362)-0

Ya-17 (UT-3, AIR-17) Twin engine trainer -C
C86(251)-6, A5(361)-0

Ya-19 (AIR-19) Twin engine transport -E
A5(361)-1, C86(299,P)-1

Ya-21 Racer, liaison -F
A5(363)-6

Yak-1 (I-26, Ya-26) Fighter -A
B145(2-50)-4, D9(6/75-297)-4, A5(364)-2, B6(421)-1, A3(3-168)-2, B164(54)-4, A6(192)-2, A10(624)-1, B135(2-93)-1, A15(219)-6, A7(243)-1, B18(2-239)-7

Yak-2 (BB-22, Ya-22) Twin engine
bomber -B
A5(363)-2, B6(418)-1, C86(222,P)-1,
C74(375)-1

Yak-3 (I-30) Fighter -A
B145(2-59)-4, A5(370)-2, B6(430)-2,
B135(2-97)-2, A3(3-175)-2, A6(194)-4,
B148(166)-4, A10(625)-1, A7(243)-1,
A15(219)-6, B18(2-249)-7, C141(164)-2

Yak-4 Twin engine attack bomber -A
B6(418)-2, D9(12/74-304)-2, A5(364)-3,
C74(375)-3, A10(626)-1, A15(219)-0,
D29(12/82-33)-2, B129(2-7)-1,
B58(145c)-2, B18(2-238)-7

Yak-5 Trainer -E
B6(445)-1, C86(255,P)-1, A5(373)-0

Yak-6 (NBB) Twin engine light
transport, bomber -A
A5(373)-2, B6(437)-1, C74(376)-2,
D3(7-63)-2, C86(306,P)-1, C116(94)-2,
A15(219)-0, B114(24-2606)-0

Yak-7 (UTI-26) Fighter, trainer -A
B145(2-67)-2, A5(367)-2, B6(424)-1,
D9(6/75-299)-1, A3(3-168)-1,
C74(375)-2, A10(627)-1, B135(2-95)-1,
C86(80,P)-1, A15(219)-0, C141(160)-2

Yak-8 Twin engine light transport -E
B6(438)-1, D3(8-28)-1, C86(311,P)-1,
A5(374)-0, A15(219)-0, B142(45)-1

Yak-9 Fighter -A
B145(2-70)-4, A5(368)-2, B6(426)-2,
B71(185)-2, A3(3-170)-2, A10(627)-2,
B148(160)-4, A6(196)-2, B135(2-93)-1,
A15(219)-6, A7(163)-1, B18(2-246)-7

Yak-10 (Yak-14) High wing liaison -M
A5(374)-1, B6(441)-1, B139(22)-2,
D3(8-28,9-89)-2, C10(195)-1, B142(44)-1,
C86(340,P)-1, B114(24-2607)-0

Yak-11 (Yak-3UTI) Trainer -H
B6(446)-2, C74(377)-2, A5(374)-1,

B139(70)-2, B72(60)-2, C86(258,P)-1,
C116(162)-2

Yak-13 (Yak-12) Liaison -E
B6(445)-1, D3(8-103)-1, C86(340,P)-1,
A5(376)-0, B142(45)-1

Yak-15 Single jet fighter -H
D9(11/74-233)-4, A5(377)-2, B142(62)-2,
B164(145)-2, B6(465)-1, B138(57)-2,
A10(629)-1, C123(54)-2, C116(97)-2,
B17(197)-7

Yak-16 Twin engine transport,
trainer -H
B6(439)-1, B139(118)-2, C74(379)-2,
B72(46)-2, B309(195)-1, C86(311,P)-1,
B16(166)-7, B142(43)-1, A5(378)-0

Yak-18 Trainer -H
B6(449)-2, B139(70)-2, A5(379)-1,
C116(164)-2, B309(193)-1, B72(64)-2,
B351(304)-1, C98(132)-1,
B114(24-2607)-0

YATSYENKO *Vladimir Panfilovich
Yatsyenko*
I-28 Fighter -C
A5(405)-2, D9(10/75-204)-2, C141(41)-1,
A3(3-178)-7, C86(65,P)-1, C10(177)-0

YERMOLAYEV *Vladimir Grigoryevich
Yermolayev*
Yer-2 (DB-240) Twin engine bomber -A
A5(406)-2, D6(10/72-181)-2, B6(546)-2,
A10(632)-1, C74(386)-2, A6(196)-3,
B87(119)-6, C86(164,P)-1, B129(2-7)-1,
A15(219)-6

Yer-4 Modified Yer-2 -E
D6(10/72-198)-0, A5(407)-0,
C86(165,P)-1, D3(7-104)-3, A15(220)-0

SPAIN

ADARO *Julio Adaro*
1-E7 Chirta (1.E.7) Sesquiplane
trainer-K
C112(1-73)-2, C78(328)-6

A.I.S.A. *Aeronautica Industrial S.A.
(INTA)*
Gil-Pazo GP-1 (GP-2) Liaison -D
C112(1-90)-2, C78(298)-1, C134(94)-1
HM-1 Trainer -M
B139(31)-2, D20(8/69-69)-1,
D3(9-128)-1, B401(60)-1, C10(253)-1,
B59(188c)-0, C134(183)-1
HM-2 Trainer -M
D3(9-128)-1, B139(71)-1, C10(253)-1,
C134(183)-1
HM-5 Trainer -M
B59(188c)-1, D3(9-128)-1, D3(5-168)-6
HM-7 Tourer -H
B139(71)-1, D3(9-128)-1
HM-9 Glider tug -H
B59(188c)-1, D3(9-128)-1, C134(183)-1
IP-2 (Dewoitine) Training glider -H
C26(291)-2, D3(9-128)-6

C.A.S.A. *Consejo de Construcciones
Aeronauticas S.A.*
Breguet XIX Biplane bomber -D
C78(247)-2, C112(1-80)-2, D7(7-168)-1,
D6(4/73-163)-1, A10(75)-1
C.A.S.A. III High wing trainer -K
C112(1-77)-2, C78(331)-1
C-1145-L (Gotha Go145) Biplane
trainer -B
B139(154)-1, C134(181)-0, B381(215)-0
C-2111 (Heinkel He 111) Twin engine
bomber -M
B406(14)-2, D25(6/59-24)-1, A10(292)-1,
B306(243)-1, B139(120)-1, B417(84)-1
C-352 (Junkers Ju 52/3m) Three engine
transport -M

B139(129)-2, D6(4/73-164)-1,
B418(69)-1, B71(177-13)-1, C134(187)-1
Dornier 'Wal' Tandem engine high
wing flying boat -D
C78(356)-1, C112(1-84)-2, C134(91)-1,
D6(4/73-163)-1, C48(93)-1, C28(34)-1
1.131 (Bücker Bü 131) Biplane
trainer -A
B71(222-269)-1, C134(181)-1
Vickers Vildebeeste Biplane bomber,
also floatplane -D
C78(252)-2, C112(1-87)-2, B11(278)-1,
A10(438)-1, C134(92)-1

HISPANO-SUIZA *La Hispano
Aviacion, Fabrica de Aviones*
**HA-132-L Chirri (HS-132L, Fiat
CR.32 quater)** Biplane fighter -B
D7(22-76)-1, C134(180)-1, B71(22-7)-0,
A15(155)-0
HA-1109 (Messerschmitt Bf 109G)
Fighter -M
B133(123)-1, B187(110)-1,
D20(7/68-412)-1, B377(134)-1,
B139(134)-1, B307(112)-1, A10(293)-0
Hispano-Nieuport 52 (59) Sesquiplane
fighter -D
C78(217)-2, C112(1-100)-2, C74(349)-2,
A10(117)-1, B411(102)-1
HS-30 (E-30) High wing reconnaissance
bomber -D
C112(1-94)-2, C78(344)-1, C134(93)-1
HS-34 Biplane trainer -D
C112(1-97)-2, B165(326)-2, C78(345)-1,
C134(93)-1
HS-42 Trainer -M
B139(35)-2, B57(137c)-1, B59(188c)-1,
B279(192)-1, C10(253)-1, C134(182)-1
HS-50 (Dewoitine D.600) Fighter -J
C27(206)-2, D20(6/67-679)-1,
C26(189)-1, C10(253)-1, C134(177)-1

SWEDEN

ASJA Svenska Jarnvagsverkstaderna AB
B 5 (Douglas/Northrop 8A) Attack bomber -B
B121(217)-1, A10(546)-1, A14(166)-1, C74(336)-2, B153(216c)-1, C89(198,232)-1, B382(145)-1, B289(61)-6, A15(206)-0

J 6 Jaktfalken II Biplane fighter -B
D6(5/72-254)-2, A10(302)-1, B15(288)-7, C70(78)-1, C89(206)-1, C122(26)-1, B293(42)-6, B297(33)-1, A15(186)-0, B114(14-1487)-0, B458(28)-2

Ö 9 (Typ 2) Biplane trainer, also floatplane -D
B219(30)-2

Sk 10 Tigerschwalbe (Raab-Katzenstein R.K.26) Biplane trainer -B
B219(72)-2, C89(182)-6, D10(7/66-253)-1, B192(102)-1

Sk 12 (Focke-Wulf Fw 44) Biplane trainer -B
B219(80)-2, B152(241c)-1, D3(8-30)-1, C89(183)-6, D7(11-49)-1, B139(154)-1

Sk 14 (North American NA-16-M) Trainer -A
B219(84)-2, B394(31)-1, B153(216c)-1, C89(183)-1, D9(5/83-232)-1, D19(2/79-102)-1, C128(11)-1

FFVS Flygforvaltningens Verkstad
J 22 (S 22) Fighter -A
D20(11/64-48)-2, B164(64)-2, D9(9/81-149)-2, B18(1-280)-7, A10(294)-2, C89(240)-2, B59(190c)-2, B297(108)-1, A15(186)-6, B458(72)-2

FLYGINDUSTRI AB Flygindustri
Fi 1 High wing training sailplane -K
D3(7-30)-3, D3(6-266)-1, D3(5-48)-6
Fi 3 High wing transport glider -C
D3(9-19)-2, D6(5/72-253)-1, B286(193)-1, C10(259)-1

GOTAVERKIN
GV-38 (Rearwin Sportster) High wing tourer -L
D6(9/72-154)-1, B139(27)-1, D3(7-211)-1, D3(6-266)-1, B279(177)-0

SAAB Svenska Aeroplan AB
B 17 (ASJA L10) Reconnaissance bomber, also floatplane **S 17** -A
D20(11/67-997)-1, A10(295)-2, B139(67)-2, C70(92)-2, C89(236)-1, B59(193c)-1, C10(31,256)-2, B297(98)-1, C31(23)-1, A15(186)-6

B 18 Twin engine bomber, reconnaissance **S 18** -B
D20(12/64-52)-2, D3(6-77)-2, C132-2, A10(296)-1, C89(238)-5, B139(128)-1, B59(192c)-1, B18(1-281)-7, C10(257)-2, B297(98)-1, A15(186)-6

T 18B Ground attack version B 18, also torpedo bomber -H
D20(12/64-53)-1, B401(42)-2, C132(74)-1, C89(190)-6, A10(296)-0, A15(187)-0

J 19 (ASJA L12) Fighter -J
D6(4/73-203)-6, D15(1-18)-3, D25(11/55-13)-6, C128(5)-6

J 21A Twin boom pusher fighter -M
D7(22-30)-4, B71(138)-2, D25(6/59-16)-2, A10(296)-2, B164(136)-2, C128-4, C89(242)-5, B17(278)-7, B292(92)-6, B59(192c)-1, D3(6-63)-2, B458(60)-2

J 23 Fighter -J
D13(1-9)-3

J 24 Twin engine fighter -J
D14(4-64)-3

Saab 90 Scandia Twin engine transport -H
B162(178)-2, B391(511)-1, D3(8-21)-2, B139(116)-2, C74(338)-2, D9(7/82-21)-1,

B16(248)-7, B176(108)-1, B60(167c)-3,
D24(1-79)-1
Saab 91 Safir (Sk 50) Trainer, tourer -H
B219(118)-2, D3(7-21)-2, B60(168c)-2,
C74(338)-2, B139(67)-1, C70(94)-2,
B351(290)-1, B401(46)-2

SPARMANN *Ing. E. Sparmann's*
Flygplanverkstad
E4 Fighter -J
C128(4)-1
S 1A (P1) Communications -B
B397(604)-1, C122(28)-1,
D10(7/66-253)-1, B192(103)-1,
C89(224)-6, D3(6-147)-1, B279(282)-0

SWITZERLAND

COMTE *Flugzeugbau Alfred Comte*
AC-1 High wing high altitude trainer -F
B421(148)-2, C26(473)-1
AC-4 Gentleman High wing trainer,
liaison -D
B421(178)-2, C74(343)-2, B391(514)-1,
C67(60)-1, D6(12/71-392)-1
AC-11 High wing survey -I
B421(250)-2, C67(77)-1
AC-12 Moskito High wing tourer -L
B139(25)-1, D3(7-204)-1

DEWOITINE *Eidg. Konstruktions-*
Werkstatte, Thun
D-9 High wing fighter trainer -B
B421(146)-2, D9(12/77-293)-2,
A10(86)-1, B411(40)-1, C26(28)-1
D-19 High wing fighter trainer -B
B421(130)-2, D9(1/78-32)-1, A10(86)-1,
C26(35)-1
D-26 High wing fighter trainer -B
B421(166,168)-2, C26(61)-1
D-27 High wing fighter -B
B421(162,172,182)-2, D9(1/78-32)-2,
D7(3-94)-2, B411(41)-1, A10(86)-1,
B14(117,127)-2, B293(58)-6, C26(51)-2,
B139(26)-1

DOFLUG *Dornier-Werke Abteilung*
Flugzeugbau
Do 212
See Germany: Dornier Do 212
D-3802 (Morane-Saulnier M.S.540)
Fighter -M

B421(278)-2, D9(4/78-200)-2,
D25(9/58-23)-2, A10(304)-1, B139(72)-1,
D3(9-162)-1, A15(97)-0, B114(7-683)-0
D-3803 Fighter -H
B421(284)-2, D20(4/69-72)-2,
D9(4/78-201)-1, D25(9/58-23)-2,
B139(72)-1, A15(97)-0, B114(7-683)-0

EFW *Eidg. Flugzeugwerke, Emmen*
C-3602 Reconnaissance, ground
support -E
B421(234)-2, D20(2/69-54)-1,
D3(5-131)-1, D15(1-19)-3, A15(187)-0
C-3603 Reconnaissance, ground
support -A
B421(240,248,270,276)-2,
D20(2/69-54)-1, A10(305)-1, C74(343)-1,
B59(195c)-1, A15(187)-6
C-3604 Reconnaissance, ground
support -M
B421(286)-2, B139(53)-2,
D20(2/69-54)-1, A10(305)-1,
B279(151)-1, D3(9-162)-1, C88(326,P)-1,
A15(187)-0, B60(171c)-1
D-3800 (Morane-Saulnier M.S.406)
Fighter -B
B421(222,230)-2, D6(10/73-184)-1,
A10(111)-1, B411(174)-1, B71(147-4)-1,
C114(102)-1, A15(97)-0, B114(7-683)-0
D-3801 (Morane-Saulnier M.S.506)
Fighter -A
B421(238)-2, D6(10/73-185)-1,
A10(304)-1, B139(72)-1, B61(49)-1,

B71(147-11)-6, A15(97)-6

EKW *Eidg. Konstruktions-Werkstatte, Thun*
C-35 Biplane reconnaissance, ground attack -B
B421(206,252)-2, D20(12/67-1068)-2, A10(304)-1, B279(151)-1, C74(345)-2, B14(126,135)-7, B293(53)-6, D3(5-124)-6, A15(187)-0

FARNER *Farner AG, Flugzeugbau*
WF.12 Mid-engine light plane -E
B279(160)-0

HÄFELI *Eidg. Konstruktions-Werkstatte, Thun*
DH-5 (MV) Biplane reconnaissance, trainer -B
B421(114,152,158,160)-2, A10(306)-1, C74(344)-2, B411(146)-1

PILATUS *Pilatus-Flugzeugwerke AG*
P2-01 Trainer, liaison -M
B421(268)-2, B139(65)-2, B60(172c)-1, D3(9-162)-1, B114(19-2060)-0
SB-2 Pelican High wing light transport -L
D3(6-9)-2, B60(172c)-1, B279(253)-0

TURKEY

KAYSERI *Kayseri Ucak Fabrikasi*
P.Z.L. P.24 High wing fighter -B
D7(28-47)-1, A1(206)-1, B71(170-6)-1, A3(3-118)-1

NURI DEMIRAG *Nuri Demirag Tayyare Fabrikasi*
Nu.D.36 Biplane trainer -B
B59(196c)-1, D3(5-208,231)-1, D3(6-24)-1, B279(242)-0
Nu.D.38 Twin engine high wing light transport -K
B56(129c)-1, D3(5-208,231)-1, B279(242)-0

T.H.K. *Türk Hava Kurumu Ucak Fabrikasi*
THK.1 Transport glider -E
D6(5/72-253)-6, B286(194)-7, D3(5-208,231)-1, D3(4-288)-1, A1(481)-0, B279(293)-0, D9(7/85-36)-6
THK.2 Trainer -B
B139(69)-2, B60(174c)-1, A1(481)-0, B279(293)-0, D9(7/85-36)-1
THK.3 Training sailplane -B
A1(481)-0, D9(7/85-36)-0
THK.4 Training glider -B
A1(481)-0, D9(7/85-36)-0
THK.5 Twin engine light transport -B
B139(128)-1, C10(261)-1, A1(481)-0, B279(293)-0, D9(7/85-36)-1

UNITED STATES OF AMERICA

AERO INDUSTRIES *Aero Industries Technical Institute Soaring Club*
TG-31 (G-2) High wing training sailplane -I
B22(A-135)-1, A8(584)-0, B10(170)-0, D20(1/67-332)-0

AERONAUTICAL PRODUCTS *Aeronautical Products, Inc.*
Model A-3 Helicopter -E
B272(45-211)-1, B302(444)-2, D3(5-168)-1, B228(206)-0, B59(198c)-0, B279(68)-0

AERONCA *The Aeronca Aircraft*
Corporation (Aeronautical Corporation of
America)
C-3 High wing light plane -L
B420(51)-4, B384(26)-1, B218(4-295)-1,
B139(23)-1, B102(92)-1,
D3(2-50,7-175)-1
Chief (Model 50-L, 65-L) High wing
tourer, club trainer -L
B218(8-13)-1, B272(41-189)-2,
B358(1-145)-1, B57(140c)-1
GB-1 High wing glide bomb -A
D25(4/63-31)-1, B163(118)-1,
C88(201,P)-1, B125(227)-1
GB-4 Glide bomb -B
D25(4/63-32)-1, B163(118)-0,
B125(227)-0, B114(10-1101)-0
GB-8 High wing glide bomb -B
D25(4/63-32)-1, C88(201,P)-1,
B190(60)-6, B163(118)-0,
B114(10-1101)-6
GT-1 High wing glide torpedo -E
C88(202,P)-1
L-3 Grasshopper (O-58) High wing
liaison, observation -A
A8(31)-2, B88(3-26)-2, B218(8-180)-1,
B59(198c)-1, A7(167)-1, B277(8)-2,
D29(2/83-48)-1, B104(96)-1,
B358(1-147)-1, B279(68)-1, B473(20)-1
Tandem (Model 65-T, Defender)
High wing trainer -A
B218(8-108)-1, B59(199c)-1,
B272(41-99,190)-2, B358(1-146)-1
TG-5 (XLNR-1, G-3) High wing
training glider -A
D16(9/81-9)-2, B88(4-24)-2, A8(32)-6,
B57(141c)-3, B58(157c)-1, B42(252)-1,
B111(63)-1, A15(187)-0

AGA *AGA Aviation Corp. (Autogiros,*
Gliders, and Airplanes)
XCG-9 (Model G-5) Twin boom
transport glider -J
B286(118)-6, A8(572)-0, B10(97)-0

XLRG-1 Twin boom, twin hull flying
boat transport glider, 40% scale model -F
B286(150)-1, A9(475)-0, B10(201)-0
XO-61
See Firestone XO-61

AIRCRAFT DEVELOPMENT
Aircraft Development Corp. (Metalclad
Airship Corp.)
ZMC-2 Training airship -D
A9(493)-1, B425(145)-1, B358(2-181)-1,
B317(48)-1, B354(350)-1, B426(222)-1,
D19(4/68-283)-1, C87(198,P)-1

AKRON-FUNK *Akron Aircraft Co.,*
Funk Aircraft Co.
UC-92 (B-75-L) High wing liaison -I
B218(8-60)-1, B56(173c)-1, B21(A-92)-1,
B358(1-151)-1, B279(171)-1, A8(571)-0,
B10(82)-0, B420(67)-1

ALLIED *Allied Aviation Corp.*
XLRA-1 'Invader' Amphibian
transport glider -E
B58(158c)-1, D6(6/72-318)-1,
B286(150)-0, A9(475)-1, B358(2-101)-1,
B22(A-135)-1, D3(4-288,7-273)-1

BARKLEY-GROW *Barkley-Grow*
Aircraft Corp.
T8P-1 Twin engine transport, also
floatplane -B
B218(7-216)-1, B153(220c)-1,
B468(87)-1, B155(5,40)-1, B139(126)-1,
B227(35)-1, B20(A-14)-1, D3(2-122)-1,
B279(92)-0

BEECHCRAFT *Beech Aircraft Corp.*
AT-7 Navigator (SNB-2, Model 18-S)
Twin engine trainer -A
B88(4-38)-2, B314(24,51)-2,
B218(8-43)-1, B59(202c)-1, A7(174)-1,
B111(40)-1, A8(36)-0, A9(42)-0,
A15(188)-0, B125(213)-1, B312(178)-1
AT-10 Wichita Twin engine trainer -A

B88(4-41)-2, B314(26,51)-2, B59(202c)-2,
A8(481)-1, A7(173)-1, B358(1-176)-2,
B288(18)-1, D3(4-63,6-15)-2, B111(41)-1,
B104(97)-1
AT-11 Kansan (SNB-1, Model 18-S)
Twin engine trainer -A
B58(162c)-2, A8(36)-1, A9(41)-1,
B314(27)-1, D16(3/85-44)-1,
B218(8-43)-1, B288(18)-1, B111(41)-1,
B104(94)-1, A15(188)-0
Biplane observation -J
D29(2/83-42)-1
**C-45 Expediter (UC-45, CQ-3, JRB,
F-2, Model 18-S,** Sweden **Tp 4)** Twin
engine transport, target control,
photographic -A
A8(36)-2, A9(41)-2, B88(6-47)-2,
B59(201c)-2, B218(8-43)-1, B288(18)-1,
D3(5-231)-2, B277(11)-1, B18(2-68)-7,
A15(187)-6, A7(174)-1
JRB-1 (Model 18-S) Twin engine
photographic, target control -B
A9(41)-1, B230(288)-1, B218(8-44)-1,
B58(161c)-1, B139(126)-1, B358(1-183)-1
Model M18R Twin engine bomber,
transport -B
D29(10/83-39)-1
UC-43 Traveller (GB, JB, Model 17)
Biplane liaison -A
A8(34)-2, B88(3-29)-2, B59(201c)-2,
B218(7-174)-1, A9(389)-1,
D29(10/79-47)-1, A7(174)-1, B18(2-67)-7,
B277(10)-1, A15(187)-6
UC-43A (Model D-17-R) Biplane
utility -I
B218(7-136)-1, D3(2-147)-2, A8(34)-0
UC-43B (Model D-17-S) Biplane
utility -I
B218(7-174)-1, A8(34)-0, C131(160)-1
UC-43C (Model F-17-D) Biplane
utility -I
B218(7-305)-1, A8(34)-0, B10(64)-0
UC-43D (Model E-17-B) Biplane
utility -I
B218(7-145)-1, A8(34)-0, B10(64)-0

UC-43E (Model C-17-R) Biplane
utility -I
B218(7-20)-1, A8(34)-0, B10(65)-0
UC-43F (Model D-17-A) Biplane
utility -I
B218(8-53)-1, A8(34)-0, C131(57)-1
UC-43G (Model C-17-B) Biplane
utility -I
B218(7-13)-1, A8(34)-0, B50(196)-1
UC-43H (Model B-17-R) Biplane
utility -I
B218(6-281)-1, A8(34)-0, B10(65)-0
UC-43J (Model C-17-L) Biplane
utility -I
B218(7-13)-1, A8(34)-0, B310(P)-2
UC-43K (Model D-17-W) Biplane
utility -I
B218(7-136)-0, A8(34)-0, B10(65)-0
XA-38 Grizzly Twin engine ground
attack -E
D16(11/78-10)-5, D4(10/68-6)-2,
B60(180c)-1, A14(191)-1, B352(10)-1,
D18(9/70-6,10/70-18)-2, B111(40)-1,
D14(3-50)-3, D17(1-22)-1, B312(203)-1

BELL *Bell Aircraft Corp.*
L-39 Swept wing research version
P-63 -H
B259(46)-1, B350(112)-1,
D25(5/59-11)-1, D19(3/63-186)-1,
D3(7-132)-1
Model 30 Helicopter -F
B53(73)-1, B59(208c)-1, B228(212)-1,
B151(145)-1, D19(1/84-74)-1,
B127(95)-1, B161(32)-6, B447(112)-1,
B23(20)-6, B358(2-135)-1
**P-39 Airacobra (A-7, TP-39, F2L,
TDL, P-400)** Mid-engine fighter -A
D9(1/82-31,2/82-78)-4, B146(1-3)-4,
B71(165)-2, A8(45)-2, A3(4-4)-2, B259-2,
A6(197)-2, A10(446)-2, B277(12)-2,
B215(95)-2, C23(198)-1, A15(188)-6
P-59 Airacomet Twin jet fighter,
trainer -B
D9(3/80-132)-4, B146(1-15)-4,

D19(3/66-155)-2, A3(4-19)-2,
B215(150)-2, A8(54)-2, A6(198)-2,
B164(119)-2, B59(204c)-2, A10(447)-1,
B277(14)-7, B310(P)-2, A14(296)-1

P-63 Kingcobra (RP-63) Mid-engine
fighter -A
B146(1-21)-2, B259(30)-2, A3(4-15)-2,
A8(51)-2, B277(17)-2, A6(198)-2,
A10(448)-1, B215(167)-2, A7(175)-1,
A15(188)-6, A14(297)-1, B18(2-100)-7

XFL-1 Airabonita Mid-engine carrier
fighter -E
B147(3)-2, D9(1/82-33)-2, A3(4-13)-2,
B216(164)-2, B259(48)-1, B350(76)-2,
D6(3/73-143)-2, A14(385)-1, B109(66)-1

XP-39E Mid-engine fighter -E
D19(1/82-55)-2, B259(30)-1,
D9(2/82-81)-1, B146(1-6)-1, A14(270)-1,
B118(1-6)-1

XP-52 Twin boom pusher fighter -J
B215(131)-3, A14(288)-0, B347(64)-0

XP-59 Twin boom pusher fighter -J
B215(150)-3, D9(3/80-132)-3, C88(53)-6,
A14(288)-0, B347(64)-0

XP-77 Fighter -E
D19(4/81-311)-2, B146(1-25)-2,
A3(4-22)-2, B215(196)-2, A14(301)-1,
B104(116)-1, D6(4/73-200)-2,
B59(207c)-1, B221(132)-1, B347(195)-3

XP-83 Twin jet fighter -E
D16(1/82-18)-2, B146(1-27)-2,
A3(4-24)-2, B215(211)-2, B138(55)-2,
D6(4/73-200)-2, A14(446)-1, B347(90)-1,
B111(59)-1, B312(195)-1, B60(183c)-1

XS-1 (X-1) Rocket-propelled supersonic
research -H
B169(32)-1, D7(5-68)-2, B310(P)-2,
B138(64)-2, B268(14)-2, B52(102)-1,
B395(93)-1, B405(24)-1, B168(106)-1,
B60(183c)-1

YFM-1 Airacuda Twin engine pusher
fighter -C
B273(106)-2, D25(7/63-53)-2,
D6(3/73-142)-2, B88(3-31)-2, A8(482)-1,

A14(248)-1, B347(46)-2, B221(63)-1,
B104(70)-1, B111(59)-1

YR-13 (HTL-1, Model 47) Training
helicopter -H
B326(158)-0, A9(45)-1, B228(213)-0,
A8(56)-0, D3(7-310,8-286)-1

BELLANCA *The Bellanca Aircraft Corp.*
C-27 (Model 66-70 Aircruiser)
Sesquiplane transport -B
A8(483)-1, B358(2-16)-2, B218(6-226)-1,
B152(250c)-1, B139(24)-1, B468(71)-1,
D19(3/58-184)-1, B385(71)-1,
B42(236)-1, B111(47)-1, A15(188)-0

CH-300 Pacemaker Sesquiplane
transport, also floatplane -B
B276(104)-1, B155(6,44)-1, B385(54)-1,
B218(2-85)-1, B139(24)-1, C131(126)-1,
D19(3/58-181)-1, B279(96)-1, B227(28)-1

**JE-1 (Model 31-42 Senior
Pacemaker)** Sesquiplane transport -B
A9(391)-1, B218(6-277)-1, B385(59)-1,
B230(241)-1, B154(159c)-1, B20(A-20)-1,
D19(3/58-184)-1, B10(198)-0

L-11 (Model 31-50 Senior Skyrocket)
Sesquiplane liaison -I
B218(6-233)-1, B385(59)-1, B468(46)-1,
D19(3/58-184)-1, B139(24)-1,
B276(106)-1, A8(576)-0, B10(130)-0

Model 14-9 Crusair Junior Tourer -L
B218(8-64)-1, B385(71)-1, B56(137c)-1,
B22(A-59)-1, B272(41-198)-3

Model 14-12 Crusair Tourer -L
B218(8-160)-1, B57(147c)-1,
B22(A-59)-1, B358(1-84)-0

Model 28-90 Flash (Model 28-110)
Reconnaissance bomber, fighter -B
D20(12/67-1068)-2, A10(448)-1,
D11(9/66-24)-1, D19(3/74-170)-1,
A14(169)-1, B16(17)-7, C112(2-25)-2,
B154(158c)-1, C78(287)-1, B471(48)-1

Model 77-140 Twin engine sesquiplane
bomber, also floatplane -K
A10(449)-1, B385(71)-1, B152(250c)-1,
A14(198)-1, D19(3/81-254)-1,

D9(10/84-182)-1, D25(4/63-45)-1,
B411(180)-0, B20(A-21)-1

Model T-14-14 Trainer -E
B57(148c)-1, B261(95)-0, B358(1-84)-0

XRE (Model CH-400 Skyrocket)
Sesquiplane utility -D
B229(77)-1, B218(4-70)-1, B385(58)-1,
D19(3/58-181)-1, B230(123)-1,
C131(141)-1, A9(391)-0, B218(5-228)-1,
B10(217)-0, B468(46)-1

YO-50 High wing STOL observation -E
D9(7/81-32)-1, B312(184)-1,
D29(2/83-41)-1, B22(A-60)-1,
B111(53)-1, D4(11/71-54)-1,
B272(41-182)-1, A8(578)-0

BENDIX *Bendix Helicopters Inc.*
Model K Coaxial rotor helicopter -F
B228(239)-1, B302(453)-1, C16(107)-1

BERLINER-JOYCE *Berliner-Joyce
Aircraft Corp.*
OJ-2 Biplane observation -D
A9(392)-1, B230(276)-1, B229(90)-1,
D19(2/74-143)-1, A14(327)-1,
B352(27)-1, B96(10)-1

BOEING *The Boeing Aircraft Co.*
AB-17 Reed Project improved armament
version B-17 -E
D16(1/84-10)-1, D26(116)-3,
B125(155)-1

B-17 Flying Fortress (F-9, PB-1) Four
engine bomber -A
B41-4, B37(244)-2, B134(1-24)-2,
B71(77,205)-2, B214(45)-2, A6(200)-4,
A8(74)-2, A10(454)-2, D9(12/74-279)-4,
B277(20)-2, B352(39)-4, B93-2,
B171(39)-1, B298(64)-1, B252(17)-2,
A7(32)-1, A15(189)-6, A14(209)-1

B-29 Superfortress (F-13, P2B) Four
engine bomber -A
B37(275)-2, B134(2-108)-2, B71(101)-2,
A8(84)-2, B158(86,135)-5, B324-4,

B237-4, A6(202)-2, A10(455)-1, B210-1,
B214(97)-2, B277(28)-2, B298(87)-1,
B252(20)-2, B171(47)-1, A7(34)-1,
A15(191)-6, B451-2, A14(398)-1

BQ-7 Aphrodite Flying bomb
conversion B-17 -B
B163(32)-1, B41(191)-1, B42(247)-1,
B37(267)-0, B125(101,162)-1,
A15(190)-0, D19(4/85-290)-1

C-73 (Model 247) Twin engine
transport -I
D7(9-43)-4, D19(4/64-239)-2,
B37(185)-2, B162(80)-4, A8(484)-1,
B155(6,47)-1, B277(34)-1, B15(252)-7,
B298(56)-1, A15(189)-0, B310(P)-2

C-75 (Model 307 Stratoliner) Four
engine transport -I
D7(10-58)-4, B37(204)-2, B162(129)-2,
A8(484)-1, B236(56)-2, A7(178)-1,
B58(167c)-2, B277(35)-1, B298(71)-1,
A15(189)-6, B468(96)-1

C-97 Stratofreighter Four engine
transport -M
B37(305)-2, A8(96)-2, B162(144)-2,
B88(6-36)-2, B298(94)-1, B59(211c)-2,
D3(6-28)-2, D7(18-38)-1, B171(51)-1,
B352(64)-1

C-98 (Model 314 Clipper) Four engine
high wing transport flying boat -I
B37(207)-2, B200(1-174)-2, B162(133)-2,
B59(213c)-2, A9(393)-1, B88(5-43)-2,
B277(33)-1, B298(74)-1, B431(167)-5,
A15(189)-6, B468(92)-1

C-108 (CB-17) Transport conversion
B-17 -B
B37(268)-1, B41(194)-1, A8(82)-1,
B60(193c)-1, D3(6-88)-2, B171(43)-1,
B236(60)-1, A15(189)-0

F4B Biplane carrier fighter, target
drone -D
B37(167)-2, A9(59)-2, B71(27)-2,
B230(191)-1, D6(3/74-133)-2,
B352(28)-2, A10(452)-1, B216(71)-2,
B298(39)-1, A15(188)-0, A14(142)-1,
B310(P)-2

Model 80A Three engine biplane transport -L
B37(123)-2, B162(48)-2, D7(22-64)-4, B218(3-23)-1, B271(112)-1, B298(37)-1, B15(234)-7, B171(24)-1, B291(13)-1, B78(23)-0, B461-2, B468(41)-1

Model 95 Biplane mail, light bomber -D
B37(129)-2, B298(48)-1, B218(2-22)-1, B171(26)-1, B78(26)-1

Model 100E (P-12E, Japan **AXB)** Biplane fighter trainer -C
D25(11/57-17)-1, B171(29)-1, B242(P)-1, C100(6-114)-1, B37(154)-0, A15(188)-0

Model 203 Biplane trainer -L
B37(133)-2, B218(3-37)-1, B298(53)-1, B171(26)-1, B78(27)-1

Model 256 (Model 267) Biplane fighter, version F4B -B
C131(43,123,124)-1, B37(170)-1, B298(46)-1, B171(33)-1

P-12 (A-5) Biplane fighter, target drone -D
B37(163)-2, B71(2)-2, A8(65)-2, D6(2/74-78)-2, A10(452)-2, B215(42)-2, B24(34)-1, B298(43)-1, A14(63)-1, B221(91)-1, A15(188)-0

P-26 'Peashooter' Fighter -B
D7(14-1)-4, B37(193)-2, A8(70)-2, B71(14)-2, B148(62)-4, B38-5, B24(34)-1, A10(453)-2, B277(36)-2, B215(68)-2, A15(188)-6, B243-2, A14(233)-1, B310(P)-2

PB2B
See Canada: Boeing Catalina IVB

XAT-15 Crewmaker (Stearman X-120) Twin engine high wing trainer -E
B37(235)-2, B88(4-46)-2, B298(85)-1, B255(27)-1, B314(28,52)-2, B312(178)-1, D16(3/85-49)-1, A8(567)-0, B10(42)-0

XB-15 (XBLR-1, XC-105) Four engine bomber, transport -F
B37(199)-2, B214(36)-2, B41(7)-1, B298(62)-1, A8(485)-1, B93(4)-1, B277(37)-1, A14(200)-1, B221(118)-1, B273(92)-1, A15(189)-0

XB-38 Allison engine conversion B-17, Vega -E
B41(183)-1, B236(24)-2, B214(132)-2, B120(213)-2, B37(266)-1, A14(211)-1, B298(67)-1, D1(5-14)-1, B60(193c)-1, A15(189)-0

XB-39 'Spirit of Lincoln' Allison engine conversion YB-29 -E
B214(135)-2, B37(290)-1, B134(2-113)-1, A14(401)-1, B171(49)-1, B60(191c)-1, D3(7-270)-1, B111(45)-1

XB-44 Pratt & Whitney engine conversion B-29 -F
B214(150)-2, B37(291)-1, A14(417)-1, B60(191c)-1, B171(49)-1, B111(64)-1, D3(7-96)-1, B210(5)-1

XBT-17 (Stearman X-90/91) Trainer -E
B37(231)-2, B298(83)-1, B255(26)-1, B314(18)-1, D3(6-132)-1, A8(569)-0, B10(61)-0, B111(46)-1, B312(177)-1

XF8B Carrier fighter -E
B37(217)-2, B147(4)-2, A3(4-26)-2, B216(193)-2, D6(3/74-135)-2, B350(90)-2, B298(101)-1, A14(396)-1, B60(188c)-1, B78(65)-1

XPBB Sea Ranger Twin engine high wing patrol flying boat -E
B37(216)-2, A3(5-145)-2, D29(12/84-8)-2, B58(166c)-2, B298(86)-1, B277(38)-2, A7(266)-1, A14(319)-1, D3(3-258)-2, B78(64)-1, D19(1/85-45)-1, B473(39)-1

YB-40 (XB-40, TB-40) Escort fighter conversion B-17 -B
B214(138)-2, B41(184)-1, B37(266)-1, B120(212)-1, D16(1/84-12)-1, A8(80)-1, A14(212)-1, B125(154)-1, B93(34)-1, A15(189)-0

BOWLUS Bowlus Sailplanes Inc.
TG-24 (Bowlus-DuPont) Training sailplane -I
B10(170)-0, A8(583)-0, B111(37)-0, D20(1/67-332)-0

XCG-7 High wing transport glider -E
B286(115)-2, B180(89)-3, B121(346)-1,
D6(6/72-318)-1, A8(572)-1, B111(63)-1,
D3(6-86)-1

XCG-8 High wing transport glider -E
B180(89)-2, B286(115)-1, B121(346)-1,
D6(6/72-318)-1, A8(572)-1,
B358(2-115)-1

XTG-12 (BA-102) Training glider -I
B165(351)-2, B10(170)-0, A8(583)-0,
B111(37)-0, D20(1/67-332)-0

BRANTLY Brantly Helicopter Corp.
B-1 Coaxial rotor helicopter -H
B447(62)-1, B279(104)-1, D3(8-90)-1,
B228(248)-0

*BREWSTER Brewster Aeronautical
Corp.*
Brewster Fleet 10 (B-1, Model 16F)
Biplane trainer -E
B153(231c)-1, B276(343)-0,
B358(2-22)-0, B218(6-86)-0

F2A Buffalo Carrier fighter-A
D7(1-66)-5, B147(5)-4, B71(217)-2,
A3(4-28)-2, A9(67)-2, C68-1, A10(458)-2,
A6(205)-2, B277(41)-2, B118(2-5)-2,
B164(48)-2, A15(191)-6, A14(379)-1

F3A Corsair (Vought F4U) Carrier
fighter -A
A9(381)-0, B147(18)-0, A14(386)-0,
A15(211)-0

P-33 Twin boom pusher carrier fighter -J
D19(2/85-127)-1

P-37 High wing carrier bomber -J
D19(2/85-127)-1

SB2A Buccaneer (A-34, Bermuda)
Carrier bomber, target tug -B
A9(69)-2, D20(3/66-420)-2, B277(46)-2,
A10(459)-1, A11(479)-1, B88(3-13)-2,
D29(4/85-10)-1, B58(169c)-2, A7(181)-1,
A14(358)-1, A15(191)-0, D19(2/85-120)-1

XA-32 Attack bomber -E
D20(4/66-500)-2, A14(190)-1,
D29(4/85-16)-1, D25(1/61-40)-1,

B312(203)-1, B111(39)-1, C88(223,P)-1

XSBA (SBN) Carrier scout bomber -E
D9(7/78-43)-1, A9(394)-1, A14(357)-1,
A10(458)-1, B277(45)-1, D29(4/85-12)-1,
B153(230c)-1, B275(14)-1, B230(238)-1,
A15(205)-0, D19(2/85-118)-1

*BRIEGLEB Sailplane Corporation of
America*
TG-13 (BG-8) High wing training
glider -I
D3(7-253)-1, A8(583)-0, B10(170)-0,
B111(37)-0, D20(1/67-332)-0

XTG-9 (BG-6) High wing training
glider -I
B22(A-138)-1, B358(2-107)-0, A8(583)-0,
B10(170)-0, B111(37)-0

BRISTOL Bristol Aeronautical Co.
XLRQ-1 Amphibian transport glider -E
D6(6/72-319)-2, B286(148)-2,
D3(4-266)-2, B358(2-100)-1, A9(475)-1,
D4(12/73-56)-1, C88(266,P)-1

*BUDD Edward G. Budd Manufacturing
Co.*
RB-1 Conestoga (C-93) Twin engine
high wing transport -C
D19(1/67-54)-1, D20(7/68-413)-2,
B218(8-194)-1, B59(215c)-2,
D3(5-171)-2, B288(37)-1, B96(75)-1,
C88(261,P)-1, A9(510)-0, B468(103)-1

BUNYARD Bunyard Aircraft Co.
BAX-3 Sportsman High wing pusher
liaison amphibian -H
B60(194c)-1, B434(34)-1,
D19(4/61-274)-1, B279(109)-0

CESSNA The Cessna Aircraft Co.
AT-8 (Crane, Model T-50) Twin
engine trainer -B
D22(17-83)-2, A8(118)-1, B256(32)-1,
B314(24)-1, B218(8-85)-1, B88(2-43)-2,
D3(3-195)-2, A15(197)-0, B111(40)-1

AT-17 Bobcat (Crane, Model T-50)
Twin engine trainer -A
D22(17-83)-2, A8(118)-1, B314(24,52)-2,
B88(4-39)-2, B256(32)-1, A7(184)-1,
B218(8-85)-1, B277(47)-3, B18(2-66)-7,
A15(197)-0

Model P-10 Twin engine trainer -E
B256(37)-1, C22(62)-1,
D11(Winter/60-55)-1, D11(8/64-38)-6

Model T-50A (P-7) Twin engine light
transport -E
B256(36)-1, C22(60)-1

UC-77 (Model DC-6A) High wing
utility -I
B256(15)-1, B218(3-127)-1, C22(28)-1,
A15(191)-0, B10(80)-0

UC-77A (Model DC-6B) High wing
utility -I
B256(15)-1, B218(3-130)-1, A15(191)-0,
B10(80)-0, B468(40)-1

UC-77B (Model C-34) High wing
utility -I
B256(25)-1, B218(6-260)-1, D3(2-63)-2,
B449(104)-1, A15(191)-0, B468(72)-1

UC-77D (Model C-37) High wing
utility -I
B256(27)-1, B218(7-84)-1, B102(93)-1,
C70(88)-1, A15(191)-0, B468(83)-1

UC-78 Bobcat (JRC, Model T-50)
Twin engine light transport -A
D22(17-81)-2, A8(118)-2, B256(34)-2,
B59(217c)-2, A9(395)-1, B218(8-85)-1,
B277(47)-1, B104(100)-1, B125(212)-1,
A15(191)-0

UC-94 (Model C-165 Airmaster) High
wing utility -I
B256(29)-1, B218(8-9)-1, B153(232c)-1,
D11(Winter/60-53)-2, A15(191)-0,
B10(82)-0, B468(90)-1, B21(A-64)-1

XC-106 Loadmaster (Model P-260)
Twin engine high wing transport -E
B256(37)-1, D3(5-159)-2, C22(64)-1,
C8(147)-1, D11(Winter/60-55)-1

CHANCE VOUGHT See Vought

CHASE *Chase Aircraft Co.*
XCG-14 (Stroukoff MS-1 Avitruck)
High wing transport glider -E
B286(127)-2, D6(6/72-319)-1,
B111(63)-1, C8(64)-1, A8(572)-0

CHRISTOPHER *Christopher Aircraft*
XAG-1 Armed assault glider -J
D6(3/72-131)-0, B286(155)-0, A8(566)-0,
B10(39)-0

COLUMBIA *Columbia Aircraft Corp.*
XJL-1 (Grumman G-42) Utility
amphibian -H
D19(2/84-136)-2, D6(11/72-262)-2,
D3(8-268)-2, D25(4/61-47)-2,
B254(18)-1, B60(200c)-1, D7(23-54)-1,
B434(42)-1, A9(507)-0

CONSOLIDATED *The Consolidated
Vultee Aircraft Corp.*
B-24 Liberator (F-7, BQ-8, LB-30)
Four engine high wing bomber -A
B35-2, B134(1-83)-2, B71(19)-2,
A8(132)-2, A6(204)-4, B158(103)-5,
A10(462)-2, B159(42)-8, B277(48)-2,
B214(71)-2, B352(113)-5, B252(27)-2,
A7(42)-1, B18(2-79)-7, A15(192)-6,
A11(132)-2, A14(213)-1

B-32 Dominator (TB-32) Four engine
high wing bomber -B
B175-1, B124(63)-2, D9(2/79-93)-2,
D19(2/68-80)-1, B214(106)-2,
B277(56)-2, A6(202)-2, A8(488)-1,
A10(464)-1, B59(220c)-2, A14(402)-1

BT-7 (PT-12) Biplane trainer -B
B88(4-35)-2, B314(8,47)-2, A8(127)-1,
B430(168)-1, B359(2-24)-3

C-87 Liberator Express (RY, AT-22)
Transport version B-24 -A
B59(224c)-2, B35(114)-1, A8(140)-1,
D3(4-58)-2, A15(193)-0

C-109 Fuel tanker version B-24 -A
D19(4/81-272)-1, B35(125)-1, A8(140)-0,
A15(193)-0

Model 16 Commodore Twin engine high wing transport flying boat -I
C131(143)-1, B162(66)-2, B430(122)-1, B225(95)-2, B440(117)-1, B197(35)-1, B15(240)-6, B452(37)-1, B218(3-167)-1

N2Y (Fleet I) Biplane trainer -D
A9(397)-1, B230(188,306)-1, D19(2/58-104)-1, D19(1/68-56)-1

N4Y (PT-11, Model 21-A) Biplane trainer -B
A9(397)-1, B230(299)-1

O-17 Courier Biplane observation version PT-3, also floatplane -D
A8(127)-1, B430(36)-1, B155(8,80)-1, A14(86)-1, B114(19-2025)-0

P2Y Ranger (Japan **HXC**) Twin engine biplane patrol flying boat -B
A9(74)-2, A14(304)-1, A10(459)-1, B225(103)-2, C100(6-132)-1, B411(139)-1, B450(40)-1, B230(292)-1, D7(26-1)-1, A15(191)-0

PB-2 (P-30) Fighter -D
A8(130)-2, B215(74)-2, B347(40)-2, D9(10/75-202)-2, B273(36)-1, A10(460)-1, A14(236)-1, B411(138)-1, B221(53)-1, D16(3/83-14)-1

PBY Catalina (P3Y, 0A-10) Twin engine high wing patrol flying boat, amphibian -A
D22(17-54)-2, B71(183)-2, A9(76)-2, A3(5-147)-2, B225(106,158)-2, A6(208)-2, B277(57)-2, B360-2, D19(1/71-27,2/71-113,3/71-200)-1, A10(460)-1, D3(3-173)-4, B58(176c)-2, B252(28)-2, A15(191)-6, A14(308)-1

PB2Y Coronado Four engine high wing patrol, transport flying boat -A
A9(81)-2, A3(5-158)-2, B277(63)-2, B225(142)-2, B58(177c)-2, A6(210)-2, A10(462)-1, B18(2-48)-7, A7(185)-1, A15(192)-0, A14(314)-1

PB4Y-1 Liberator Four engine high wing patrol bomber -A
B88(6-29)-2, A9(83)-1, B35(68)-1,
B134(1-95)-1, B450(82)-1, A7(42)-1, A14(320)-1, B96(81)-1, B297(84)-1, A15(192)-0

PB4Y-2 Privateer Four engine high wing patrol bomber -A
B88(6-31)-2, A9(83)-2, B35(75)-1, B59(226c)-2, B277(64)-2, A6(209)-2, A10(464)-1, A14(321)-1, A7(186)-1, A15(193)-6, B18(2-109)-7

PT-3 Husky (NY-1) Biplane trainer -D
A8(126)-1, B314(5)-1, B218(1-205)-1, D11(10/63-59)-7, A9(71)-1, B312(174)-1, B111(60)-1, B14(150,159)-6, C131(35)-1

PT-11 Biplane trainer -D
B314(8)-1, D3(5-258)-1, A8(127)-0, B111(60)-1, B312(174)-1

RY-3 Four engine high wing transport -B
B59(224c)-2, B88(6-30)-2, B35(76)-1, C9(111,149)-2, A9(85)-0, A15(193)-0

TBY Sea Wolf (Vought XTBU) Carrier torpedo bomber -C
A9(398)-1, D3(6-248)-2, C9(94)-2, A14(363)-1, C82(223)-1, B275(55)-1, B203(25)-1, B114(21-2305)-0

XA-41
See Vultee XA-41

XB-36 Six engine pusher bomber -H
D19(4/70-224)-4, D16(11/74-8)-1, B204(4)-1, D3(8-17)-2, B214(124)-2, A14(420)-1, B104(127)-1, B352(133)-1, B111(45)-1, B60(206c)-1

XB-41 Escort fighter conversion B-24 -E
B214(141)-2, B35(100)-1, A14(216)-1, B134(1-88)-1, A15(192)-0

XB-46 Four jet bomber -H
D16(9/76-8)-1, B214(156)-2, A14(425)-1, B138(66)-2, B60(202c)-1

XC-99 Six engine pusher transport -H
D6(9/73-148)-1, D3(8-293)-2, B204(41)-1, A8(489)-1, B430(258)-1, B261(83)-1, B408(376)-1, B272(46-315)-3

XL-13 High wing liaison -H
D3(8-29)-2, B139(14)-2, A8(489)-1, B60(207c)-1, B419(71)-1

XP-81 Tandem piston/jet engine
fighter -E
D9(11/75-252)-2, A3(4-34)-2,
B146(1-28)-2, B215(205)-2, B138(57)-2,
B347(89)-2, A14(444)-1, B277(67)-1,
B8(80)-1, B111(59)-1, B60(203c)-1

XP4Y Corregidor (Model 31) Twin
engine high wing patrol flying boat -E
D19(2/82-136)-1, A3(5-164)-2,
B88(4-56)-2, D29(12/84-13)-1,
B277(66)-2, A14(318)-1, B56(148c)-2,
B358(2-61)-2, B452(62)-1

XPB3Y Four engine high wing patrol
flying boat -J
D19(1/85-52)-1, A14(319)-0, B10(212)-0,
A9(510)-0

XR2Y (Model 39 Liberator Liner)
Four engine high wing transport -E
B35(122)-1, D25(8/62-45)-1,
B59(225c)-2, B88(6-30)-1, C9(111)-2,
B402(572)-1, D3(5-195)-2, B261(36)-1,
B162(148)-7, A9(510)-0, C15(166)-1

Y1C-22 (Model 17 Fleetster) High
wing transport, also floatplane -D
B218(4-216)-1, B430(153)-1,
B318(152)-1, C15(48)-1, D3(3-50)-1,
C112(2-38)-2, C78(312)-1, A8(570)-0,
B10(62)-0, B468(45)-1

CORNELIUS Cornelius Aircraft Corp.
Mallard Tailless light plane -E
B439(88)-1, D3(5-36)-1

XBG-3 Tailless bomb glider -J
B163(118)-0, A8(569)-0, B10(59)-0,
B279(132)-0

XFG-1 Tailless fuel transport glider -E
D6(6/72-320)-2, B286(145)-2,
B439(89)-1, D7(25-43)-1, A8(574)-0,
D9(4/84-188)-1, B60(210c)-1,
D3(7-200)-1, B109(78)-1, C88(215,P)-1

CULVER Culver Aircraft Corp.
Cadet (Model LCA, LFA) Light
plane -L
B218(8-115)-1, B358(1-87)-1,

B57(162c)-1, B272(41-169)-1,
B420(71)-1, B279(133)-1

**PQ-8 (A-8, TDC-2, Model LAR-90
Cadet)** Target drone -A
A8(490-1), B60(208c)-1, D3(8-18)-1,
B218(8-170)-1, B277(68)-1, B42(246)-1,
B111(62)-1

PQ-14 (TD2C, Model NR-D) Target
drone -A
A8(490)-1, A9(401)-1, B60(209c)-1,
D3(8-18)-1, D20(12/65-251)-1,
B277(69)-2, B42(246)-1, B444(1-73)-1,
D7(23-62)-1, D29(6/82-30)-1

XPQ-9 Target drone -E
D3(8-18)-1, C8(224)-1, A8(581)-0,
B10(157)-0

*CURTISS The Curtiss-Wright
Corporation, Airplane Division*
A-12 Shrike Attack bomber -D
B71(128)-2, D19(2/65-129)-1,
B39(329)-2, A8(180)-2, A10(476)-1,
D16(9/79-13)-1, B411(139)-1,
A14(162)-1, B273(48)-1, A15(193)-0

A-25 Helldiver (Shrike, SB2C-1A)
Dive bomber, target tug -A
B39(432)-1, B88(4-20)-2, A8(496)-1,
A10(480)-1, A14(183)-1, B389(15)-1,
B111(39)-1, A15(195)-0, B312(202)-1

AT-9 Jeep (Model CW-25 Fledgling)
Twin engine trainer -A
B39(469)-2, B88(4-40)-2, A8(495)-1,
B314(25,51)-2, B57(169c)-1, B277(70)-2,
D29(10/81-50)-1, B444(1-38)-1,
B352(161)-1, B356(193)-1

BFC (F11C Goshawk, Hawk II)
Biplane fighter, also floatplane -D
B39(274,281)-1, D9(7/76-48)-2,
B216(109)-2, A9(135)-1, A10(475)-1,
B350(59)-2, B411(35)-1, B293(49)-6,
B471(82)-1, A15(193)-0, A14(371)-1

BF2C (Hawk III) Biplane carrier
fighter -D
D6(10/72-193)-4, B39(276,283)-2,
B148(68)-4, B216(109)-2, B368(78)-5,

A10(476)-2, B350(61)-2, B356(123)-1, A14(371)-1, A15(193)-6

C-46 Commando (C-55, R5C, Model CW-20) Twin engine transport -A
B39(451)-2, A8(193)-2, A6(214)-2, B277(71)-2, B59(237c)-2, B162(134)-2, A9(405)-1, A7(46)-1, B218(8-250,298)-1, A15(195)-6, B18(2-90)-7

C-76 Caravan (Model CW-27) Twin engine high wing transport -C
B39(471)-1, B88(4-60)-2, D3(4-183)-2, D16(5/74-60)-1, B277(72)-1, B288(54)-1, B356(182)-1, D29(6/85-16)-1, B109(30)-1, A8(571)-0

CW-C14 Osprey Biplane military -D
B39(404)-1, B218(5-242)-1, D7(2-208)-1, B152(53b)-1, D3(3-98)-1

CW-16 Biplane trainer -B
B39(408)-1, D7(26-8)-1, B218(5-87,185)-1, C131(129)-1

CW-19R Attack fighter, trainer -B
B39(410)-2, D9(2/77-98)-1, B218(7-108)-1, B153(241c)-1, B356(192)-1, D29(10/81-40)-1, B397(312)-1, B471(49)-1

CW-21 'Demon' Fighter -B
D7(16-33)-4, B39(461)-2, A3(4-76)-2, D9(1/77-47)-2, B277(97)-2, A10(480)-1, C59(114)-1, D29(10/81-50)-1, D7(18-77)-1, A15(195)-6, A14(249)-1

CW-22 Falcon Reconnaissance bomber -B
B39(463)-1, D9(2/77-99)-1, C59(94,125)-1, B56(160c)-1, D3(5-208)-1, A15(196)-0

CW-23 Trainer -E
B39(413)-1, D9(1/77-47)-1, D7(16-36)-1, D29(10/81-49)-1, B154(180c)-1

CW-24B Canard pusher -F
A3(4-62)-1, B146(1-69)-1, B39(466)-1, B439(116)-1, B42(9)-1, D9(12/83-288)-1, D29(6/85-10)-1, D14(5-79,6-90)-3

Hawk 75 Fighter -A
A3(4-45)-2, B146(1-33)-2, B39(354)-1, B71(80)-2, D9(9/76-150)-2, A10(478)-1,

A14(244)-1, B368(90)-1, B277(78)-0, A15(194)-0

N2C Fledgling (A-3) Biplane trainer, target drone -D
B39(200)-2, A9(128)-2, B230(252)-1, D9(1/82-17)-1, B356(110)-1, B368(14)-1, B218(2-262)-1, D3(5-208)-1, C131(113)-1

O-1 Falcon (A-3) Biplane reconnaissance, also floatplane -D
B39(285,311)-2, A8(174)-2, D4(11/75-66)-4, D7(2-208,26-7)-1, A14(80)-1, D9(10/84-182)-1, C131(117)-1, D19(3/84-173)-8, A15(193)-0

O-52 Owl High wing observation, trainer -B
B39(433)-2, D20(11/64-57)-2, A8(495)-1, D3(4-257)-2, B88(3-23)-2, B277(87)-3, D29(2/83-42)-1, A14(158)-1, B57(166c)-2, A15(194)-0

P-36 (Mohawk, Hawk 75A) Fighter -A
D6(11/71-307,12/71-374,1/72-47)-4, B146(1-29)-4, B71(80)-2, A7(186)-1, B39(348)-2, B148(82)-4, A3(4-36)-2, A8(182)-2, B368(91)-5, B61(52)-2, A6(210)-8, A10(478)-2, B215(85)-2, B277(73)-7, A15(194)-6, B273(18)-1

P-40 Warhawk (Tomahawk, Kittyhawk) Fighter -A
D9(1/77-28,2/77-75,3/77-132)-4, B146(1-48)-4, B71(35,136)-2, B39(474)-2, B148(116)-4, A8(186)-2, A3(4-47)-2, B368(113)-4, A6(210)-2, A10(481)-2, B277(78)-2, D16(5/83-9)-1, B258-2, A15(194)-6, A14(252)-1

R4C Condor II (YC-30, Model T-32) Twin engine biplane transport, bomber, also floatplane -B
D7(6-94)-1, D19(1/67-3)-1, B39(391)-2, B162(59)-2, A9(404)-1, A10(476)-1, A14(198)-1, B15(250)-7, B289(51)-6, A15(195)-0, B471(83)-1, B468(59)-1

SBC Helldiver (Cleveland) Biplane carrier dive bomber -A
D7(5-1)-4, B39(368)-2, A9(141)-2,

A10(477)-1, D29(4/85-19)-1, B88(1-40)-2,
A7(187)-1, B277(88)-6, A14(350)-1,
A15(194)-6

SB2C Helldiver (A-25, SBF, SBW)
Carrier dive bomber -A
B389-2, B65(90)-4, B71(124)-2,
B39(423)-2, A9(145)-2, A6(214)-2,
B277(90)-2, B252(30)-2, B275(61)-5,
A10(480)-1, A15(195)-6, A14(359)-1

SC Seahawk Scout rescue floatplane,
also wheeled -B
B39(446)-2, A3(6-166)-2, A9(148)-2,
A14(342)-1, D29(2/85-33)-1, A7(187)-1,
D19(2/61-89)-1, B277(94)-3, B88(6-34)-2,
B18(2-108)-7, A15(195)-0, B60(213c)-1

SNC Falcon (Model CW-22N)
Trainer -A
D1(7-38)-2, B39(463)-2, B88(4-63)-2,
B57(169c)-2, D29(10/81-47)-1,
A9(404)-1, B356(193)-1, B229(110)-1,
B277(94)-1, A15(196)-0

SOC Seagull (SON-1) Biplane scout
floatplane, also wheeled -A
B71(194)-2, B39(339)-2, A3(6-157)-2,
A9(138)-2, D29(2/85-32)-1, A14(335)-1,
B88(3-15)-2, B411(141)-1, B277(96)-3,
A15(193)-6

SO3C Seagull (Seamew) Scout
observation floatplane, also wheeled -A
A3(6-161)-2, B39(419)-2, A9(143)-2,
A12(78)-2, D29(2/85-33)-1, B88(3-16)-2,
A14(341)-1, B288(67)-1, B277(95)-3,
A15(194)-0

Twin engine fighter Version P-40 -J
D16(5/83-11)-1, B39(495)-1, B258(31)-1

XA-40
See XSB3C

XBTC-2 Carrier dive torpedo bomber -H
D9(7/79-50)-2, B39(445)-1,
D25(3/61-13)-2, D29(6/85-17)-1,
A14(366)-1, B60(213c)-1, B275(57)-1,
D3(7-251)-1, B356(195)-0

XBT2C Carrier dive torpedo bomber -H
D9(7/79-50)-2, B39(449)-1,
D25(3/61-13)-2, D29(6/85-17)-1,

A14(366)-1, B60(212c)-1, B450(124)-1,
D3(7-227)-1, B356(195)-1

XF14C Carrier fighter -E
B147(30)-2, B39(439)-2, B216(180)-2,
A3(4-74)-2, D29(6/85-11)-1,
D9(12/76-293)-2, A14(393)-1,
B350(86)-2, B450(124)-1, B60(212c)-1

XF15C Tandem piston/jet engine carrier
fighter -E
D7(3-98)-2, B147(31)-2, B39(506)-2,
B216(221)-2, D29(6/85-17)-1,
D9(12/76-293)-2, A14(501)-1,
B350(101)-2, B450(124)-1, B60(211c)-1

XP-42 Fighter -E
D19(2/74-82)-2, B215(105)-2,
B39(364)-1, B146(1-31)-1, A14(244)-1,
D9(11/76-236)-1, D16(3/83-19)-1,
B221(59)-1, B368(127)-1, B40(87)-1

XP-46 Fighter -E
B146(1-68)-2, B39(435)-2, A3(4-60)-2,
B215(110)-2, D19(1/81-26)-1,
D9(11/76-236)-2,
D16(5/83-10,5/85-12)-1, A14(255)-1,
B347(63)-1

XP-53 Fighter -G
B215(133)-3, B258(36)-3, B146(1-72)-0,
B39(437)-0, A14(290)-0

XP-55 Ascender Canard pusher
fighter -E
B146(1-69)-2, B39(466)-2, A3(4-62)-2,
B215(139)-2, B231(53)-2,
D9(11/76-236,12/83-288)-2, B347(64)-2,
B439(116)-1, A14(289)-1,
D29(6/85-10)-1, B277(100)-1,
B50(106)-1, B42(10)-1, B59(231c)-1

XP-60 Fighter -E
B146(1-72)-2, A3(4-66)-2, B39(437)-2,
B215(155)-2, D9(11/76-237)-2,
D16(5/83-10,5/85-10)-1, B258(36)-1,
A14(290)-1, B277(98)-1

XP-62 Fighter -E
B146(1-76)-2, A3(4-72)-2, B39(438)-1,
B215(164)-2, D16(5/85-45)-1,
D9(12/76-292)-2, A14(291)-1,
B347(64)-2, B8(80)-1, B60(214c)-1

XP-71 Twin engine pusher fighter -J
B215(187)-3, A14(300)-1,
D29(6/85-11)-1, D20(5/64-61)-3,
C88(101)-6

XSB3C (XA-40) Carrier torpedo dive
bomber -J
B389(48)-1, A14(192)-0, B10(35,221)-0

XSO2C Biplane scout observation -E
A14(336)-1, D29(2/85-40)-1,
B230(225)-1, B39(343)-0

Y1A-18 Shrike Twin engine attack
bomber -D
B39(365)-2, A8(494)-1, B273(52)-1,
A10(478)-1, B444(2-15)-1, B411(181)-1,
A14(171)-1, D29(12/71)-1, B221(137)-1,
A15(194)-0

YP-37 Fighter -E
D19(1/77-12)-2, B215(88)-2, B39(362)-1,
D9(9/76-151)-2, A14(243)-1,
D16(3/83-17)-1, B221(87)-1,
B273(140)-1, B368(112)-1, B153(236c)-1

CUSTER *Custer Channel Wing Corp.*
CCW-1 Twin engine pusher channel
wing -F
B50(121)-1, B42(106)-0

DOAK *Doak Aircraft Co., Inc.*
Model DRD-1 Trainer -E
B21(A-88)-1

DOUGLAS *The Douglas Aircraft Co.,
Inc.*
A-20 Havoc (DB-7, Boston, F-3, BD)
Twin engine bomber -A
B121(281)-2, B134(2-59)-2, B71(202)-2,
B180(55)-2, A8(230)-2, B262-2,
D6(12/71-379)-5, B124(48)-2, A6(216)-1,
B277(100)-2, A10(487)-2, B252(38)-2,
A7(56)-1, B18(2-76)-7, A15(198)-6,
A14(172)-1, B464(28)-1, A11(188)-2

A-24 Banshee (SBD Dauntless) Dive
bomber -A
A8(228)-2, B121(271)-1, A14(182)-1,

B104(90)-1, B390(17,47)-1, B81(103)-1,
A15(197)-0, B277(124)-6, A10(486)-1,
B312(202)-1, B464(45)-1

A-26 Invader (JD-1) Twin engine
bomber -A
D7(7-215)-4, B121(348)-2, B180(69)-2,
A8(237)-2, B277(106)-2, A10(491)-2,
A6(218)-2, B252(39)-2, B263-2,
B464(36)-1, A7(191)-1, A15(198)-6,
A14(187)-1

B-18 Bolo (DB-1, C-58, Digby) Twin
engine bomber, transport -A
B121(200)-2, A8(218)-2, B214(51)-2,
A6(219)-1, D4(10/81-20)-1, A10(485)-1,
B277(110)-1, A14(203)-1, B273(80)-1,
A15(197)-0, B464(22)-1, C131(162)-1

B-23 Dragon (UC-67) Twin engine
bomber, transport -B
D16(11/80-28)-1, B121(313)-2,
B214(68)-2, A8(500)-1, B277(111)-1,
A10(490)-1, A14(204)-1, B221(121)-1,
B273(84)-1, A15(197)-0, B464(23)-1

BT-2 (0-32, 0-2M, A-4) Biplane trainer,
target drone -D
B121(88)-1, A8(207)-1, B314(16)-1,
A14(91)-1, D29(2/84-48)-1, B42(245)-1,
D11(Summer/61 -55)-1, D3(8-18)-1,
B111(46,62)-1, D19(4/85-315)-1

BTD Destroyer Carrier dive torpedo
bomber -C
B121(366)-1, D9(5/78-240)-2,
B180(100)-2, B88(7-36)-2, A9(408)-1,
A10(490)-1, A14(364)-1, B277(112)-3,
B275(56)-1, B450(123)-1, B60(222c)-1

**C-32 (DC-2, C-33, C-34, C-38, C-39,
C-41, C-42, R2D,** Japan **'Tess')** Twin
engine transport -A
D7(19-60)-4, B121(181)-2, A8(215)-2,
B88(3-36)-2, B277(112)-1, A9(407)-1,
C70(73)-2, B162(92)-2, B36(38)-2,
A15(197)-6, B104(60)-1, A2(498)-1,
B464(96)-2, B465(3)-1, B468(64)-1

**C-47 Skytrain (DC-3, C-41A, C-48,
C-49, C-50, C-51, C-52, C-53, C-68,
C-84, C-117, R4D, Dakota)** Twin

engine transport -A
B121(239)-1, B71(96,220,249)-2,
A8(221)-2, A9(165)-2, A6(220)-2,
A11(192)-2, D16(1/81-3)-1, B465-4,
D29(2/81-5)-1, B277(114)-2,
B162(106)-2, B36-2, A7(58)-1,
B252(41)-2, A3(6-172)-2, B59(241c)-2,
A15(197)-6, B18(2-36)-7, B464(97)-2

**C-54 Skymaster (DC-4, R5D,
XC-114, XC-116)** Four engine
transport -A
D7(15-38)-4, B121(325)-2, A8(242)-2,
A9(169)-2, B162(138)-4, A6(219)-2,
B277(120)-2, B59(243c)-2, A7(60)-1,
A15(198)-6, B18(2-78)-7, B464(119)-2

C-74 Globemaster I Four engine
transport -M
D19(2/80-82)-2, B121(406)-2,
B88(7-45)-2, D3(7-75)-2, A8(500)-1,
B408(369)-2, B60(216c)-1, B444(1-81)-1,
B104(136)-1, B139(141)-1, B464(176)-2

D-558-1 Skystreak Single jet transonic
research -H
B121(434)-2, B169(56)-5, B180(141)-2,
B138(66)-2, D3(8-65)-2, B405(77)-1,
B168(141)-1, B395(84)-1, B450(127)-1,
B410(112)-1, D16(9/85-36)-4,
B464(196)-2

DC-4E (Japan **LXD**) Four engine
transport -E
B121(277)-2, B162(118)-2, B464(118)-1,
D29(6/81-10)-1, D7(15-38)-1,
B291(66)-1, C100(6-166)-2, A2(423)-1,
B153(244c)-1, B352(177)-1, B281(257)-1,
B354(404)-1, B468(94)-1

DF (Japan **HXD**) Twin engine high wing
transport flying boat -C
B121(263)-2, C100(6-146)-2, A2(497)-1,
D3(3-206)-1, B226(188)-1, C6(282)-1,
A15(196)-0, B452(54)-1, B464(21)-1

**Model 8A (A-33, Northrop A-17,
ASJA B 5)** Dive bomber -A
B121(217)-1, A14(166)-1, B464(28)-1,
D20(3/65-41)-1, B277(108)-1,
B111(39)-1, C89(198,232)-1,

D19(1/85-41)-1, B153(246c)-1,
D23(79-70)-1, A15(206)-0

O-25 Biplane observation -D
B121(83)-1, A8(205)-1, A14(90)-1,
B111(52)-1, B473(14)-1

O-31 High wing observation -D
B121(127)-1, A8(212)-1,
D19(3/63-205)-1, B312(183)-1,
A14(153)-1, B104(46)-1, B111(52)-1,
B114(19-2028)-8

O-38 (O-2MC, A-6) Biplane
observation, target drone -B
B121(85)-2, A8(207)-2, A14(91)-1,
B312(183)-1, B114(19-2927)-6,
B352(169)-1, D7(26-5)-1, B471(82)-1,
B81(26)-1, B111(52)-1, B464(15)-1

O-43 High wing observation -D
B121(130)-1, A8(213)-1,
D19(3/63-205)-1, A14(155)-1,
B312(183)-1, D29(2/84-51)-1,
B111(52)-1, B114(19-2028)-0,
A15(197)-0

O-46 High wing observation -B
B121(131)-2, A8(212)-2, B464(20)-1,
D19(3/63-205)-1, A14(156)-1,
B104(46)-1, B24(34)-1, B13(1-55,236)-1,
B444(1-5)-1, B473(18)-1, A15(197)-0

P-70 Nighthawk (DB-7) Twin engine
night fighter -A
D7(27-61)-2, B146(2-3)-2, A3(4-78)-2,
B121(295)-1, D9(7/78-44)-2, A8(235)-1,
B215(184)-2, D29(6/86-44)-1,
B164(30)-2, A6(216)-2, B262(48)-1,
A14(293)-1

RD Dolphin (OA-3, OA-4) Twin
engine high wing transport amphibian -B
A3(5-167)-2, D16(11/82-10)-1,
B121(121)-2, A8(210)-2, A9(158)-2,
B277(122)-1, B218(6-24)-1, B321(32)-1,
B104(50)-1, A15(196)-0, B464(16)-2

R3D (DC-5, C-110) Twin engine high
wing transport -B
B121(308)-2, B180(79)-2, B88(4-61)-2,
A9(407)-1, D19(2/84-96)-2, B230(287)-1,
B229(88)-1, B277(121)-3, B153(245c)-1,

A15(197)-6, B464(122)-2, B468(93)-1

SBD Dauntless (A-24, BT-2) Carrier dive bomber -A
B65(52)-4, B121(266)-2, B71(196)-2, A9(162)-2, D3(5-185)-4, B390-2, A6(220)-2, B277(123)-2, B180(43)-2, A10(486)-2, A7(61)-1, B59(249c)-2, B252(40)-2, B18(2-38)-7, A15(197)-6, B275(43)-1, A14(355)-1, A7(61)-1, B310(P)-2, B464(43)-1

TBD Devastator Carrier torpedo bomber, also floatplane -B
B71(171)-2, B121(196)-2, A9(160)-2, A6(222)-2, A7(192)-1, B202-2, B464(42)-1, A10(485)-1, A14(348)-1, B275(32)-2, B277(128)-7, A15(197)-6, B18(2-16)-7

VB-10, VB-12 Roc Guided bomb -E
B163(119)-1, B272(46-43)-1, D3(7-310)-1, B464(190)-1

XB-19 (XBLR-2) Four engine bomber, transport -F
B121(319)-2, B214(55)-2, A8(499)-1, D20(10/66-157)-2, A14(206)-1, B464(25)-1, D4(10/81-28)-1, D19(3/82-160)-1, B277(129)-3, B221(119)-1, B273(96)-1

XB-31 (Model 423) Four engine high wing bomber -J
B214(103)-2, B121(713)-3, A14(398)-0

XB-42 Mixmaster Twin mid-engine pusher high wing bomber -E
B121(372)-2, D9(8/75-100)-2, B214(144)-2, A14(229)-1, B50(185)-1, B88(7-35)-2, B60(223c)-1, B410(121)-1, B104(114)-1, B111(45)-1, B464(39)-1

XB-43 Twin jet high wing bomber -H
B121(422)-2, D9(8/75-100)-2, B214(147)-2, A8(501)-1, A14(424)-1, B138(60)-2, B60(224c)-1, B50(187)-1, B410(123)-1, B104(114)-1, B464(41)-1

XBT2D Skyraider (AD) Carrier dive torpedo bomber -M
B121(384)-2, B71(60)-2, B180(136)-2, A9(171)-2, B277(109)-1, A14(484)-1,

D3(7-195)-2, B275(56)-1, B60(222c)-1, B450(124)-1, B464(47)-1

XC-112A (DC-6, C-118, R6D) Four engine transport -H
B121(409)-2, D7(16-45)-2, A8(501)-1, B162(162)-2, B60(217c)-1, D3(7-227)-1, A9(409)-1, B16(52)-7, B464(127)-0

XCG-17 Transport glider conversion C-47 -E
B286(138)-2, B121(244)-1, B465(8)-1, D6(6/72-320)-1, B36(90)-1, B42(253)-1, D29(2/81-44)-1, C88(267,P)-1, B464(108)-1

XP-48 (Model 312) Fighter -J
B215(119)-7, B121(712)-3, A14(287)-0, B347(64)-0

XSB2D Carrier dive torpedo bomber -E
B121(366)-1, B180(96)-2, B464(46)-1, D9(5/78-240)-1, A14(364)-1, B275(56)-1

XT3D Biplane carrier torpedo bomber, engine test -E
B121(140)-2, A14(114)-1, B230(122)-1

XTB2D Skypirate Carrier torpedo bomber -E
B121(377)-2, D9(5/78-241)-2, B464(46)-1, D29(12/81-42)-1, B180(106)-2, A14(365)-1, B275(56)-1, B450(124)-1

YOA-5 (YB-11, YO-44) Twin engine high wing rescue amphibian -C
B121(192)-2, B214(33)-2, A14(307)-1, B81(35)-1, B434(64)-1, D16(11/82-25)-1, B312(185)-1, B111(53)-1

EDO *Edo Aircraft Co. (Earl D. Osborn)*
XOSE-1 Scout floatplane -H
D25(5/61-48)-2, B60(226c)-2, D19(1/79-78)-1, D3(7-215)-1, A14(344)-1, B96(64)-1, B279(151)-1, A9(508)-0

ERCO *Engineering & Research Corp.*
XPQ-13 (Model 415-C Ercoupe) Target drone -E
B60(226c)-1, D3(8-18)-1, B218(8-74)-1, B111(62)-1, A8(581)-0

YO-55 (Model 415-C Ercoupe)
Observation -E
B59(250c)-1, B218(8-72)-1, D3(8-129)-2,
B272(41-62,223)-2, B420(69)-2,
B279(153)-1, B22(A-90)-1, A8(578)-0,
B10(139)-0

FAIRCHILD *The Fairchild Engine &
Airplane Corp.*
AT-21 Gunner Twin engine trainer,
target tug -A
A8(256)-2, B59(255c)-2, B288(81)-1,
A7(193)-1, B139(126)-1,
D20(7/67-748)-1, B277(130)-2, C8(203)-3
C-8 (Model 71, F-1) High wing
photographic, also floatplane -D
A8(507)-1, D19(2/74-98)-2, B111(47)-1,
B218(3-254)-1, D22(17-38)-1,
D11(8/63-28)-1, B352(189)-0,
B411(183)-0, B473(6)-1
C-82 Packet (Model F-78) Twin engine
twin boom high wing transport -M
A8(261)-2, B59(252c)-2, B88(6-32)-2,
B139(96)-2, D3(7-209)-2, B104(124)-1,
C8(147,188)-2, B111(49)-1,
B444(2-115)-1, B312(208)-1
JK (Model F-45, UC-88) Light
transport -I
A9(413)-1, B218(7-17)-1, B277(131)-1,
B230(248)-1, B152(268c)-1, B139(72)-1,
D3(3-242)-1, A15(199)-0
Lark Surface-to-air missile -M
B163(196)-1, B428(98)-1,
D19(1/82-26)-1, B190(60)-7,
B114(16-1706)-6
Model KR-34 (Kreider-Reisner) Biplane
utility -D
B218(1-219)-1, B279(206)-0,
D19(1/57-69)-1
Model F-46A (Clark Duramold) Light
transport, engine test -L
D19(1/74-46)-1, B218(9-196)-1,
B279(149)-0

Model 51 (UC-61D) High wing utility,
also floatplane -B
B218(4-186)-1, D19(2/74-96)-1,
B155(11,114)-1, B227(34)-1,
D22(17-31)-1
**Model 91 Baby Clipper (Model
A-942-B, Jungle Clipper,** Japan **LXF)**
High wing transport amphibian -I
B88(4-52)-2, D6(1/72-35)-1, D3(4-3)-2,
B218(7-24)-1, B225(200)-1, A2(497)-1,
B284(4-171)-1, C100(6-32,144)-2,
D29(10/82-50)-1, A15(199)-6
PT-19 Cornell (Model M-62)
Trainer -A
D1(8-34)-2, A8(258)-1, B314(13,48)-2,
B218(8-93)-1, B277(132)-1, B59(254c)-1,
B88(2-28)-2, A7(193)-1, B292(52)-6,
B111(61)-1
PT-23 Cornell Trainer -A
A8(258)-1, D1(8-34)-1, B314(15)-1,
B218(8-96)-1, B58(192c)-1, B312(175)-1,
B288(82)-1, B104(76)-1, B111(61)-1
PT-26 Cornell Trainer -A
B88(4-52)-2, A8(258)-3, D1(8-34)-1,
B314(15)-1, B218(8-96)-1, A6(222)-7,
B155(12,120)-1, B58(192c)-1
**UC-61 Forwarder (Model 24-W, GK,
Argus)** High wing utility -A
A8(508)-1, B200(2-19)-2, A11(493)-1,
B88(3-30)-2, D19(3/83-225)-1,
B58(191c)-2, D3(8-140)-4, A9(412)-1,
A7(194)-1, B277(129)-3, C131(154)-1
UC-61B (Model 24-J) High wing
utility -I
B218(7-220)-1, B153(248c)-1, C70(88)-1,
C121(1-52)-1, B10(78)-0
UC-61C,F (Model 24-R) High wing
utility -I
B218(8-27)-1, B10(78)-0
UC-61D (Model 51-A) High wing
utility -I
B218(4-188)-1, D19(2/74-96)-1,
B155(11,114)-1, B10(78)-0

UC-61E (Model 24-K) High wing
utility -I
B218(7-232)-1, B153(248c)-1, B10(78)-0
UC-61H (Model 24-G) High wing
utility -I
B218(7-119)-1, B10(78)-0
UC-61J (Model 24-C, J2K) High wing
utility -I
B218(7-42)-1, B229(117)-1, A9(412)-1,
D11(8/63-29)-1, B10(78)-0
UC-61K Forwarder (Model 24-R)
High wing utility -A
B59(253c)-2, B218(8-27)-1, B10(78)-0
UC-86 Forwarder (Model 24R40)
High wing utility -I
B88(5-44)-2, B218(8-27)-1, B111(49)-1,
B10(82)-0, A8(571)-0
UC-96 (Model FC-2W2) High wing
photographic -I
D22(17-25)-2, B218(1-159)-1,
D19(2/74-97)-1, B310(P)-2, B276(305)-1,
B15(231)-6, A15(199)-0, B10(82)-0
XAT-13 Yankee Doodle Twin engine
trainer -E
B88(4-43)-2, B314(28)-1, B57(180c)-1,
B312(178)-1, B111(41)-1,
D25(8/57-35)-1, B272(43-128)-1,
A8(256)-0
XAT-14 Bombardier Twin engine
trainer -E
B88(4-44)-2, B314(28)-1, D25(8/57-35)-1,
B111(41)-1, A8(256)-0
XBQ-3 Flying bomb version AT-21 -E
B60(228c)-1, D3(8-19)-1, B111(62)-1,
C8(225)-1, D19(4/85-290)-1, A8(569)-0
XNQ-1 (YT-31) Trainer -H
D19(1/77-48)-1, B60(228c)-1,
D3(7-275)-1, B314(37,54)-2, B110(27)-1,
A9(508)-0, B10(202)-0

FIRESTONE *Firestone Aircraft Co.*
(G. & A. Aircraft Inc).
XO-61 (Pitcairn PA-44) Twin boom
pusher observation autogiro -E
B467(84)-2, B375(308)-1,

D16(3/83-47)-1, D5(Fall/77 -111)-1,
B228(268)-0, B59(257c)-0, D3(6-84)-1,
A8(578)-0, B10(140)-0
XR-9 (Model 45) Liaison helicopter -H
B375(310)-1, B326(212)-1, B60(231c)-1,
B228(268)-1, B279(163)-1,
D3(7-108,251)-1, D16(3/83-47)-1,
B111(61)-1, A8(502)-0, B10(162)-0

FLEET *Fleet Aircraft, Inc. Division of*
Consolidated Aircraft
Model 7 Biplane trainer -B
C131(119)-1, B218(4-229)-1
Model 10 Biplane trainer, also
floatplane -B
B218(6-84)-1, B276(341)-1,
D6(4/72-219)-1, B430(150)-1,
D3(3-302)-1, C131(125)-1
Model 11 Biplane trainer -A
B218(6-84)-1, B276(341)-1,
D6(4/72-219)-0
Model 21 Biplane trainer -B
B276(347)-1, D9(11/81-248)-1,
B430(167)-1, D19(3/85-241)-3

FLEETWINGS *Fleetwings, Inc. Division*
of Kaiser Cargo Co.
A-1 Target drone -K
C8(224)-1, A8(566)-0, B10(35)-0
BT-12 Sophomore Trainer -C
B88(4-36)-2, B314(17,49)-2, B111(46)-1,
B272(41-100,227)-2, B277(134)-3,
B22(A-93)-1, B358(1-88)-1,
C8(149,205)-1, A8(569)-0, B312(176)-1
Model 33 Trainer -E
B13(1-22,227)-1, D3(3-314)-1,
B279(163)-0
Model F-5 Seabird High wing
amphibian -L
D19(3/71-227)-1, B218(7-277)-1,
B139(150)-1, B13(2-86,231)-1,
B153(249c)-1, B434(72)-1, B449(130)-1,
B301(P)-1, B21(A-91)-1
XBQ-1 Twin engine flying bomb -E
D3(8-19)-1, B163(32)-0, A8(569)-0,
B10(60)-0

XBQ-2 Twin engine flying bomb -E
B60(232c)-1, D3(8-19)-1, B163(32)-0,
A8(569)-0, B10(60)-0, D19(4/85-290)-1
XBTK-1
See Kaiser-Fleetwings
YPQ-12A Target drone -C
B60(232c)-1, D3(8-18)-1, B111(62)-1,
C8(225)-1, D11(8/64-37)-6, A8(581)-0,
B10(157)-0

FLETCHER Fletcher Aviation Corp.
FBT-2 Trainer -E
B56(173c)-1, B358(1-87)-1, B22(A-93)-1,
D3(3-314)-1, B279(163)-0
XBG-1 Bomb glider version PQ-11 -E
B286(155)-0, B10(59)-0, B60(233c)-0,
B163(118)-0
XPQ-11 Target drone -J
B10(157)-0, A8(581)-0, B60(233c)-0
YCQ-1A Target control -E
B60(233c)-1, D3(8-18)-1, B111(62)-1,
D11(8/64-38)-6, A8(573)-0, B279(163)-0

FORD Ford Motor Co.
4-AT, 5-AT Trimotor (C-4, C-9, RR)
Three engine high wing transport -I
D7(8-38)-4, B71(156)-2, B162(42)-4,
B323(57)-1, B218(5-28,120)-1, D3(3-3)-2,
A8(510)-1, B408(152)-2, B352(196)-2,
A15(199)-0, B310(P)-2, B468(32)-1

FRANKFORT Frankfort Sailplane Co.
(Aircraft Division, Globe Corp.)
TD3D (OQ-16) Target drone -K
A9(513)-0, B10(228)-0
TG-1 (Cinema) High wing training
glider -B
A8(510)-1, B59(257c)-1, B22(A-137)-1,
B42(135)-1, B10(169)-0
XCG-1 (Model TCC-41) High wing
transport glider -G
B286(100)-1, A8(572)-0, B10(96)-0
XCG-2 (Model TCC-21) High wing
transport glider -J
B286(100)-0, B10(96)-0, A8(572)-0

FRANKLIN-STEVENS
TG-15 (PS-2) Training glider -I
B10(170)-0, A8(583)-0, B111(37)-0,
D20(1/67-332)-0
TG-17 Training sailplane -I
B10(170)-0, A8(583)-0, B111(37)-0,
D20(1/67-332)-0

FUNK
See Akron-Funk

G & A AIRCRAFT
See Firestone

GENERAL General Aircraft Corp.
Skyfarer (G1-80) High wing tourer -L
B218(8-150)-1, B56(174c)-1,
B272(41-63,227)-2, B22(A-94)-1,
B13(2-88,231)-1, B279(172)-0

GENERAL AIRBORNE General
Airborne Transport Inc.
XCG-16 (Model MC-1A) Twin boom
transport glider -E
D6(6/72-320)-2, B286(133)-2,
B59(258c)-1, B111(63)-1, C8(152)-1,
C88(265,P)-1, A8(572)-0, B10(97)-0

GENERAL AVIATION General
*Aviation Corp. (Fokker Aircraft Corp. of
America)*
Fokker Super Universal High wing
transport -B
B328(74)-1, B218(1-137)-1, C101(151)-1,
B226(343)-1, B468(26)-1, A15(178)-0
PJ-1 (FLB, Model AF-15) Twin engine
high wing pusher rescue flying boat -D
A9(415)-1, B328(87)-1, B230(198)-1,
D19(4/71-252)-1, B394(8)-1, B96(18)-1,
C60(1-P)-1, D19(3/57-173)-1
PJ-2 Antares (FLB, Model AF-15)
Twin engine high wing rescue flying
boat -D
A9(415)-1, B328(87)-1, B230(183)-1,
D19(4/71-253)-1, C60(1-P)-1,
D9(10/77-191)-1

GENERAL MOTORS *Eastern Aircraft Division, General Motors Corp.*
FM Wildcat (Grumman F4F) Carrier fighter -A
A3(4-82)-2, B147(42)-1, B88(6-39)-2, B135(2-45)-1, A9(207)-1, D3(5-235)-2, B59(262c)-2, B352(212)-2, B216(159)-1, A15(200)-0, A14(384)-1
TBM Avenger (Grumman TBF) Carrier torpedo bomber -A
B65(123)-1, A9(213)-1, A14(361)-1, B275(50)-5, B59(261c)-2, B203(10)-1, B277(152)-0, A6(224)-3, A15(200)-0, B71(214)-2

GENERAL MOTORS *Fisher Body Division, General Motors Corp.*
P-75 Eagle Mid-engine long range escort fighter -C
B146(2-6)-2, A3(4-85)-2, B215(192)-2, D9(5/79-259)-2, A14(301)-1, B347(88)-2, B59(256c)-1, B277(135)-1, B8(79)-1, B104(118)-1

GENERAL MOTORS *General Motors Research Laboratories*
A-1 'Bug' (Kettering) High wing flying bomb -E
D19(4/85-285)-1

GLOBE *The Globe Aircraft Corp.*
Model GC-1 Swift Tourer -L
B57(183c)-2, B218(8-186)-0, B218(9-96)-1, B13(2-87,233)-1, B279(176)-1

GOODYEAR *Goodyear Aircraft Corp.*
FG Corsair (Vought F4U) Carrier fighter -A
B135(2-84)-1, B147(18)-1, B71(150-5)-1, B60(235c)-1, B392(36)-1, A14(386)-1, C82(247)-1, A15(211)-0, A9(381)-0, B277(235)-6
F2G Corsair Carrier fighter -C
A3(4-88)-2, B147(26)-1, D9(10/80-194)-2, B135(2-90)-1, A9(381)-1, B216(179)-1, A14(389)-1, B415(194)-1, B392(36)-1, A15(211)-0

GA-1 Pusher amphibian -F
D19(2/60-90)-2, D3(7-120)-1, B218(8-292)-0
G Type Training airship -B
A9(485)-1, B358(2-171)-1, B13(2-120,233)-1, D11(4/63-15)-1, D19(1/82-10)-1, B426(201)-1, B425(156)-1, D19(2/85-141)-1
J Type Patrol airship -D
A9(487)-1, D11(4/63-13)-1, D19(1/82-12,1/83-16)-1, B426(200)-1
K Type Patrol airship -A
A9(487)-1, B358(2-172)-1, B13(2-120,233)-1, D11(4/63-14)-1, B3(83)-1, B426(201)-1, B425(157)-1, B57(88b)-1, A15(199)-0, D19(2/85-142)-1
L Type Training airship -B
A9(489)-1, B358(2-176)-1, B13(2-120,133)-1, D19(1/82-12)-1, D19(1/83-17)-1, B426(201)-1, B425(157)-1, B96(54)-1, B450(57)-1
M Type Patrol airship -B
A9(490)-1, B358(2-176)-1, B13(2-120,233)-1, D11(4/63-15)-1, B3(106)-1, B426(207)-1, B425(157)-1, C88(272,P)-1, A15(199)-0, D19(2/85-150)-1
TC-13 Training airship -B
A9(494)-1, B358(2-171)-1, D19(2/85-142)-1
TC-14 Training airship -B
A9(494)-0, B358(2-171)-1, B3(104)-1, D19(1/82-12)-1, B426(196)-1, D11(4/63-14)-1

GREAT LAKES *Great Lakes Aircraft Corp.*
BG-1 Biplane carrier dive bomber -D
A9(192)-2, D16(11/79-44)-1, B229(68)-1, B230(214)-1, A10(498)-1, A14(346)-1, B411(145)-1, B450(22)-1, B275(10)-1, A15(199)-0

TG (Martin T4M) Biplane carrier
torpedo bomber -D
A9(290)-1, B230(213)-1,
D16(11/79-38)-1, A14(114)-1,
A10(526)-1, D19(1/82-21)-1, A15(203)-0
XB2G-1 Biplane carrier dive bomber,
command -E
D16(11/79-48)-1, B229(78)-1,
B230(195)-1, A14(347)-1, D3(4-86)-1
*GRUMMAN The Grumman Aircraft
Engineering Corp.*
FF (Japan **AXG**) Biplane carrier fighter -D
D7(9-26)-4, A9(194)-2, B254(8,78)-2,
B216(92)-2, A10(499)-1, B229(96)-1,
B222(74)-2, A14(368)-1, B15(254)-7,
A15(200)-0
F2F Biplane carrier fighter -D
D9(3/76-124,3/81-150)-2, A9(196)-2,
B254(19,80)-2, B216(125)-2, A10(499)-1,
A14(373)-1, B230(292)-1, B297(373)-1,
A15(200)-0
F3F Biplane carrier fighter -A
D9(3/76-124)-4, B71(92)-2, A9(196)-2,
B148(80)-4, A10(499)-2, B254(22,82)-2,
B216(140)-2, B411(63)-1, B101(85)-1,
A15(200)-0, A14(376)-1
F4F Wildcat (FM, Martlet) Carrier
fighter -A
D7(3-49)-4, B147(33)-4, B71(53)-2,
A3(4-90,6-180)-2, A9(204)-2,
D19(4/61-223)-2, B65(40)-4, A7(84)-1,
B148(108)-4, B135(2-36)-2, B277(136)-2,
A6(233)-2, A10(500)-2, B252(59)-2,
B216(155)-2, A15(200)-6, A14(381)-1
F6F Hellcat Carrier fighter -A
B147(47)-4, D9(4/76-176)-4, A3(4-102)-2,
B148(158)-4, B277(139)-2, A6(230)-4,
A9(216)-2, B65(167)-4, B216(183)-2,
B252(60)-2, B453-2, A10(502)-1,
A7(85)-1, B18(2-92)-7, A15(200)-6,
B135(2-104)-2, A14(390)-1
F7F Tigercat Twin engine carrier
fighter -M
D9(4/84-180)-4, B147(57)-2, A3(4-106)-2,
A9(219)-2, D29(8/73-20)-1, B216(188)-2,

B164(129)-2, A6(224)-2, B277(145)-2,
B59(259c)-2, A14(393)-1
F8F Bearcat Carrier fighter -M
D9(5/80-233)-4, B71(107)-2, A3(4-109)-2,
B147(62)-2, A9(222)-2, B148(172)-4,
B164(130)-4, B277(147)-2, B216(197)-2,
A10(504)-1, A14(394)-1
G-23
See Canada: C.C.F. G-23 Goblin
G-42
See Columbia: XJL-1
G-63 Kitten Light tourer -E
D11(10/67-24)-1, B414(223)-1,
B261(59)-1, D3(9-100)-1
G-65 Tadpole Pusher sport
amphibian -E
D11(10/67-24)-1, B414(224)-1,
B261(61)-1, B434(92)-1
JF Duck Biplane utility amphibian -B
D7(23-46)-1, A3(6-175)-1, B254(12)-1,
B230(298)-1, A9(201)-0, A15(200)-0
J2F Duck (OA-12) Biplane utility
amphibian -A
D7(23-46)-4, A3(6-175)-2, A9(201)-2,
B88(3-18)-2, D9(1/77-45)-2, B277(150)-2,
B254(14)-1, A7(200)-1, B18(2-50)-7,
A15(200)-6, A14(330)-1
J4F Widgeon (OA-14) Twin engine
high wing utility amphibian -A
A3(5-172)-2, B59(264c)-2, B88(3-20)-2,
A9(416)-1, A12(367)-1, B139(146)-2,
B277(149)-3, B254(46)-1, A7(200)-1,
A15(200)-6, B468(97)-1
JRF Goose (XJ3F, OA-9, OA-13) Twin
engine high wing amphibian -A
A3(5-169)-2, A9(210)-2, B59(263c)-2,
B88(3-19)-2, A11(500)-1, B139(146)-2,
B277(148)-3, B254(39)-1, A7(201)-1,
A15(200)-6, B468(85)-1
SF Biplane carrier scout -D
D7(9-28)-1, A9(194)-1, B230(276)-1,
A14(331)-1, B254(10)-1, B445(291)-1,
B297(45)-1, A15(200)-6
TBF Avenger (TBM, Tarpon) Carrier
torpedo bomber -A

B65(117)-4, B71(214)-2, A9(212)-2,
A12(196)-2, A6(224)-2, B203-2,
B277(151)-2, A10(501)-2, B58(197c)-2,
B88(4-22)-2, B252(62)-2, A7(86)-1,
B18(2-74)-7, B275(48)-5, B352(216)-2,
A15(200)-6, A14(361)-1
UC-103 (G-32, Gulfhawk III) Biplane
utility, version F3F -I
B254(24,25)-1, D9(3/76-131)-0,
A8(571)-0, B10(84)-0, B218(9-196)-1
XF4F-1 (Model G-16) Biplane carrier
fighter -J
B216(155)-3, B254(25)-6, A3(4-90)-0,
D7(3-49)-3, B147(33)-0
XF5F Skyrocket Twin engine carrier
fighter -E
A3(4-97)-2, B254(51,88)-2, B147(46)-2,
B216(167)-2, B350(75)-2,
D9(4/81-207)-2, A14(385)-1,
B352(215)-1, B445(303)-1
XJR2F Albatross (UF, SA-16) Twin
engine high wing amphibian -H
A9(228)-2, D16(5/85-33)-1, D3(9-77)-2,
B139(145)-2, B17(94)-7
XP-50 Twin engine fighter -E
A3(4-100)-2, B215(124)-2,
B254(52,90)-2, D9(4/81-207)-2,
A14(287)-1, B347(64)-2, B40(92)-1,
B111(57)-1, B312(192)-1
XP-65 (F7F) Twin engine fighter -J
B215(173)-2, B147(60)-0, A14(287)-0,
A8(580)-0, B10(153)-0
XTB2F Twin engine high wing carrier
torpedo bomber -J
D9(6/82-313)-2, B414(213)-1,
A14(365)-1, B450(124)-1,
D27(9/70-77)-1, D14(1-13)-3, A9(225)-0
XTB3F Guardian (AF) Tandem
piston/jet engine carrier bomber -H
D19(4/73-218)-1, D3(9-137)-2,
A14(498)-1, A9(225)-2, B139(57)-2,
B203(53)-1, B17(26)-7, A10(505)-1
XTSF-1 Carrier torpedo bomber version
F7F -J
D9(6/82-313)-0, B10(228)-0, A9(513)-0

HALL *The Hall-Aluminum Aircraft
Corp.*
PH Twin engine biplane patrol flying
boat -B
A3(5-175)-2, A9(248)-2, B88(4-53)-2,
A14(103)-1, D9(10/77-191)-1,
B230(297)-1, B277(154)-3, B225(87)-1,
B444(2-7)-1, A15(200)-0

HALLER
TG-28 (Hawk Junior) Training glider -I
B10(170)-0, A8(583)-0, B111(37)-0,
D20(1/67-332)-0

HAMILTON *Hamilton Aero
Manufacturing Co.*
UC-89 (H-47 Metalplane) High wing
transport -I
B218(1-232)-1, B217(266)-1, B468(31)-1,
B353(147)-6, B10(82)-0, A8(571)-0

HARLOW *Harlow Aircraft Corp.*
PC-5 (H.A.L. PC-5A) Trainer -E
B218(8-129)-1, B358(1-83)-1,
B21(A-98)-1, D3(4-110)-1, B56(181c)-0,
B279(185)-0
UC-80 (PJC-2) Liaison -I
B218(7-206)-1, B56(181c)-1,
B21(A-98)-1, B358(1-82)-1, B139(73)-1,
A15(201)-0, B272(41-232)-3, B10(81)-0,
B279(185)-0

HARPER-CORCORAN
TG-23 Training sailplane -I
B10(170)-0, A8(583)-0, B111(37)-0,
D20(1/67-332)-0

HIGGINS *Helicopter Division, Higgins
Industries Inc.*
EB-1 Helicopter -F
B59(265c)-1, B151(148)-1, D3(5-18)-1,
B228(285)-0, B279(190)-0

HILLER *Hiller Industries, Aircraft Div.
(United Helicopters Inc.)*
X-235 (Hiller-Kaiser) Coaxial rotor
helicopter -F
B228(287)-0

XH-44 Hiller-Copter Coaxial rotor
helicopter -F
B310(P)-2, B228(287)-1, B59(266c)-1,
D3(6-76)-2, B447(51)-1, B23(20)-6

HOWARD *Howard Aircraft Corp.*
DGA-18 (DGA-125,145,160)
Trainer -B
B218(8-142)-1, B154(197c)-1,
B57(189c)-3, B20(A-55)-1,
B13(1-20,227)-1, B279(194)-0
GH Nightingale (NH, DGA-15) High
wing utility, trainer, ambulance -A
B88(4-62)-2, A9(419)-1, B218(8-68)-1,
C9(113,155)-2, B277(155)-1,
B58(201c)-1, D19(1/83-53)-1,
B358(1-152)-2, B96(74)-1, A15(201)-0
UC-70 (DGA-15P) High wing utility -I
B218(8-68)-1, B279(194)-1, B111(49)-1,
A15(201)-0, A8(513)-0
UC-70A (DGA-12) High wing utility -I
B218(7-161)-1, A8(513)-0, B10(79)-0
UC-70B (DGA-15J) High wing utility -I
A8(513)-1, B218(8-69)-1, D3(5-183)-2,
B10(79)-0
UC-70C (DGA-8) High wing utility -I
B218(7-49)-1, B152(274c)-1, A8(513)-0,
B10(79)-0, D19(1/57-69)-1
UC-70D (DGA-9) High wing utility -I
B218(7-161)-1, A8(513)-0, B10(79)-0

HUGHES *Hughes Aircraft Co.*
D-2 (XA-37?) Twin engine twin boom
attack bomber -E
D8(1-17)-2, B30(102)-1, D29(6/77-44)-6,
A14(191)-0, B352(229)-0, B470(79)-1
H-4 Hercules (HK-1) Eight engine high
wing transport flying boat -H
B30(11)-2, B225(193)-1, B311-2, B179-1,
B16(41)-7, B408(378)-2, B470(83)-1,
D29(12/82-10)-1, D19(4/85-294)-1,
D20(9/69-75)-1, B279(194)-1, B452(69)-1
XF-11 Twin engine twin boom
reconnaissance -H
D29(6/77-44)-1, D20(9/69-75)-2,

D8(1-20)-2, B179(14)-1, B43(45)-1,
B60(243c)-1, B30(103)-1, D26(202)-3,
B473(69)-1, B470(81)-1

INTERSTATE *Interstate Aircraft &
Engineering Corp.*
L-6 Grasshopper (XO-63, S-1-B) High
wing liaison -A
B88(4-27)-2, A8(514)-1, B277(156)-1,
B218(8-188)-1, B58(202c)-1, B111(51)-1,
D3(4-303)-2, A15(201)-0, B312(185)-1
L-8 (S-1-A Cadet) High wing liaison,
trainer -A
B218(8-136)-1, B56(182c)-1, B420(71)-1,
B272(41-81)-1, A8(576)-0, B21(A-101)-1,
B358(1-148)-0, B10(130)-0
TDR (XBQ-4) Twin engine flying
bomb -B
B60(243c)-1, B288(94)-1, B111(62)-1,
D19(4/77-308,1/82-25,4/85-290)-1,
B444(1-57)-1, D10(9/67)-1, A15(201)-0
XBQ-5 Twin engine flying bomb -E
B60(243c)-0, B111(37)-0, B10(60)-0
XTD2R Twin engine flying bomb -J
B10(228)-0, A9(513)-0
XTD3R Twin engine flying bomb -E
B60(243c)-0, B10(228)-0, A9(513)-0

KAISER-FLEETWINGS *Fleetwings
Division, Kaiser Cargo Co.*
XA-39 Attack bomber -J
A14(192)-0, B109(8)-0, B10(35)-0,
A8(566)-0
XBTK-1 Carrier torpedo bomber -E
D20(11/66-217)-2, A14(366)-1,
C9(30,92)-2, B279(202)-1, D3(8-244)-1,
D26(152)-3

KELLETT *The Kellett Aircraft Corp.*
XR-2 (YG-1C) Autogiro -G
B467(132)-2, D5(Fall/77-19)-1,
B326(242)-0, A8(514)-0, B10(161)-0
XR-3 (YG-1B) Autogiro -F
B467(134)-2, B151(70)-1,
D5(Fall/77-110)-1, B326(242)-0,
A8(514)-0, B10(161)-0

XR-8 Twin rotor helicopter -E
B60(244c)-1, B326(245)-1, B228(324)-1,
B447(51)-1, B355(139)-1, D3(6-144)-1,
B111(61)-1, B23(20)-6, A8(582)-0,
B358(2-256)-1
XR-10 (XH-10) Twin engine twin rotor
ambulance helicopter -H
B228(325)-1, D3(8-175)-2, B326(246)-1,
B447(70)-1, B355(139)-1, B110(24)-1,
A8(582)-0, B10(162)-0
YG-1 (KD-1) Observation autogiro -D
B467(107)-2, A8(514)-1, B218(8-50)-1,
D25(6/60-53)-1, B326(242)-1,
B151(44)-1, B152(275c)-1, B355(80)-1,
B468(91)-1, B111(61)-1, B296(21)-6
YO-60 Observation autogiro -C
B467(126)-2, B88(5-46)-2, B310(3P4)-2,
D3(5-111)-2, B59(268c)-1, B111(53)-1,
B326(242)-1, B228(323)-1, B23(15)-6,
A8(514)-0, B10(140)-0

*KEYSTONE Keystone Aircraft Corp.
(Huff-Daland Airplane Co.)*
B-3A Panther (LB-10A) Twin engine
biplane bomber -D
B214(17)-1, A14(35)-1, B411(83)-1,
B24(33)-1, B111(42)-1, B104(38)-1,
A8(277)-0, A10(510)-0, B114(15-1589)-1
Pelican Biplane trainer floatplane -B
D16(1/78-56)-1, B152(47b)-1

*KINNER Kinner Airplane & Motor
Corp.*
XRK-1 (C-7 Envoy, Japan LXK) Light
transport -B
A9(421)-1, B218(6-107)-1, B226(502)-1,
C100(6-156)-1, B230(223)-1,
B279(205)-0

*LAISTER-KAUFFMANN Laister-
Kauffmann Aircraft Corp.*
TG-4 (LK-10 Yankee Doodle)
Training glider -A
B59(269c)-1, A8(515)-1, B358(2-104)-1,
B111(63)-1, B277(156)-0, B22(A-137)-1

TG-20 (Göppingen) High wing training
sailplane -I
A8(583)-0, B10(170)-0, B111(37)-0,
D20(1/67-332)-0
XCG-10 Trojan Horse High wing
transport glider -E
D6(6/72-320)-2, B286(119)-2,
B59(269c)-2, B111(63)-1, B277(156)-3,
D20(3/64-61)-1, D3(6-3)-2, C8(151)-1,
B109(44)-1, C88(265,P)-1

*LANDGRAF The Landgraf Helicopter
Co.*
H-2 Twin rotor helicopter -E
B59(270c)-1, D3(6-146)-1, B228(327)-0,
B279(208)-0

*LANGLEY Langley Aircraft Corp.
(Andover Kent Aviation Corp.)*
XNL-1 (Langley Twin) Twin engine
trainer -E
B218(8-191)-1, B58(203c)-1,
B358(1-184)-1, C9(119)-1, B317(60)-1,
B22(A-50)-1, A9(508)-0, B10(202)-0

*LOCKHEED The Lockheed Aircraft
Corp.*
A-29 Hudson (A-28, AT-18, PBO)
Twin engine bomber -A
D9(11/85-240)-4, B120(145)-2,
B71(253)-2, A11(320)-2, A8(286)-2,
D29(4/84-26)-5, D16(5/84-8)-1,
B88(4-47)-2, A6(226)-2, A10(510)-2,
B59(279c)-2, B252(96)-2, B277(160)-1,
A9(424)-1, B18(2-18)-7, A15(202)-6,
A14(180)-1, A7(111)-1
Airtrooper (V-308) Light transport,
version Little Dipper -J
D11(6/63-39)-8, B120(256)-0,
B194(108)-0, B261(76)-0
B-34 Ventura (B-37, 0-56, Lexington)
Twin engine bomber -A
A8(288)-2, A11(326)-2, B214(118)-2,
B88(3-34)-2, B120(200)-1, A14(228)-1,
D3(3-150)-2, B362(5)-1, B277(162)-3,
A15(202)-0

C-56 Lodestar (C-57, C-60, C-66, R50, Model 18) Twin engine transport -A
B120(185)-2, A8(284)-2, B58(207c)-2, B162(123)-2, B218(8-89)-1, A9(423)-1, A11(504)-1, B277(158)-1, A7(112)-1, B288(97)-1, A15(202)-0, B18(2-35)-7, C131(157)-1, B468(95)-1

C-69 Constellation (R70, Model 49) Four engine transport -B
D7(14-29)-4, B120(219)-2, D19(3/83-190)-2, A8(298)-1, A7(213)-1, B59(207c)-2, B162(165)-2, B71(120)-1, B277(164)-1, A15(203)-0, B18(2-104)-7

C-111 (R40, Model 14 Super Electra) Twin engine transport -I
B120(135)-2, B162(122)-2, B218(7-199,229,253)-1, B230(254)-1, B96(43)-1, D3(1-131)-2, B194(52)-1, A8(284)-0, A15(202)-0, B468(88)-1

L-133 Single jet canard fighter -J
B120(468)-3, D7(11-54)-7, B138(20)-3, B194(87)-6

Little Dipper (V-304, Model 33) Light plane -E
B120(256)-2, D11(6/63-39)-2, B420(73)-2, B194(108)-1, B261(76)-1, B60(252c)-1, D3(7-215)-1

Model 8A Sirius Liaison -K
B120(96)-2, B4(116)-2, B218(3-283)-1, C78(300)-6

P-38 Lightning (F-5, P-322) Twin engine twin boom fighter -A
B146(2-8)-4, B120(158)-2, A3(4-112)-2, B71(106)-2, B148(122)-8, A8(290)-2, A6(227)-2, A10(511)-2, B277(165)-2, B164(69)-2, B455-2, B252(93)-2, A7(113)-1, B18(2-53)-7, A15(203)-6, B215(91)-2, A14(260)-1

P-80 Shooting Star (TO-1) Single jet fighter -M
D7(11-54)-4, B438-4, B120(232)-2, B146(2-26)-2, A3(4-126)-2, B148(170)-4, A8(302)-2, A10(514)-2, B59(272c)-2, B215(202)-2, A14(441)-1, A15(203)-6

PV-1 Ventura Twin engine patrol bomber -A
B120(201)-2, A9(252)-2, B361(6,50)-2, B277(162)-1, A6(228)-2, B362-2, B285(2-50)-2, B58(205c)-2, A10(513)-1, A15(202)-6, A14(320)-1, A7(114)-1

PV-2 Harpoon Twin engine patrol bomber -A
B120(258)-2, A9(252)-2, B361(11,53)-2, B362(39)-2, B59(276c)-1, A10(514)-1, C9(31,101)-2, A14(320)-1, A7(213)-1, A15(203)-0, B18(2-101)-7

P2V Neptune Twin engine patrol bomber -M
B120(258)-2, B88(7-52)-2, D3(7-123)-2, A9(256)-1, B71(204)-1, B393-2, B60(253c)-1, A14(475)-1, C9(34,104)-2, B362(49)-1

UC-36 (UC-37, R20, R30, Model 10 Electra, Japan **KXL)** Twin engine transport -B
B120(116)-2, B88(4-23)-2, A8(517)-1, A9(422)-1, B162(87)-2, B218(6-184)-1, D3(1-139)-2, B277(157)-1, B152(276c)-1, B176(86)-1, B468(67)-1

UC-40 (JO, Model 12 Electra Junior) Twin engine transport -B
D6(5/72-261)-4, B120(127)-2, A8(517)-1, A9(423)-1, B277(158)-1, B88(3-28,76)-2, D3(2-41)-4, B218(7-62)-1, B56(184c)-1, A15(202)-0, C131(134)-1, B468(82)-1

UC-85 (Model 9-D2 Orion) Light transport -I
B4(164,192)-2, B120(110)-2, B162(75)-2, B218(6-51,9-187)-1, B468(53)-1, D19(1/56-9,1/71-40)-5, C78(300)-1, B139(23)-1, B15(241)-7

UC-101 (Model 5 Vega) High wing light transport -I
B4(181,187)-2, A8(515)-1, B120(75)-2, B162(44)-2, B408(211)-2, D19(1/57-5)-1, B352(245)-5, B15(228)-7, B222(62)-1, A15(201)-0, B468(25)-1

XB-30 (Model 249) Four engine bomber, version C-69 -J

B214(100)-2, D19(3/83-197)-3,
B210(1)-1, C88(179)-6, A14(398)-0
XC-35 (Version Model 10E Electra)
Twin engine high altitude -F
D16(9/81-37)-1, B120(120)-1,
B194(44)-1, A8(516)-1, C8(194)-1,
B152(278c)-1, B312(206)-1, B402(465)-1,
A15(201)-0
XP-49 Twin engine twin boom fighter -E
B120(216)-2, A3(4-122)-2, B215(121)-2,
B146(2-14)-1, A14(287)-1, D9(1/85-44)-2,
B347(59)-1, B455(5)-1, B60(255c)-1
XP-58 Chain Lightning Twin engine
twin boom escort fighter -E
D19(2/82-120)-4, D29(6/80-18)-1,
D16(7/80-8)-2, B146(2-25)-2,
B120(252)-2, A3(4-124)-2, B215(147)-2,
B347(59)-2, A14(292)-1, B60(254c)-1
XR60 Constitution Four engine
transport -H
B120(281)-2, D16(3/77-10)-1,
B60(247c)-1, D3(9-17)-2, A9(424)-1,
B194(100)-1, B139(141)-1, B450(108)-1,
B408(372)-1, B261(82)-1, C15(166)-1
Y1C-23 (Model DL-2A Altair)
Liaison -D
B120(104)-2, B4(157,191)-2, A8(516)-1,
B352(248)-1, B111(47)-1

LUSCOMBE Luscombe Airplane Co.
Phantom High wing liaison -I
C131(55)-1, B218(6-188)-1,
B152(278c)-1, B420(54)-1
UC-90 (Model 8 Silvaire) High wing
utility -I
B218(7-320)-1, B57(196c)-1,
B272(41-160,239)-2, B358(1-154)-1,
B139(17)-2, B420(70)-1, B449(137)-1,
B10(82)-0, A8(571)-0

MANAGEMENT AND RESEARCH
Management and Research Inc. (Tuscar
Metals)
H-70-71 Pusher flying wing -E
B439(61)-1

MARTIN The Glenn L. Martin Co.
B-26 Marauder (AT-23, JM) Twin
engine bomber -A
B134(1-107)-2, B71(112)-2, B260(29)-4,
A8(334)-2, B214(88)-2, A6(229)-2,
A10(529)-2, B277(180)-2, A11(334)-2,
B124(30)-2, B252(103)-2, B33-2,
B59(284c)-2, A7(117)-1, A15(207)-6
BM Biplane carrier bomber -D
A9(294)-2, B230(250)-1, A10(526)-1,
B411(150)-1, A14(117)-1, D16(9/85-10)-1
JRM Mars Four engine high wing
transport flying boat -H
B225(184)-2, B88(7-48)-2, A9(429)-1,
B60(263c)-1, B139(150)-1, D8(1-13)-2,
B76(114)-1, B277(186)-1, B281(307)-1,
B5(124)-1
M-130 China Clipper Four engine high
wing transport flying boat -I
D19(3/65-172)-1, B162(99)-2,
B225(131)-2, A9(429)-1, B15(266)-7,
B431(153)-5, B440(137)-1,
B218(6-301)-1, B294(60)-6, A15(203)-0
M-139 (B-10, B-12) Twin engine
bomber -B
A8(330)-2, B214(30)-2, D7(22-1)-5,
D20(8/65-49)-1, A10(527)-1,
B277(178)-7, B273(63)-2, A6(246)-7,
A15(203)-6, A14(196)-1
M-156 'Soviet Clipper' (USSR **PS-30**)
Four engine high wing patrol flying
boat -C
B218(7-335)-1, B197(145)-1,
B154(206c)-1, A15(203)-0, B20(A-64)-1
M-166 Twin engine bomber -B
B88(3-80)-2, A10(528)-1, D25(1/63-45)-1,
A14(199)-1, B153(262c)-1, C59(62,48)-1,
D20(8/65-51)-0, A15(203)-0
M-167 Maryland (XA-22) Twin engine
bomber -A
B71(232)-1, D16(1/75-16)-1, A11(330)-2,
B56(191c)-2, B252(101)-2, A6(228)-1,
D9(12/74-303)-1, B277(174)-1,
A10(528)-1, A15(204)-6, A14(178)-1
M-187 Baltimore (A-30, XA-23) Twin

engine bomber -A
B71(232)-2, D16(1/75-16)-1, A11(332)-2,
B58(212c)-2, B252(102)-2, D1(3-12)-2,
B277(175)-2, A6(245)-1, A10(530)-1,
A15(204)-6, A14(179)-1, A7(214)-1

P3M (Consolidated XPY-1) Twin
engine high wing patrol flying boat -D
A9(296)-2, B230(108)-1, B197(35)-1,
A10(526)-1, A14(303)-1, B452(25)-1

P4M Mercator Twin tandem piston/jet
engine patrol bomber -H
D3(8-53)-2, A9(430)-1, B139(113)-2,
A10(531)-1, A14(478)-1, B473(103)-1,
D29(12/84-28)-1, B450(145)-1

PBM Mariner Twin engine high wing
patrol flying boat -A
A3(5-177)-2, A9(298)-2, B225(145)-2,
B59(283c)-2, B277(187)-7, A10(528)-2,
B139(147)-2, A6(245)-1, B18(2-64)-7,
A15(204)-6, A14(316)-1, A7(215)-1

T4M Biplane carrier torpedo bomber -D
A9(290)-2, B230(171)-1, A10(526)-1,
B411(92)-1, A14(114)-1, B14(144,154)-7,
B101(89)-1, B275(9)-1, B96(21)-1,
A15(203)-0

XB-27 Twin engine bomber -J
B214(91)-2, D14(6-100)-3, C88(178)-6,
A14(229)-0

XB-33 Twin or four engine bomber -J
B214(112)-2, D14(3-47)-2, C88(154)-6,
A14(404)-0

XB-48 Six jet bomber -H
B214(163)-2, D3(8-125)-2,
D9(11/76-240)-2, B138(67)-2, A14(425)-1

XBTM Mauler (AM) Carrier
bomber -M
D16(7/74-8)-2, A9(301)-2, D3(8-268)-2,
B60(261c)-1, B277(177)-2, B139(61)-2,
C9(93)-2, A14(366)-1, B275(60)-1,
B450(122)-1

XPB2M Mars Four engine high wing
patrol, transport flying boat -E
A3(5-184)-2, B225(182)-2, B197(208)-1,
A14(318)-1, B59(281c)-1, D3(3-207)-2,

B352(272)-1, B277(186)-3, B444(2-4)-1,
B294(74)-6

McDONNELL *McDonnell Aircraft
Corp.*

FD-1 Phantom Twin jet carrier
fighter -M
B147(64)-2, B121(380)-2, B148(176)-4,
A3(4-132)-2, A9(281)-2, B216(225)-2,
B164(141)-2, A10(521)-2, B60(257c)-2,
B138(54)-2, A14(502)-1, B464(72)-2,
D9(1/86-44)-2, B310(P)-2

LBD-1 Gargoyle (KSD-1) Rocket-
propelled glide bomb -E
B163(121)-1, B60(259c)-1, B195(219)-1,
B115(158)-1, B114(10-1090)-0,
B464(190)-0

Model 1 Mid-engine twin pusher
fighter -J
D14(5-69)-3, B121(370)-0, A3(4-129)-0,
B146(2-28)-0, B215(179)-0

XF2D Banshee Twin jet carrier
fighter -H
B121(426)-2, A9(283)-2, B216(239)-2,
B164(164)-2, B350(104)-2, B138(64)-2,
A10(522)-1, A14(504)-1, B195(88)-1,
B17(64)-7, B464(72)-1, D9(1/86-44)-2

XHJD-1 Whirlaway Twin engine twin
rotor helicopter -H
B121(420)-2, B326(255)-1, B228(335)-1,
B195(251)-1, B447(73)-1, D3(7-206)-1,
C45(96)-1, C91(46)-1, B410(79)-1

XP-67 Twin engine fighter -E
A3(4-129)-2, B121(370)-2, B146(2-28)-2,
B215(179)-2, B277(189)-1, B111(58)-1,
D9(11/75-256)-2, D29(12/73-44)-1,
A14(299)-1, B347(65)-2, B312(194)-1,
D9(12/85-301,1/86-44)-2

XTD2D Katydid (KDD-1) Pulse jet
target drone -E
B60(258c)-1, B195(219)-1, B10(228)-0,
A9(513)-0, B464(190)-0

MELHOUSE
TG-22 Training sailplane -I

B10(170)-0, A8(583)-0, B111(37)-0,
D20(1/67-332)-0

MERCURY *Mercury Aircraft Corp.*
BT-120 Aerobat Biplane trainer -E
B218(8-157)-1, B21(A-114)-1,
B56(193c)-0, D3(5-75)-1

MEYERS *Meyers Aircraft Co.*
ME-165W Trainer -E
B57(200c)-1, B21(A-115)-1,
B272(43-265)-1, D3(5-111)-1
OTW-145, OTW-160 Biplane trainer -B
B218(8-132)-1, B57(199c)-2,
B59(286c)-1, B22(A-112)-1, B314(45)-1,
B139(155)-1, B420(63)-1, B279(228)-0
O2 High wing trainer -E
B56(194c)-1, D3(5-111)-1

MIDWEST *Midwest Sailplane Co.*
(Steinhauser)
TG-18 (MU-1) High wing training
glider -I
B22(A-140)-1, A8(583)-0, B10(170)-0,
B111(37)-0, D20(1/67-332)-0

MONOCOUPE
See Universal

MORROW *Morrow Aircraft Corp.*
Model 1-L Victory Trainer Trainer -E
B57(201c)-1, B22(A-113)-1, B56(195c)-3,
D3(5-171)-1, B279(232)-0

N.A.F. *Naval Aircraft Factory (Naval
Air Material Center)*
KAN Little Joe Anti-aircraft missile -E
B163(196)-1, D3(7-311)-1, B190(61)-6,
B428(98)-0, B114(16-1752)-6
KDN Single jet target drone -K
B60(265c)-1, D3(7-311)-1
N3N 'Yellow Peril' Biplane trainer, also
floatplane -A
A9(318)-2, A3(6-182)-2, B88(4-59)-2,
B56(196c)-1, B277(190)-3,

D19(3/62-230)-2, B230(253,299)-1,
B450(72)-1, B279(235)-1
OS2N Kingfisher (Vought OS2U)
Observation, also floatplane -A
A3(6-192)-1, A9(378)-1, B71(251-114)-0,
B22(A-114)-1, A15(211)-0, A14(339)-0
PBN Nomad (Consolidated PBY-6)
Twin engine high wing patrol flying
boat -A
A3(5-152)-2, B59(287c)-2, B88(6-46)-2,
A14(312)-1, B360(36)-1, A9(79)-0,
A15(191)-0
SBN (Brewster XSBA) Carrier scout
bomber, trainer -B
D9(7/78-43)-2, B230(284)-1,
B57(202c)-1, A14(312)-1, A9(394)-0,
D29(4/85-13)-1, B275(15)-1, B277(45)-3,
A15(205)-0, B114(21-2273)-0
SON Seagull (Curtiss SOC) Biplane
carrier scout -B
D19(3/58-168)-1, B230(247)-1,
B39(343)-1, B22(A-114)-1, A9(139)-0,
A15(194)-0, A14(337)-0
TDN Twin engine high wing flying
bomb -B
D3(8-19)-1, C88(205,P)-1, B10(228)-0,
A9(513)-0
XLRN-1 High wing transport glider -E
B286(151)-1, B10(201)-0, A9(507)-0
XN5N-1 Trainer, glider tug -E
B230(289)-1, C9(119,167)-1,
D3(7-207)-1, A9(508)-0, B10(202)-0
XOSN-1 Biplane scout -E
B230(239)-1, A14(338)-1, B10(205)-0,
A9(509)-0

NASH-KELVINATOR *Nash-
Kelvinator Corp.*
XJRK Four engine transport flying
boat -J
B10(200)-0, A9(507)-0

NAVAL BUREAU OF ORDNANCE
**Bat (RCA Dragon, NBS Pelican,
SWOD Mk 9)** High wing glide bomb -A
B163(120)-1, B428(102)-1,

D19(1/82-26)-1, B288(49)-1,
B115(152)-1, D3(6-312)-1, C88(204,P)-1,
B190(51)-6, B114(3-282)-5
Gorgon Rocket, jet-propelled missiles -F
B163(120,222)-1, B428(102)-0,
B190(60)-6, D19(1/82-28)-0,
B114(11-1154)-8, B60(265c)-0

NORTH AMERICAN *North American
Aviation, Inc.*
A-27 (NA-69) Light bomber version
NA-16 -B
B394(42)-1, A14(170)-1,
D19(4/68-246)-1, A15(205)-0, B10(34)-0
A-36 Invader Dive bomber version
P-51 -A
A8(364)-2, B58(216c)-2, B88(5-30)-2,
B394(52)-1, A14(185)-1, D3(4-230)-2,
D9(9/83-133)-1, B94(14)-1, B371(114)-1,
D16(7/85-15)-5
AT-6 Texan (BC-1, SNJ, Harvard)
Trainer -A
D22(16-35)-2, A8(348)-2, A9(321)-2,
B394(20)-1, B277(206)-2, B57(205c)-2,
D19(2/79-107)-1, A6(246)-1, A11(344)-2,
A7(139)-1, B18(2-40)-7, B463-4
B-25 Mitchell (AT-24, PBJ, F-10)
Twin engine bomber -A
B134(1-97)-2, B260(6)-4, A8(352)-2,
B71(59)-2, B277(191)-2, A6(247)-2,
D29(6/72-38)-5, B274-4, B257-2,
A10(535)-2, B214(84)-2, B252(130)-2,
B18(2-44)-7, A14(219)-1, A15(205)-6,
B394(34)-1, A7(140)-1, A11(348)-2
BT-9 (NJ, Yale, NA-46) Trainer -A
A8(344)-2, B394(16)-1, B314(17)-1,
D19(2/79-100)-1, B104(59)-1,
D29(2/84-48)-1, B153(268c)-1,
C23(180)-1, B156(34)-1, B444(1-14)-1
BT-14 (Yale) Trainer -A
B56(200c)-2, B88(2-41)-2, B314(18,50)-2,
B394(17)-1, B156(36)-1, B312(177)-1,
D19(2/79-110)-1, A8(344)-0, B463(P)-1
L-17 Navion Liaison -H
B218(8-283)-1, B394(80)-1, A8(522)-1,

B139(66)-2, B60(266c)-1, B444(1-112)-1,
B10(131)-0
NA-16 (Japan **KXA**) Trainer, light
bomber -A
B394(14,20,25)-1, D19(2/79-99)-1,
D22(16-35)-1, B156(34)-1, B153(268c)-1
NA-35 (Vega 35) Trainer -E
B120(195)-2, B218(8-147)-1, B394(32)-1,
B314(44)-1, B20(A-96)-1,
B272(41-110,279)-2, D29(8/85-52)-1
NA-40 Twin engine high wing
bomber -E
B214(81)-2, B394(34)-1, B134(1-97)-1,
A14(68)-1, D29(4/84-13)-1, B273(104)-1,
B260(24,140)-1, B153(267c)-1,
B257(3)-1, B397(334)-1
NA-44 (NA-69,72,74) Light bomber,
version NA-16 -B
B394(42)-1, B155(15,163)-1,
C131(144)-1, D19(3/83-223)-1,
B153(267c)-1, B358(1-72)-1, A14(170)-0,
B57(5a)-1
NA-50 Fighter -B
B394(44)-1, D19(4/78-296)-1,
D29(10/72-40)-1, B153(266c)-1,
A10(534)-1, B156(37)-1, A14(250)-0,
A15(205)-0, B20(A-70)-1
O-47 Observation, trainer -A
D22(13-185)-2, D16(1/75-30)-1,
A8(346)-2, B88(3-21)-2, A14(157)-1,
D20(6/64-71)-2, B394(13)-1,
D29(2/83-41)-1, B221(139)-1, A15(205)-6
P-51 Mustang (A-36, F-6, Apache,
Sweden **J 26)** Fighter -A
B146(2-30)-4, D9(9/83-130,10/83-179)-4,
B135(1-91)-2, B71(8,100)-2, A3(4-136)-2,
A8(360)-2, D7(2-191)-5, B156-4, B90-2,
B164(102)-4, B148(140)-4, A6(242)-5,
B277(196)-2, B215(127)-2, A10(536)-2,
B94-2, B59(288c)-2, B107-1,
B252(127)-2, D16(7/85)-5, A7(141)-1,
A15(206)-6, A14(280)-1, B18(2-82)-7
P-64 (NA-68) Fighter, trainer -B
B146(2-29)-2, D19(4/78-296,3/83-216)-2,
A3(4-134)-2, B215(170)-2,

D29(10/72-40)-1, A8(521)-1, B394(44)-1,
A10(534)-1, B277(204)-3, A14(250)-1

P-82 Twin Mustang Twin engine twin
fuselage fighter -M
B146(2-49)-2, D7(6-121)-4, A3(4-153)-2,
A8(368)-2, B215(208)-2, B277(205)-2,
B164(150)-2, D9(11/83-235)-4,
B156(138)-5, A10(538)-1, A14(444)-1

XB-21 Dragon Twin engine bomber -E
B214(65)-2, B394(32)-1, D29(4/84-13)-5,
B273(104)-5, A14(203)-1,
D9(4/77-189)-1, B260(24,140)-1,
B111(43)-1, B312(198)-1

XB-28 Twin engine high altitude
bomber -E
D19(2/79-82)-2, D9(4/77-189)-2,
D16(5/75-36)-1, D18(10/72-7)-2,
B214(94)-2, A14(229)-1, B394(46)-1,
B60(271c)-1, B111(44)-1

XB-45 Four jet bomber -H
A8(370)-2, B214(153)-2, B138(65)-2,
B139(142)-2, B394(65)-1, A10(539)-1,
A14(425)-1, B104(133)-1, B17(36)-7,
B114(23-2507)-1

XFJ-1 Fury Single jet carrier fighter -H
A9(324)-2, B71(42)-2, B216(234)-2,
B138(63)-2, D3(8-269)-2, A14(503)-1,
B164(160)-2, B350(103)-2, B394(67)-1,
A10(538)-1, B60(267c)-1

XSN2J Carrier trainer -H
B394(78)-1, D3(8-281)-2, B10(223)-0,
A9(511)-0

NORTHROP Northrop Aircraft, Inc.
A-17 Nomad Attack bomber -A
B121(210)-2, A8(388)-2, B273(118)-1,
D20(3/65-41)-2, B180(28)-3, A11(507)-1,
A10(545)-2, A7(225)-1, A14(165)-1,
A15(206)-6, B18(2-14)-7, D16(9/85-18)-1

BT Carrier dive bomber -B
B121(223)-2, A9(339)-2, B180(34)-2,
A14(354)-1, B152(287c)-1, B230(263)-1,
B390(4)-1, B275(17)-1, B96(42)-1,
A15(206)-0, D16(9/85-11)-1, B464(42)-1

Delta (RT-1, Canadian Vickers)

Transport, bomber -B
B121(157)-2, B162(76)-2, B218(6-192)-1,
B323(84)-1, B279(241)-1, B230(185)-1,
C112(2-67)-2, C78(326)-1, B15(255)-7,
A15(206)-0, B468(68)-1

Gamma 2E (Japan **BXN**) Attack
bomber -B
B121(151)-1, D19(1/81-81)-1,
C100(6-125)-2, A14(164)-1, B273(118)-1,
B471(51)-1

Gamma 2L Engine test -F
B121(153)-1, D19(1/81-81)-0,
B200(2-398)-1

JB-1 (MX-543 Bat) Glider version
JB-1A -F
B7(70)-1, B60(275c)-1, B439(127)-1

JB-1A Twin jet flying wing bomb -E
B7(70)-3, B439(127)-1, B163(33)-1,
D19(1/81-86)-1, D29(2/86-39)-3

JB-10 (MX-544) Pulse-jet flying wing
bomb -C
B7(74)-2, B439(127)-1, B163(33)-1,
C88(205,P)-1, D29(2/86-39)-3

Model 8A
See Douglas Model 8A

MX-324 (XP-79 model) Rocket-
propelled flying wing fighter -E
B7(65)-2, B138(51)-2, B137(84)-2,
D25(12/55-15)-2, B439(119)-1,
B410(44)-1, D19(1/81-86)-1,
B215(201)-1, B246(P)-1, C36(307)-1

MX-334 Glider version MX-324 -F
B7(65)-1, B439(119)-1, B137(82)-1,
D25(12/55-15)-1, B60(274c)-1

N-1M Jeep Twin engine pusher flying
wing -F
B439(97)-2, B7(26)-2, D6(4/72-220)-2,
B42(45)-1, B168(95)-1, B60(272c)-1,
B410(34)-1, B352(330)-1, D3(2-250)-2,
B310(P)-2, D29(2/86-36)-2

N-3PB Patrol bomber floatplane -B
D29(2/81-24)-1, B7(21)-2, A3(6-185)-2,
B88(2-40)-2, A10(546)-1, B57(206c)-2,
A11(508)-1, B352(328)-1, A14(314)-1,
A15(206)-6

161

N-9M Twin engine pusher flying wing model XB-35 -F
B7(48)-2, B439(133)-1, B60(273c)-1, D19(1/81-85)-1, B214(121)-1, B42(46)-1, B410(37)-1, B168(95)-1

N-23 Pioneer Three engine high wing transport -H
B7(118)-2, D3(8-45)-2, D19(1/81-86)-1, B468(111)-1

P-61 Black Widow (F2T) Twin engine twin boom night fighter -A
B146(2-50)-4, D7(4-137)-5, B7(53)-2, A3(4-158)-2, A8(390)-2, B148(156)-4, B277(208)-2, A6(248)-2, B118(1-58)-2, B164(122)-2, B215(161)-2, B8(64)-4, A10(546)-1, B252(131)-2, A15(206)-6

UC-100 (Gamma 2D) Light transport -I
B121(148)-1, B218(6-177)-1, D19(1/81-82)-1, A8(571)-0, B10(83)-0

XB-35 Flying Wing Four engine pusher flying wing bomber -H
B7(91)-2, B214(121)-2, B439(145)-1, D6(3/72-150)-2, B410(37)-5, B168(96)-1, A8(523)-1, A14(418)-1, D3(8-17)-2, B60(273c)-1, D29(2/86-36)-4

XF-15 Reporter (XP-61E) Twin engine twin boom photographic -H
B7(114)-2, D3(7-111)-2, D25(6/63-45)-2, B88(7-49)-2, A14(296)-1, B60(276c)-1, B215(163)-1, C8(139)-1, A15(206)-0

XP-56 Black Bullet Pusher flying wing fighter -E
B7(61)-2, B146(2-60)-2, A3(4-155)-2, B215(142)-2, B439(114)-1, A14(289)-1, B42(46)-1, B59(296c)-1, B8(79)-1, B168(103)-6

XP-79 Rocket-propelled flying wing fighter -J
B137(80)-3, B7(76)-0, B439(119,126)-0, A14(441)-0

XP-79B (MX-365, Flying Ram) Twin jet flying wing fighter -H
B7(76)-2, B215(199)-2, B138(56)-2, B439(125)-1, B168(95)-1, B60(275c)-1, A14(441)-1, B347(88)-1, B410(45)-1,
B167(117)-1, D29(2/86-39)-1

YB-49 Eight jet flying wing bomber -H
B7(118)-2, B214(166)-2, B138(73)-2, B439(156)-1, B410(40)-5, A8(523)-1, A14(419)-1, B168(92)-1, B42(50)-1, D29(2/86-44)-4

NOTRE DAME University of Notre Dame
TG-21 (ND-1) Training glider -I
B10(170)-0, A8(583)-0, B111(37)-0, D20(1/67-332)-0

ORDCIT Ordnance Project, California Institute of Technology
Private Ballistic missile -E
B26(73)-1, B428(103)-0
Wac Corporal Sounding rocket -F
B26(74)-1, B428(104)-0

PENTECOST Horace T. Pentecost
Hoppicopter Coaxial rotor strap-on helicopter -E
B228(301)-1, B310(P)-1, B161(36)-6, B279(193)-0

PHILLIPS Phillips Aviation Co.
CT-1 Skylark Biplane trainer -E
B218(8-118)-1, B21(A-126)-1, D3(5-255)-1, B279(251)-0
Model 725 Phillips-Fleet Biplane trainer -E
B21(A-126)-1, D19(1/68-56)-1, B218(9-199)-1
XPT (Aeroneer 1-B) Trainer -E
B218(7-317)-1, B21(A-125)-1, D3(5-255)-1, B153(219c)-0

PIASECKI Piasecki Helicopter Corp. (P-V Engineering Forum, Inc.)
PV-2 Helicopter -F
B53(57)-1, B228(348)-1, B59(297c)-1, B447(53)-1, B151(152)-1, B358(2-138)-1, D3(4-300)-1, B23(20)-6, B310(P)-2
XHRP-X 'Dogship' (PV-3) Tandem

rotor transport helicopter -M
B53(58)-1, B326(260)-1, A9(437)-1,
D3(6-192,8-90)-1, B279(253)-1,
B447(53)-1, B139(158)-1, B229(136)-1,
B42(78)-1, B296(86)-6

PIPER *The Piper Aircraft Corp.*
**AE-1 (J-5 Cub Cruiser, HE-1, L-4F,
L-4G, UC-83) High wing ambulance,
liaison, utility -A**
B218(8-98)-1, B59(299c)-1, B218(9-95)-1,
B288(125)-1, A9(438)-0, D3(4-34)-2,
B22(A-121)-1, B42(220)-1, A8(401)-0,
A15(206)-0
**J-3 Cub (L-4C, L-4D, UC-83A) High
wing trainer, liaison -A**
B218(8-310,314,338)-1, B310(P)-2,
B272(41-104,258)-2, D29(2/83-44)-1,
B57(208c)-1, B139(19)-2, D3(4-34)-2,
B354(419)-1, A8(401)-0
**J-4 Cub Coupe (L-4E, UC-83B) High
wing liaison, patrol -I**
B218(8-145)-1, B272(41-185,257)-2,
B59(298c)-1, D3(4-34)-2, B358(1-140)-1,
B420(71)-1, A8(401)-0, B10(81,129)-0
**L-4 Grasshopper (0-59, NE-1) High
wing liaison -A**
A8(400)-2, B88(3-27)-2, A9(438)-1,
B59(297c)-1, D29(2/83-40)-1,
B288(124)-1, A7(227)-1, B277(212)-3,
D19(1/76-72)-1, A15(206)-0, B18(2-51)-7
PT-1 Trainer -E
B261(95)-1, B60(278c)-1, B358(1-85)-1,
B13(2-87,245)-1
Skycoupe Twin boom pusher light
plane -E
D20(1/67-332)-1, D3(6-132)-1,
B60(278c)-0
**TG-8 (XLNP-1) High wing training
glider version L-4 -A**
D16(9/81-15)-1, B88(4-26)-2,
B58(220c)-1, B22(A-121)-1, A8(400)-6,
B358(2-108)-1, C88(246,P)-1,
A15(206)-0, B42(252)-0
XLBP Glomb High wing glider

bomb -E
B286(152)-0, B272(46-360)-0,
B10(200)-0, A9(507)-0
YL-14 Army Cruiser High wing
liaison -C
B218(8-208,9-97)-1, D4(11/71-59)-1,
D3(6-156,9-20)-1, A8(401)-0

PITCAIRN *Pitcairn Autogiro Co.*
PA-36 Whirlwing Autogiro -E
B375(274)-2, B154(214c)-1,
B272(41-165,259)-2, D16(3/83-43)-1,
B151(50)-1, B42(192)-1, B22(A-95)-1,
D5(Fall/77-112)-1, B467(73)-2
PA-39 Observation autogiro -C
B375(295)-2, B211(294)-1, B467(77)-2,
D16(3/83-46)-1, D5(Fall/77-19)-1,
B1(Sec.J)-2, B358(2-124)-3
YG-2 (XOP-2, PA-33, PA-34)
Observation autogiro -E
B375(236)-2, B326(272)-1,
D16(3/83-42)-1, B152(288c)-1,
B151(44)-1, B230(196)-1,
D5(Fall/77-15)-1, B42(86)-1, B355(81)-1,
B111(61)-1, B467(62)-2

PLATT-LePAGE *Platt-LePage
Aircraft Co.*
XR-1 (PL-3) Twin rotor helicopter -E
B53(176)-1, B151(64)-1, B121(317)-1,
B326(273)-1, B375(283)-1, B59(299c)-1,
B447(54)-1, B355(176)-1, B472(185)-1,
D3(5-216,264)-1, B111(61)-1

PORTERFIELD *The Porterfield
Aircraft Co.*
**Collegiate (CP-65, LP-65) High wing
trainer -A**
B218(8-78,7-307)-1, B272(41-105,260)-2,
B153(272c)-1, B20(A-77)-1
35-70 Flyabout High wing trainer,
communications -L
B218(6-239)-1, B200(2-407)-1,
D3(3-82)-2, B153(271c)-1, B139(29)-1,
B420(55)-1, B20(A-77)-1

145 Biplane trainer -K
D3(5-267)-1

PRATT-READ Pratt, Read and Co.
(Gould Aeronautical Division)
LNE-1 (TG-32) Training sailplane -B
A9(472)-1, B57(88a)-1,
D3(5-291,7-207)-1, B10(170,200)-0
XLBE Glomb Glider bomb -E
D19(4/70-260)-1, D3(7-165)-1,
B115(158)-1, B163(120)-0, A9(507)-0

RADIOPLANE Radioplane Co.
(Reginald Denny)
OQ-1 (RP-4) Twin propeller high wing
target drone -C
B409(25)-1, D29(8/85-52)-1
OQ-2 (A-2, TDD-1) High wing target
drone -A
B111(37)-0, B10(142,228)-0, A9(513)-0,
B409(25)-0
OQ-3 (TDD-2) High wing target
drone -A
D3(8-19)-1, B111(63)-1, B409(25)-1,
A9(513)-0, B10(142,228)-0
OQ-6 High wing target drone -E
D3(8-19)-1
OQ-14 (TDD-3) High wing target
drone -A
D3(8-19)-0, B111(37)-0, B409(25)-0,
B10(142,228)-0

RAWDON Rawdon Bros Aircraft, Inc.
R-1 Trainer -E
B218(8-325)-0
T-1 Trainer -E
B218(8-325)-1, B279(258)-0

READ-YORK
XCG-12 High wing transport glider -J
B286(122)-1, A8(572)-0, B10(97)-0

REARWIN Rearwin Aircraft & Engines,
Inc. (Commonwealth Aircraft)
UC-102 (Model 9000KR Sportster)

High wing utility -I
B218(7-90)-1, B92(32)-1, B153(273c)-1,
B420(58)-1, B22(A-70)-1
UC-102A (Model 8135 Cloudster)
High wing utility -I
B358(1-149)-1, B272(43-205)-1,
A8(571)-0, B10(84)-0, B21(A-131)-1

REPUBLIC The Republic Aviation Corp.
AT-12 Guardsman (Seversky 2PA,
Sweden **B 6)** Trainer -B
A8(526)-1, B245(85,117)-2, B88(4-42)-2,
B314(28,52)-2, A14(241)-1, C89(197)-1,
D1(7-36)-1, B56(208c)-1, B273(16)-1,
D29(10/83-8)-1
JB-2 (KUW-1 Loon) Pulse-jet flying
bomb, V-1 copy -C
B442(152)-1, B163(33,81)-1, B111(62)-1,
D3(6-36)-1, B114(16-1767)-0
P-43 Lancer Fighter, reconnaissance -A
A3(4-166)-2, B146(2-62)-2, A8(404)-2,
B245(88)-2, B215(107)-2, B164(36)-2,
B448(4)-1, A10(549)-1, B277(215)-2,
A15(206)-6, A14(273)-1, A7(230)-1
P-47 Thunderbolt Fighter -A
D9(1/78-26,2/78-81,3/78-132,5/78-228)-
4, B146(2-64)-4, B448-2, B126-4,
B71(7,262)-2, A3(4-169)-2, A8(406)-2,
B148(144)-4, A6(249)-4, B277(216)-2,
A10(550)-2, B164(106)-4, B215(113)-2,
B252(137)-2, B8(19)-4, A7(146)-1,
B135(1-84)-2, A15(207)-6, A14(274)-1
XF-12 Rainbow (XR-12) Four engine
reconnaissance -H
D6(2/74-84)-2, B60(282c)-2,
D19(4/76-282)-1, B181(1-154)-1,
D3(7-15)-2, B261(81)-1, B444(2-102)-1,
B111(50)-1, A8(573)-0, B473(66)-1
XP-44 Rocket (Model AP-4J,L)
Fighter -J
B215(107)-6, B245(92,122)-3,
D29(12/82-21)-6, A14(273)-0,
B347(60)-0, B448(5)-0, A8(404)-0,
D16(7/85-10)-6
XP-47 Fighter -J

B215(113)-3, B448(5)-0, B126(17)-0,
A14(274)-0, A8(406)-0
XP-69 Mid-engine fighter -J
B215(182)-2, D14(1-11)-3, A14(299)-1,
B347(88)-1, D3(7-215)-1, D25(3/60-9)-1
XP-72 Fighter -E
B146(2-82)-2, A3(4-184)-2, B215(189)-2,
A14(300)-1, B8(75)-1, B126(63,132)-1,
B109(62)-1, B448(49)-1, B111(58)-1
XP-84 Thunderjet Single jet fighter -H
A8(413)-2, B60(283c)-1, B215(214)-2,
B148(178)-4, B138(58)-2, A10(551)-2,
A14(446)-1, B347(91)-2, B111(59)-1,
B17(38)-7
YOA-15 (RC-2 Seabee) High wing
pusher amphibian -L
D22(16-82)-2, B218(8-241,9-98)-1,
D3(6-16,7-177)-2, B59(303c)-1,
B139(148)-2, B434(144)-1,
B272(46-235,369)-2, B452(82)-1,
B10(142)-0

ROTOR-CRAFT Rotor-Craft Corp.
XR-11 Dragonfly (X-2A) Tandem rotor
helicopter -H
B326(275)-1, B228(365)-0, B60(286c)-0,
B279(265)-0, A8(582)-0

RYAN The Ryan Aeronautical Co.
FR Fireball Tandem piston/jet engine
carrier fighter -M
D19(4/63-231)-2, B147(66)-2,
B74(37,116)-2, A3(4-186)-2,
B216(213)-2, A9(341)-2, B164(140)-2,
B277(223)-2, A10(553)-1, A14(501)-1
I-10 Model SCW-145) Liaison -L
B218(7-203)-1, B74(35,105)-2,
B153(274c)-1, B77(168)-1, B139(49)-1,
B10(130)-0, A8(576)-0, B22(A-124)-1
PT-20 (Model STA-2) Trainer -B
A8(423)-1, B88(4-31)-2, B71(158-4)-1,
B74(26)-1, B154(221c)-1, B314(14)-1,
B104(73)-1, A15(208)-0, B77(163)-1
PT-21 (NR-1) Trainer -B
A8(423)-2, B74(32)-1, B218(8-173)-1,

B314(14,48)-2, A9(439)-1, B71(158-4)-1,
B88(4-32)-2, A15(208)-0, B77(193)-1
PT-22 Recruit (Model ST-3)
Trainer -A
B71(158-2)-2, B277(224)-2, B57(212c)-2,
B74(33)-1, B314(14)-1, B218(8-173)-1,
B279(266)-1, B111(61)-1, A8(423)-0,
A15(208)-0
ST-3 Trainer, also floatplane -E
B74(30)-1, B71(158-7)-1, B57(213c)-1,
B358(2-42)-1, B77(193)-1
STM (STA Special) Fighter trainer -B
B74(24,89)-1, B71(158-6)-1,
B218(7-283)-1, D3(4-291)-2, B77(157)-1
STM-2 Trainer, also floatplane -A
B74(28,89,90)-1, A3(6-188)-2,
B56(211c)-2, C58(2-22,41)-1,
B323(59)-1, B77(157)-1, A15(208)-6
XF2R Dark Shark Tandem
turboprop/jet engine carrier fighter -H
B216(217)-2, D19(4/63-240)-2,
B350(100)-2, B138(63)-2, B74(38)-1,
D3(8-208)-2, B60(287c)-1,
D16(5/84-46)-1, A14(501)-1, B77(218)-1
YO-51 Dragonfly High wing STOL
observation -E
B74(36)-1, B154(220c)-1,
D29(2/83-41)-1, B77(208)-1, B111(53)-1,
B312(184)-1, B358(1-156)-1, C8(137)-1,
C93(46)-1, A8(578)-0, B473(17)-1
Y1PT-16 (Model STA-1) Trainer-B
B71(158-4)-1, B74(24)-1, B314(10)-1,
B153(274c)-1, B288(130)-1,
D19(1/84-79)-1, B104(72)-1, B111(60)-1,
A8(423)-0, A15(208)-0, B312(175)-1
YPT-25 (Model ST-4) Trainer -C
B74(34)-1, B88(4-33)-2, D6(9/71-220)-1,
B58(223c)-1, C8(148)-1, B312(176)-1,
B111(15)-1, A8(424)-0, A15(208)-0,
B77(204)-1, B22(A-125)-1

SAILPLANE
See Briegleb

*ST LOUIS St Louis Aircraft Corp., Div.
of the St Louis Car Co.*

PT-LM-4 Trainer -E
B22(A-128)-1, B272(41-123)-1,
D3(6-207)-1, B261(95)-0
XCG-5 High wing transport glider -E
B286(114)-3, D6(6/72-321)-1,
D16(9/81-8)-1, B111(63)-1, A8(572)-0,
B10(97)-0
YPT-15 (PT-1W) Biplane trainer -B
A8(526)-1, B88(4-30)-2, B314(9,47)-2,
B57(214c)-2, B277(229)-1, B312(175)-1,
B272(41-106,268)-2, B111(60)-1

SCHWEIZER *Schweizer Aircraft Corp.*
TG-2 (LNS-1, Model SGS 2-8)
Training glider -B
A9(473)-1, D16(9/81-8)-1,
D11(10/64-28)-2, B358(2-102)-1,
B229(93)-1, B22(A-139)-1, C9(171)-3,
B57(88a)-1, B10(169,201)-0
TG-3 (Model SGS 2-12) Training
glider -A
A8(526)-1, D11(10/64-28)-2,
B59(304c)-1, B111(63)-1, B22(A-139)-1,
B358(2-103)-1, B10(169)-0

SECURITY *American Aircraft Co.*
S-1-B Airster Tourer -L
B218(8-24)-1, B152(293c)-1,
B21(A-117)-1, C100(6-150)-1

SEVERSKY *Seversky Aircraft Corp.*
BT-8 (Model X-1-P) Trainer -B
A8(527)-1, B245(21,109)-2,
B314(17,49)-2, B152(295c)-1, B273(9)-1,
D19(4/58-267)-1, D29(12/82-19)-1,
B279(271)-1, D1(5-21)-1, B111(46)-1
EP-1 (Sweden **J 9**) Fighter,
reconnaissance -B
B245(75,116)-4, D7(10-17,27-79)-1,
C89(207)-1, D25(5/61-22)-2,
D19(4/58-267)-1, A14(240)-1, C31(16)-1,
B293(89)-6, A15(208)-0, B458(48)-2
P-35 (AP-1) Fighter -A
D7(10-8)-5, A3(4-163)-2, B146(2-61)-2,
A8(426)-2, B148(90)-4, B245(43,112)-2,

B118(2-60)-2, B215(82)-2, A10(554)-1,
B273(6)-5, B277(213)-7, A14(239)-1,
B411(154)-1, B104(61)-1, A15(208)-6
SEV-2PA Convoy Fighter (Japan **A8V
'Dick'**) General purpose military, also
floatplane -B
B245(47,68)-1, A14(240)-1, A10(554)-1,
C100(6-150)-2, B152(294c)-1, A2(497)-1,
D19(4/58-267,2/84-157,3/85-214)-1,
D1(7-33)-1, A15(208)-0, B466(7)-1
SEV-3M-WW Reconnaissance
floatplane -B
B245(80)-1, A14(238)-1,
D19(4/58-267)-1, D1(5-21)-1,
B126(11)-1, B221(52)-1, B297(39)-1,
D7(18-34)-1
XP-41 (AP-4D) Fighter -E
B215(103)-2, B245(60,120)-2,
A14(273)-1, D29(10/81-32,12/82-21)-1,
D7(10-15)-1, D16(3/83-24)-1,
B347(50)-1, B448(4)-1, A15(206)-0

SIKORSKY *Sikorsky Aircraft Division of
United Aircraft Corp. (Vought-Sikorsky)*
JRS (S-43, OA-8, OA-11) Twin engine
high wing utility amphibian -B
A3(5-186)-2, D19(3/81-178)-1,
A9(440)-1, A8(528)-1, B162(105)-2,
B277(225)-1, B57(223c)-1, B440(136)-1,
B230(267)-1, A15(208)-0, B468(74)-1
R-4 (HNS, Hoverfly) Observation,
rescue helicopter -B
A8(428)-2, B59(305c)-2, B277(226)-2,
D3(5-224)-5, B310(P)-2, B326(279)-1,
B151(76)-1, B53(18)-1, B161(24)-5,
A7(233)-1, B88(5-47)-2, B447(45)-1,
A12(391)-1, B296(34)-6, A15(209)-6
R-5 (HO2S) Observation, rescue
helicopter -B
A8(430)-2, B59(306c)-2, B326(284)-1,
B228(378)-1, B53(22)-1, B151(133)-1,
B277(227)-3, C74(551)-2, B447(48)-1,
A15(209)-0
R-6 (HOS, Hoverfly II) Observation,
rescue helicopter -B

B88(7-44)-2, B59(306c)-1, A8(529)-1,
B326(282)-1, B151(142)-1, B53(23)-1,
B447(50)-1, B228(377)-1, A9(441)-1,
B296(36)-6, B471(155)-1

S-38 (RS-3) Twin engine twin boom
sesquiplane transport amphibian -D
B225(210)-2, A9(343)-2, B218(2-166)-1,
A14(104)-1, B440(116)-1, B452(22)-1,
B15(232)-7, B468(28)-1

S-39-B Amphibion (C-28) High wing
twin boom amphibian -L
D19(1/62-3)-2, B225(212)-2, B197(78)-1,
B301(P)-1, B139(151)-1, B218(4-234)-1,
B440(117)-1, D19(3/59-155)-2

S-40 American Clipper Four engine
high wing twin boom transport
amphibian -I
D19(4/79-244)-2, B162(68)-2,
B225(126)-2, C74(549)-2, B197(81)-1,
B218(6-223)-1, B222(81)-1, B431(146)-1,
B440(132)-1, B452(40)-1, B468(55)-1

S-42 Clipper Four engine high wing
transport flying boat -L
D19(4/79-248,2/84-82)-4, B162(86)-2,
B218(6-328)-1, B197(90)-1,
B154(234c)-1, B431(148)-1, B15(264)-7,
B440(134)-1, B222(80)-1, B468(65)-1

VS-44A Excalibur (XJR2S) Four
engine high wing transport flying boat -I
D20(6/64-67)-2, B468(102)-1,
D19(4/79-25,4/75-237)-1, B162(142)-2,
B283(70)-1, B225(134)-5, B57(224c)-2,
B218(8-183)-1, B279(122)-1, A15(208)-0

VS-300 Helicopter -F
B53(47)-1, B151(74)-1, B228(374)-1,
B326(277)-1, B56(225c)-1, B447(38)-1,
B222(98)-1, B443(68)-1, B296(33)-6,
B42(76)-1, B22(A-126)-1

XPBS-1 Flying Dreadnought Four
engine high wing patrol flying boat -E
D16(1/77-50)-2, D19(4/75-236)-1,
A9(440)-1, A14(314)-1, B283(69)-1,
B154(235c)-1, B230(224)-1, B452(64)-1,
C82(502)-1, A15(208)-0, B21(A-146)-1

SMITH
TG-30 (Bluebird) Training glider -I
B10(170)-0, A8(584)-0, B111(37)-0,
D20(1/67-332)-0

SNEAD Snead & Company
XCG-11 High wing transport glider -J
B286(122)-1, B10(97)-0, A8(572)-0
XLRH-1 Twin hull amphibian transport
glider -J
B286(152)-0, B10(201)-0, A9(507)-0

SOUTHERN Southern Aircraft Corp.
BM-10 Biplane trainer -E
B272(41-107,269)-2, B21(A-138)-1,
D3(6-147)-1, B56(213c)-0, B279(282)-0

SPARTAN The Spartan Aircraft Co.
FBW-1 Zeus Light bomber -C
A10(555)-1, A14(170)-1, B279(282)-1,
D3(6-171)-1, B411(184)-0, B153(277c)-0,
B114(24-2618)-0
NP-1 (Model NS-1, C-3) Biplane
trainer -A
B88(4-58)-2, B57(215c)-2, A9(444)-1,
B230(290)-1, B277(228)-1,
B272(41-59,270)-2, C9(119,166)-2
UC-71 (Model 7-W Executive) Light
transport -I
B218(7-104)-1, A8(530)-1,
D19(2/80-145)-1, D3(2-22)-2,
C78(305)-1, D11(3/67-40)-3,
B58(228c)-1, C112(2-73)-2, A15(209)-0

*STEARMAN Stearman Aircraft
Division of the Boeing Aircraft Co.*
Model 76 Biplane trainer, armed
trainer -B
B255(18)-1, B56(216c)-2, B298(76)-1,
B24(34)-1, B397(338)-1, C131(133)-1
NS-1 (Model 73) Biplane trainer -B
B255(16)-1, B230(183)-1, B153(278c)-1,
B298(76)-1, A9(357)-0
PT-13 Kaydet (N2S, Model 75)
Biplane trainer -A

B37(219)-2, A9(357)-2, A8(442)-3,
B255(18,22)-1, B314(8)-1, B56(214c)-2,
B88(4-28)-2, B277(39)-2, B298(77)-1,
A7(179)-1, C131(142)-1

PT-17 Kaydet (N2S) Biplane trainer -A
B37(219)-1, A8(442)-1, B314(11,47)-2,
B255(23)-1, A6(204)-2, B57(153c)-1,
B298(77)-1, B104(62)-1, B111(61)-1,
B14(334,339)-7

PT-18 Kaydet Biplane trainer -A
B37(223)-1, B255(22)-1, B314(12)-1,
D19(4/57-219)-1

PT-27 Kaydet Biplane trainer -A
B37(228)-1, B255(28)-1, B155(17,178)-1,
B314(12)-1, A8(442)-0, D19(3/85-167)-1

XA-21 (Model X-100) Twin engine high
wing attack bomber -E
B37(233)-2, B255(21)-1, C8(40,131)-2,
A14(171)-1, B298(84)-1, B397(342)-1,
B111(39)-1, B312(202)-1, B21(A-57)-1

XOSS-1 Biplane scout, also floatplane -E
B230(239)-1, B255(20)-1, A14(338)-1,
D19(4/57-217)-1, B440(160)-1

YPT-9 (Model 6 Cloudboy) Biplane
trainer -D
A8(440)-2, B255(11)-1, B314(7)-1,
B218(4-205,5-173)-1, B312(174)-1

STEARMAN-HAMMOND *Stearman-
Hammond Aircraft Co.*
JH-1 (Model Y-1-S) Twin boom pusher
radio control -F
A9(445)-1, B218(7-157)-1, B230(212)-1,
B152(300c)-1, B20(A-88)-1,
D19(1/82-16)-1, B420(67)-1,
B284(3-142)-0, B10(198)-0, B297(284)-0

STEIGLEMAIER
TG-14 (Model S-24) Training glider -I
B10(170)-0, A8(583)-0, B111(37)-0,
D20(1/67-332)-0

STINSON *The Stinson Division of the
Consolidated Vultee Aircraft Corp.*
AT-19 (V-77, SR-10J Reliant) High
wing trainer -A

B59(309c)-2, B88(4-45)-2, B314(31,53)-2,
B419(64)-2, A7(234)-1, A12(298)-1,
B277(229)-1, B111(41)-1, A8(532)-0,
A15(209)-0, B312(178)-1

C-91 (SM-6000A) Three engine high
wing transport -I
B419(45)-1, B218(4-211)-1, B271(51)-1,
B15(243)-6, D19(2/57-115)-1,
B468(48)-1, B10(82)-0, A8(571)-0

L-1 Vigilant (0-49, CQ-2, Model 74)
High wing liaison, target control, also
floatplane -A
A8(444)-2, A3(6-196)-2, B88(3-22)-2,
B277(230)-2, B419(66)-1, B57(228c)-2,
A7(241)-1, A11(519)-1, D29(2/83-41)-1,
A15(209)-0

L-5 Sentinal (0-62, OY-1, Model 76)
High wing liaison -A
A8(446)-2, B59(308c)-2, B88(6-48)-2,
B218(8-222)-1, B277(231)-2, B419(67)-1,
A9(398)-1, A11(519)-1, B125(214)-1,
A15(209)-6, A7(234)-1, B18(2-60)-7

L-9 (Model 10 Voyager) High wing
liaison -I
B218(8-139)-1, B419(72)-1,
B272(41-153,275)-2, B358(1-159)-1,
A15(209)-0, B10(130)-0, A8(446)-0

L-12 (Model SR-5 Reliant, XR3Q)
High wing liaison -I
B419(55)-1, B218(6-126,130)-1,
B200(2-437)-1, A9(445)-1,
B284(3-142)-1, B10(130)-0, A8(576)-0

Model A Three engine transport -L
B419(51)-1, B162(73)-2, B218(6-201)-1,
B139(130)-1, B291(49)-1, B468(69)-1,
D16(1/85-52)-1, D6(12/72-388)-1,
D3(6-76)-1

Model O High wing ground attack,
trainer -B
B218(6-67)-1, B419(54)-1

Model R Junior High wing
communications -I
B218(5-170)-1, B419(47)-1, D3(3-34)-2,
D11(10/63-24)-1, B200(2-436)-1,
B284(3-142)-0

Model SR-6 Reliant High wing
tourer -L
B419(57)-1, B218(6-284)-1, D3(3-34)-2,
B200(2-437)-1
UC-81 (Model SR-8B Reliant) High
wing utility -I
B218(7-33)-1, B200(2-438)-1,
B277(229)-3, A15(209)-6, B10(81)-0
UC-81A (Model SR-10G Reliant)
High wing utility -I
B218(7-270)-1, B419(64)-3, B10(81)-0
UC-81B (Model SR-8E Reliant) High
wing utility -I
B218(7-38)-1, B154(226c)-1, B10(81)-0
UC-81C (Model SR-9C Reliant) High
wing utility -I
B218(7-80)-1, D11(10/63-27)-1,
B10(81)-0
UC-81E (Model SR-9F Reliant) High
wing utility -I
B218(7-142)-1, B419(65)-1, A8(532)-1,
D11(10/63-27)-1
UC-81F (Model SR-10F Reliant) High
wing utility -I
B218(7-293)-1, B419(65)-1, B10(81)-0
UC-81G (Model SR-9D Reliant) High
wing utility -I
B218(7-93)-1, B200(2-439)-1,
B284(3-144)-1, B419(62)-1, B468(61)-1
UC-81H (Model SR-10E Reliant)
High wing utility -I
B218(7-274)-1, B152(301c)-1, B10(81)-0
UC-81J (Model SR-9E Reliant) High
wing utility -I
B218(7-93)-1, B154(226c)-1, B24(33)-1,
B10(81)-0
UC-81K (Model SR-10C Reliant)
High wing utility -I
B218(7-270)-1, B419(63)-1,
B200(2-439)-1, D11(10/63-28)-1
UC-81L (Model SR-8C Reliant) High
wing utility -I
B218(7-33)-1, B10(81)-0
UC-81M (Model SR-9EM Reliant)
High wing utility -I

B218(7-93)-1, B10(81)-0
UC-81N (Model SR-9B Reliant) High
wing utility -I
B218(7-80)-1, B419(64)-3, B10(81)-0
V-77B High wing liaison -E
D19(1/63-52)-1
XC-81D (Model SR-10F Reliant)
High wing glider pick-up -I
B419(63)-1, B218(7-293)-1, B10(81)-0
YO-54 (Model 105 Voyager) High
wing observation -B
B419(66)-1, B218(8-39)-1, B154(227c)-1,
B111(53)-1, D21(1/1-34)-1, B227(34)-1,
D29(2/83-44)-1, D3(3-99)-2, C131(58)-1,
D4(11/71-56)-1, A15(209)-0, B471(116)-1

STOUT *Stout Research Division,*
Consolidated Vultee Aircraft Corp.
Skycar IV (Spratt controllable wing)
High wing pusher -F
B42(194)-1, D3(6-120)-1, B80(P)-1,
B207(81)-0
UC-107 (Skycar III) High wing pusher
twin boom utility -E
C8(195)-0, A8(571)-0, B111(27)-0,
B10(84)-0
XC-65 (Skycar) High wing pusher twin
boom utility -E
C8(147,195)-1, B21(A-142)-1, A8(571)-0,
B111(26)-0, B10(79)-0

TAYLOR-YOUNG *Taylor-Young*
Airplane Co.
Model A Taylorcraft High wing
tourer -I
B218(7-153)-1, B284(3-145)-0

TAYLORCRAFT *Taylorcraft Aviation*
Corp.
L-2 Grasshopper (YO-57, Model
DC-65 Tandem Trainer) High wing
liaison -A
A8(448)-2, B59(311c)-2, B88(3-25)-2,
B218(8-163)-1, B288(133)-1,
B277(232)-1, A7(236)-1, B104(94)-1,

B111(50)-1, A15(210)-0, B473(19)-1

L-2D (Model DL-65) High wing glider trainer -I
B218(8-163)-1, A8(449)-0, B10(129)-0

L-2E (Model DF-65) High wing glider trainer -I
B218(8-163)-1, A8(449)-0, B10(129)-0

L-2F (Model BL-65, UC-95) High wing liaison, glider trainer -I
B218(7-330)-1, A8(449)-0, B20(A-94)-1

L-2G (Model BFT-65) High wing glider trainer -I
B218(7-342)-1, A8(449)-0, B10(129)-0

L-2H (Model BC-12-65) High wing glider trainer -I
B218(7-330)-1, A8(449)-0, B10(129)-0

L-2J (Model BL-12-65) High wing glider trainer -I
B218(7-345)-1, B154(228c)-1, A8(449)-0, B10(129)-0

L-2K (Model BF-12-65) High wing glider trainer -I
B218(7-342)-1, A8(449)-0, B10(129)-0

L-2L (Model BF-50) High wing glider trainer -I
B218(7-342)-1, A8(449)-0, B10(129)-0

LBT Glomb High wing glide bomb -C
B286(153)-1, A9(507)-0, B10(200)-0

TG-6 (LNT-1, Model ST-100) High wing training glider -A
D16(9/81-13)-1, A8(450)-1, B88(4-25)-2, A9(474)-1, B111(63)-1, B58(232c)-1, A15(210)-0, B42(252)-0, B22(A-129)-1

XTG-33 Prone pilot version TG-6 -F
D16(9/81-18)-0, A8(584)-0, B10(170)-0, D20(1/67-332)-0

THOMAS-MORSE *Thomas-Morse Aircraft Corp.*
O-19E Biplane observation -D
A8(456)-2, A14(88)-1, B111(51)-1, B104(40)-1, B352(393)-1, B312(182)-1

TIMM *Timm Aircraft Corp. (Aetna Aircraft Corp.)*

Aerocraft (Aetna Model 2 SA) Trainer -C
B218(8-123)-1

Model PT-160-K Aeromold (PT-175-K) Trainer -C
B218(8-167)-1, B56(220c)-1, B20(A-95)-1, B279(291)-0

N2T-1 Tutor (Model PT-220-C Aeromold) Trainer -A
B218(8-177)-1, A9(449)-1, B88(4-64)-2, B58(232c)-1, B229(122)-1, B277(233)-2, C9(119,166)-2, B358(1-99)-1, B279(291)-0, B22(A-130)-1

XAG-2 Assault glider -J
B286(153)-1, D6(3/72-131)-0, A8(566)-0, B10(39)-0

TUCKER *Tucker Aviation Co.*
XP-57 (Model AL-5) Fighter -J
B215(145)-3, D20(10/63-62)-3, C88(109)-6, A14(288)-0, B347(65)-0

UNIVERSAL *Monocoupe Division of Universal Moulded Products Corp.*
L-7 (Model 90AF Monocoupe) High wing liaison -I
B88(5-45)-2, B358(1-144)-2, B218(4-25)-1, B21(A-116)-1, D3(4-279)-2, B153(264c)-1, C112(2-62)-2, A15(210)-0, B10(130)-0

UNIVERSAL-BLACKHAWK
TG-26 (Model BT-2) Training glider -I
B10(170)-0, A8(583)-0, B111(37)-0, D20(1/67-332)-0

VEGA *Vega Airplane Co.*
Model 40 High wing target drone -E
D29(8/85-52)-1, B120(17)-0, B279(296)-0
Vega 35
See North American NA-35

VIKING *Viking Flying Boat Co.*
OO-1 (V-2, Schreck FBA-17) Biplane pusher patrol flying boat -D

A9(439)-1, B230(199)-1, B218(4-194)-1,
B279(298)-0, B10(204)-0

VOLMER-JENSEN *Volmer S. Jensen*
TG-29 (Model VJ-10) Training
sailplane -I
B21(A-159)-1, A8(584)-0, B10(170)-0,
B111(37)-0, D20(1/67-332)-0

VOUGHT *Chance Vought Division of
United Aircraft Corp. (Vought-Sikorsky)*
F4U Corsair (FG, F3A) Carrier
fighter -A
B147(16)-4, B65(78)-4, B71(47,150)-2,
B135(2-79)-2, A3(4-188)-2, B283(81)-2,
A9(280)-2, B148(136)-4, A6(252)-2,
B277(234)-2, B415-2, B392-2,
A10(557)-2, A12(66)-2, B216(171)-2,
C82(234)-2, B252(155)-2, A7(41)-1,
B18(2-87)-7, B8(46)-4, A15(211)-6
O2U Corsair Biplane observation, also
floatplane -D
A9(367)-2, B283(39)-2, B230(221)-1,
B411(158)-1, A14(124)-1, C82(88)-2,
B275(11)-1, B96(27)-1, B15(224)-7,
A15(210)-0
O3U Corsair Biplane observation, also
floatplane -B
A9(370)-2, B283(48)-2, B230(291)-1,
A14(129,324)-1, C82(112)-2, A15(210)-0
OS2U Kingfisher Observation, also
floatplane -A
B71(251)-2, A9(378)-2, A3(6-190)-2,
B283(72)-2, B277(242)-2, A12(318)-2,
C82(208)-2, B58(235c)-2, A14(338)-1,
A15(210)-6, A7(239)-1, B18(2-21)-7
SBU (V-142) Biplane carrier scout
bomber -B
A9(374)-2, B283(59)-2, B230(261)-1,
C82(156)-2, A10(556)-1, A14(332)-1,
B411(158)-1, B154(231c)-1, B96(69)-1,
A15(210)-0
**SB2U Vindicator (V-156,
Chesapeake)** Carrier scout bomber -A
D7(8-1)-4, B65(20)-4, A9(376)-2,

B283(62)-2, D23(61-102)-1, B277(239)-1,
A12(316)-2, A10(557)-1, C82(171)-2,
A15(210)-6, A14(352)-1, A7(240)-1
SU Corsair Biplane carrier scout -B
B283(49)-2, C82(114)-2, A9(371)-1,
B230(270)-1, A14(322)-1, B96(22)-1,
B289(30)-6, A15(210)-0, B114(6-638)-6
V-65 (V-93, V-97, V-99) Export versions
03U -B
B283(55)-1, A14(325)-1, C82(128)-2,
D9(4/75-205)-1, A15(210)-0,
C131(120)-1, B471(47)-1
V-66 Export version SU, also
floatplane -D
B283(55)-1, A14(325)-1, C82(130)-1,
C131(46)-1
V-93S Corsair Biplane military -B
B283(57)-1, D7(25-25)-1,
D9(11/81-256)-1, D19(3/83-217)-1,
A14(326)-1, C82(140)-1
V-100 Corsairo Junior Biplane
trainer -B
B283(57)-1, D9(11/81-256)-1, C82(147)-1
V-143 (V-141, Northrop 3-A, Japan
AXV1) Fighter -E
D6(10/72-199)-2, B283(66)-2,
C100(6-148)-2, D19(2/56-106)-1,
C82(194)-2, D16(3/83-16)-1, A14(237)-1,
B153(286c)-1, C129(398)-1,
D16(11/85-10)-4
V-162 Circular wing flying model -F
D4(8/75-18)-1, B283(98)-1, C82(302)-1
V-173 Twin engine circular wing -F
B283(97)-2, D6(6/73-287)-1,
D4(8/75-16)-1, C82(303)-2, B42(93)-1,
B216(205)-1, B50(128)-1, B439(88)-1,
B405(51)-1, B352(403)-1, B60(198c)-1
VS-326 High altitude engine test version
XTBU -F
B283(80)-2, C82(225)-2,
D6(10/72-199)-1,
D19(2/71-154,1/68-67)-1, D1(8-42)-1,
B415(194)-1
XF5U Twin engine circular wing carrier
fighter -G

D6(6/73-287)-4, D4(8/75-16)-2,
B283(99)-2, B216(201)-2, A9(406)-1,
C82(308)-2, B350(91)-2, A14(396)-1,
B50(130)-1, B42(95)-1, B60(197c)-1
XF6U Pirate Single jet carrier fighter -H
D29(12/77-24)-2, D9(5/76-256)-2,
B283(102)-2, B216(229)-2, B350(101)-2,
B138(62)-2, C82(321)-2, A9(449)-1,
A10(560)-1, A14(503)-1, B60(197c)-1
XSB3U Biplane carrier bomber -E
B283(61)-1, A14(352)-1, B230(196)-1,
C82(168)-1
XSO2U Scout observation, also
floatplane -E
B283(102)-2, C82(201)-2,
D25(10/62-57)-2, A14(341)-1,
B230(272)-1, D29(2/85-41)-1,
C9(109,147)-2, B71(251-134)-1
XTBU Sea Wolf (Consolidated TBY)
Carrier torpedo bomber -C
B283(79)-2, A14(363)-1, B230(293)-1,
C82(218)-1, A10(559)-1, B277(241)-1,
D25(10/57-11)-1, B275(55)-1, B203(8)-1

VULTEE *Vultee Aircraft, Inc.*
(Consolidated Vultee Aircraft)
A-35 Vengeance (A-31, V-72) Dive
bomber -A
D7(5-29)-1, A8(458)-2, A11(454)-2,
B7(31)-2, B88(3-14)-2, B277(245)-1,
B58(178c)-2, A10(561)-1, A6(253)-7,
A15(212)-6, A14(184)-1, A7(161)-1,
D16(9/85-8)-1, D29(10/85-34)-1,
C131(175,191)-1
BC-3 (Model 51) Trainer -E
B314(22)-1, B312(179)-1, B154(237c)-1,
B21(A-11)-1, B111(41)-1,
D16(3/85-14)-1, A8(460)-0, B10(59)-0
BT-13 Valiant (SNV, Model 54)
Trainer -A
A8(460)-2, B88(4-37)-2, B314(18,49)-2,
B56(226c)-2, A9(451)-1, A7(240)-1,
B277(246)-1, B104(74)-1,
B14(336,340)-7, B292(30)-6
BT-15 Valiant Trainer -A

B314(18)-1, A8(460)-0, C131(174)-1
P-66 Vanguard (Model V-48, Sweden
J 10) Fighter -B
A3(4-195)-2, B146(2-83)-2, B215(176)-2,
A8(534)-1, B277(247)-1,
D19(2/84-102)-2, D16(3/85-10)-1,
A10(561)-1, A14(250)-1, A15(212)-0
V-1A Transport, liaison -B
D6(7/72-27)-2, D4(6/76-64)-1,
B468(66)-1, D20(5/68-298)-2,
D29(10/82-10)-1, B162(94)-2,
B218(6-162)-1, C78(279)-2, B15(258)-6,
A15(211)-0, D19(2/56-38)-1
V-11 (USSR **Kochyerigin BSh-1**)
Attack bomber, also floatplane -B
D6(7/72-31)-5, B273(102)-1, A14(168)-1,
A10(560)-1, B411(184)-1,
D19(1/57-69)-1,
D29(12/82-32,10/83-40)-5, B152(306c)-1,
D6(7/71-111)-1, A15(212)-6, C131(138)-1
V-12 (AB-2) Attack bomber -B
D6(7/72-38)-5, B273(101)-5, A14(168)-1,
D16(9/85-14)-1, B149(25)-1,
D29(10/83-40)-1, A15(212)-0
V-85 (XA-31B) Engine test -F
D16(9/85-52)-1, A14(184)-0, D7(5-31)-0
XA-41 (Model 90) Attack bomber -E
D20(10/62-59)-2, B60(205c)-1,
A14(192)-1, B312(203)-1, B109(8)-1,
B111(40)-1, C88(223,P)-1, C8(136)-3
XBT-16 (Vidal) Plastic fuselage version
BT-13 -E
A8(460)-0, B314(58)-0, B10(61)-0
XP-54 'Swoose Goose' (Model 84)
Twin boom pusher fighter -E
A3(4-200)-2, B215(135)-2, B146(2-84)-2,
B347(62)-2, A14(288)-1, B312(193)-1,
D9(11/75-252)-2, B59(229c)-1,
B439(116)-1, D29(6/85-14)-1
XP-68 Tornado Twin boom pusher
fighter -J
B215(138)-0, A14(299)-0, B10(153)-0
YA-19 (V-11) Attack bomber, engine
test -C
D6(7/72-38,12/72-295)-1, A8(534)-1,

A14(168)-1, B154(236c)-1, B312(202)-1,
D16(9/85-13)-1, B273(102)-1,
B111(38)-1, A15(212)-0

WACO *The Waco Aircraft Co.*
CG-3 (Model NYQ, Commonwealth)
High wing training transport glider -B
B286(100)-2, D6(6/72-321)-1, A8(536)-1,
B59(315c)-1, B277(248)-1, B22(A-133)-1,
D16(9/81-17)-1, B111(63)-1
CG-4 (LRW, Hadrian, Haig) High
wing transport glider -A
A8(462)-2, B286(103)-2, D6(6/72-322)-1,
B88(4-50)-2, A7(241)-1, B59(314c)-2,
A6(253)-2, A9(474)-1, B277(249)-3,
A15(212)-6
CG-13 (Ford) High wing transport
glider -B
B286(124)-2, B59(314c)-2,
D6(6/72-322)-1, B88(5-42)-2, A7(242)-1,
A8(536)-1, D3(5-127)-2, B277(250)-1,
B18(2-86)-7, A15(213)-0, D19(1/85-19)-3
CG-15 (LR2W, Model NEU) High
wing transport glider -A
B286(130)-2, B59(313c)-2, A8(462)-1,
D6(6/72-322)-1, B111(63)-1,
B277(251)-1, B288(145)-1, A15(213)-0
J2W (Model EQC-6) Biplane light
transport -B
A9(450)-1, B230(199)-1, B218(7-139)-1,
B411(184)-0, A15(212)-0
Model CJC Biplane light transport -B
C131(50,128)-1, B218(6-134)-1,
B54(31)-1, D19(1/85-17)-3
Model D (JHD, S2HD, S3HD, WHD)
Biplane military -B
D9(4/76-205)-2, B218(7-243)-1,
B218(6-154,288)-1, B56(229c)-1,
D19(2/64-134,3/84-220,1/85-16)-2,
B54(38)-1, B397(356)-1, B21(A-153)-1
Model F (CPF, UPF) Biplane trainer -B
B54(39,54)-1, B218(7-148,6-294)-1,
D19(2/64-134,3/84-219)-1, B139(156)-1,
D9(7/85-34)-1, C131(51,121,130,131)-1

Model O (BSO, CSO, CTO) Biplane
utility -B
B218(2-196,3-164)-1, B54(10,11,12)-1,
D19(3/84-217)-1, C131(47,122,127)-1
Model QDC Biplane trainer -I
B92(19)-1, B218(5-37)-1, B54(18)-1,
D9(9/77-154)-1, D19(1/85-17)-3
Model UKC (Sweden **Tp 8**) Biplane
utility -I
D19(2/83-145)-1, B218(6-92)-1,
B54(29)-1, C89(214)-0
PG-2 (Northwestern) Twin engine
version CG-4 -C
A8(463)-1, B155(18,189)-1,
D3(7-215,8-148)-1, B286(154)-0
PT-14 (Model UPF-7) Biplane
trainer -B
B88(4-29)-2, B314(8,47)-2, B21(A-154)-1,
B218(7-148)-1, A8(535)-1, B139(156)-1,
B54(54,60)-1, B58(237c)-1, B312(175)-1,
D19(3/84-220)-1, B111(60)-1
UC-72 (Model SRE) Biplane utility -I
A8(535)-1, D9(4/77-190)-2, B218(8-56)-1,
B54(59)-1, B277(252)-3, A15(212)-0,
B10(79)-0
UC-72A (Model ARE) Biplane utility -I
B218(8-56)-1, B54(58)-1, B139(156)-1,
B58(237c)-1, B10(79)-0, D19(1/85-19)-2
UC-72B (Model EGC-8) Biplane
utility -I
B218(7-226)-1,
D19(2/83-145,3/84-220)-1, B54(49)-1,
D3(5-292)-2, B218(9-93)-1, C131(137)-1
UC-72C (Model HRE) Biplane utility -I
B218(8-56)-1, B10(79)-0
UC-72D (Model VKS-7) Biplane
utility -I
B218(7-170)-1, B54(53,61)-1,
B139(156)-1, B58(237c)-1, B279(302)-1
UC-72E (Model ZGC-7) Biplane
utility -I
B218(7-101)-1, B54(47)-1, B10(79)-0,
D19(1/85-18)-3
UC-72F (Model CUC-1) Biplane
utility -I

B218(6-268)-1, B54(35)-1, B10(79)-0
UC-72G (Model AQC-6) Biplane
utility -I
B218(6-353)-1, B54(50)-1,
B155(18,188)-1, B10(79)-0
UC-72H (Model ZQC-6) Biplane
utility -I
B218(6-353)-1, B54(42)-1, B10(79)-0
UC-72J (Model AVN-8) Biplane
utility -I
B218(7-267)-1, B54(56)-1, B154(241c)-1,
B19(943)-1, D19(3/84-221)-1
UC-72K (Model YKS-7) Biplane
utility -I
B218(7-97)-1, B54(46,53)-1, D3(7-3)-1,
B10(79)-0, D19(1/85-19)-3
UC-72L (Model ZVN-7) Biplane
utility -I
B218(7-267)-1, B54(57)-1, B10(79)-0
UC-72M (Model ZKS-7) Biplane
utility -I
B218(7-97)-1, B54(52)-1, A15(212)-0,
B10(79)-0
UC-72N (Model YOC-1) Biplane
utility -I
B218(6-246)-1, D17(3/84-218)-1,
B54(36)-1, B10(79)-0

UC-72P (Model AGC-8) Biplane
utility -1
B218(7-223)-1, B54(51)-1, B19(943)-1,
B10(79)-0
XJW-1 (Model UBF) Biplane airship
hook-on trainer -D
A9(450)-1, B230(269)-1, B54(24)-1,
D20(12/65-234)-1, B218(5-210)-1,
D19(2/58-107,3/84-219)-1, B411(184)-0,
B10(199)-0
XPG-1 (Northwestern) Twin engine
version CG-4 -E
B42(255)-1, B111(63)-1, C88(265,P)-1,
B286(154)-0, A8(464)-0
XPG-3 Twin engine version CG-15 -E
D20(11/64-56)-1, C8(221)-1,
D3(7-215)-1, B286(154)-0, A8(465)-0
YC-62 Twin engine high wing
transport -J
D19(2/81-140,3/84-222)-1,
D3(4-218,7-3)-1, B10(78)-0, A8(571)-0

WICHITA *Wichita Engineering*
XTG-10 Training glider -K
B10(170)-0, A8(583)-0, B111(37)-0,
D20(1/67-332)-0

YUGOSLAVIA

IKARUS *Ikarus Akcionarsko Drustwo*
Aero 2 Trainer -H
B139(30)-2, D9(1/84-10)-1, B406(65)-1,
B136(320)-0
B-5 Pionir Twin engine prone pilot -F
D20(9/65-60)-1
Bristol Blenheim Twin engine
bomber -B
D7(28-71)-1, B143(1-58)-1, B27(268)-1,
B44(36)-1, B71(93-11)-1, B134(2-8)-1
IK-2 High wing fighter -B
B71(242)-2, A3(4-203)-2, B88(2-77)-2,
B153(293c)-1, A10(632)-1,

D9(5/80-250,2/83-98)-2, C74(287)-2,
B18(1-282)-7, A15(220)-6
Orkan Twin engine high wing fighter
bomber -E
D6(3/72-148)-1, D14(6-95)-3,
B153(293c)-0, B20(A-311)-0

ROGOZARSKI *Prva Srpska Fabrika*
Aeroplana Zivojin Rogozarski A.D.
Fizir Biplane reconnaissance -B
C32(166)-1, C33(103)-1, A15(220)-0
IK-Z (IK-3) Fighter -B
B71(242)-2, A3(4-205)-2, D9(8/80-85)-1,

A10(633)-1, B293(93)-6, B18(1-283)-7,
A15(220)-0, B114(13-1419)-0
IK-5 Twin engine fighter -J
B71(242)-3, A3(4-207)-0
PVT (Version Morane-Saulnier
M.S.233) High wing trainer, also
floatplane -B
A3(6-198)-2, B152(314c)-1, D3(6-15)-1,
C33(101)-1, A15(220)-0
R-313 Twin engine reconnaissance
bomber -E
D6(7/71-111)-2, C87(115,P)-1,
D14(5-77)-3, B153(295c)-0, A15(220)-0
SIM-VI A Trainer -K
B153(294c)-1, D3(6-15)-1
SIM-XI High wing trainer -K
B153(294c)-1, D3(6-15)-1

SIM-XII-H High wing trainer
floatplane -B
A3(6-200)-2, B153(294c)-1, D3(6-15)-1
SIM-XIV-H Twin engine
reconnaissance floatplane -B
A3(6-201)-2, C20(11-79)-2, A10(634)-1,
B153(295c)-1, C80(228)-1,
D25(3/63-49)-2, B397(610)-1,
A15(220)-0, B114(21-2330)-0

ZMAJ *Fabrika Aeroplani I Hidroplani
'Zmaj'*
R 1 Twin engine light bomber -E
D6(6/73-309)-2, B153(295c)-0,
B20(A-312)-0

Part Two:
BIBLIOGRAPHY

SECTION A

A1   Cynk, Jerzy B. *Polish Aircraft 1893-1939* London: Putnam, 1971

A2   Francillon, R.J. *Japanese Aircraft of the Pacific War* London: Putnam, 1970

A3   Green, William *War Planes of the Second World War* London: Macdonald

    Volume 1 *Fighters* Australia, Belgium, Bohemia-Moravia, Finland, France, Germany, 1960

    Volume 2 *Fighters* Great Britain, Italy, 1961

    Volume 3 *Fighters* Japan, Netherlands, Poland, Rumania, Soviet Union, 1961

    Volume 4 *Fighters* United States, Yugoslavia, 1961

    Volume 5 *Flying Boats* 1962

    Volume 6 *Float Planes* 1962

    Volume 7 *Bombers and Reconnaissance Aircraft* Australia, Belgium, Bohemia-Moravia, Bulgaria, Canada, Finland, France, 1967

    Volume 8 *Bombers and Reconnaissance Aircraft* France, Germany 1967

    Volume 9 *Bombers and Reconnaissance Aircraft* Germany, 1967

    Volume 10 *Bombers and Reconnaissance Aircraft* Germany, 1968

    Listed as A3 (Volume-Page)

A4   Green, William *Warplanes of the Third Reich* London: Macdonald, 1970

A5   Gunston, Bill *Aircraft of the Soviet Union* London: Osprey Publishing 1983

A6   Gunston, Bill *The Illustrated Encyclopedia of Combat Aircraft of World War II* London: Salamander Books, 1978. New York: Bookthrift Publishers, 1978

A7   Munson, Kenneth *Aircraft of World War II* London: Ian Allen, 1972

A8   Swanborough, F.G. *United States Military Aircraft Since 1909* London: Putnam, 1963

A9   Swanborough, Gordon and Peter Bowers *United States Navy Aircraft Since 1911* London: Putnam, 1963

A10   Taylor, John W.R. *Combat Aircraft of the World* London: Ebury Press and Michael Joseph. 1969

A11   Thetford, Owen *Aircraft of the Royal Air Force 1919-58* London: Putnam, 1958

A12   Thetford, Owen *British Naval Aircraft 1912-58* London: Putnam, 1958

A13   Thompson, Jonathan *Italian Civil and Military Aircraft 1930-1945* Los Angeles: Aero Publishers, 1963

A14   Wagner, Ray *American Combat Planes* Garden City: Doubleday, 1982

A15   Weal, Elke C. *Combat Aircraft of World War Two* London: Lionel Leventhal, 1977. New York: Macmillan, 1977

SECTION B

B1　Air Ministry *Recognition Handbook of British Aircraft* Air Publication 1480A, Part 1 Sections A-D, Part 2 Sections E-J, ca. 1941-1945

B2　Air Ministry *Silhouettes of British Aircraft* London: H.M. Stationery Office, 1940

B3　Allen, Hugh *Goodyear Aircraft* Cleveland: Corday & Gross, 1947

B4　Allen, Richard S. *Revolution in the Sky* Brattleboro: Stephen Greene Press, 1964

B5　Alexander, Jean et al *The Encyclopedia of Aviation* London: Reference International Pub., 1977. New York: Charles Scribner's Sons, 1977

B6　Alexander, Jean *Russian Aircraft Since 1940* London: Putnam, 1975

B7　Anderson, Fred *Northrop An Aeronautical History* Los Angeles: Northrop Corporation, 1976

B8　Anderton, David *American Fighters of World War II* London: Hamlyn, 1982. New York: Crescent Books, 1982

B9　Andrade, John M. *Latin American Military Aviation* Leicester: Midland Counties Pub., 1982

B10　Andrade, John M. *U.S. Military Aircraft Designations and Serials Since 1909* Leicester: Midland Counties Pub., 1979

B11　Andrews, C.F. *Vickers Aircraft Since 1908* London: Putnam, 1969

B12　Andrews, C.F. and E.B. Morgan *Supermarine Aircraft Since 1914* London: Putnam, 1981

B13　Andrews, Phillip *Air News Yearbook* New York: Duell, Sloane, and Pierce, Volume 1 1942, Volume 2 1944

Listed as B13 (Volume-Page)

B14　Angelucci, Enzo *The Rand McNally Encyclopedia of Military Aircraft 1914-1980* Chicago: Rand McNally, 1981

B15　Angelucci, Enzo and Paolo Matricardi *World Aircraft 1918-1935* Maidenhead: Sampson Low, 1977

B16　Angelucci, Enzo and Paolo Matricardi *World Aircraft Commercial 1935-1960* Chicago: Rand McNally, 1979

B17　Angelucci, Enzo and Paolo Matricardi *World Aircraft Military 1945-1960* Chicago: Rand McNally, 1980

B18　Angelucci, Enzo and Paolo Matricardi *World War II Airplanes* (2 volumes) Chicago: Rand McNally, 1978

Listed as B18 (Volume-Page)

B19　Angle, Glenn D. *Aerosphere-1939* New York: Aircraft Pub., 1940

B20　Angle, Glenn D. *Aerosphere-1941* New York: Aircraft Pub., 1941

B21　Angle, Glenn D. *Aerosphere-1942* New York: Aircraft Pub., 1942

B22　Angle, Glenn D. *Aerosphere-1943* New York: Aerosphere Inc., 1944

B23　Apostolo, Giorgio *The Illustrated Encyclopedia of Helicopters* New York: Bonanza Books, 1984

B24　Aquino, Florendo A. Jr., Francisco C. Vasallo, Alberto A. Anido *50 Years Philippine Air Force* Manila: 1971

B25　Arena, Nino *Air War in North Italy 1943-1945* Modena: S.T.E.M. Mucchi, 1975

B26　Baker, David *The Rocket* London: New Cavendish, 1978, New York:

Crown Pub., 1978

B27 Barnes, C.H. *Bristol Aircraft Since 1910* London, Putnam, 1964

B28 Barnes, C.H. *Handley Page Aircraft Since 1907* London: Putnam, 1976

B29 Barnes, C.H. *Shorts Aircraft Since 1900* London: Putnam, 1967

B30 Barton, Charles *Howard Hughes and His Flying Boat* Fallbrook: Aero Publishers, 1982

B31 Beaman, John R. Jr. and Jerry L. Campbell *Messerschmitt Bf 109 in Action* Carrollton: Squadron/Signal, 1980, Part 2 1983

B32 Bignozzi, Giorgo and Roberto Gentili *Aeroplani S.I.A.I. 1915-1935* Firenze: Edizione Aeronautiche Italiane S.r.l., 1982 (Italian/English text)

B33 Birdsall, Steve *B-26 Marauder in Action* Carrollton: Squadron/Signal, 1981

B34 Birtles, Philip *Mosquito A Pictorial History of the DH98* London: Jane's, 1980

B35 Blue, Allan G. *The B-24 Liberator* London: Ian Allen, 1976

B36 Borge, Jacques, Nicolas Viasnoff *The Dakota the DC-3 Story* New York: VILO, 1982

B37 Bowers, Peter M. *Boeing Aircraft Since 1916* London: Putnam, 1966

B38 Bowers, Peter M. *Boeing P-26 Variants* Aerofax Minigraph 8, Arlington: Aerofax, 1984

B39 Bowers, Peter M. *Curtiss Aircraft 1907-1947* London: Putnam 1979

B40 Bowers, Peter M. *Forgotten Fighters and Experimental Aircraft U.S. Army 1918-1941* New York: Arco, 1971

B41 Bowers, Peter M. *Fortress in the Sky* Granada Hills: Sentry Books, 1976

B42 Bowers, Peter M. *Unconventional Aircraft* Blue Ridge Summit: TAB Books, 1984

B43 Bowers, Peter M. and Paul R. Matt *Aircraft Photo Album Vol.1* Temple City: Historical Aviation Album, 1969

B44 Bowyer, Chaz *Bristol Blenheim* London: Ian Allen, 1984

B45 Bowyer, Chaz *The Encyclopedia of British Military Aircraft* London: Bison Books, 1982. New York: Crescent Books, 1982

B46 Bowyer, Chaz *Hampden Special* London: Ian Allen, 1976

B47 Bowyer, Michael J.F. *Aircraft for the Royal Air Force* London: Faber and Faber, 1980

B48 Bowyer, Michael J.F. *Aviation Photo Album* Cambridge: Patrick Stephens, No.1 1978, No.2 1980

B49 Bowyer, Michael J.F. *Interceptor Fighters for the Royal Air Force 1935-45* Wellingborough: Patrick Stephens, 1984

B50 Boyne, Walter J. *The Aircraft Treasures of Silver Hill* New York: Rawson Associates, 1982

B51 Boyne, Walter J. *Messerschmitt Me 262 Arrow to the Future* Washington: Smithsonian Institution, 1980

B52 Boyne, Walter J. and Donald S. Lopez *The Jet Age* Washington: National Air and Space Museum, 1979

B53 Boyne, Walter J. and Donald S. Lopez *Vertical Flight the Age of the Helicopter* Washington: Smithsonian Institution Press, 1984

B54 Brandly, Raymond H. *Waco Airplanes* Raymond Brandly, 1978

B55 Bridgman, Leonard *Aircraft of the British Empire 1940* London: Sampson Low, 1940

B56 Bridgman, Leonard *Jane's All the World's Aircraft 1941* London: Sampson Low, Marston & Co., 1942

B57 Bridgman, Leonard *Jane's All the World's Aircraft 1942* London:

Sampson Low, Marston & Co., 1943

B58 Bridgman, Leonard *Jane's All the World's Aircraft 1943-44* London: Sampson Low, Marston & Co., 1944

B59 Bridgman, Leonard *Jane's All the World's Aircraft 1945-46* London: Sampson Low, Marston & Co., 1946

B60 Bridgman, Leonard *Jane's All the World's Aircraft 1947* London: Sampson Low, Marston & Co., 1947

B61 Brindley, John F. *French Fighters of World War Two* Windsor: Hylton Lacy, 1971

B62 Brown, David, Christopher Shores, Kenneth Macksey *The Guinness History of Air Warfare* Enfield: Guinness Superlatives, 1976

B63 Brown, Don L. *Miles Aircraft Since 1925* London: Putnam, 1970

B64 Brown, Eric *Wings of the Luftwaffe* London: Macdonald and Jane's, 1977

B65 Brown, Eric *Wings of the Navy* London: Jane's Publishing Co., 1980

B66 Brown, Captain Eric *Wings of the Weird & Wonderful* Shrewsbury: Airlife Publishing, 1983, Vol.2 1985 Listed as B66(Volume-Page)

B67 Bueschel, Richard M. *Japanese Aircraft Insignia, Camouflage, and Markings* West Roxbury: World War I Aero Publishers, 1966

B68 Bueschel, Richard M. *Japanese Code Names* West Roxbury: World War I Aero Publishers, 1966

B69 Butler, P.H. *British Gliders* Liverpool: Merseyside Aviation Society, 1980

B70 Butler, P.H. *Irish Aircraft* Liverpool: Merseyside Aviation Society, 1972

B71 Cain, Charles W. (editor) *Aircraft in Profile* Leatherhead and Windsor: Profile Publications, 1965-1974. Numbers 1 through 262 published

separately, several bound editions. Referenced profiles listed below.

Listed as B71 (Profile Number-Page)

No.2 Peter M. Bowers *Boeing P-12E*

No.3 Martin C. Windrow *Focke-Wulf Fw 190A*

No.6 C.F. Andrews *Bristol Bulldog*

No.7 E.G. Shacklady *Republic P-47D Thunderbolt*

No.8 E.G. Shacklady *North American P-51D Mustang*

No.10 Francis K. Mason *Gloster Gauntlet*

No.11 Philip J.R. Moyes *Handley Page Halifax III, VI, VII*

No.14 Peter M. Bowers *Boeing P-26A*

No.15 Martin C. Windrow *Heinkel He 111H*

No.16 Dott. Ing. Gianni Cattaneo *Fiat C.R.42*

No.18 Francis K. Mason *Hawker Fury I*

No.19 Roger A. Freeman *Consolidated B-24J Liberator*

No.22 Dott. Ing. Gianni Cattaneo *Fiat C.R.32*

No.23 Martin C. Windrow *Messerschmitt Bf 110*

No.24 Francis K. Mason *Hawker Hurricane IIc*

No.27 Peter M. Bowers *Boeing F4B-4*

No.28 Dott. Ing. Gianni Cattaneo *Macchi C.202*

No.29 Martin C. Windrow *Junkers Ju 88A*

No.32 C.F. Andrews *Westland Wapiti*

No.33 Francis K. Mason *Gloster Gamecock*

No.34 Philip J.R. Moyes *Fairey Battle*

No.35 Ray Wagner *Curtiss P-40*

No.40 Martin C. Windrow *Messerschmitt Bf 109E*

No.41 Philip J.R. Moyes *Supermarine Spitfire I & II*

B71 (continued)   BIBLIOGRAPHY

No.42 Francis K. Mason *North American FJ Fury*

No.44 Francis K. Mason *Fairey IIIF*

No.46 Francis K. Mason & Rene J. Francillon *Nakajima Ki-43 Hayabusa*

No.47 Jay Frank Dial *Chance Vought F4U-1 Corsair*

No.52 Philip J.R. Moyes *deHavilland Mosquito I-IV*

No.53 Frank L. Greene *Grumman F4F-3 Wildcat*

No.57 Francis K. Mason *Hawker Hart*

No.58 Philip J.R. Moyes *Handley Page Hampden*

No.59 Ray Wagner *North American B-25A-G Mitchell*

No.60 Harry Gann *Douglas Skyraider*

No.63 G.H. Kamphuis *Fokker D.XXI*

No.64 Dott. Ing. Gianni Cattaneo *Macchi MC.200*

No.65 Brian Goulding and M. Garbett *Avro Lancaster I*

No.69 J. Richard Smith *Henschel Hs 129*

No.70 Rene J. Francillon *Nakajima Ki-84 Hayate*

No.75 Witold Liss *P.Z.L. P-11*

No.76 J. Richard Smith *Junkers Ju 87A & B*

No.77 Charles D. Thompson *Boeing B-17E & F Flying Fortress*

No.80 Peter M. Bowers *Curtiss Hawk 75*

No.81 Francis K. Mason *Hawker Typhoon*

No.82 Rene J. Francillon *Mitsubishi Ki-46*

No.84 Geoffrey Norris *Short Empire Boats*

No.87 G.H. Kamphuis *Fokker C.V*

No.88 Witold Liss *Ilyushin Il-2*

No.89 G. Apostolo *Savoia-Marchetti S.M.79*

No.92 Lt. Cdr. Benton Reams *Grumman F3F-Series*

No.93 Philip J.R. Moyes *Bristol Blenheim I*

No.94 J. Richard Smith *Focke-Wulf Fw 190D/Ta 152*

No.96 Arthur Pearcy Jr. *Douglas DC-3 (pre-1942)*

No.98 Francis K. Mason *Gloster Gladiator*

No.99 J. Richard Smith *Focke-Wulf Fw 200*

No.100 Richard Atkins *North American P-51B & C Mustang*

No.101 Mitch Mayborn *Boeing B-29 Superfortress*

No.104 J.B. Cynk *P.Z.L. P-23 Karas*

No.105 Rene J. Francillon *Kawasaki Ki-45 Toryu*

No.106 Le Roy Weber *Lockheed P-38J-M Lightning*

No.107 Hal Andrews *Grumman F8F-1 Bearcat*

No.110 G. Apostolo *Fiat B.R.20*

No.111 Francis K. Mason *Hawker Hurricane I*

No.112 Ray Wagner *Martin B-26B & C Marauder*

No.113 J. Richard Smith and Ian Primmer *Messerschmitt Bf 109G & K*

No.117 Michael Bowyer *Boulton-Paul Defiant*

No.118 Rene J. Francillon *Kawasaki Ki-6l Hien*

No.120 Holmes Anderson *Lockheed Constellation*

No.122 Witold Liss *Polikarpov I-16*

No.123 C. Cattaneo *Reggiane Re.2000*

No.124 Hal Andrews *Curtiss SB2C-1 Helldiver*

No.125 C.F. Andrews *Vickers Wellington I & II*

No.126 Francis K. Mason *Hawker Sea Fury*

No.128 Kenneth Rust and W.M. Jefferies *Curtiss A-12 Shrike*

No.129 Rene J. Francillon *Mitsubishi A6M2 Zero-Sen*

No.130 J. Richard Smith *Messerschmitt Me 262*

No.132 A.J. Jackson *deHavilland Tiger Moth*

No.134 B. van der Klaauw *Fokker G-1*

No.135 Raymond Danel *Dewoitine 520*

No.136 Ray Wagner *Curtiss P-40 Kittyhawk I-IV*

No.137 Philip J.R. Moyes *Bristol Beaufighter I & II*

No.138 Bo Widfeldt *Saab 21 A & R*

No.140 Francis K. Mason *Hawker Audax & Hardy*

No.141 Dr. M.F. Hawkins *Nakajima B5N "Kate"*

No.142 Geoffrey Norris *Short Stirling*

No.144 Peter W. Moss *deHavilland Rapide*

No.146 Giorgio Apostolo *Savoia-Marchetti S.M.81*

No.147 Gaston Botquin *Morane Saulnier 406*

No.148 Alfred Price *Junkers Ju 88 Night Fighters*

No.149 Witold Liss *Lavochkin La 5 & 7*

No.150 Jay Frank Dial *Chance Vought F4U-4 to F4U-7 Corsair*

No.152 Josef Krybus *Avia B.534*

No.153 Philip J.R. Moyes *Armstrong Whitworth Whitley*

No.154 Philip J.R. Moyes *Commonwealth Wirraway*

No.156 William T. Larkins *Ford Tri-Motor*

No.158 Mitch Mayborn *Ryan PT/ST Series*

No.159 Francis K. Mason *Westland Lysander*

No.160 Rene J. Francillon *Mitsubishi G3M "Nell"*

No.161 J. Richard Smith *Messerschmitt Me 210/410 Series*

No.164 J. Richard Smith *Dornier Do 17E - Z Series*

No.165 Jay Frank Dial *Bell P-39 Airacobra*

No.166 Ted Hooton *Supermarine Spitfire V Series*

No.168 Donald M. Hannah *Avro York*

No.170 Jerzy B. Cynk *P.Z.L. P-24*

No.171 Thomas E. Doll *Douglas TBD Devastator*

No.172 Rene J. Francillon *Mitsubishi Ki-21*

No.173 Raymond Danel *Liore et Olivier LeO 45 Series*

No.174 P.J. Birtles *deHavilland Hornet*

No.176 B. van der Klaauw *Fokker T.VIII*

No.177 J. Richard Smith *Junkers Ju 52 Series*

No.178 Rene J. Francillon *Commonwealth Boomerang*

No.182 Philip J.R. Moyes *Handley Page Heyford*

No.183 Everett Cassagneres *Consolidated PBY Catalina*

No.184 Martin C. Windrow *Messerschmitt Bf 109F*

No.185 Witold Liss *Yak 9 Series*

No.188 Dott. Ing. Gianni Cattaneo *Fiat G.50*

No.189 Geoffrey Norris *Short Sunderland*

No.190 Rene J. Francillon *Mitsubishi A6M3 Zero-Sen "Hamp"*

No.191 Philip J.R. Moyes *Westland Whirlwind*

No.194 William T. Larkins *Curtiss S0C Seagull*

No.195 Raymond Danel *Potez 63 Series*

No.196 David Brazelton *Douglas SBD Dauntless*

No.197 Francis K. Mason *Hawker Tempest Mks.I to VI*

No. 201 Michel Cristesco *M. Bloch 151/152*

No.202 Harry Gann *Douglas A-20 Series (7A to Boston III)*

No.203 J. Richard Smith & William Conway *Heinkel He 162*

No.204 Holmes G. Anderson *Lockheed P2V Neptune*

No.205 Roger A. Freeman *Boeing B-17G Flying Fortress*

No.206 Peter Moss & Len Bachelor *Supermarine Spitfire Mks.IX & XVI*

No.207 Alfred Price *Messerschmitt Bf 110 Night Fighters*

No.209 Michael J.F. Bowyer *deHavilland Mosquito Mk.IV*

No.210 Rene J. Francillon *Mitsubishi G4M "Betty" & Ohka Bomb*

No.211 Richard P. Bateson *Junkers Ju 87D Variants*

No.212 Ian G. Stott *Fairey Swordfish Mks.I-IV*

No.213 Rene J. Francillon *Kawanishi N1K Shiden "George"*

No.214 Rene J. Francillon *Grumman TBF/Eastern TBM Avenger*

No.215 Richard P. Bateson *Arado Ar 234 Blitz*

No.216 Malcolm Passingham & Waclaw Klepacki *Petlyakov Pe-2*

No.217 Christopher F. Shores *Brewster Buffalo Variants*

No.218 James D. Oughton *Bristol Blenheim Mk.IV*

No.219 Richard P. Bateson *Heinkel He 219 Uhu*

No.220 Arthur Pearcy Jr. *Douglas C-47 (R.A.F. Dakotas)*

No.221 Len Bachelor *Supermarine Seafires (Merlins)*

No.222 L.F. Serjeant *Bücker Bü 131 Jungmann*

No.224 David Brown *Supermarine Walrus I & Seagull V*

No.225 Oberstleutnant a.D. Wolfgang Spate and Richard P. Bateson *Messerschmitt Me 163 Komet*

No.228 Richard P. Bateson *Fieseler Fi 156 Storch*

No.229 Norman Barfield *Vickers Warwick Mks.I-VI*

No.231 Jerzy B. Cynk *Lublin R-XIII Variants*

No.232 Christopher F. Shores *Martin Maryland and Baltimore (RAF)*

No.233 M.C. Richards *Kawanishi 4-Motor Flying Boats (H6K "Mavis" and H8K "Emily")*

No.234 Alfred Price *Heinkel He 177 Greif*

No.235 Bruce Robertson *Avro Lancaster Mk.II*

No.236 M.C. Richards and Donald S. Smith *Mitsubishi A6M5/8 Zero-Sen*

No.240 David Brown *Fairey Barracuda Mks.I-V*

No.241 M.C. Richards and Donald S. Smith *Aichi D3A "Val" & Yokasuka D4Y "Judy" Carrier Bombers*

No.242 Sime I. Ostric and Cedomir J. Janic *IK Fighters (Yugoslavia: 1930-40s)*

No.244 John F. Brindley *Caproni Reggiane Re.2001 Falco II, Re.2002 Ariete & Re.2005 Sagittario*

No.246 L.J. (Len) Bachelor *Supermarine Spitfire (Griffons) Mks.XIV & XVIII*

No.249 Arthur Pearcy Jr. *Douglas R4D Variants (US Navy's DC-3/C-47s)*

No.251 T.F. Doll and B.R. Jackson *Vought-Sikorsky OS2U Kingfisher*

No.253 Christopher F. Shores *Lockheed Hudson Mks I to VI*

No.254 David Brown *Fairey Fulmar Mks I & II*

No.255 John F. Brindley *Nakajima Ki-44 Shoki "Tojo"*

No.256 Norman Barfield *Vickers Wellesley Variants*

No.257 Armand van Ishoven *Udet (BFW) U-12 Flamingo Variants*

B71 (continued) **BIBLIOGRAPHY**

No.258 Jerzy B. Cynk *P.Z.L. P.37 Łos*
No.260 Chaz Bowyer *Avro Manchester*
No.261 Alfred Price *Dornier Do 217 Variants*
No.262 Roger A. Freeman *Republic P-47N Thunderbolt*

B72 Cain, Charles W. and Denys J. Voaden *Military Aircraft of the U.S.S.R.* London: Herbert Jenkins, 1952

B73 Camelio, Paul & Christopher Shores *Armee de l'Air The French Air Force 1937-1945* Warren: Squadron/Signal, 1976

B74 Carpenter, Don B. and Mitch Mayborn *Ryan Guidebook* Dallas: Flying Enterprise Publications, 1975

B75 Casey, Louis S. and John Batchelor *Naval Aircraft 1914-1939* London: Phoebus Publishing, 1977

B76 Casey, Louis S. and John Batchelor *The Illustrated History of Seaplanes and Flying Boats* London: Phoebus Publishing, 1980. New York: Exeter Books, 1980

B77 Cassagneres, Ev *The Spirit of Ryan* Blue Ridge Summit: TAB Books, 1982

B78 Chant, Christopher *Boeing The World's Greatest Planemakers* Hadley Wood: Winchmore Pub., 1982. Secaucus: Chartwell, 1982

B79 Clayton, Donald C. *Handley Page An Aircraft Album* London: Ian Allen, 1969

B80 Cleveland, Reginald M. and Frederick P. Graham *The Aviation Annual of 1946* Garden City: Doubleday, 1946

B81 Cloe, John Hale *Top Cover for America The Air Force in Alaska 1920-1983* Missoula: Pictorial Histories Pub., 1984

B82 Coates, Andrew *Jane's World Sailplanes and Motor Gliders* New York: Ziff-Davis Publishing Co., 1978

B83 Collier, Basil *Japanese Aircraft of World War II* London: Sidgwick & Jackson, 1979

B84 Conway, H.G. *Bugatti - le pour sang des automobiles* London: G.T. Foulis, 1963

B85 Cooke, David C. *War Planes of the Axis* New York: Robert M. McBride & Co., 1942

B86 Cooksley, Peter G. *Flying Bomb* New York: Charles Scribner's Sons, 1979

B87 Cooper, Bryan *The Story of the Bomber 1914-1945* London: Octopus Books, 1974

B88 Cooper, H.J., O.G. Thetford, E.J. Riding *Aircraft of the Fighting Powers* Leicester: The Harborough Publishing Co. Vol.I 1940, Vol.II 1941, Vol.III 1942, Vol.IV 1943, Vol.V 1944, Vol.VI 1945, Vol.VII 1946.

Listed as B88(Volume-Page)

B89 Courtney, Frank T. *The Eighth Sea* Garden City: Doubleday, 1972

B90 Cross, Roy and Gerald Scarborough *P-51 Mustang Classic Aircraft No.3* London: Patrick Stephens, 1973

B91 Cynk, Jerzy B. *History of the Polish Air Force 1918-1968* Reading: Osprey Pub., 1972

B92 Darby, Charles *RNZAF The First Decade 1937-46* Melbourne: Kookaburra Technical Pub., 1978

B93 Davis, Larry *B-17 in Action* Carrollton: Squadron/Signal, 1984

B94 Davis, Larry *P-51 Mustang in Action* Carrollton: Squadron/Signal, 1981

B95 Dickson, Bonner W.A. *Aircraft from Airship to Jet Propulsion 1908-1948* London: Naldrett Press, ca. 1948

B96   Doll, Thomas E., Berkley R. Jackson, William A. Riley *Navy Air Colors Vol.1 1911-1945* Carrollton: Squadron/Signal, 1983

B97   Donnet, Michael *Flight to Freedom* London: Ian Allen, 1974

B98   Durant, Frederick C. III and George S. James *First Steps Toward Space* Smithsonian Annals of Flight No.10, Washington: Smithsonian Institution, 1974

B99   Duval, G.R. *British Flying Boats and Amphibians 1909-1952* London: Putnam, 1966

B100   Elfrath, Ulrich *Aircraft of the Luftwaffe 1935-1945* London: Almark Publishing Co., ca.1973 *(Das waren die deutschen Kriegsflugzeuge 1935-1945* Dorheim: Podzun-Verlag)

B101   Ellis, Chris *A History of Combat Aircraft* London: Hamlyn, 1979

B102   Ellis, Chris *The World of Aviation* London: Hamlyn, 1977

B103   Ellis, Paul *Aircraft of the RAF A Pictorial Record 1918-1978* London: Macdonald and Jane's, 1978

B104   Ellis, Paul *Aircraft of the U.S.A.F. Sixty Years in Pictures* London: Jane's, 1980

B105   Elstob, Peter *Condor Legion* New York: Ballantine, 1973

B106   Ethell, Jeffrey *Komet The Messerschmitt 163* London: Ian Allen, 1978

B107   Ethell, Jeffrey *Mustang A Documentary History* London: Jane's, 1981

B108   Everett-Heath, John *Soviet Helicopters* London: Jane's, 1983

B109   *Fabulous Flying Flops* Air Classics Vol.2, 1985, Canoga Park: Challenge Publications

B110   Fahey, James C. *USAF Aircraft 1947-1956* Falls Church: Ships and Aircraft, 1956

B111   Fahey, James C. *U.S. Army Aircraft 1908-1946* Falls Church: Ships and Aircraft, 1946

B112   Feist, Uwe *Luftwaffe in Action, Aircraft No. Two* Warren: Squadron/Signal, 1972

B113   Feist, Uwe *The Luftwaffe in World War II Part Two* Fallbrook: Aero Publishers, 1979

B114   Fitzsimmons, Bernard *The Illustrated Encyclopedia of 20th Century Weapons and Warfare* (24 volumes) London: Phoebus Pub., 1977. New York: Columbia House, 1978 Listed as B114(Volume-Page)

B115   Ford, Brian J. *Allied Secret Weapons The War of Science* New York: Ballantine, 1971

B116   Ford, Brian J. *German Secret Weapons Blueprint for Mars* New York: Ballantine, 1969

B117   *Forty Years On* London: Handley Page Ltd., 1949

B118   Francillon, Rene J *American Fighters of World War II* Windsor: Hylton Lacy, Vol.1 1968, Vol.2 1972 Listed as B118(Volume-Page)

B119   Francillon, Rene J. *Imperial Japanese Navy Bombers of World War Two* Windsor: Hylton Lacy, 1969

B120   Francillon, Rene J. *Lockheed Aircraft Since 1913* London: Putnam, 1982

B121   Francillon, Rene J. *McDonnell Douglas Aircraft Since 1920* London: Putnam, 1979

B122   Francillon, Rene J. *The Royal Australian Air Force & Royal New Zealand Air Force in the Pacific* Fallbrook: Aero Publishers, 1970

B123   Franklin, Neville and Gerald Scarborough *Lancaster Classic Aircraft*

No. 6 Cambridge: Patrick Stephens, 1979

B124   Freeman, Roger A. *American Bombers of World War Two* Windsor: Hylton Lacy, 1973

B125   Freeman, Roger A. *Mighty Eighth War Manual* London: Jane's Publishing Co., 1984

B126   Freeman, Roger A. *Thunderbolt A Documentary History of the Republic P-47* London: Macdonald and Jane's, 1978 (prior publication as *Republic Thunderbolt* London: Ducimus Books)

B127   Gablehouse, Charles *Helicopters and Autogiros* Philadelphia: J.B. Lippincott, 1967

B128   Gentili, Roberto & Luigi Gorena *Macchi C.202 in Action* Carrollton: Squadron/Signal, 1980

B129   Geust, Carl-Fredrik, Kalevi Keskinen, Klaus Niska, Kari Stenman *Red Stars in the Sky* Espoo: Tietoteos, No.1 1979, No.2 1981, No.3 1983 (Finnish/English text)
Listed as B129(Number-Page)

B130   Gibbs-Smith, C.H. *The Aircraft Recognition Manual* London: George Newnes, 1944

B131   Glushko, V.P. *Rocket Engines GDL-OKB* USSR Academy of Sciences, Novosty Press Agency, 1975

B132   Goulding, James & Philip Moyes *RAF Bomber Command and It's Aircraft* London: Ian Allen, Volume 1 (1936-1940) 1975, Volume 2 (1941-1945) 1978
Listed as B132(Volume-Page)

B133   Green, William *Augsburg Eagle The Story of The Messerschmitt 109* London: Macdonald, 1971

B134   Green, William *Famous Bombers of the Second World War* London: Macdonald, 1959, Volume 2 1960
Listed as B134(Volume-Page)

B135   Green, William *Famous Fighters of the Second World War* London: Macdonald, 1957, Second Series, 1962
Listed as B135(Volume-Page)

B136   Green, William *The Observer's World Aircraft Directory* London: Frederick Warne & Co., 1961

B137   Green, William *Rocket Fighter* New York: Ballantine Books, 1971

B138   Green, William and Roy Cross *The Jet Aircraft of the World* London: Macdonald, 1955

B139   Green, William and Gerald Pollinger *The Aircraft of the World* London: Macdonald, 1953

B140   Green, William and Gordon Swanborough *The Focke-Wulf 190* Newton Abbot: David & Charles, 1976

B141   Green, William and Gordon Swanborough *Japanese Army Fighters* World War 2 Fact Files, London: Macdonald and Jane's, Part 1 1976, Part 2 1977
Listed as B141(Part-Page)

B142   Green, William and Gordon Swanborough *The Observer's Soviet Aircraft Directory* London: Frederick Warne & Co., 1975

B143   Green, William and Gordon Swanborough *RAF Bombers* World War 2 Fact Files, London: Macdonald and Jane's, Part 1 1979, Part 2 1981
Listed as B143(Part-Page)

B144   Green, William and Gordon Swanborough *RAF Fighters* World War 2 Fact Files, London: Macdonald and Jane's, Part 1 1978, Part 2 1979, Part 3 1981
Listed as B144(Part-Page)

B145   Green, William and Gordon Swanborough *Soviet Air Force Fighters* World War 2 Fact Files, London: Macdonald and Jane's, Part 1 1977, Part 2 1978
Listed as B145(Part-Page)

B146 Green, William and Gordon Swanborough *U.S. Army Air Force Fighters* World War 2 Fact Files, London: Macdonald and Jane's Part 1 1977, Part 2 1978
Listed as B146(Part-Page)

B147 Green, William and Gordon Swanborough *U.S. Navy and Marine Corps Fighters* World War 2 Fact Files, London: Macdonald and Jane's, 1976

B148 Green, William and Gordon Swanborough *The World's Great Fighter Aircraft* London: Salamander Books, 1981, New York: Crescent Books, 1981

B149 Green, William, Gordon Swanborough, and Pushpindar Singh Chopra *The Indian Air Force and Its Aircraft* London: Ducimus, 1982

B150 Gregory, Barry and John Batchelor *Airborne Warfare 1918-1945* New York: Exeter Books, 1979, London: Phoebus Pub., 1979

B151 Gregory, Hollingsworth Franklin *The Helicopter* South Brunswick: A.S. Barnes and Co., 1976 (includes *Anything a Horse Can Do: The Story of the Helicopter* 1944)

B152 Grey, C.G. and Leonard Bridgman *Jane's All the World's Aircraft 1938* London: Sampson Low, Marston & Co., 1938

B153 Grey, C.G. and Leonard Bridgman *Jane's All the World's Aircraft 1939* London: Sampson Low, Marston & Co., 1939

B154 Grey, C.G. and Leonard Bridgman *Jane's All the World's Aircraft 1940* London: Sampson Low, Marston & Co., 1941

B155 Griffin, J.A. *Canadian Military Aircraft Serials and Photographs* Ottawa: Canadian War Museum, 1969

B156 Gruenhagen, Robert W. *Mustang The Story of the P-51 Fighter* New York: Genesis Press — Arco, 1969

B157 Gunston, Bill *British Fighters of World War II* London: Hamlyn, 1982. New York: Crescent Books, 1982

B158 Gunston, Bill *Classic Aircraft Bombers* London: Hamlyn, 1978. New York: Grosset & Dunlap, 1978

B159 Gunston, Bill *The Encyclopedia of the World's Combat Aircraft* London: Salamander Books, 1976. New York: Chartwell, 1976

B160 Gunston, Bill *Fighters 1914-1945* London: Phoebus Pub., 1978. New York: Crescent Books, 1978

B161 Gunston, Bill *Helicopters at War* London: Phoebus Pub., 1977. Secaucus: Chartwell Books, 1977

B162 Gunston, Bill *The Illustrated Encyclopedia of Propeller Airliners* London: Phoebus Pub., 1980. New York: Exeter Books, 1980

B163 Gunston, Bill *The Illustrated Encyclopedia of the World's Rockets & Missiles* London: Salamander Books, 1979. New York: Crescent Books, 1979

B164 Gunston, Bill *The Illustrated History of Fighters* London: Phoebus Pub., 1981. New York: Exeter Books, 1981

B165 Guthman, L.C. *The Aeronautics Aircraft Spotter's Handbook* New York: National Aeronautics Council, 1943

B166 Hall, Alan W. and Eric Taylor *Avro Anson Marks I, III, IV, & X* London: Almark Publishing Co., 1972

B167 Halley, James J. *The Role of the Fighter in Air Warfare* Windsor: Profile Publications, 1978. New York: Ziff-Davis, 1978

B168 Hallion, Richard P. *Designers and Test Pilots* Alexandria: Time-Life Books, 1983

B169 Hallion, Richard P. *Supersonic Flight* New York: Macmillan Co., 1972

B170 Hannah, Donald *Avro — Flypast Reference Library* Stamford: Key Pub., 1983

B171 Hannah, Donald *Boeing — Flypast Reference Library* Stamford: Key Pub., 1983

B172 Hannah, Donald *DeHavilland — Flypast Reference Library* Stamford: Key Pub., 1982

B173 Hannah, Donald *Hawker — Flypast Reference Library* Stamford: Key Pub., 1982

B174 Hannah, Donald *Shorts — Flypast Reference Library* Stamford: Key Pub., 1983

B175 Harding, Stephen and James I. Long *Dominator The Story of the Consolidated B-32 Bomber* Missoula: Pictorial Histories, 1984

B176 Hardy, Michael *World Civil Aircraft Since 1945* New York: Charles Scribner's Sons, 1979

B177 Harlin, E.A. and G.A. Jenks *Avro An Aircraft Album* London: Ian Allen, 1973

B178 Harrison, W.A. *Swordfish Special* London: Ian Allen, 1977

B179 Hatfield, D.D. *Howard Hughes H-4 Hercules* Los Angeles: Historical Airplanes, 1972

B180 Heinemann, Edward H. and Rosario Rausa *Ed Heinemann Combat Aircraft Designer* Annapolis: Naval Institute Press, 1980

B181 Higham, Robin, Abigail Siddall, and Carol Williams *Flying Combat Aircraft of the USAAF-USAF* Ames: Iowa State University Press, 1975, Volume 2, 1978
Listed as B181(Volume-Page)

B182 Hirsch, R.S. and Uwe Feist *Heinkel 100, 112* Fallbrook: Aero Publishers, 1967

B183 Hirsch, R.S. and Uwe Feist *Heinkel 177* Fallbrook: Aero Publishers, 1967

B184 Hitchcock, Thomas H. *Junkers 287* Acton: Monogram Aviation Pub., 1974

B185 Hitchcock, Thomas H. *Junkers 288* Acton: Monogram Aviation Pub., 1974

B186 Hitchcock, Thomas H. *Junkers 290* Acton: Monogram Aviation Pub., 1975

B187 Hitchcock, Thomas H. *Messerschmitt O-Nine Gallery* Acton: Monogram Aviation Pub., 1973

B188 Hitchcock, Thomas H. *Taifun* Boylston: Monogram Aviation Pub., 1979

B189 Hogg, I.V. *German Secret Weapons of World War 2* London: Lionel Leventhal, 1970. New York: Arco, 1970

B190 Hogg, Ian V. and John Batchelor *Allied Secret Weapons* London: Phoebus Pub., 1975

B191 Hotson, Fred, W. *The deHavilland Canada Story* Toronto: CANAV Books, 1983

B192 Hunt, Leslie *Veteran and Vintage Aircraft* Third Edition, London: Garnstone Press, 1970

B193 Imai, Jin *General View of Japanese Military Aircraft in the Pacific War* Tokyo: Kantosha, 1958 (includes English text volume)

B194 Ingells, Douglas J. *L-1011 TriStar and the Lockheed Story* Fallbrook: Aero Publishers, 1973

B195 Ingells, Douglas J. *The McDonnell Douglas Story* Fallbrook: Aero Publishers, 1979

B196 Ishoven, Armand van *Messerschmitt Aircraft Designer* London: Gentry Books, 1970

B197 Jablonski, Edward *Sea Wings The Romance of the Flying Boats* Garden City: Doubleday, 1972

B198 Jackson, A.J. *Avro Aircraft Since 1908* London: Putnam, 1965

B199 Jackson, A.J. *Blackburn Aircraft Since 1909* London: Putnam, 1968

B200 Jackson, A.J. *British Civil Aircraft 1919-1959* London: Putnam, 1959, Volume 2 1960
Listed as B200(Volume-Page)

B201 Jackson, A.J. *DeHavilland Aircraft Since 1909* London: Putnam, 1978

B202 Jackson, B.R. and T.E. Doll *Douglas TBD-1 "Devastator"* Fallbrook: Aero Publishers, 1973

B203 Jackson, B.R. and T.E. Doll *Grumman TBF/TBM "Avenger"* Fallbrook: Aero Publishers, 1970 (supplement 1970)

B204 Jacobsen, Meyers K. & Ray Wagner *B-36 in Action* Carrollton: Squadron/Signal, 1980

B205 James, Derek N. *Gloster Aircraft since 1917* London: Putnam, 1971

B206 James, Derek N. *Hawker An Aircraft Album* London: Ian Allen, 1972

B207 Jerram, Michael F. *Incredible Flying Machines* London: Marshall Cavendish, 1980. New York: Exeter Books, 1980

B208 Jerram, Michael F. *Tiger Moth* Yeovil: Haynes Pub., 1984

B209 Jeudy, J-G and M. Tararine *The Jeep* New York: VILO, 1981

B210 Johnsen, Frederick A. *The B-29 Book* Tacoma: Bomber Books, 1978

B211 Johnson, Brian *The Secret War* London: British Broadcasting Co., 1978. New York: Methuen, 1978

B212 Johnson, Brian & Terry Heffernan *A Most Secret Place Boscombe Down 1939-45* London: Jane's, 1982

B213 Johnson, G.H.R. *The Miles Magister* Newark: Newark Air Museum, ca. 1968

B214 Jones, Lloyd S. *U.S. Bombers 1928 to 1980's* Fallbrook: Aero Publishers, 1980

B215 Jones, Lloyd S. *U.S. Fighters 1922 to 1980's* Fallbrook: Aero Publishers, 1975

B216 Jones, Lloyd S. *U.S. Naval Fighters 1922 to 1980's* Fallbrook: Aero Publishers, 1977

B217 Josephy, Alvin M. *The American Heritage History of Flight* New York: American Heritage Publishing Co., 1962

B218 Juptner, Joseph P. *U.S. Civil Aircraft* Fallbrook: Aero Publishers, 9 volumes 1962-1981
Listed as B218(Volume-Page)

B219 Karlstrom, Bjorn *Flygplans-Ritningar 1 Swedish Air Force Trainers 1926-83* Stockholm: Allt om Hobby, 1983 (Swedish/English text)

B220 Kay, Antony L. *Buzz Bomb* Acton: Monogram Aviation Pub., 1977

B221 Kelsey, Benjamin S. *The Dragon's Teeth?* Washington: Smithsonian Institution Press, 1982

B222 King, H.F. and John W.R. Taylor *Kittyhawk to Concorde Jane's 100 Significant Aircraft* London: Jane's All the World's Aircraft Publishing Co., 1970

B223 King, J.B. and John Batchelor *German Secret Weapons* London: Phoebus Pub., 1974

B224 Klee, Ernst and Otto Merk *The Birth of the Missile — The Secrets of Peenemünde* New York: E.P. Dutton & Co., 1965

B225 Knott, Richard C. *The American Flying Boat* Annapolis: Naval Institute Press, 1979

B226 Kohri, Katsu, Ikuo Komori, and Ishiro Naito *Aireview's The Fifty Years of Japanese Aviation 1910-1960* Tokyo: Kantosha, 1961 (includes English text volumes) Listed as B226(Photo Number)

B227 Kostenuk, S. and J. Griffin *RCAF Squadrons and Aircraft* Toronto: A.M. Hakkert, 1977

B228 Lambermont, Paul *Helicopters & Autogiros of the World* South Brunswick: A.S. Barnes and Co., 1970

B229 Larkins, William T. *U.S. Marine Corps Aircraft 1914-1959* Concord: Aviation History Pub., 1959

B230 Larkins, William T. *U.S. Navy Aircraft 1921-1941* Concord: Aviation History Pub., 1961

B231 Lennon, Andy *Canard: A Revolution in Flight* Hummelston: AViation Publishers, 1984

B232 Lerche, Hans-Werner *Luftwaffe Test Pilot* London: Jane's, 1980

B233 Lewis, Peter *The British Bomber Since 1914* London: Putnam, 1967

B234 Lewis, Peter *The British Fighter Since 1912* London: Putnam, 1965

B235 Lippisch, Alexander *The Delta Wing History and Development* Ames: Iowa State University Press, 1981

B236 Lloyd, Alwyn T. *B-17 Flying Fortress in Detail & Scale Part 2* Fallbrook: Aero Publishers, 1983. London: Arms & Armour Press, 1983

B237 Lloyd, Alwyn T. *B-29 Superfortress in Detail & Scale* Fallbrook: Aero Publishers, 1983. London: Arms & Armour Press, 1983

B238 Lukins, A.H. *The Book of Miles Aircraft* Leicester: Harborough Publishing Co., 1946

B239 Lukins, A.H. *The Book of Westland Aircraft* Leicester: Harborough Publishing Co., ca. 1945

B240 Lumsden, Alec *Wellington Special* London: Ian Allen, 1974

B241 Luukkanen, Eino *Fighter Over Finland* London: Macdonald, 1963

B242 Maloney, Edward T. *Boeing P-12, F4B* Fallbrook: Aero Publishers, 1966

B243 Maloney, Edward T. *Boeing P-26 "Peashooter"* Fallbrook: Aero Publishers, 1973

B244 Maloney, Edward T. *Kamikaze* Fallbrook: Aero Publishers, 1966

B245 Maloney, Edward T. *Sever the Sky Evolution of Seversky Aircraft* Corona del Mar: World War II Pub., 1979

B246 Maloney, Edward T. and Uwe Feist *Messerschmitt 163* Fallbrook: Aero Publishers, 1968

B247 Mason, Francis K. *British Fighters of World War Two* Windsor: Hylton Lacy, Vol. One 1969

B248 Mason, Francis K. *German Warplanes of World War II* London: Temple Press, 1983. New York: Crescent Books, 1983

B249 Mason, Francis K. *The Gloster Gladiator* London: Macdonald, 1964

B250 Mason, Francis K. *Hawker Aircraft Since 1920* London: Putnam, 1961

B251 Mason, Francis K. *The Hawker Hurricane* London: Macdonald, 1962

B252 Mason, Francis K. *The Illustrated Encyclopedia of Major Aircraft of World War II* London: Temple Press, 1983. New York: Crescent Books, 1983

B253 Masters, David *German Jet Genesis* London: Jane's Publishing Co., 1982

B254 Mayborn, Mitch *Grumman Guidebook Volume 1* Dallas: Flying Enterprise Pub., 1976

B255 Mayborn, Mitch *Stearman Guidebook* Dallas: Flying Enterprise Pub., 1967

B256 Mayborn, Mitch and Bob Pickett *Cessna Guidebook Volume 1* Dallas: Flying Enterprise Pub., 1973

B257 McDowell, Ernest R. *B-25 Mitchell in Action* Warren: Squadron/Signal, 1978

B258 McDowell, Ernest R. *Curtiss P-40 in Action* Warren: Squadron/Signal, 1976

B259 McDowell, Ernie *P-39 Airacobra in Action* Carrollton: Squadron/Signal, 1980

B260 Mendenhall, Charles *Deadly Duo The B-25 and B-26 in WW-II* Osceola: Specialty Press, 1981

B261 Mertens, Randy *Closet Cases* Kansas City: Pilot News Press, 1982

B262 Mesko, Jim *A-20 Havoc in Action* Carrollton: Squadron/Signal, 1983

B263 Mesko, Jim *A-26 Invader in Action* Carrollton: Squadron/Signal, 1980

B264 Mikesh, Robert C. *Aichi M6A1 Seiran* Boylston: Monogram Aviation Pub., 1975

B265 Mikesh, Robert C. *Japan's World War II Balloon Attacks on North America* Smithsonian Annals of Flight Number 9, Washington: Smithsonian Institution, 1973

B266 Mikesh, Robert C. *Kikka* Boylston: Monogram Aviation Pub., 1979

B267 Mikesh, Robert C. *Zero Fighter* Tokyo: Zokeisha Pub., 1981. New York: Crown Pub., 1981

B268 Miller, Jay *The X-Planes X-1 to X-29* Marine on St. Croix: Specialty Press, 1983

B269 Miller, Russell *The Soviet Air Force at War* Alexandria: Time-Life Books, 1983

B270 Millot, Bernard *Divine Thunder* London: Macdonald, 1971

B271 Mills, Stephen E. *Arctic War Birds* New York: Bonanza Books, 1978

B272 Mingos, Howard *The Aircraft Yearbook* New York: Aeronautical Chamber of Commerce of America, Inc., Aircraft Industries Association of America, Inc., Lanciar Publishers, Inc. (published annually)
Listed as B272(Year-Page)

B273 Mizrahi, J.V. *Air Corps* Northridge: Sentry Books, 1970

B274 Mizrahi, J.V. *North American B-25* North Hollywood: Challenge Pub., 1965

B275 Mizrahi, J.V. *U.S. Navy Dive & Torpedo Bombers* Sentry Books, 1967

B276 Molson, K.M. and H.A. Taylor *Canadian Aircraft Since 1909* London: Putnam, 1982

B277 Mondey, David *American Aircraft of World War II* London: Hamlyn/Aerospace, 1982

B278 Mondey, David *British Aircraft of World War II* London: Hamlyn/Aerospace, 1982

B279 Mondey, David *The Complete Illustrated Encyclopedia of the World's Aircraft* London: Quarto, 1978. New York: A.& W. Publishers, 1978

B280 Mondey, David *Concise Guide to Axis Aircraft of World War II* Feltham: Temple Press Aerospace, 1984

B281 Mondey, David *The International Encyclopedia of Aviation* London: Octopus Books, 1977. New York: Crown Pub., 1977

B282 Mondey, David *Westland Planemakers: 2* London: Jane's Publishing Co., 1982

B283 Moran, Gerald P. *Aeroplanes Vought 1917-1977* Temple City: Historical Aviation Album, 1978

B284 Moss, Peter W. *Impressments Log* Southend: Air Britain, Vol.1 1962, Vol.2 1963, Vol.3 1964, Vol.4 1966
Listed as B284(Volume-Page)

B285 Moyes, Philip J.R. *Royal Air Force Bombers of World War Two* Windsor: Hylton Lacy, Vol.One 1968, Vol.Two 1968
Listed as B285(Volume-Page)

B286 Mrazek, James E. *Fighting Gliders of World War II* London: Robert Hale, 1977

B287 Munson, Kenneth *Airliners Between the Wars 1919-39* London: Blandford Press, 1972

B288 Munson, Kenneth *American Aircraft of World War 2 in Colour* Poole: Blandford Press, 1982

B289 Munson, Kenneth *Bombers Between the Wars 1919-1939* London: Blandford Press, 1970

B290 Munson, Kenneth *Bombers, Patrol, and Transport Aircraft 1939-45* London: Blandford Press, 1969

B291 Munson, Kenneth *Civil Aircraft of Yesteryear* London: Ian Allen, 1967

B292 Munson, Kenneth *Fighters, Attack and Training Aircraft 1939-45* London: Blandford Press, 1969

B293 Munson, Kenneth *Fighters Between the Wars 1919-1939* London: Blandford Press, 1970

B294 Munson, Kenneth *Flying Boats and Seaplanes Since 1910* London: Blandford Press, 1971

B295 Munson, Kenneth *German Aircraft of World War 2 in Colour* Poole: Blandford Press, 1978

B296 Munson, Kenneth *Helicopters and Other Rotorcraft Since 1907* London: Blandford Press, 1968

B297 Munson, Kenneth *Warplanes of Yesteryear* London: Ian Allen, 1965

B298 Munson, Kenneth and Gordon Swanborough *Boeing An Aircraft Album* London: Ian Allen. 1971

B299 Murray, R.T. *Focke-Wulf Ta 154* London: Iso Publications, 1979

B300 Myhra, David *Horten 229* Boylston: Monogram Aviation Pub., 1983

B301 Neprud, Robert E. *Flying Minute Men* New York: Duell, Sloan, and Pearce, 1948

B302 Neville, Leslie E. *Aircraft Designers' Data Book* New York: McGraw Hill Book Co., 1950

B303 Nicholl, G.W.R. *The Supermarine Walrus* London: G.T. Foulis, 1966

B304 Nohara, Shigeru *A6M Zero in Action* Carrollton: Squadron/Signal, 1983

B305 Nowarra, Heinz J. *The Focke-Wulf 190 A Famous German Fighter* Letchworth: Harleyford, 1965

B306 Nowarra, Heinz *Heinkel He 111 A Documentary History* London: Jane's, 1980

B307 Nowarra, Heinz J. *The Messerschmitt 109 A Famous German Fighter* Letchworth: Harleyford, 1963

B308 Nowarra, Heinz J. and Edward T Maloney *Dornier Do 335* Fallbrook: Aero Publishers, 1966

B309 Nowarra, Heinz J. and G.R. Duval *Russian Civil and Military Aircraft 1884-1969* London: Fountain Press, 1970

B310 Oakes, Claudia M and Kathleen L. Brooks-Pazmany *Aircraft of the National Air and Space Museum* Washington: Smithsonian Institution Press, 1985

B311 Odekirk, Glenn E. *Spruce Goose HK-1 Hercules* Frank Alcanter, Inc., 1982

B312 *The Official Pictorial History of the AAF* New York: Duell, Sloan, and Pearce, 1947

B313 Ogden, Bob *Dornier — Flypast Reference Library* Stamford: Key Pub., 1983

B314 O'Hara, Wm., J. Ward Boyce *Training Aircraft of the U.S. Air Force 1925-1965* North Hollywood: Challenge Pub., 1965

B315 O'Neill, Richard *Suicide Squads: W.W.II* London: Salamander Books, 1981. New York: St. Martin's Press, 1981

B316 Oughton, James D. *Bristol An Aircraft Album* London: Ian Allen, 1973

B317 Palmer, Henry R. Jr. *Remarkable Flying Machines* Seattle: Superior Publishing Co., 1972

B318 Palmer, Henry R. Jr. *This Was Air Travel* Seattle: Superior Publishing Co., 1960

B319 Pentland, Geoffrey *Aircraft & Markings of the R.A.A.F. 1939-45* Melbourne: Lansdowne Press, 1970

B320 Pentland, Geoffrey *Commonwealth Boomerang Described* Kingston-upon-Thames: Kookaburra Technical Pub., ca.1963

B321 Pentland, Geoffrey *RAAF Camouflage & Markings 1939-45* Melbourne: Kookaburra, 1980

B322 Pentland, Geoffrey *Wirraway and Boomerang Markings* Toronto: Kookaburra Technical Pub., ca.1967

B323 Pentland, Geoffrey and Peter Malone *Aircraft of the RAAF 1921-71* Melbourne: Kookaburra Technical Pub., 1971

B324 Pimlott, John *B-29 Superfortress* London: Bison Books, 1980

B325 Pocock, Rowland F. *German Guided Missiles* London: Ian Allen, 1967

B326 Polmar, Norman and Floyd D. Kennedy *Military Helicopters of the World* London: Arms & Armour Press, 1981

B327 Poolman, Kenneth *Flying Boat* London: William Kimber, 1962

B328 Postma, Thijs *Fokker Aircraft Builders to the World* London: Jane's Publishing Co., 1980

B329 Potgieter, Herman and Willem Steenkamp *Aircraft of the South African Air Force* London: Jane's Publishing Co., 1981

B330 Prato, Piero *The Caproni-Reggiane Fighters 1938-1945* Genoa: Intyrama, 1969

B331 Price, Alfred *German Air Force Bombers of World War Two* Windsor: Hylton Lacy, Vol.One 1968, Vol.Two 1969
Listed as B331(Volume-Page)

B332 Price, Alfred *The Luftwaffe 1933-1945 Vol.IV* Warbirds Illustrated No.6, London: Arms & Armour Press, 1982

B333 Price, Alfred *The Spitfire Story* London: Jane's, 1982

B334 Rawlings, John D.R. *The History of the Royal Air Force* London: Temple Press, 1984. New York: Crescent Books, 1984

B335 Reed, Arthur & Roland Beamont *Typhoon and Tempest at War* London: Ian Allen, 1974

B336 Reid, P.R. *Escape from Colditz* Philadelphia: J.B. Lippincott Co., 1953

B337 Reitsch, Hanna *The Sky My Kingdom* London: The Bodley Head, 1955

B338 Ries, Karl *Deutsche Luftwaffe uber der Schweiz 1939-1945* Mainz: Verlag Dieter Hoffmann, 1978 (German/English text)

B339 Ries, Karl *Luftwaffe Vol.1 The Moles 1919-1935* Mainz: Verlag Dieter Hoffmann, 1970 (German/English text)

B340 Ries, Karl *Luftwaffen Story 1935-1939* Mainz: Verlag Dieter Hoffmann, 1974 (German/English text)

B341 Ries, Karl *Markings and Camouflage of Luftwaffe Aircraft in World War II* Mainz: Verlag Dieter Hoffman, 1963, Vol.II 1965, Vol.III 1967, Vol.IV 1972 (German/English text)
Listed as B341(Volume-Page)

B342 Robertson, Bruce *Aircraft Markings of the World 1912-1967* Letchworth: Harleyford Pub., 1967

B343 Robertson, Bruce *Beaufort Special* London: Ian Allen, 1976

B344 Robertson, Bruce *Lancaster The Story of a Famous Bomber* Letchworth: Harleyford Pub., 1964

B345 Robertson, Bruce *Lysander Special* London: Ian Allen, 1977

B346 Robertson, Bruce *Spitfire The Story of a Famous Fighter* Letchworth: Harleyford Pub., 1960

B347 Robertson, Bruce *United States Army and Air Force Fighters 1916-1961* Letchworth: Harleyford Pub., 1961

B348 Robertson, Bruce *Westland Whirlwind Described* Toronto: Kookaburra Technical Pub., 1965

B349 Robertson, Bruce and Gerald Scarborough *Hawker Hurricane Classic Aircraft No.4* Cambridge: Patrick Stephens, 1974

B350 Robertson, Bruce and Paul R. Matt *United States Navy and Marine Corps Fighters 1918-1962* Letchworth: Harleyford, 1962

B351 Robinson, Anthony *Dictionary of Aviation* London: Orbis Pub., 1984. New York: Crescent Books, 1984

B352 Robinson, Anthony *The Encyclopedia of American Aircraft* London: Orbis Pub., 1979. New York: Galahad Books, 1979

B353 Rolfe, Douglas and Alexis Dawydoff *Airplanes of the World From Pusher to Jet 1490 to 1954* New York: Simon and Schuster, 1954

B354 Roseberry, C.R. *The Challenging Skies* Garden City: Doubleday, 1966

B355 Ross, Frank Jr *Flying Windmills The Story of the Helicopter* New York: Lothrop, Lee, and Shephard Co., 1953

B356 Rubenstein, Murray and Richard M. Goldman *To Join With the Eagles* Garden City: Doubleday, 1974

B357 Russell, D.A. *The Book of Bristol Aircraft* Leicester: Harborough Publishing Co., 1946

B358 Saville-Sneath, R.A. *Aircraft of the United States* Harmondsworth: Penguin Books, Vol.1 1945, Vol.2 1946
Listed as B358(Volume-Page)

B359 Saville-Sneath, R.A. *British Aircraft* Harmondsworth: Penguin Books, Vol.1 1944, Vol.2 1944
Listed as B359(Volume-Page)

B360 Scarborough, Capt. W.E. *PBY Catalina in Action* Carrollton: Squadron/Signal, 1983

B361 Scrivner, Charles L. *Empire Express* Temple City: Historical Aviation Album, 1976

B362 Scrivner, Charles L. & W.E. Scarborough *Lockheed PV-1 Ventura in Action* Carrollton: Squadron/Signal, 1981

B363 Scutts, Jerry *Halifax in Action* Carrollton: Squadron/Signal, 1984

B364 Sekigawa, Eiichiro *Aireview's German Military Aircraft in Second World War* Tokyo: Kantosha, 1959 (includes English text volume)

B365 Sekigawa, Eiichiro *Pictorial History of Japanese Military Aviation* London: Ian Allen, 1974

B366 Sgarlato, Nico *Italian Aircraft of

World War II Warren: Squadron/Signal, 1979

B367 Shacklady, Edward *The Gloster Meteor* London: Macdonald, 1962

B368 Shamburger, Page & Joe Christy *The Curtiss Hawks* Kalamazoo: Wolverine Press, 1972

B369 Sharp, C. Martin and Michael J.F. Bowyer *Mosquito* London: Faber and Faber, 1967

B370 Shores, Christopher F. *Finnish Air Force 1918-1968* Aircam Aviation Series No.S2, Canterbury: Osprey Pub., ca.1969

B371 Shores, Christopher *Ground Attack Aircraft of World War II* London: Macdonald and Jane's, 1977

B372 Shores, Christopher *Regia Aeronautica A Pictorial History of the Italian Air Force 1940-1943* Warren: Squadron/Signal, 1976

B373 *SIAI Ali Nella Storia* Firenze: Edizione Aeronautiche Italiane, 1979 (Italian/English text)

B374 *SIAI Momenti di Storia* Firenze: Edizione Aeronautiche Italiane, 1977 (Italian/English text)

B375 Smith, Frank Kingston *Legacy of Wings — The Harold F. Pitcairn Story* New York: Jason Aronson, 1981

B376 Smith, J. Richard *Focke-Wulf an Aircraft Album* London: Ian Allen, 1973

B377 Smith, J. Richard *Messerschmitt An Aircraft Album* London: Ian Allen, 1971

B378 Smith, J. Richard and Eddie J. Creek *Dornier 335* Boylston: Monogram Aviation Pub., 1983

B379 Smith, J. Richard and Eddie J. Creek *Jet Planes of the Third Reich* Boylston: Monogram Aviation Pub., 1982

B380 Smith, J.R. and J.D. Gallaspy *Luftwaffe Camouflage & Markings 1935-45 Vol.3* Melbourne: Kookaburra Technical Pub., 1977

B381 Smith, J.R. and Antony L. Kay *German Aircraft of the Second World War* London: Putnam, 1972

B382 Smith, Peter C. *Dive Bomber:* Annapolis: Naval Institute Press, 1982. Ashbourne: Moorland Publishing Co., 1982

B383 Smith, Peter C. *The History of Dive Bombing* Annapolis: The Nautical & Aviation Publishing Company of America, 1981

B384 Spenser, Jay P. *Aeronca C-2* Washington: Smithsonian Institution Press, 1978

B385 Spenser, Jay P. *Bellanca C.F.* Washington: Smithsonian Institution Press, 1982

B386 Spenser, Jay P. *Moskito* Boylston: Monogram Aviation Pub., 1983

B387 *Spot-Photo No.1* Voison: Club de l'Air 1939/45, ca.1970 (French/English text)

B388 Stahl, P.W. *KG200 The True Story* London: Jane's 1981

B389 Stern, Robert *SB2C Helldiver in Action* Carrollton: Squadron/Signal, 1982

B390 Stern, Rob *SBD Dauntless in Action* Carrollton: Squadron/Signal, 1984

B391 Stroud, John *European Transport Aircraft Since 1910* London: Putnam, 1966

B392 Sullivan, Jim *F4U Corsair in Action* Warren: Squadron/Signal, 1977

B393 Sullivan, Jim *P2V Neptune in Action* Carrollton: Squadron/Signal, 1985

B394 Swanborough, Gordon *North American An Aviation Album* London: Ian Allen, 1973

B395 Sweetman, Bill *High Speed Flight* London: Jane's, 1983

B396   Talbot-Boothe, E.C. *Aircraft of the World* London: Sampson Low, Marston & Co., ca.1939

B397   Talbot-Boothe, E.C. *Fighting Planes of the World* London: Sampson Low, Marston & Co., 3rd edition, ca.1940

B398   Tapper, Oliver *Armstrong Whitworth Aircraft Since 1913* London: Putnam, 1973

B399   Taylor, H.A. *Airspeed Aircraft Since 1931* London: Putnam, 1970

B400   Taylor, H.A. *Fairey Aircraft Since 1915* London: Putnam, 1974

B401   Taylor, John W.R. *Continental Military Aircraft* London: Ian Allen, 1954

B402   Taylor, John W.R. *Flight* New York: Peebles Press, 1974 (*A Picture History of Flight* London: Hulton Press)
Listed as B402(Photo Number)

B403   Taylor, John W.R. *The Lore of Flight* Gothenburg: Tre Tryckare Cagner & Co., 1970

B404   Taylor, John W.R. *Record-Breaking Aircraft* London: Macdonald and Jane's, 1978

B405   Taylor, John W.R. *Research and Experimental Aircraft* London: Macdonald and Jane's, 1976

B406   Taylor, John W.R. *Warplanes of the World* London: Ian Allen, 1960

B407   Taylor, John W.R. and Maurice F. Allward *Westland 50* London: Ian Allen, 1965

B408   Taylor, John W.R. and Kenneth Munson *History of Aviation* London: New English Library, 1972. New York: Crown Pub., 1972

B409   Taylor, John W.R. and Kenneth Munson *Jane's Pocket Book of Remotely Piloted Vehicles* New York: Collier Books, 1977

B410   Taylor, Michael J.H. *Fantastic Flying Machines* London: Jane's, 1981

B411   Taylor, Michael J.H. *Warplanes of the World 1918-1939* London: Ian Allen, 1981

B412   Thorpe, Donald W. *Japanese Army Air Force Camouflage and Markings World War II* Fallbrook: Aero Publishers, 1968

B413   Thorpe, Donald W. *Japanese Naval Air Force Camouflage and Markings World War II* Fallbrook: Aero Publishers, 1977

B414   Thruelson, Richard T. *The Grumman Story* New York: Praeger Pub., 1976

B415   Tillman, Barrett *Corsair The F4U in World War II* Annapolis: Naval Institute Press, 1979

B416   Titz, Zdenek *Czechoslovakian Air Force 1918-1970* Aircam Aviation Series No.S5, Canterbury: Osprey Pub., 1971

B417   Turner, P. St. John *Heinkel An Aircraft Album* London: Ian Allen, 1970

B418   Turner, P. St. John & Heinz J. Nowarra *Junkers An Aircraft Album* London: Ian Allen, 1971

B419   Underwood, John *The Stinsons* Glendale: Heritage Press, 1976

B420   Underwood, John and George Collinge *The Lightplane Since 1909* Glendale: Heritage Press, 1975

B421   Urech, Jakob *The Aircraft of the Swiss Air Force Since 1914* Dubendorf: Verlag Th. Gut & Co., 1975

B422   Van Haute, Andre *Pictorial History of the French Air Force* London: Ian Allen, Vol.1 (1909-1940) 1974, Vol.2 (1941-1974) 1975
Listed as B422(Volume-Page)

B423   Vanags-Baginskis, Alex *Stuka Ju*

87 New York: Crown Pub., 1982.
Tokyo: Zokeisha Pub., 1982

B424   Vergnano, Piero *The FIAT
Fighters 1930-1945* Genoa: Intyrama,
1969

B425   Ventry, Lord and Eugene M.
Kolesnik *Airship Saga* Poole:
Blandford Press, 1982

B426   Ventry, Lord and Eugene M.
Kolesnik *Jane's Pocket Book of Airships*
New York: Collier Books, 1977

B427   Vincent, Carl *The Blackburn
Shark* Stittsville: Canada's Wings,
1974

B428   Von Braun, Wernher and
Frederick I. Ordway III *History of
Rocketry & Space Travel* New York:
Thomas Y. Crowell Co., 1966

B429   Wagner, Ray and Heinz Nowarra
German Combat Planes Garden City:
Doubleday, 1971

B430   Wagner, William *Reuben Fleet and
the Story of Consolidated Aircraft*
Fallbrook: Aero Publishers, 1976

B431   Wall, Robert *Airliners* Englewood
Cliffs: Prentice-Hall, 1980. London:
Quarto, 1980

B432   Ward, Richard *50 Fighters
1938-1945* Canterbury: Osprey Pub.,
Vol.1 Aircam Aviation Series No.S17
1973, Vol.2 Aircam Aviation Series
No.S18 1973
Listed as B432(Volume-Page)

B433   West, Kenneth S. *The Captive
Luftwaffe* London: Putnam, 1978

B434   Wigton, Don C. *Those Fabulous
Amphibians* Detroit: Harlo Press, 1973

B435   Windrow, Martin *German Air
Force Fighters of World War Two*
Windsor: Hylton Lacy, Vol.1 1968,
Vol.2 1970
Listed as B435(Volume-Page)

B436   Winter, William *Warplanes of the*

Nations London: George G. Harrup &
Co., 1944

B437   Wood, Tony and Bill Gunston
Hitler's Luftwaffe London: Salamander
Books, 1977. New York: Crescent
Books, 1977

B438   Wooldridge, E.T. Jr *The P-80
Shooting Star Evolution of a Jet Fighter*
Washington: Smithsonian Institution,
1979

B439   Wooldridge, E.T. *Winged
Wonders The Story of the Flying Wings*
Washington: Smithsonian Institution
Press, 1983

B440   Wragg, David *Boats of the Air*
London: Robert Hale, 1984

B441   Wragg, David *Wings Over the Sea*
New York: Arco, 1979

B442   Young, Richard Anthony *The
Flying Bomb* London: Ian Allen, 1978.
New York: Sky Books Press, 1978

B443   Young, Warren R. *The Helicopters*
Alexandria: Time-Life Books, 1982

ADDENDA

B444   Ethell, Jeffrey L. *American
Warplanes World War II — Korea* Vol.I
and II, London: Arms & Armour
Press, 1983
Listed as B444(Volume-Page)

B445   Jablonski, Edward *Man With
Wings* Garden City: Doubleday, 1980

B446   Smith, J. Richard & Eddie J.
Creek *Arado 234B* Boylston:
Monogram Aviation Pub., 1983

B447   Taylor, Michael J. *History of
Helicopters* London: Hamlyn Pub.,
1984. *The Illustrated Encyclopedia of
Helicopters* New York: Exeter Books,
1984

B448   Davis, Larry *P-47 Thunderbolt in
Action* Carrollton: Squadron/Signal,
1984

B449 Dwiggins, Don *The Complete Book of Cockpits* Blue Ridge Summit: TAB Books, 1982

B450 Lawson, Robert L *The History of U.S. Naval Air Power* Feltham: Temple Press, 1985. New York: The Military Press, 1985

B451 Birdsall, Steve *B-29 Superfortress in Action* Warren: Squadron/Signal, 1977

B452 Duval, G.R. *American Flying Boats* Truro: D. Bradford Barton, 1974

B453 Sullivan, Jim *F6F Hellcat in Action* Carrollton: Squadron/Signal, 1979

B454 Campbell, Jerry L. *Messerschmitt Bf 110 Zerstorer in Action* Warren: Squadron/Signal, 1977

B455 Stafford, Gene B. *P-38 Lightning in Action* Warren: Squadron/Signal, 1976

B456 Feist, Uwe *Junkers Ju 52 in Action* Warren: Squadron/Signal, 1973

B457 Mackay, R.S.G. *Lancaster in Action* Carrollton: Squadron/Signal, 1982

B458 Karlstrom, Bjorn *Flygplans-Ritningar 2 Swedish Air Force Fighters 1926-84* Stockholm: Allt om Hobby, 1985 (Swedish/English text)

B459 Ogilvy, David *The Shuttleworth Collection* Shrewsbury: Airlife Pub., 1982

B460 Kennedy, Gregory P. *Vengeance Weapon 2 The V-2 Guided Missile* Washington: Smithsonian Institution Press, 1983

B461 Bowers, Peter M. *Flying the Boeing Model 80* Seattle: Museum of Flight, 1984

B462 Bateson, Richard P. *Saro A/1 Fighter Flying Boat* London: ISO Publications, 1985

B463 Morgan, Len *The AT-6 Harvard* New York: Arco Publishing Co., 1965

B464 Yenne, Bill *McDonnell Douglas A Tale of Two Giants* London: Bison Books, 1985. New York: Crescent Books, 1985

B465 Gradidge, J.M.G. *The Douglas DC-3 and It's Predecessors* Tonbridge: Air Britain, 1984

B466 Mikesh, Robert C. and Osamu Tagaya *Moonlight Interceptor Japan's "Irving" Night Fighter* Washington: Smithsonian Institution Press, 1985

B467 Townson, George *Autogiro The Story of "the Windmill Plane"* Fallbrook: Aero Publishers, 1985

B468 Munson, Kenneth *U.S. Commercial Aircraft* London: Jane's, 1982

B469 Rimell, Raymond Laurence *R.A.F. Between the Wars* London: Arms & Armour Press, 1985

B470 Maguglin, Robert *Howard Hughes His Achievements & Legacy* Long Beach: Wrather Port Properties, 1984

B471 Rosholt, Malcolm *Flight in the China Air Space 1910-1950* Rosholt: Rosholt House, 1984

B472 LePage, Wynn Laurence *Growing Up With Aviation* Ardmore: Dorrance & Co., 1981

B473 O'Leary, Michael *U.S. Sky Spies Since World War I* Poole: Blandford Press, 1986
Listed as B473 (Photo Number)

B474 Gentili, Roberto *Savoia-Marchetti S.79 in Action* Carrollton: Squadron/Signal, 1986

B475 Burns, Michael G. *Spitfire! Spitfire!* Poole: Blandford Press, 1986

SECTION C

C1   Abate, Rosario *Gli Aeroplani Della Caproni Aeronautica Bergamasca* Volume Primo, Roma: Edizione Bizzarri, 1975. Volume Secondo, Roma: Edizione Dell'Ateneo & Bizzarri, 1978
Listed as C1(Volume-Page)

C2   Abate, Rosario and Giulio Lazzate *I Velivoli Macchi dal 1912 al 1963* Milano: Al Nel Tempo, 1963

C3   *Aireview's British Military Aircraft of World War II* No.138, Tokyo: Kantosha, 1961

C4   *Aireview's Japanese Army Aircraft in the Pacific War* Tokyo: Kantosha, ca.1970

C5   *Aireview's Japanese Army Aircraft 1910-1945* No.150, Tokyo: Kantosha, 1962

C6   *Aireview's Japanese Navy Aircraft in the Pacific War* Tokyo: Kantosha, ca.1975

C7   *Aireview's Representative Japanese Aircraft Vol.2* No.118, Tokyo: Kantosha, ca.1960

C8   *Aireview's U.S. Army Aircraft of World War II* No.183, Tokyo: Kantosha, 1964

C9   *Aireview's U.S. Navy Aircraft of World War II* No.231, Tokyo: Kantosha, 1967

C10   *Aireview's World War II Military Aircraft of France, Italy, Soviet, and 21 Other Countries* No.196, Tokyo: Kantosha, 1965

C11   Akimoto, M. *A Pictorial History of Japanese Army Air Force* Tokyo: Shuppan Kyodo, 1961
Listed as C11(Section-Photo Number)

C12   Anttonen, Ossi and Hannu Valtonen *Luftwaffe Suomessa — In Finland 1941-1944* Helsinki: Piirrokset Petteri Patolinna, Vol.1 1976, Vol.2 1980 (partial English text)
Listed as C12(Volume-Page)

C13   Apostolo, Giorgio *Guida Agli Aeroplani d'Italia* Verona: Arnoldo Mondadori Editore, 1981

C14   *Arado Flugzeuge* Steinebach: Luftfahrt-Verlag Walter Zuerl, ca.1968

C15   Arena, Nino *Dai Wright All'Avvento Del Jet* Roma: Edizione Bizzarri, 1976

C16   Besser, Rolf *Technik und Geschichte der Hubschrauber Band 1* München: Bernard & Graefe Verlag, 1982

C17   Bignozzi, G. and B. Catalanotto *Storia Degli Aerei d'Italia dal 1911 al 1961* Roma: Edizione Cielo, ca.1961

C18   Bonte, Louis *l'Histoire des Essais en Vol 1914-1940* Paris: Docavia/Editions Lariviere, 1975

C19   Borgiotti, Alberto and Cesare Gori *Il Savoia Marchetti S.M.79 Sparviero 1933-1940* Modena: S.T.E.M. Mucchi, 1980

C20   Brotzu, Emilio, Michele Caso, Gherardo Casolo, Giancarlo Garello *Aerei Italiani Nella 2ª Guerra Mondiale* Dimensione Cielo, Roma: Edizione Bizzarri and Edizione Dell 'Ateneo & Bizzarri

Vol.1   *Caccia-Assalto* 1971
Vol.2   *Caccia-Assalto* 1971
Vol.3   *Caccia-Assalto* 1972
Vol.4   *Bombardieri-Recognitori* 1972
Vol.5   *Bombardieri-Recognitori* 1973
Vol.6   *Bombardieri-Recognitori* 1974
Vol.7   *Trasporto* 1974
Vol.8   *Trasporto* 1975

Vol.9 *Trasporto* 1976
Vol.10 *Scuola-Collegamento* 1977
Vol.11 *Scuola-Collegamento* 1977
Listed as C20(Volume-Page)

C21 Brotzu, Emilio, Gherado Casolo,
Ciancarlo Garello *Immagini*
Dimensione Cielo, Roma: Edizione
Bizzarri and Edizione Dell 'Ateneo &
Bizzarri
Vol.A1 *Caccia-Assalto* 1972
Vol.B1 *Caccia-Assalto* 1973
Vol.C2 *Caccia-Assalto* 1978
Vol.D3 *Caccia-Assalto* 1978
Vol.E4 *Bombardieri* 1978
Vol.F4 *Bombardieri* 1974
Vol.G5 *Bombardieri* 1978
Vol.H6 *Bombardieri* 1979
Listed as C21(Volume-Page)

C22 *Cessna-Flugzeuge* Steinebach:
Luftfahrt-Verlag Walter Zuerl,
ca.1964

C23 Cuich, Myrone *De l'Aeronautique
Militaire 1912 a l'Armee de l'Air 1976*
M.N. Cuich, 1978

C24 Cuny, Jean and Raymond Danel
*l'Aviation de Chasse Francaise
1918-1940* Paris: Docavia/Editions
Lariviere, 1973 (partial English text)

C25 Danel, Raymond and Jean Cuny
*l'Aviation Francaise de Bombardement
et de Renseignement* Paris:
Docavia/Editions Lariviere 1980

C26 Danel, Raymond and Jean Cuny
Les Avions Dewoitine Paris:
Docavia/Editions Lariviere, 1982

C27 Danel, Raymond and Jean Cuny *le
Dewoitine D.520* Paris:
Docavia/Editions Lariviere, ca.1975
(partial English text)

C28 *Dornier-Flugzeuge* München:
Luftfahrt-Verlag Walter Zuerl,
ca.1963

C29 Ebert, Hans *Messerschmitt Bölkow
Blohm 111 MBB Flugzeuge 1913-1973*
Stuttgart: Motorbuch Verlag, 1974

C30 Ehrengardt, C-J *Bloch 152 Special*
Paris: International Plastic Modellers'
Society, Branch Francaise, 1969

C31 Emanuelsson, C.O., Stig Jarlevik,
Sven Kull *Svenskt Spaningsflyg
Swedish Reconnaisance* Göteborg: Rare
Aviation Publishers, 1981

C32 Emiliani, Angelo, Giuseppe
Ghergo, Achille Vigna *Regia
Aeronautica Balcani e Fronte Orientale*
Milano: Intergest, 1974
Listed as C32(Photo Number)

C33 Emiliani, Angelo, Giuseppe
Ghergo, Achille Vigna *Regia
Aeronautica Colori e Insegne 1935-1943*
Milano: Intergest, 1974
Listed as C33 (Photo Number)

C34 Engelmann, Joachim *Raketen Die
Den Krieg Entscheiden Sollten*
Friedberg: Podzun-Pallas-Verlag,
ca.1982

C35 Evangelisti, Giorgio *Cento
Aeroplani e un Grande Cuore* Milano-
Modena: Artiole Editore, 1969

C36 Evangelisti, Giorgio *Macchine
Bizzarre Nella Storia Dell Aviazione*
Firenze: Editoriale Olimpia, 1980

C37 Eyermann, Karl-Heinz *Die
Luftfahrt de UdSSR 1917-1977* Berlin
(DDR): Transpress, 1977

C38 Eyermann, Karl-Heinz
Lufttransport Spiegelbild der Luftmacht
Berlin (DDR): Deutscher
Militarverlag, 1967

C39 *Famous Airplanes of the World*
Tokyo: Bunrin-Do
No.50 *Mitsubishi Type 4 Medium
Bomber Hiryu* June 1974
No.68 *Kawanishi Type 2 Flying Boat*
December 1975

BIBLIOGRAPHY

No.76 *Japanese Army Experimental Fighters (1)* August 1976

No.90 *Nakajima Navy Experimental Attack-Bomber Shinzan/Renzan* October 1977

No.102 *Kyushu Navy Experimental Interceptor Fighter Shinden* October 1978

Listed as C39 (Number-Page)

C40 *Flugzeuge der GWF (Gothaer Waggonfabrik AG)* Steinebach: Luftfahrt-Verlag Walter Zuerl, ca.1968

C41 *Focke-Wulf Flugzeuge* Steinebach: Luftfahrt-Verlag Walter Zuerl, ca.1964

C42 Garello, Giancarlo *Il Piaggio P.108* Roma: Edizione Bizzarri, 1973

C43 Gentili, Roberto *l'Aviazione da Caccia Italiana 1918-1939* Firenze: Editrice Aeronatica Italiana, ca.1978, Vol.2 1982

Listed as C43(Volume-Page)

C44 Gerard, Herve *Histoire de l'Aviation Belge* Bruxelles: Paul Legrain, 1978

C45 Gersdorff, Kyrill von and Kurt Knobling *Hubschrauber und Tragschrauber* München: Bernard & Graefe Verlag, 1982

C46 Glass, Andrzej *Polskie Konstruckcje Lotnicze 1893-1939* Warszawa: Wydawnictwa Komunikacji Lacznosci, 1977

C47 Gudju, I., G. Iacobescu, O. Ionescu *Constructii Aeronautice Romanesti 1905-1970* Bucharest: Editura Militara, 1970

C48 Gutschow, Fred *Die Deutschen Flugboote* Stuttgart: Motorbuch Verlag, 1978

C49 Haubner, Fred *Die Flugzeuge der Österreichischen Luftskreitkräfte vor* 1938 Graz: H. Weishaupt Verlag, 1982

C50 Havet, Andre *Les Avions Renard* Bruxelles: Editions A.E.L.R., 1984

C51 Hooftman, Hugo *Burgerluchtvaard in Nederland Deel 3* Nederlandse Vliegtuig Encyclopedie Nr.13, Bennekom: Cockpit-Uitgeverij, 1981

C52 Hooftman, Hugo *Fokker D-XXI* Nederlandse Vliegtuig Encyclopedie Nr.5, Bennekom: Cockpit-Uitgeverij, 1978

C53 Hooftman, Hugo *Fokker G-1* Nederlandse Vliegtuig Encyclopedie Nr.2, Bennekom: Cockpit-Uitgeverij, 1977

C54 Hooftman, Hugo *Fokker Neerlands Grootse Vliegtuigbouwer* Nr.36, Alkmar: Alkenreeks Beeld-Encyclopedie, ca.1963

C55 Hooftman, Hugo *Fokker T-V en T-IX* Nederlandse Vliegtuig Encyclopedie Nr.8, Bennekom: Cockpit-Uitgeverij, 1979

C56 Hooftman, Hugo *Scheldemusch en Scheldemeuw* Nederlandse Vliegtuig Encyclopedie Nr.7, Bennekom: Cockpit-Uitgeverij, 1978

C57 Hooftman, Hugo *Van Brik tot Starfighter* Zwolle: LaRiviere & Voorhoeve, Vol.I 1963, Vol.II 1962

Listed as C57(Volume-Page)

C58 Hooftman, Hugo *Van Farman tot Neptune* Zwolle: LaRiviere & Voorhoeve, Vol.I 1964, Vol.II 1965

Listed as C58(Volume-Page)

C59 Hooftman, Hugo *Van Glenn Martins en Mustangs* Zwolle: LaRiviere & Voorhoeve, 1967

C60 Hooftman, Hugo *Zeldzame Vliegtuigfoto's Rare Aircraft Photographs* Zwolle: LaRiviere & Voorhoeve, Ser.1 1966, Ser.2 1968, Ser.3 1972 (partial English text)

Listed as C60(Series-Page)

C61   *The Japanese Army Wings of the Second World War* Tokyo: Bunrin-Do, 1972

C62   *Japanese Imperial Army Aircraft* Koku-Fan Illustrated No.4, Tokyo: Bunrin-Do, ca.1980

C63   *Japanese Navy Wings of the Second World War* Tokyo: Bunrin-Do, 1974

C64   Jouhaud, Reginald *Stampe SV4* Rennes: Ouest France, 1981

C65   *Junkers Flugzeug und Flugmotoren* Steinebach: Luftfahrt-Verlag Walter Zuerl, ca.1964 (2 volumes) Listed as C65(Volume-Page)

C66   Kens, Karlheinz and Heinz Nowarra *Die Deutschen Flugzeuge 1933-1945* München: J.F. Lehmann Verlag, 1977

C67   Keller, Ulrich *Propeller Flugzeuge in Dienste Schweizerischen Fluglinienverkehrs 1919-38* Basel: Birkhauser Verlag, 1969

C68   Keskinen, Kalevi *Brewster B-239 ja Humu* Suomen Ilmavoimien Historia 1, Tampere: Litopaino, 1970

C69   Keskinen, Kalevi, Kari Stenman, Klaus Niska *Suomen Ilmavoimien Lentokoneet 1918-38* Helsinki: Tietoteos, 1976 (partial English text)

C70   Keskinen, Kelevi, Klaus Niska, Kari Stenman *Suomen Ilmavoimien Lentokoneet 1939-72* Helsinki: Tietoteos, 1972 (partial English text)

C71   Keskinen, Kalevi, Kari Stenman, Klaus Niska *Venalaiset Pommittajat Soviet Bombers* Suomen Ilmavoimien Historia 9, Espoo: Tietoteos, 1982 (partial English text)

C72   Kober, Franz *Die ersten Strahlbomber der Welt* Friedberg: Podzun-Pallas-Verlag, 1980

C73   Kofoed, Hans *Danske Militaerfly Gennem 50 Ar 1912-1962* Kobenhavn:

Flyv's Forlag, Ejvind Christensen, 1962

C74   Kopenhagen, Wilfried and Dr. Rolf Neustadt *Das Grosse Flugzeuge Typenbuch* Berlin (DDR): VEB Verlag für Verkehrswesen, 1982

C75   Kowalski, Tomasz J. *Godto i Barwa w Lotnictwie Polskim 1918-1939* Warszawa: Wydawnictwa Komunikacji i Lacznosci, 1981

C76   Kruse, Karl-Albin *Das Grosse Buch der Fliegerei und Raumfahrt* München: Sudwest Verlag, 1973

C77   Lange, Bruno *Das Buch der Deutschen Luftfahrttechnik Bildteil* Mainz: Verlag Dieter Hoffmann, 1970

C78   Laureau, Patrick *L'Aviation Republicaine Espagnole (1936-1939)* Paris: Docavia/Editions Lariviere, 1978

C79   Leonard, Herbert *Les avions de chasse Polikarpov* Rennes: Ouest France, 1981

C80   Malizia, Nicola *Vita e Vicende de l'Aeronautica Militaire Italiana* Roma: Edizione Dell'Ateneo & Bizzarri, 1979

C81   *Messerschmitt Flugzeuge* München: Luftfahrt-Verlag Walter Zuerl, ca.1963

C82   Millot, Bernard *Les Avions Vought* Paris: Docavia/Editions Lariviere, 1983

C83   Morgala, Andrzej *Polskie Samoloty Wojskowe 1918-1939* Warszawa: Wyndawnictwo Ministertwa Obrony Narodowej, 1972

C84   Nagaishi, M. and M. Akimoto *A Pictorial History of Japanese Naval Air Force* Tokyo: Shuppan Kyodo, 1960 Listed as C84(Section-Photo Number)

C85   Nemecek, Vaclav *Ceskoslovenska Letadla 1918-1945* Praha: Nase Vojsko, 1983

C86 Nemecek, Vaclav *Sovetska Letadla* Praha: Nase Vojsko, 1969

C87 Nemecek, Vaclav *Vojenska Letadla 2 Mezi Duema Svetovymi Valkami* Praha: Nase Vojsko, 1975

C88 Nemecek, Vaclav *Vojenska Letadla 3 Letadla Druhe Svetove Valky* Praha: Nase Vojsko, 1977

C89 Norrbohm, Gosta and Bertil Skogsberg *Att Flyga ar att Leva Flygvapnet 1926-1976* Hoganas: Bokforlaget Bra Bocker, 1975

C90 Nowarra, Heinz J. *Deutsche Lastensegler an Allen Fronten* Friedberg: Podzun-Pallas-Verlag, 1978

C91 Nowarra, Heinz J. *Die Deutschen Hubschrauber 1928-1945* Friedberg: Podzun-Pallas-Verlag, 1980

C92 Nowarra, Heinz J. *Fernaufklarer 1915-1945* Stuttgart: Motorbuch Verlag,1982

C93 Nowarra, Heinz J. *Fieseler 156 Storch* Friedberg: Podzun-Pallas-Verlag, 1979

C94 Nowarra, Heinz J. *Die Grossen Dessauer Ju G38-Ju 89-Ju 90-Ju 290-Ju 390* Friedberg: Podzun-Pallas-Verlag, 1983

C95 Nowarra, Heinz *Heinkel und seine Flugzeuge* München: J.F. Lehmanns Verlag, 1975

C96 Nowarra, Heinz J. *Luftgiganten uber See BV222-Wiking-BV238* Friedberg: Podzun-Pallas-Verlag, 1978

C97 Nowarra, Heinz J. *Russische Jagdflugzeuge 1920-1941* Friedberg: Podzun-Pallas-Verlag, 1978

C98 Nowarra, Heinz *Die Sowjetischen Flugzeuge 1941-1966* München: J.F. Lehmanns Verlag, 1967

C99 Nowarra, Heinz J. *"Uhu" — He 219* Friedberg: Podzun-Pallas-Verlag, 1982

C100 Nozawa, Tadashi *Encyclopedia of Japanese Aircraft* Tokyo: Shuppan-Kyodo, Vol.1 Mitsubishi's Aircraft 1966, Vol.2 Aichi, Kugisho, Vol.3 Kawanishi, Hirosho 1963, Vol.4 Kawasaki Aircraft 1966, Vol.5 Nakajima Aircraft 1963, Vol.6 Import Aircraft 1972, Vol.7 Tachikawa 1980, Vol.8 Kyushu 1980 Listed as C100(Volume-Page)

C101 Nozawa, Tadashi *A Pictorial History of Aviation in Japan 1910-1960* Tokyo: Shuppan-Kyodo, 1960 Listed as C101(Photo Number)

C102 Okamura and Iwaya *Airplanes of Japan, Series I: Navy Aircraft* ca.1960

C103 Pawlas, Karl *Die Giganten Me 321 — Me 323* Luftfahrt Monographie LS3, Nurnberg: Pawlas, ca.1974

C104 Pawlas, Karl *Kampf — und Lastensegler DFS 230 — DFS 331* Luftfahrt Monographie LS1, Nurnberg: Pawlas, ca.1974

C105 Pawlas, Karl *Die Sturm — und Lastensegler Go 242 - Go 244 - Go 345 - P39 - Ka 430* Luftfahrt Monographie LS2, Nurnberg: Pawlas, ca.1974

C106 Pereira de Andrade, Roberto *A Construcao Aeronautica No Brasil 1910/1976* Sao Paulo: Editora Brasiliense, 1976

C107 *Pictorial German Warplanes of the World War II* Tokyo: Bunrin-Do, 1969

C108 *Pictorial History Japanese Army Aircraft* Tokyo: Bunrin-Do, 1969

C109 *Pictorial History Japanese Navy Aircraft* Tokyo: Bunrin-Do, 1970

C110 Pilecki, Szymon and Jerzy Domanski *Samoloty Bojowe 1910-1967* Warszawa: Wydawnictwo Ministertwa Obrony Narodowej, 1969

C111 Pohlmann, Hermann *Chronik Eines Flugzeugwerke 1932-1945* Stuttgart: Motorbuch Verlag, 1979

C112   Rello, Salvador *La Aviacion en la Guerra Espana* Madrid: San Martin, Vol.1 Collescion Alea 11 1969, Vol.2 Collescion Alea 13 1969, Vol.3 Collescion Alea 14 1971, Vol.4 Collescion Alea 15 1972
Listed as C112(Volume-Page)

C113   Ries, Karl *Dora Kurfurst und rote 13 Bildband: Flugzeug der Luftwaffe 1933-1945* Finthen bei Mainz: Verlag Dieter Hoffmann, Vol.1 1964, Vol.2 1964, Vol.3 1966, Vol.4 1969
Listed as C113(Volume-Page)

C114   Ries, Karl *Luftwaffe Photo Report 1919-1945* Stuttgart: Motorbuch Verlag, 1984

C115   Rolbetzki, Hanns *Focke-Wulf Fw 58 Weihe* Luftfahrt Bild-Dokumente LBD2, Nurnberg: Pawlas, ca.1977

C116   Schmidt, Heinz *Sowjetische Flugzeuge* Berlin (DDR): Transpress VEB Verlag für Verkehrswesen, 1971

C117   Schneider, Helmut *Flugzeug Typenbuch* Leipzig: Herm. Beyer Verlag, 1944 (reprint Olms Presse, Hildesheim, 1980)

C118   Selinger, Peter F. *Segelflugzeuge vom Wolf zum Mini-Nimbus* Stuttgart: Motorbuch Verlag, 1978

C119   Shavrov, V.B. *Istoriya konstructsy samoletov v SSSR do 1938* Moscow: Mashinostroyeniye, 1969

C120   Shavrov, V.B. *Istoriya konstructsy samoletov v SSSR 1938-1950* Moscow: Mashinostroyeniye, 1978

C121   Sorsa, Toivo *Lentajan Albumi* Oulu: PM-julkaisut, Vol.1 1977, Vol.2 1979, Vol.3 1979, Vol.4 1981 (partial English text)
Listed as C121(Volume-Page)

C122   *Svenskt Militarflyg 50 Ar* Stockholm: Utgiven Av Flygstabens Press-detalj, 1962

C123   Travnicek, Zdenek *Reaktivni Letouny* Praha: Nase Vojsko, 1965

C124   Vogt, Richard *Weltumspannende Memoiren eines Flugzeug-Konstrukteurs* Steinebach: Luftfahrt-Verlag Walter Zuerl, ca.1978

C125   Wagner, Wolfgang *Kurt Tank — Konstrukteur und Testpilot bei Focke-Wulf* München: Bernard & Graefe Verlag, 1980

C126   Wesselink, Theo and Thijs Postma *Koolhoven Nederlands Vliegtuigbouwer in de Schaduw van Fokker* Bussum: Uniboek, 1981

C127   Wesselink, Theo and Thijs Postma *De Nederlandse Vliegtuigen* Haarlem: Romen, 1982

C128   Westerberg, Rolf *SAAB 21* Flyghistorisk Revy Nr29, Stockholm: Svensk Flyghistorisk Forening, 1981 (partial English text)

ADDENDA

C129   Millot, Bernard *Les Chasseurs Japonais* Paris: Docavia/Editions Lariviere, 1977

C130   Liron, J. *Les Avions Farman* Paris: Docavia/Editions Lariviere, 1984

C131   Pereira Netto, Francisco C. *Aviacao Militar Brasiliera 1916-1984* Rio de Janeiro: Revista Aeronautica Editora, 1984

C132   Westerberg, Rolf *SAAB 18* Flyghistorisk Revy Nr31, Stockholm: Svensk Flyghistorisk Forening, 1984 (partial English text)

C133   Keimel, Reinhard *Flugzeuge und Projekte von Theodor Hopfner* Graz: H. Weishaupt Verlag, 1983

C134   Pecker, Beatriz, Carlos Perez Grange *Cronica de la Aviacion Espanola* Madrid: Silex, 1983

C135   Pohlmann, Hermann *Prof. Junkers nannte es "Die Fliege"* Stuttgart: Motorbuch Verlag, 1983

C136   Glass, Andrzej, Krzysztof Cieslak *Barwa w Lotnictwie Polskim l Samoloty i Szybowce do 1939 Roku* Warszawa: Wydawnictwa Komunikacji i Lacznosci, 1985

C137   Horten, Reimar, Peter F. Selinger *Nurflügel Die Geschichte der Horten-Flugzeuge 1933-1960* Graz: H. Weishaupt Verlag, 1985 (partial English text)

C138   Köhler, H. Dieter *Ernst Heinkel – Pionier der Schnellflugzeuge* Koblenz: Bernard & Graefe Verlag, 1983

C139   Nowarra, Heinz J. *Die Deutsche Luftrüsting 1933-1945 Band 1: Flugzeugtypen AEG-Dornier* Koblenz: Bernard & Graefe Verlag, 1985

C140   Nowarra, Heinz J. *Die Verbotenen Flugzeuge 1921-1935* Stuttgart: Motorbuch Verlag, 1980

C141   Kopenhagen, Wilfried *Sowjetische Jagdflugzeuge* Berlin (DDR): Transpress VEB Verlag für Verkehrswesen, 1985

C142   Peter, Ernst *Tragschrauber Hubschrauber Österreichs Pioniere* Graz: H. Weishaupt Verlag, 1985

SECTION D

D1   *Aero Album* Fallbrook: Aero Publishers, Vol.1 Spring 1968 through Vol.8 Winter 1969
Listed as D1(Volume-Page)

D2   *Aerophile* San Antonio: Aerophile, Inc.
Listed as D2(Volume/Number-Page)

D3   *The Aeroplane Spotter* London: Temple Press, Vol.1 & 2 1941 through Vol.9 1948
Listed as D3(Volume-Page)

D4   *Air Classics* Canoga Park: Challenge Publications

D5   *Air Classics Quarterly Review* Canoga Park: Challenge Pub.
Listed as D5(Season/Year-Page)

D6   *Air Enthusiast* London: Fine Scroll Ltd.

D7   *Air Enthusiast (Quarterly)* London: Fine Scroll Ltd., Pilot Press Ltd.
Listed as D7(Number-Page)

D8   *Air Historian* Kogarah, Australia: Regency House
Listed as D8 (Book Number-Page)

D9   *Air International* London: Fine Scroll Ltd.

D10   *Air Pictorial* London: Air League, Rolls House Publishing Co., Windsor: Profile Books

D11   *Air Progress* New York: Conde Nast Publications, Street & Smith

D12   *Aircraft Recognition* H.M. Stationery Office, London: Sampson Clark & Co., Vol.1 Sept 1942 through Vol.3 Sept 1945

D13   *Airplane 3-View Journal* Midland Park: B.C.F.K. Publications
Listed as D13(Number-Page)

D14   *Airplane Five-View Album* Midland Park: B.C.F.K. Publications
Listed as D14(Number-Page)

D15   *Airplane Scale Views* Midland Park: B.C.F.K. Publications
Listed as D15(Number-Page)

D16   *Airpower* Granada Hills: Sentry Books Inc.

D17   *Air Scene* London: Ian Allen
Listed as D17(Number-Page)

D18 *l'Album du fanatique de l'Aviation*
Paris: Editions Lariviere

D19 *A.A.H.S. Journal* Santa Ana:
American Aviation Historial Society
Listed as D19(Quarter/Year-Page)

D20 *Flying Review International*
London: Haymarket Publishing
Group, Macdonald & Co.

D21 *High Flight* Stittsville: Canada's
Wings
Listed as D21(Volume/Number-Page)

D22 *The Historical Aviation Album*
Temple City: Paul Matt
Listed as D22(Volume-Page)

D23 *Icare — Revue de l'Aviation
Francais* Paris: Icare

Listed as D23(Number-Page)

D24 *Luftfahrt International* Nurnberg:
Karl Pawlas
Listed as D24(Number-Page)

D25 *Royal Air Force Flying Review*
London: Royal Air Force Review Ltd.

D26 *Three-Views of Aircraft* Midland
Park: B.C.F.K. Publications
Listed as D26(Number)

D27 *United States Naval Institute
Proceedings* Annapolis: U.S. Naval
Institute

D28 *Vliegtuig Parade* Bennekom:
Cockput-Uitgeverij

D29 *Wings* Granada Hills: Sentry
Books Inc.

Part Three: INDEX

The index lists all aircraft alphabetically by most commonly used and other designations. Following each index entry is the corresponding general listing manufacturer, designation (if different) and package number. For aircraft types grouped by manufacturer, consult the general listing. Names of manufacturers or designers are indexed if full capitals. Numerical designations are indexed following the alphabetical section. Roman numeral designations are listed alphabetically. Aircraft are indexed as model or type number, which see, if so designated in the general listing. United States experimental and service test aircraft are indexed under the corresponding X or Y prefix letter.

INDEX

E

G

H

L

M

INDEX

243

N

O

S

U

Z

Numerical

INDEX